THEY CAME TO EAST TEXAS

500-1850

IMMIGRANTS AND IMMIGRATION PATTERNS

Compiled by
Joe E. Ericson

Edited by
Carolyn R. Ericson

HERITAGE BOOKS
2007

HERITAGE BOOKS
AN IMPRINT OF HERITAGE BOOKS, INC.

Books, CDs, and more—Worldwide

For our listing of thousands of titles see our website at
www.HeritageBooks.com

Published 2007 by
HERITAGE BOOKS, INC.
Publishing Division
65 East Main Street
Westminster, Maryland 21157-5026

Copyright © 2005 Joe E. Ericson

Other books by the author:
Early East Texas: A History from Indian Settlements to Statehood
The Nacogdoches Story: An Informal History

All rights reserved. No part of this book may be reproduced or transmitted in any form or by any means, electronic or mechanical, including photocopying, recording or by any information storage and retrieval system without written permission from the author, except for the inclusion of brief quotations in a review.

International Standard Book Number: 978-0-7884-3327-6

DEDICATION
To Carolyn R. and Linda D. who always help and encourage.

TABLE OF CONTENTS

	Foreword	i
PART 1	Introduction: The Beginning	1
	Spanish Missions	1
	Indian Settlement	2
	European Penetration	4
PART II	The Indians	5
	The Caddos	7
	The Cherokees	11
PART III	The Spanish, Mexicans and Anglos	21
	Colonials	22
	Texas 1832-1835	88
PART IV	The Texians (Texans)	123
	The Revolutionary Years	125
	Post Revolution Days	136
	East Texas Pioneers	152
	1850 Census Data	166
	Pioneers of Southeast Texas	167
	Population Analysis	174

APPENDIX I Nacogdoches Census (1809) 179

APPENDIX II Nacogdoches Census (1826) 191

INDEX 195

LIST OF TABLES

Table 1	Indian Militiamen (1838-1839)	18
Table II	Military Roster of the Presidio Nuestra Senora del Pilar	24
Table III	Signers: Petition of 1773	27
Table IV	1792 Census for the Village of Nacogdoches	30
Table V	List of Foreigners in Nacogdoches	37
Table VI	Census of Foreigners in Nacogdoches (1805)	43
Table VII	Nacogdoches Census (1826)	53
Table VIII	Men in Ayish Bayou (1826)	61
Table IX	Participants: Battle of Nacogdoches (1832)	69
Table X	Some Early Settlers of Liberty Municipality	75
Table XI	Some Early Settlers of San Augustine Municipality	77
Table XII	Some Early Settlers of Sabine Municipality	80
Table XIII	Some Early Settlers of Tenahaw-Shelby Municipality	83
Table XIV	Some Early Settlers of Jasper Municipality	85
Table XV	Some Early Settlers of Red River Municipality	86
Table XVI	Immigrants (1835)	99
Table XVII	Participants: Cordovan Rebellion	132
Table XVIII	1850 Census: Northeast Texas	143
Table XIX	1850 Census Central East Texas	165
Table XX	1850 Census Southeast Texas	173

LIST OF MAPS

Immigration Patterns..	Frontispiece
Map I	Caddoes	Following p. 6
Map II	Cherokee Lands	Following p. 12
Map III	Nacogdoches District 1792	Following p. 30
Map IV	Texas Departments (1835)	Following p. 50
Map V	Nacogdoches and Liberty Municipalities (1831)	Following p. 74
Map VI	San Augustine Municipality (1834)	Following p. 76
Map VII	Sabine, Shelby, Jasper & Red River Municipalities ..	Following p. 78

TRAILS TO TEXAS

By
G. Loyd Collier

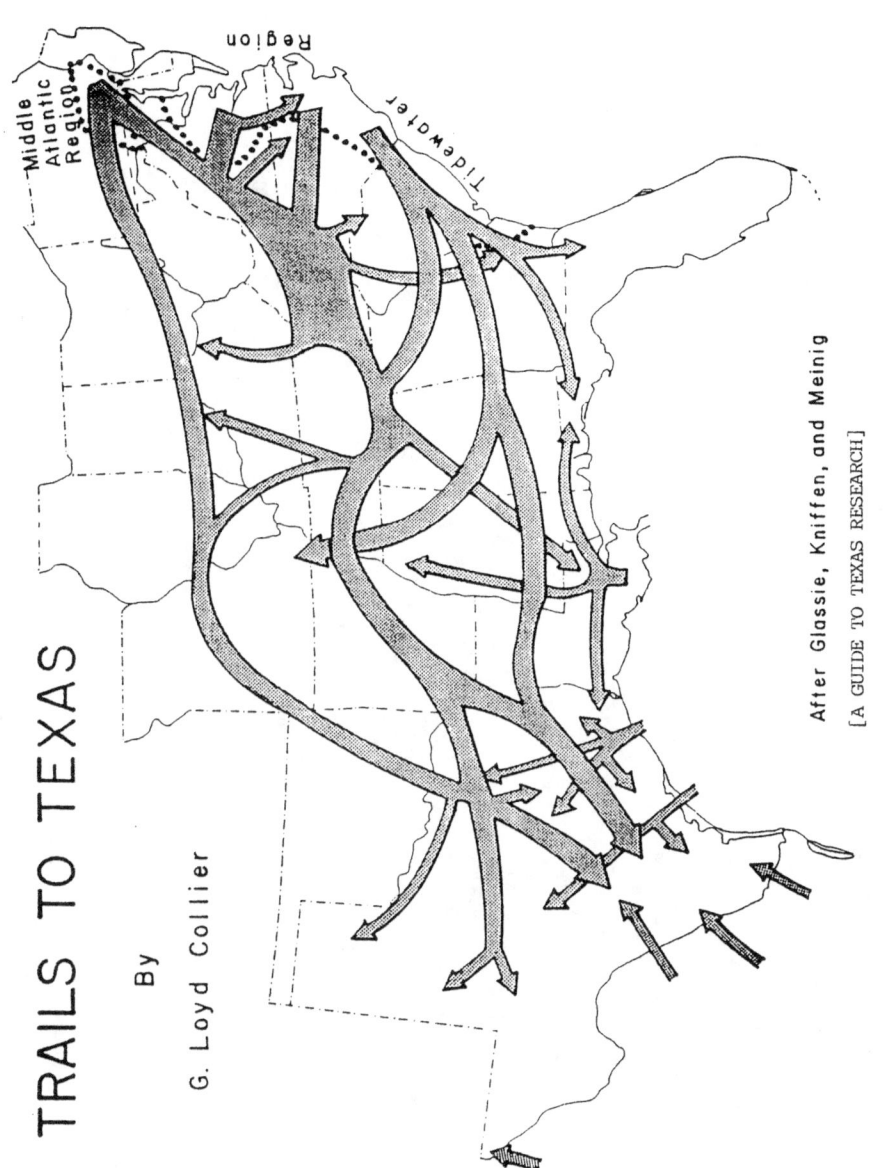

After Glassie, Kniffen, and Meinig
[A GUIDE TO TEXAS RESEARCH]

FOREWORD

This volume is another in a continuing series of works dedicated to the preservation of the history of East Texas. It focuses on the names of the early settlers from the arrival of the Caddos and associated Indian tribes about A.D. 500, the later arrival of and settlement by Spanish colonials in the seventeenth and eighteenth centuries, and the influx of Anglo-Americans and European immigrants in the nineteenth century.

It seeks to identify and provide data on heads of families, their wives where known, their date of arrival in Texas, and their place of birth, failing that, the place from which they emigrated. In addition to that genealogical information, maps and physical descriptions of places of settlement, Spanish, Mexican, and U. S. Census data, patterns of immigration for the three regions of East Texas--northeastern, central, and southeastern--are provided.

Information from Spanish, Mexican, and Republic of Texas is included, regional and county histories were reviewed, and family biographies were consulted and correlated. Compilation of data, especially the three volumes of Residents of Texas (1782-1836) by the Institute of Texan Cultures; *Gateway to Texas(1772-1849)*, Volume I, by Carolyn R. Ericson; the various volumes entitled *First Settlers of East Texas* counties by Gifford White and his *Citizens of Texas 1830 and 1840*; and the seven volume set of *Founders and Patriots of the Republic of Texas* (1963-2002) by the Daughters of the Republic of Texas were especially useful and are gratefully acknowledged.

Other works in this series include *Early East Texas: A History from Indian Settlements to Statehood* and *The Nacogdoches Story: An Informal History*. These volumes contain biographies of prominent early settlers of East Texas, for example, John S. Roberts, Martin Parmer, and Haden Edwards; histories of Nacogdoches, Sabine, San Augustine, and Shelby Counties; articles in historical journals and genealogical publications. In all of these, the willing help and encouragement offered by Carolyn R. Ericson was the incentive to begin and conclude each. They could not and would not have been produced with out that assistance.

PART 1

INTRODUCTION

THE BEGINNING

The first Europeans began finding their way into eastern regions of Texas in the Eighteenth Century, although both Spanish and French explorers had penetrated its forests and crossed its streams as early as the mid years of the Sixteenth Century. In 1542, Luis de Moscoso de Alvarado leading the remnants of Hernando de Soto's Expedition set foot in the region following de Soto's death May 21 of fever at the Mississippi River in present-day Arkansas. From there Moscoso's force possibly crossed into northeast Texas near the site of the modern city of Texarkana, Bowie County, drifted southward through country inhabited by Caddoan Indians, and encountered the Ais Indians and the Hasinai Confederacy of Caddos.

Almost a century and a half passed before the French explorer Robert Cavelier, Sieur de La Salle's Expedition mistakenly landed at Matagorda Island and Lavaca Bay on the Texas Gulf coast. In 1687 La Salle was killed by members of his force, and Henri Joutel assumed command of the survivors. Joutel led the survivors in a long trek to Canada. Along the way from the Gulf Coast, the Frenchmen passed through eastern Texas and the land of the Caddos.

In the 1680s, rumors of French intrusion and the urging of missionaries in the 1680s prompted a series of Spanish explorations led by Governor Alonso de Leon of New Mexico. On the fourth of his Seventeenth Century explorations, de Leon's route led him into the forests of East Texas. Later he reported to his superiors in Mexico City that the country of the Tejas Indians[1] "was a goodly land with fertile soil, sturdy trees, plenty of game, and a salubrious climate" and that the Tejas Indians were a superior primitive people."[2]

Spanish Missions. The Spanish Viceroy in Mexico City and his advisors determined that such a country and such a people could no longer be neglected. Churchmen and military alike were eager to enter Texas. The East Texas Caddos asked for missionaries and soon

---

[1] No individual tribe of Texas Indians called themselves Tejas. but the Caddoan bands of East Texas used the word to refer to their allies in the Cadddoan Confederacy. Early Spanish-speaking peoples translated the word to mean "friend" and used it to refer to East Texas Indians generally.

[2] Rupert N. Richardson, <u>Texas, the Lone Star State</u> (New York: Prentice Hall, Inc., 1943), p. 23.

churchmen and military leaders jointly petitioned the Viceroy, the Count de Galvez, to authorize and support a missionary expedition to Texas. Thus, in 1690, Father Damian Massanet and three other priests with a military escort of more than 100 men under Governor de Leon, returned to East Texas and established a mission, San Francisco de los Tejas, which was located a few miles west of the Neches River, near the present village of Weches in Houston County. Three years later the Viceroy's council recommended the abandonment of the mission, and on the night of October 25, 1693, the missionaries set fire to their mission and made their way back to Mexico.

Indian Settlement. However, centuries before these first Europeans set foot in East Texas moving along established Indian trails through the dense forests and crossing its many waterways, the remote ancestors of the natives they encountered on their wanderings already inhabited the area. About 500 A. D. a new American Indian culture began to spread north from the Mississippi basin. It had originated along the Gulf of Mexico and had followed the curve of the sea wherever the forests ran.[3]

In time it crossed the Sabine River and moved into the western edge of the vast Southern pine forest. Its bearers became known as the Mound Builders from the remains of the immense earthen truncated pyramids they left behind them when they abandoned an area Although they demonstrated marked Mexican influences on it, their culture was fundamentally Cirum-Caribbean in origin. No reliable evidence of the mode of their passage into and across East Texas has yet been unearthed. Nevertheless, they established within the bounds of modern East Texas the Caddoan Confederacies of the Piney Woods that were made up of Indians who were for a time the most numerous and powerful native groups in all of Texas.[4]

When early European explorers first observed the Tejas and other Caddoan tribes a historian of the time and place has observed, "they were closely related culturally to those Native Americans inhabiting what is now the United States' Southern Woodlands, home of such societies as the Five Civilized Tribes (Cherokee, Choctaw, Chickasaws, Creeks, and

---

[3] W. N. Newcomb, Jr., The Indians of Texas from Prehistoric Times to Modern Times (Austin: The University of Texas Press, 1961), p. 21.

[4] Ibid.

Seminoles), as well as the Natchez and other woodlands groups. Some time after 500 A. D. the Caddoes [had] settled in the East Texas piney woods and parts of Western Louisiana."[5]

The Caddoes had fought to maintain possession of their lands in the Southeast. But to the west and north of them were such warlike nations as the Osage, the Wichita, and the Apache. Between these tribal bands animosity developed over time due, in part, to a "pinball" effect begun by migrating white settlers. Smallwood contends that "every time the white frontier pushed westward, that movement forced the Native Americans on the frontier to move further west [and south] where they in turn infringed on the territory of another tribe. Constant Indian struggles for range were a result."[6] Thus, when the white frontier moved toward Texas, it pushed the Caddos westward causing the Apaches, Wichitas, and Osages to launch savage attacks on their villages.

By the time early European explorers reached their area the Caddos were united in two large confederacies, the Hasinai and the Kadohadocho, and more than twenty tribes. Their territories halted abruptly where the Piney Woods ended. Thus, they became preeminently an East Texas people. Their language was bound to that of the lower Yazoo River region. It resembled that of the Choctaws, Cherokees, and Creeks, all descended from a common ancestor.

Since they were an agricultural people growing and harvesting two varieties of corn and a great assortment of vegetables, they were almost totally unwarlike, and were markedly friendly to Europeans who visited them in their villages of timbered, thatched houses. Both Spanish and French explorers found their culture and life style more related to their own than that of any other Texas Indians.[7]

The Hasinias Caddos located in East Texas were known as Cenis by the French and Tejas or Texas by the Spanish. Late in the Seventeenth Century they they were organized in

---

[5] James Smallwood, Born in Dixie, The History of Smith County, Texas (2 vols., Austin: Eakin Press, 1999), Vol. I, p. 4.

[6] Ibid., p, 19.

[7] See: T. R,. Farenbach, Lone Star, A History of Texas and the Texans (New York: Collier Books, 1968), pp. 10-13.

nine tribes, each in its own village, with a total of some 2,400 to 2,800 people; but they had lost 3,000 of their number, more than one-half of their earlier population, in an epidemic in the spring of 1691.

By the early Nineteenth Century they had been worn down by the onslaught of such raiders as the Osage and Wichitas; but of more significance were the sweeping epidemics that killed thousands of them. "Once found in their mighty and large confederacies, the Caddos numbered only 2,000 by 1820. Later, in 1828, Mexican General Manuel Mier y Teran. . .estimated that only 300. . .families remained where once there had been several thousand."[8]

European Penetration. Although a number of persons other than individuals of Spanish descent did not begin to push their way into eastern Texas until after the Louisiana Purchase (1803), they were not altogether uncommon at that time. In 1792, for example, a Spanish census listed some 125 foreigners living in the province, eighty-six of them in the frontier Spanish settlement at Nacogdoches. These late Eighteenth Century Spanish reports do not attempt to estimate the number of foreigners who had crossed the boundary illegally and roamed over or settled in the region. Anglo-Americans had begun to trickle into East Texas as early as 1789. Many of them traded with the Indians of the area, some quietly took up unoccupied land and engaged in farming and stock raising, others launched filibustering expeditions, and still others sought to escape from American law enforcement officers.

The earliest effort to introduce European settlers and their cultures was made by the Spanish in the mid years of the Eighteenth Century. When their first bands of settlers, military forces, and missionaries reached the Piney Woods, they came in contact with Caddo Indians living in ancient villages with Caddo names and demonstrating a well-advanced culture.

---

[8] Smallwood, Born in Dixie, Vol. I, p. 25.

PART II

THE INDIANS

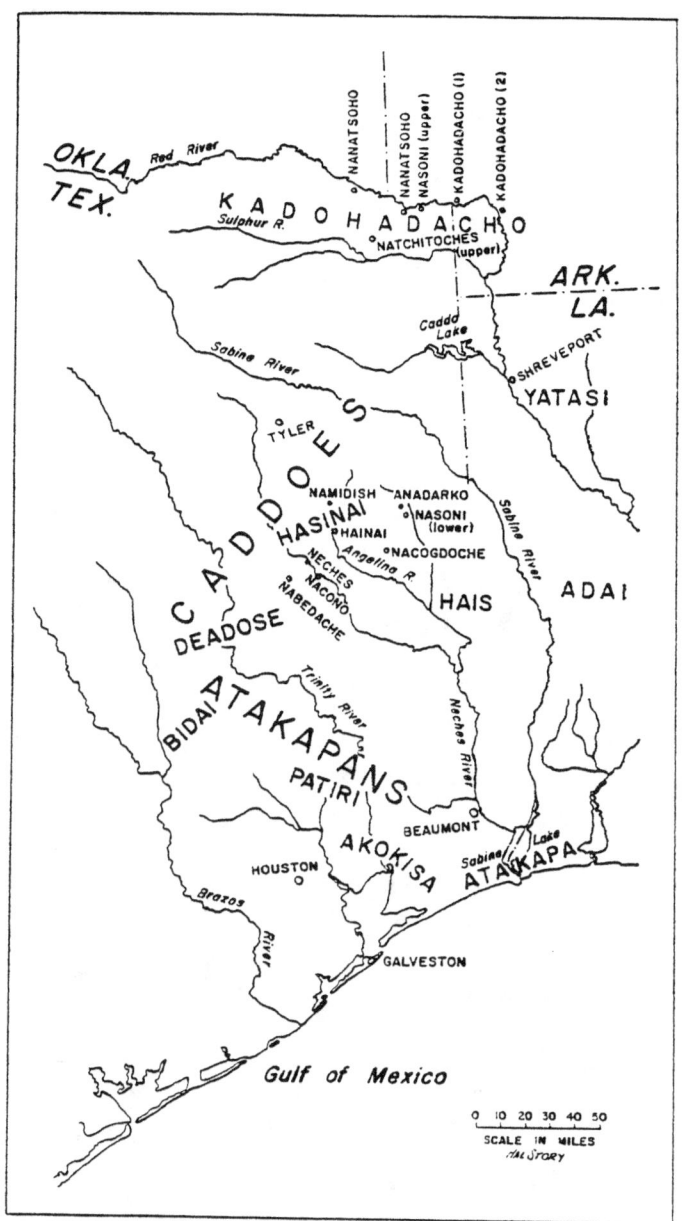

Map 4. Texas Tribes of the Southeast Culture Area

THE INDIANS

Almost certainly the Caddos were the first immigrants to enter and take up permanent residence in the forests of East Texas. With their allies the Kadohadachos of northeastern Texas and southwestern Arkansas and the Natchitoches of western Louisiana, the Hasinai (sometimes known as the Asenai, the Assoni, the Asenay, or the Cenis), they were members of loose alliances known as the Caddo Confederacies. Individual members of these confederacies called one another tayshas, meaning "allies" or "friends," and from this greeting gave the region its and its people the European designation "Tejas" or "Texas."

The Caddos

When first encountered by Europeans, they had evolved into three confederacies: The largest of these was the Hasinai who occupied the upper reaches of the Neches and Angelina River valleys; the Kadohadachos who occupied the great bend of the Red River in northeastern Texas and southwestern Arkansas; and the Natchitoches who lived in the vicinity of present-day Natchitoches Parish in Louisiana. Between the Natchitoches and the Kadohadachos was an independent tribe, the Yatasi which later split into segments, one joining each of the neighboring confederacies. Other independent tribes were Adais, living north of Natchitoches on the Red River and the Eyeish (Hais or Ayish) near San Augustine, Texas. (See Map I.)

East Texas Caddos. In due time, following their appearance about 500 A. D., they established themselves in a number of villages strung out along the waterways. Caddos were highly successful agriculturists who produced an abundant food supply making possible a dense population and a high degree of cultural development. Linguistically, they were related to tribes to their north and northwest, including the Arikara and the Pawnee. Culturally, however, their affiliations were with the Creeks, Chickasaws, Choctaws, Cherokees, and Natchez to their east and southeast.

A Caddo village of the time when they were first visited by European explorers consisted of a number of small units of varying size often strung out for perhaps twenty miles along a watercourse within a valley. A sedentary people, they established their villages along streams and built conical houses by setting upright poles in the ground and covering them with clay-plastered wattle.

Their crops were planted, cultivated, and harvested by communal effort. Both men and women worked the plots, using crude tools fashioned from animal bones or wood. Fire was sometimes employed to burn over old fields or to assist in clearing new ones. Despite their use of primitive methods, the Caddos planted and harvested corn, several varieties of beans, squash, muskmelons, watermelons, sunflower seeds, and tobacco. To supplement those food sources, they gathered nuts, wild fruits, berries, roots, and tubers from the surrounding forests. Hunting provided them with meat from deer, buffalo, and bear, as well as a variety of small mammals and birds; and they also took fish from the nearby streams.

The principal food staple was corn which was roasted, presumably by placing the green, unhusked ears in a bed of ashes. It was also boiled, either alone or with beans or other vegetables. Dried corn was ground as were nuts and seeds, in large mortars made from hollowed out tree trunks. Women pounded the corn with large wooden pestles. The resulting flour was used in soups and gruel and when winnowed to make bread and tortillas. Meat was preserved by smoking and also jerked by sun drying or fire drying.

They were also widely known for their ceramic arts, acknowledged as among the finest in the New World. They produced large amounts of pottery, utilizing numerous forms, patterns, and decorations. In addition, they created baskets and mats of reeds. They fashioned bows of bois d'arc (Osage orange) and musical instruments such as rattles, flutes, flageolets, and drums.

Caddos had evolved a well organized system of government containing a series of graded officers, each with a specific duty. Each confederacy was headed by a xinzsei, a hereditary office whose holder was accorded a great deal of respect and obedience. Next came the caddices, or tribal chieftains also hereditary office holders. Large tribes would also have a number of subordinate chiefs known as canhas. The canha assisted the caddi by making his orders known throughout the tribe, calling meetings of the elders, and on occasion presiding in the absence of the caddi.

Under the canhas were the chayas who were in charge of executing commands and other orders of their superior officers. Yet another series of officers, the tammas, acted as sergeants-at-arms or law enforcement officers.

In addition to serving as the temporal leaders of the community, the xinesi and the caddices also acted as its spiritual leaders as well, serving as priests and "voices of the gods." Although the Caddos were not monotheistic, they did believe in an omnipotent male deity who had created the universe, and now punished evil and rewarded good.

On occasions the xinesi called the tribes of the confederacy together at the temple, a structure similar to an ordinary house, only larger, furnished with various religious articles and having a perpetual fire burning in its center. Nearby were the two small houses of the cocinicis, two boys who served as intermediaries between the supreme god and the xinesi and through which the xinesi learned the will of the deity for his people. Caddos also had shamans (medicine men) who acted as healers and had close contact with the spirit world.

Among the most important religious occasions for these people were the feasts of thanksgiving for the harvest season and ceremonies in wintertime aimed at insuring a successful planting season.

Their ceremonial centers were clustered around temple mounds that varied considerably in size and shape. These earthen mounds were usually square or rectangular in shape with flat tops, having a stairway on at least one side. The prodigious labor required to build them indicates that the tribes' agricultural lifestyle afforded them enough free time to undertake such massive projects. They also indicate that their political system was developed to the point where it could induce, direct, and organize the people into units to fashion such structures. The mounds were almost certainly used for religious ceremonies conducted by a priestly caste.[9]

Their clothing consisted of tanned hides decorated with small white seeds or fringe. Men kept their hair short except for a small patch on top of the head which they allowed to grow to waist length, greased, and decorated with feathers. Women styled their hair more simply, parting it in the middle, combing it into a queue, and tying it into a knot at the neck with pieces of dyed animal skin. They were fond of ornamentation, painting their faces and bodies and wearing shells, bones, feathers, and pretty stones in their ears, noses, and hair, as

---

[9] Newcombe, The Indians of Texas, pp. 283-284.

well as wearing necklaces, armlets, and wristlets.¹⁰

Children received a birth-name which might be kept throughout their lives, or dropped for a nickname or that of a guardian spirit. By the time males became skilled and successful warriors, they were considered ready for marriage. When a man decided to wed a particular girl he brought her presents, but more importantly he endeavored to win the favor of her parents and brothers. Notice of an impending marriage was usually given to the caddi, but no further ceremony was required. Couples could dissolve their marriage by "divorcing themselves," and seek a marriage with some other partner.

An early Spanish explorer, Fray Isidro de Espinosa, described the Caddos he knew as being "naturally quick, intelligent, friendly, high-minded, and without low thoughts. As to personal appearance, they are well built and robust, but at the same time light and strong, always ready for war expeditions and of good courage. They preserve an inviolable peace, but they never form a truce or make friends with the enemy."¹¹ Other observers commented on the cranial deformation practiced by some of them as well as their habit of tattooing their faces and bodies.

The natives used needles or other sharp-pointed objects to prick the skin until the blood flowed, these they rubbed powdered charcoal in the wounds creating vivid tattoos. They tattooed "scores or streaks on their faces, from the top of the forehead down the nose to the tip of the chin," while intricate plant and animal designs were tattooed on their bodies. Women were marked as much as the men, perhaps even more extensively, adding designs at the corners of the eyes, "and on other parts of their bodies, whereof they make more particular show on their bosom."¹²

In addition, their faces and bodies were painted for special occasions. The woman painted themselves "from the waist up to the shoulders in various colored streaks, particularly the breasts." Men painted their bodies for war with a vermillion color combined with bear

---

¹⁰ For additional information about Caddo life and lifestyle, see: Cecile Elkins Carter, Caddo Indians, Where We Came From (Norman: University of Oklahoma Press, 1995), pp. 14-19.

¹¹ Partin, et al, Nacogdoches, p. 4.

¹² Newcombe, The Indians of Texas, pp.289-290,

grease.

With the coming of Europeans to East Texas, they were exposed to European tools, firearms, and new diseases. Missions were established among them, and in time colonists crowded into their lands and displaced them. In 1835, these tribes were joined together with other Caddos from Louisiana and, confronted by Cherokees, they were forced westward. By 1859, the Caddos were forced westward to the Brazos River valleys and finally by 1859 to reservations in Oklahoma. The remnants in East Texas gradually faded away under the steady pressure of increasing European settlement.

A contemporary student of Texas Indians and their cultures summed up the fate of the East Texas Caddos, saying:

> The mighty are sometimes brought as low as the humble with as much or even more ease by conquering powers. This was the case of the Caddo Indians of East Texas, although their conquest seems to have been primarily brought about by epidemics rather than by war. The collapse of these confederacies was so rapid, and their decline in numbers so great that the onrushing American frontier hardly took notice of the Caddos, the dregs of what had been two centuries earlier rich, splendid, barbaric theocracies.[13]

Persons searching for their ancestors among the East Texas Caddos face a near impossible task. Unfortunately, the Caddos, despite their relatively advanced native culture, never developed a written language, and thus information concerning their names, parentage, gender, birth and death dates, burial places, or other relevant data has not survived. Moreover, although Spanish colonial regulations required that an annual census be taken in each of their overseas colonies, the East Texas Caddos were not enumerated. Therefore, virtually all of those people are lost to recorded history.

The Cherokees

Cherokee Indians were first reported in the Province of Texas in 1807 when a small band of these natives established a village on the Red River in its northeastern corner. That same year a delegation of Cherokees, Pascagoulas, Chickasaws, and Shawnees attempted to gain permission from Spanish officials in Nacogdoches to settle members of their tribes in the

---

[13] Newcombe, The Indians of Texas, p. 313.

region. Their request was approved as the Spaniards believed the Indians would settle and thereby create a buffer against the expansion of Anglo-Americans. For several years thereafter, a small number of them drifted in and out of northeastern and north central Texas; but between 1812 and 1819, increasing American pressure in Arkansas compelled more Cherokees to migrate south into eastern Texas. They were accompanied by associated tribes and bands of Quapaws (from the area around the mouth of the Arkansas River), Biloxis (from southern Alabama and Mississippi near Mobile), Choctaws (from central Mississippi), Delawares (from New York around Statten Island), Kickapoos (from southern Wisconsin and northern Illinois), and Shawnees (from southern Kentucky).

East Texas Cherokees. In 1819, they began settling in Lost Prairie, an area between the Sulfur Fork and the Red River in today's Miller County, Arkansas. But the next year they migrated further south, moving into present-day Cherokee and Smith Counties to join the sparse numbers of Indians already there. Other Cherokee bands from Arkansas and Oklahoma also entered, as did members of the other associated tribes. For example, Chief Bowles (also known as Duwali) led a band of some sixty families into Texas. Bowles was born in North Carolina about 1756. Tradition holds that his father was a Scotch-Irish trader and his mother a Cherokee.

Some of these bands first settled on Three Forks of the Trinity River in present-day Dallas County; but pressure from the attacks of hostile Indians of the region compelled them to more eastward into a virtually uninhabited region north of Nacogdoches settling in present-day Rusk County.[14] This land had once belonged to the Caddos who had been greatly reduced in numbers by warfare and disease. By 1822, this group of Cherokees had increased in population to some three hundred men, women, and children. Ultimately they would occupy a large portion of today's East Texas Counties of Smith, Cherokee, Rusk, and Van Zandt.

The Cherokees were a large powerful tribe of the Iroquoian linguistic family. Their society organized into clans or kin groups reflected an elaborate social, political, and

---

[14] Bowles established his village about fifty miles north of Nacogdoches.

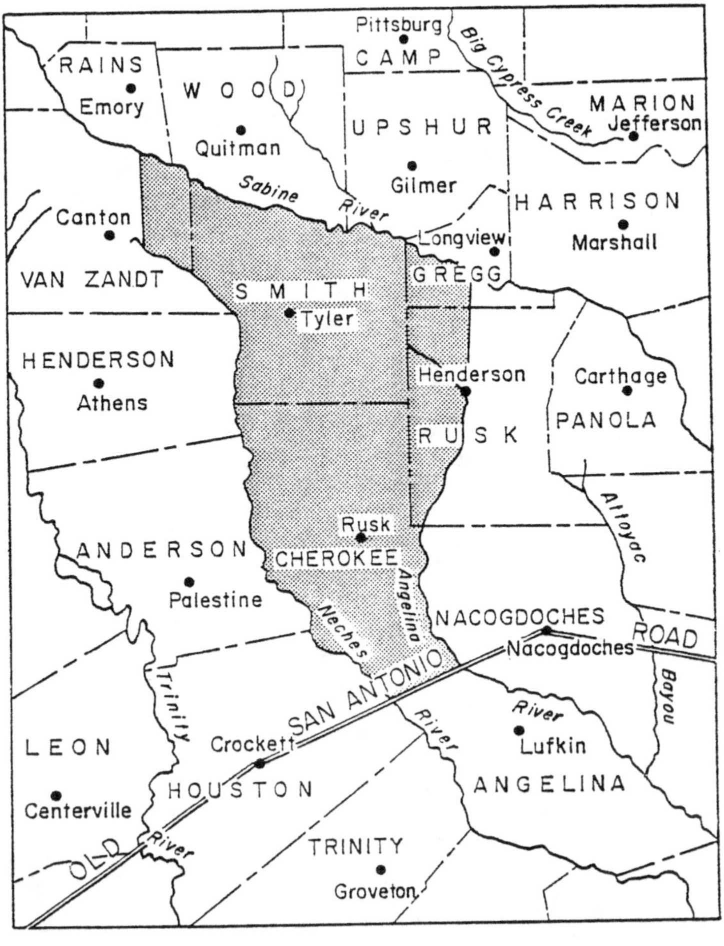

Shaded area shows the Cherokee Land Grant in Texas.

Adapted from Dorman H. Winfrey,
et al. (eds.), *Texas Indian Papers*

[CHIEF BOWLES AND THE TEXAS CHEROKEES]

ceremonial structure.[15] Their basic political unit was the town, which consisted of all the people who were drawn to a single ceremonial center. Within each town, a council dominated by older men handled political affairs. Individual towns sent representatives to regional councils to discuss diplomatic and military policy.

Cherokee towns were made up of thirty to forty households, clustered around a central townhouse which was used as a meeting place. Their houses were square or rectangular huts constructed of locked poles, weatherproofed with wattles and daub plaster and roofed with bark.[16]

Although they remained loyal to the Americans during the Revolution, many of them, under pressure of westward moving American settlers, immigrated to the present State of Arkansas. Discovery of gold in the lands of the Cherokee Nation in the 1830s and increased Anglo-American pressure, caused them, in 1835, to sell their lands in the American southeast and remove to Indian Territory (present-day Oklahoma). Having earlier adapted many white institutions to their own way of life, they established schools, adopted a constitution which created a government modeled upon that of the United States, and developed an alphabet becoming a literate people. At the same time many of them, particularly the women, adopted American-type clothing.[17] Men wore a turban, cloth tunic or coat bound at the waist by a sash, skin leggings with garters below the knee, and moccasins. Their adaptation came at a high cost, for contact with American settlers also brought calamitous wars, epidemics, and food shortages.

Their ancestral home was in the southeastern United States where they located after having been driven from the Pennsylvania region by other Iroquoian tribes. They ultimately settled in North Carolina and came to consider the entire Allegheny mountain country as their

---

[15] Emmet Star, History of the Cherokee Indians, reprint edition (Baltimore: Genealogical Publishing Com., 2003), Chapter I. This volume contains valuable information on hundreds of Cherokees, most of whom were residents of Indian Territory (Oklahoma).

[16] Carol A. Limscomb, "Cherokee Indians," The New Handbook of Texas, (Austin: Texas State Historical Society, 19--), 7 vols., Vol. 2, p. 61.

[17] Ibid.

own land. That region included parts of Virginia, Tennessee, North Carolina, South Carolina, Georgia, and Alabama.

The Cherokees and associated tribes flourished in East Texas. By 1828 approximately 300-400 of them (100 or more families) lived in Smith County and its vicinity alone, and by 1833 their total population had increased to at least 800 individuals.

When Anglo-Americans first ventured into the lands of the Cherokee Nation, the natives were living in sixty-four towns and villages with some 6,000 fighting men. They worshiped the sun who, they believed, had given them their sacred fire which they kept burning night and day and to which their priests offered sacrifices. Their god, they also believed, had divided time into day and night and into four seasons.

Among their myths was that of a great buzzard who created the beautiful valleys and mountains in the Allegheny region. White the earth was still flat and soft, in ancient times, the great buzzard flew over the country, becoming tired his great wings dragged the ground creating the great valleys. When he turned them upward to resume his flight, he created the mountains.[18]

Demands of the encroaching white settlers resulted in a removal act signed by President Andrew Jackson which precipitated the long, heartbreaking trek of 1838-1839, known today as "the Trail of Tears." In a relatively short span most of the Cherokees living east of the Mississippi River, particularly those living in Georgia, were forced to abandon their homes and their ancestral lands and migrate to Oklahoma.[19]

Whether the Spanish government in Mexico City had given Chief Bowles and his band of Cherokees permission to settle in Texas is debatable. Regardless of legalities the Indians came to East Texas and quickly learned to love their new home. They were not crowded there by white settlers. They built their homes beneath the tall pines and cleared patches of the

---

[18] Mary Whatley Clark, <u>Chief Bowles and the Texas Cherokees</u> (Norman: University of Oklahoma Press, 1971), p. 5.

[19] Clark reported that in the mid-1960s, there were approximately 100,000 mixed blood Cherokees, 47,000 living in Oklahoma. Of this number probably from 1,000 to 1,500 are descendants of the Texas Cherokees. <u>Ibid.,</u> p. 7.

forest to plant their corn. Buffalo meat was plentiful; and natural springs provided clear, cold water. "They hoped to make this land their home forever."[20]

In time this small band of Texas Cherokees were joined by other Cherokees from the United States. The well-known chief Tahchee (also known as Dutch), one of the first Cherokees to emigrate to Arkansas from the Old Cherokee Nation east of the Mississippi, was one of them; but he later returned to the United States.

Cherokee Allies. The Texas Cherokees formed a loose confederation with other refugees from the United States, including Shawnees, Delawares, Kickapoos, Choctaws, Biloxis, Alabamas, and Coushattas. Since the Cherokees formed the largest segment, their chief, John Bowles (The Bowl) was regarded as chief and leader of them all.[21]

Richard Fields. In some four years' time, however, Bowles was superseded by Richard Fields. Fields had been born about 1780, of mixed ancestry being only one-eighth Cherokee. He had served as an interpreter in negotiations leading up to the Council House treaty in September 1812 and served as a soldier in the War of 1812. In his capacity as diplomatic chief of the tribe, he went to San Antonio de Bexar about 1820 seeking title to the lands occupied by his people. He was advised to visit the Viceroy in Mexico City.

While he negotiated with the Viceroy in Mexico City during 1821, the Spanish government was overthrown and Mexico became an independent nation. Having spent all his available funds, Fields returned to East Texas. Despairing that the Mexican government would allow a separate existence for the Texas Cherokees, Fields entered into negotiations with Anglo-Americans leading the Fredonian Rebellion.

However, as a nation, the Cherokees refused to approve participation in the ill-fated Fredonian uprising. As a consequence, Fields was tried by the Cherokee Council in February 1827 and ordered executed. He left a wife, the daughter of French trader Francois Grappe of Natchitoches, and seven minor children.

While in Mexico City, Fields and his fellow negotiators, Chief Bowles and Chief

---

[20] Ibid.

[21] Clarke, <u>Chief Bowles and the Texas Cherokees</u>, p. 17.

Nicolet, he became acquainted with Stephen F. Austin, Green DeWitt, and Haden Edwards there also seeking title to large land grants. When Fields and his fellow Cherokees ran out of funds, Haden Edwards paid their expenses for a time. In any case, Fields' conclusion that the Mexican government would never ratify the Cherokees claims to their East Texas land proved to be valid. They were never to receive any firm titles to their lands.

Chief Fields deeply resented the unjust treatment of him and his people by the Mexican authorities, and he determined to exact retribution from the Mexican government and the Anglo-Americans who persisted in settling on the rich lands claimed by the Cherokees. But he delayed in taking action on advise from Austin and other Anglo and Cherokee leaders.

John Dunn Hunter. In 1825, John Dunn Hunter, perhaps the most enigmatic figure in Texas Cherokee history, arrived among the East Texas villages. He was born about 1796, place unknown. He claimed that when a child he was captured by the Cherokees before they came to Texas. As he grew to young manhood, he adopted the name John Dunn, an English benefactor, and later added the name "Hunter" given him by the Indians in recognition of his skill as a hunter. Although he lived with the Cherokees until about 1816, he somehow obtained a good education and was able to travel about the United States and England.

After he returned to the Cherokees, Chief Richard Fields sent him to renew negotiations with Mexican officials in Mexico City in their continuing effort to obtain title to their Texas lands. He was promised land grants to individual Indian settlers but unable to get land for the tribe and permission to create a self-governing Cherokee Nation in the Piney Woods. When he returned to East Texas later in the year 1826, he and Fields began negotiations with Colonel Martin Parmer and his followers in what became known as the Fredonian Rebellion.

The Fredonians and the Indians drew up an agreement whereby East Texas would be divided between them along a line running from Sand Springs westward to the Rio Grande. Along with Richard Fields, Hunter was tried by the Cherokee Council in February 1827 and thereafter executed.[22] After some lengthy study, Clarke concluded that many journalists in

---

[22] Other Cherokees known to participate in the Fredonian Rebellion included John Bags, Cuk-To-Keh, and Ne-Ko-Take. From a list prepared by Linda Ericson Devereaux in <u>Tales From the</u>

the United States accused Hunter of being an adventurer and an imposter and others saw him rather as a maligned defender of the Indians and their rights. He was, she says, "either the first philanthropist to set foot on Texas soil or one of the shrewdest schemers ever to enter the Mexican province."[23]

Treaty Negotiations. In the 1830s the Texas Cherokees were congregated in at least three but possibly in as many as seven towns north of Nacogdoches. In February 1836 on the eve of the Texas Revolution, the Anglo-Texans, needing the friendship and support of the East Texas Cherokees, sent Sam Houston, John Forbes, and John Cameron to negotiate a treaty providing for permanent title to their lands. When this document was submitted to the Senate of the Republic of Texas after the close of the Revolution, ratification was denied.

Between 1829 and 1835, frequent clashes with their Indian enemies including the Osage, Tonkawa, Tawokani, and Comanche as well as the encroachment of American settlers further augmented unsettled conditions. Incoming settlers were rapidly penetrating the Ayish Bayou region and present-day Anderson County.

Anglo-American Pressures. At the same time, Anglo-American settlers were rapidly spreading across East Texas, impinging on the territory of the Indians living there: the Caddo remnants, the Wichitas, Tonkawas, the Kickapoos, and the Cherokees. The latter became particularly restless and frightened. They had already been pushed all the way from the mountains of Carolina and Tennessee, and now, a forest and mountain people, they were being forced out onto the plains with nowhere to go. As early as October 1835, 101 land titles had been granted to Americans in East Texas to lands claimed by the Cherokees.

The Texas Cherokees had maintained a policy of strict neutrality during the time of the Texas Revolution, although a random member of the tribe may have participated on an individual basis. After Sam Houston, a long-time friend of the Cherokees, became president of the new Republic of Texas, he sought to have the Congress of the Republic enact legislation that would guarantee the Indians title to their lands only to have his attempt angrily rejected.

Old Stone Fort (Lufkin; Piney Woods Publishing, 1976), p. 56.

[23] Chief Bowles and the Texas Cherokees, p. 30.

Although, in 1838, the Kickapos, Biloxi and Iones took part in what became known as the Cordovan Rebellion, along with a group of Mexican and Anglo Texans, the Cherokees elected not to take part in the war effort. Thus, although they had demonstrated that they were a remarkably peaceful and civilized tribe, in the minds of many, perhaps most, Texans they were a band of marauding red men standing in the path of Anglo-American progress.

Cherokee War. Following the end of the short-lived Cordovan uprising, in late 1838 and early 1839, relations between the Anglo-American Texans and the various Indian groups living to the north of them deteriorated rapidly. Discovery of a letter in May 1839 disclosing plans by the Mexican government to enlist the Indians against the Anglo settlers prompted President Mirabeau B. Lamar, now president of the Republic, to order the East Texas Indians expelled from Texas and driven into Arkansas and the Indian Territory. During the ensuing hostilities, a number of Indian warriors were killed, among them Chiefs Bowles and Egg.

During the "Cherokee War" of 1838-1839, at least two companies of Indians were recruited by General Thomas J. Rusk to join with the Anglo-American troops in fighting with the Cherokees. Many of them were not identified as to tribal affiliation in the muster rolls, but one of the companies was made up entirely of Shawnees. Table I following identifies by name and rank, those individuals whose names appeared on the rolls.

Table I

Indian Militiamen (1838-1839)

Muster Roll of Captain James H. Durst's Company of Mounted Rangers

Delores Cortines, Pvt.	Big Rump, Pvt.
Early Cordery, Pvt.	Dry, Pvt.
Big Bone, Pvt.	Otterlifter, Pvt.
James, Pvt.	Sequeah, Pvt.
Tekiansta, Pvt.	They Have Shot the Dog, Pvt.
Zekiel, Pvt.	Utalah, Pvt.
Ellis, Pvt.	Calawntalite, Pvt.
Coffee, Pvt.	William, Pvt.
Wash. Loura(?), Pvt.	Turnover, Pvt.
John Rogers, Pvt.	Lightening Bug, Pvt.
Gizzard, Pvt.	Uxtalle, Pvt.
Stanly Bowls, Pvt.	Louis, Pvt.
Moses, Pvt.	Parakeet, Pvt.

Otustuke, Pvt.	Hot House, Pvt.
Shit Ass, Pvt.	He Stops Them, Pvt.
Alloverbigness, Pvt.	Ground Hog, Pvt.
Hog Stones, Pvt.	Young Bird, Pvt.
Pleasant, Pvt.	Twister, Pvt.
Jesse, Pvt.	Watch, Pvt.
Looking At Us, Pvt.	Back Bone, Pvt.
Cat Floting, Pvt.	John, Pvt.
Over the Branches, Pvt.	He Throws Them Down, Pvt.
Coshatta Killer, Pvt.	Jackson, Pvt.
White Man, Pvt.	Night Killer, Pvt.
	Krak Killer, Pvt.

Muster Roll of Captain Panther's Company of Shawnee Indians

Panther, Capt.	George, Pvt.
Shy Buck, Interp.	Robinson, Pvt.
Possum, Pvt.	Buzzard, Pvt.
Young Shy Buck, Pvt.	Chewwah, Pvt.
Hood, Pvt.	Little John, Pvt.
Little Jim	Little Jack, Pvt.
Chewwackotah, Pvt.	Howtiskey, Pvt.
Solges, Pvt.	Killawasha, Pvt.
Lewis, Pvt.	Pocawah, Pvt.
Fox, Pvt.	Oachella, Pvt.
Big Field, Pvt.	Kishescaw, Pvt.
Possatatah, Pvt.	Whet Stone, Pvt.
Yellow Jacket, Pvt.	Big John, Pvt.
Thompson, Pvt.	Petetah, Pvt.
Jack, Pvt.	Catawah, Pvt.

Source: Original Muster Rolls, Texas State Archives transcribed by Kathryn Hooper Davis, printed as East Texas Militiamen: 1838-1839 (2 vols., Nacogdoches: Ericson Books, 1992).

By 1840, then, the Indians had been virtually eliminated as permanent residents of East Texas. They would be replaced by Spanish colonials along with a few European immigrants from other nations and some venturesome Americans.

Part III

THE SPANISH, MEXICANS AND ANGLOS

COLONIALS

The East Texas region was colonized by Europeans, principally Spanish missionaries and military personnel, centuries after the first Caddos began drifting into the forests west of the Sabine River. They would be joined much later by a scattering of Spanish-speaking settlers, French and American traders, and finally by a steady wave of Anglos, primarily Anglo-Americans.

The Spanish Colonials. Despite the failure of the first Spanish effort to occupy East Texas, the attempt provided Spanish authorities with valuable knowledge of the region's geography and its Indian inhabitants. It also demonstrated that occupation efforts could not succeed without presidios (forts) and civilian settlements to sustain them. Spurred by French exploration and expeditions into the region in the latter years of the Seventeenth and early years of the Eighteenth Centuries, Spanish officials in Mexico City, who viewed those actions as a threat to Spanish claims, determined on counter measures. Initially, they authorized a series of missions to act as a buffer against possible French encroachments from their post in Western Louisiana, Natchitoches, located just fifty miles east of the Sabine River.

Spanish Missions. By 1716, the Spanish had planted six missions, five of them extending on a line from the Neches River on the west to Los Adaes near the Red River on the east only a few miles west of Natchitoches. In addition, a garrison of troops was quartered at a new presidio erected on the Neches River. One of the new missions was planted just east of the Angelina River at the site of an important Hasinai (Caddo) village. Named Nuestra Señora de la Purisima Conception, it represented the first formal European occupation of present-day Nacogdoches County. To provide protection for the mission and its activities, a presidio was built on a hill just west to the mission and named Presidio Nuestra Señora de los Delores de los Tejas.

A second mission, Nuestra Señora de Guadalupe de los Nacogdoches, was located some nine leagues (about twenty-two miles) east-southeast. It probably stood on an a high rise overlooking Banita Creek and marked the beginning of European occupation of the site of the modern City of Nacogdoches. By July 1716, a temporary log church and dwellings for the missionaries had been constructed and placed in charge of Father Antonio Margil de Jesus who represented the College of Neustra Señora de Guadalupe de Zacatecas.

Father Margil, known to many as "the Apostle of Texas," had been born in Valencia, Spain, in 1657, entered the Franciscan order there in 1663, and in 1683 volunteered for mission work among the Indians of America. After arriving in New Spain later that year, he began preaching missions in Yucatan, Costa Rica, and Guatemala. In 1706, he was placed in charge of a new missionary College or body of clergy in Zacatecas.

Other new missions were established among the Adaes Indians some fifteen miles west of the French post at Natchitoches named Mission San Miguel de Linares de los Adaes, among the Ais indians near present-day San Augustine named Nuestra Señora de los Delores de los Ais, and among the Nazonis in northern Nacogdoches County near the Rusk County line named Nuestra Señora San Jose de los Nazonis. The missions made slow progress. Their priests and the soldiers in the presidios continually fell victims to illness, many of the soldiers deserted, and the Indians, preoccupied with hunting and gathering of their crops, refused to be congregated about the missions. Severe weather, epidemics among the Indians, and the lack of adequate supplies reduced the missions to dire circumstances.

Spanish-French Confrontations. The already precarious situation of the missions grew steadily worse in 1719 when war broke out anew between Spain and France. The French in Louisiana resented the Spanish occupation of eastern Texas. They viewed it as a hinderance to French expansion and feared the Spanish would attempt to occupy territory east of the Arroyo Hondo. The French captured the Spanish outpost of Los Adaes and threatened to drive the Spanish out of all of Texas. As a consequence, by early 1720 the Spanish abandoned East Texas for the second time and retreated to San Antonio de Bexar to waited to learn the eventual fate of colonization efforts in East Texas.

Spanish Reentry. The year following the Spanish organized an expedition aimed at reestablishing their control over East Texas by restoring the priests to their missions and establishing a military post among the Caddos. The mission near the Neches River was reestablished and renamed San Francisco de los Neches, later Mission La Purisima Conception was restored, and Mission San Jose de los Nazonis was renewed, and still later Mission Nuestra Señora de Guadalupe de los Nacogdoches was rebuilt as were Mission Nuestra Señora de los Dolores de los Ais and Mission San Miguel de Linares de los Adaes.

One half a league east of Linares, the Spanish constructed a hexagonal-shaped presidio with a stockade of pointed logs which was named Nuestra Señora de Pilar and manned by a garrison of some one hundred soldiers and six brass field pieces. In 1729, Los Adaes became the provincial capital of Texas; and its garrison was reduced from one hundred troops to sixty to lessen the expense of maintenance and to reflect the absence of local Indian threats. Moreover, in the meantime Spain, had obtained sovereignty over Louisiana thus eliminating the danger of French encroachment.

Despite strenuous and persistent efforts the Franciscan priests stationed at the nearby mission were unsuccessful resetting the local Indians around the mission. As a consequence, in 1768, the mission was abandoned, the Franciscans acknowledging defeat.

Missions Abandoned. By 1772, Los Adaes and other Spanish settlements in East Texas "composed a pocket of isolated Spanish settlement."[24] After fifty years of colonizing effort with little success, Spanish authorities ordered the abandonment of los Adaes and transferred the capital to San Antonio de Bexar. Table II below provides the names of the Spanish soldiers stationed at the Los Adaes presidio in 1730.

Table II
Military Roster of the Presidio Neustra Señora del Pilar

Don Juan Antonio de Bustillo, age 40, Captain	Guillermo Rodriguez
	Juan Antonio Ramos
Don Joseph Cayetano de Bergara, age 31, Lieut.	Joseph Sanchez
	Agustin de Abila
Don Joseph Gonzalez, age 30, Ensign	Joseph de Albarado
Manuel Antonio de Losoya, Sgt.	Lazaro Ybanez
Nicholas Hernandez(?)	Antonio de Paniaguan
Juan Gamez	Juan Joseph Marquez
Francisco de Napoles	Critobal de Santiago
Francisco de la Zerda	Juan Sanchez Tovar
Juan de Armijo	Pascual de Luna
Joseph de Arejo	Antonio Luna
Joseph Rosales	Juan de los Reyes
Blas de Villareal	Philipe del Rio
Gregorio Lopez	Cristobal del Rio
Juan Joseph de la Encarnation	Domingo del Rio

---

[24] James L. McCorkle, Jr., "Los Adaes," The New Handbook of Texas, Vol. 4, p. 292.

Juan de Villareal	Francisco de San Miguel
Juan Paulin	Juan de Torres
Antonio Gregorio Cordoves	Joseph Antonio de la Vera
Francisco Morillo	Phelipe Bermudez
Andres Sanchez	Pedro Perez
Phelipe de Sierra	Francisco de Santiago
Juan Antonio de Corvarrabias	Ypolito de Fuentres (Montes?)
Joseph de Acosta	Manuel Luis de los Reyes
Juan de Padilla	Miguel Julian Flores
Joachin de Torres	Francisco Xavier de Talamantez
Cristobal Rodriguez	Nichoas Antonio de la Cardona
Julio de los Reyes	Diego de Villafranca
Joseph Ventura de Alcala	Manual Salvador de los Posos
Mateo Ybarbo	Joseph Antonio de Acostta y Arias

Source: Archives, transcribed by Terry Oliver, published in <u>Yesterdays</u> Vol. XIV, No. 2 (September 1994), p. 1.

In 1731, Spanish settlement in East Texas consisted of the provincial capital, Los Adaes, located some fifteen miles west of the Red River and the French outpost of Natchitoches; Mission San Miguel de Linares de los Adaes, near present-day Robeline, Louisiana; Mission Nuestra Señora de Guadalupe de los Nacogdoches, located at the present site of Nacogdoches, Texas; Mission Nuestra Señora de los Ais, situated on Ayish Bayou near present-day San Augustine, Texas.

The cession of Louisiana to Spain following the end of the French and Indian War removed France as a threat to Spanish East Texas and led Spanish colonial officials to question the need of maintaining expensive outposts in that far removed part of their domain. The direct result was the total abandonment, in 1773, of the East Texas missions and presidios. A decree issued by the Spanish King in 1772 ordered that the presidio at Los Adaes be dismantled and the settlers in its vicinity be removed to the Villa de San Antonio de Bexar, and the area missions abandoned.

The approximately 500 Spanish settlers living at and near Los Adaes were aghast at the thought of leaving their homes and their lands. Some fled to Natchitoches, others hid among the Indians nearby, both groups planning to return to their homes when the soldiers left. Nevertheless, on June 25, 1773, under the command of Lieutenant Don Joseph Gonzales, the

East Texans began the long march toward San Antonio de Bexar. At the ranch of Antonio Gil Ybarbo, situated near the old Ais mission site some thirty leagues west of Los Adaes, the marchers halted to rest. Here at El Lobanillo twenty-four persons, including Ybarbo's mother, sister, and sister-in-law, were left to follow later.

By July the procession had reached Nacogdoches where two families consisting of nine persons were left at the site of Mission Guadalupe. Here also Lieutenant Gonzales and two women were left in their graves having died as a result of the hardships of the journey. At this juncture, Antonio Gil Y'barbo (Ibarvo, Ibarbo, Y'Barbo, and Y'Barvo) assumed leadership of the refugees and led them on to San Antonio. Between Nacogdoches and the Brazos River, the marchers suffered from lack of food, water, and adequate transportation. Ten children died and were interred in unmarked graves. At the Brazos a relief party met them, and on September 26, 1773, three months after being forced to leave their East Texas homes, the remaining 167 families finally arrived in San Antonio de Bexar.

Antonio Gil Y'Barbo. Y'Barbo, who was born about 1729 at Los Adaes, "was destined to become the dominant figure" in Spanish colonizing efforts in early East Texas.[25] His father, Matheo Antonio Y'Barbo, was a soldier who had been stationed at the Los Adaes garrison, and his mother, Juana Luzgarda Hernandez, was the daughter of a resident of the presidio of San Antonio de Valero. The marriage was performed at the mission church of San Antonio de Valero (known today as the Alamo). The bride was the daughter of Nicholas Hernandez and Simona de Sepulbeda (Sepulveda).

Matheo Y'Barbo was a native of Andalusia, Spain who probably arrived in Texas in 1718; and Antonio's mother was also known to be a native of Andalusia. By 1725, they were both residents of Los Adaes. By 1738, his father Matheo held the rank of alferez (brevet lieutenant) at the Los Adaes garrison.

Soon after the settlers left Los Adaes Indians began to pillage their abandoned homes;

---

[25] Joe E. and Carolyn R. Ericson, <u>Personalities on the East Texas Frontier: Brief Narratives of Their Lives and Times</u> (Nacogdoches: Ericson Books, 1998), p. 1. A comprehensive genealogy of the Gil Y'Barbo and related East Texas families may be found in Carolyn Reeves Ericson and Linda Ericson Devereaux, <u>Antonio Gil Y'Barbo: Father of Nacogdoches</u> (Nacogdoches: Ericson Books, 2001).

Frenchmen from Louisiana began drifting into the region; and the Spanish residents who had fled to Natchitoches and those who had hidden among the Indians slowly returned to their homes. The latter group were soon joined by those who had remained behind at El Lobanillo and the thirty-five others who had dropped out of the march to San Antonio de Bexar. There they awaited the return of their friends and relatives.

Surviving records demonstrate that no sooner had the "Adaesanos arrived in San Antonio than they began to agitate to return to East Texas."[26] Within eight days they presented the governor with a petition in which they claimed they could not form a settlement at San Antonio without encroaching upon the land rights of those persons already residing there. They also maintained that they were bankrupt as a result of the loss of property sustained by their removal, and that they lacked funds to construct an aqueduct to provide water. They asked to be allowed to return to Los Adaes to recover goods and livestock and to form a new settlement near the Mission Los Ais. Seventy-five of the leading Adaesanos affixed their signatures to the petition. (See Table III below.)

Table III

Signers: Petition of 1773

Antonio Gil Y'Barbo	Manuel Mora
Juan Mora	Christoval Equiz
Augustin Sanchez	Melchor Morin
Juan Jose Sanchez	Juan Josef Pachero
Rorible de la Juente	Antonio del Rio
Josef Zepeda	Miguel Ramos
Pedro Mansolo	Mariano Padilla
Bernabe del Rio	Gasper Ruiz
Joaquin Cordova	Diego Herrera
Christoval Padilla	Francisco Cerda
Manuel Mendez	Juan Martinez
Cayetene Gomez	Juan Ygnacio Guerrero
Matis Sanchez	Dimas Meya
Marcos Martines	Ygnacio del Rio
Salvador de Esperanza	Francisco Losoya

---

[26] James G. Partin, Carolyn R. Ericson, Joe E. Ericson, and Archie P. McDonald, Nacogdoches (Lufkin: Best of East Texas Publishers, 1995), p. 31.

Juan Chirino	Gabriel Padilla
Candide San Miguel	Francisco de Torres
Pedro de Luna	Gil Flores
Manuel Lisonde	Lazare de Torres
Francisco Cruz	Francisco Guerrero
Juan de Tobar	Juan Josef Santa Cruz
Nepemucene de la Cerda	Thomas Y'Barbo
Melchor Benitez	Pedro Rincos
Christoval Ballexe	Patricio Padilla
Josef Calderon	Gregorio Soto
Manuel Trexe	Juan de Torres
Manuel Barrela	Jacinto Mora
Christoval Garcia	Nicholas Mora
Domingo Carmena	Jose Domingo Barcenas
Jose Maria Cambero	Victor Mansolo
Juaquin Mansolo	Manuel Cruz
Ambrosio Vasquez	Augustin del Rio
Vicente Cepeda	Manuel del Rio
Pedro de Sierra	Augustin Morillo
Barte Soto	Usiderie Equnio
Thomas Guitierrez	Ramos Verero

Governor Juan Maria Vicencio de Ripperda recommended that the Adaesanos present their petition to the Viceroy in Mexico City, and Antonio Gil Y'Barbo was elected to carry the petition to the vice regal court. In 1774, Y'Barbo made the formal presentation and received tentative approval. Ultimately, however, the East Texas refugees were permitted to return only as far east as a site on the Trinity River at Paso Tomas where the Old San Antonio Road (El Camino Real) and the La Bahia (Goliad) Roads crossed the river, near today's village of Randolph in Madison County.

The Old San Antonio Road (El Camino Real or King's Highway), although believed by many to be a single road, can be more accurately described as a network of trails, with different routes used for different purposes at different times. It began at Paso del Francia on the Rio Grande, passed near Cotulla and Poteet, and entered San Antonio, from there it passed between Hays and Caldwell Counties, then proceeded through Bastrop, Lee, and Burleson Counties, formed then the boundary between Robertson, Brazos, Madison, and Leon Counties, and then passed through Houston, Cherokee, Nacogdoches, San Augustine, and Sabine

Counties before crossing the Sabine River at Gaines Ferry--a distance of some 540 miles.[27] It was only one of five different routes used at various times; all of which began at the Presidio del Rio Grande, also known as San Juan Bautista which was located at Guerrero, Coahuilla, five miles from the Rio Grande and approximately thirty-five miles southeast of present-day Eagle Pass. Each of them led across South Texas and converged on San Antonio.[28]

Bucarelli. Nuestra Señora del Pilar de Bucarelli was the name chosen for the new settlement, and preparations for the move began in August 1774, but not all of the refuges were ready at the time and planned to come later. Y'Barbo with some seventy adult men went ahead and proceeded to lay out the new settlement around the traditional Spanish plaza. For a time Bucarelli prospered, but by 1778 an epidemic and Comanche Indian raids demoralized the people. Finally, in January, 1779, most of them, including Y'Barbo's family, left Bucarelli, while Y'Barbo and twenty men stayed behind to protect the remaining settlers, the people's goods, and their livestock.

At the same time, a fire destroyed approximately half the village, and the remainder was destroyed by a flooded Trinity River. Finding their position untenable, YBarbo and the men left behind headed eastward along the Camino Real. On their way to Nacogdoches, Y'Barbo picked up stragglers from the earlier moves. By late April, 1779, the whole band had arrived at the site of the old Mission Guadalupe in the present-day City of Nacogdoches, and permanent European settlement in East Texas became a reality.

Return to Nacogdoches. Y'Barbo was made captain of militia and lieutenant governor of the Pueblo of Nacogdoches. He soon established order in the village, and for some fifteen years he was virtually the absolute ruler of the settlement. In late 1779, he started construction on a stone house on a corner of the Plaza Principal, issued grants of land to the settlers, attempted to pacify the local Indians, and framed a code of laws for the community.

The Stone House he had constructed later became known as the "Stone Fort," although it was not really a fort but rather was a residence and trading post. From its rooms he issued

---

[27] The New Handbook of Texas, Vol. 4, p. 1139.

[28] Ibid.

land grants, although he had no legal authority to grant land or issue titles. His grants, some of them for as much as eleven leagues, were of necessity verbal in nature.

Spanish colonial regulations required that a population census be taken each year, and surviving records show that the Pueblo of Nacogdoches comprised of the village itself and much of the surrounding land numbered a total of 349 persons in 1783, 399 in 1784, 433 in 1786, 480 in 1790, 555 in 1791, 472 in 1792, 539 in 1793, and 453 in 1794, the last year of Y'Barbo's term as lieutenant governor.[29] (See Map III following.)

The earliest Spanish colonial census for East Texas extant is that taken by Antonio Gil Y'Barbo in December 1792. (See Table IV below.)

Table IV

1792 Census for the Village of Nacogdoches

ANTONIO GIL Y'BARBO, native of Los Adaes, age 63, married to Dona Maria Padilla, native of Los Adaes, 59.
CRISTOVAL de CORDOVA, native of San Luis Potosi, 68, widower.
NICHOLAS de MORA, native of Los Adaes, 46, widower with three children.
JUAN IGNACIO GUERRERO, native of San Antonio de Bexar, 61, married to Maria Antonia Ibarvo, native of Los Adaes, 40, two sons.
JOSE FLORES, native of Los Adaes, 36, married to Anna Maria Guerrero, native of Los Adaes, 25, one son and two daughters.
FRANCISCO PEREZ, native of San Antonio de Bexar, 26, married to Maria Antonia Darvan, native of Natchitoches, 32, to sons and one daughter.
JACINTE MORA, native of Los Adaes, 36, married to Maria Barrera, half-caste, native of Natchitoches, 18.
CAYSTANE SEPADA, native of San Antonio de Bexar, 48, married to Beatrice Sanchez, half-caste, native of Los Adaes, 31, one son and two daughters.
ANTONIO CORTINAS, servant, half-caste, native of Los Adaes, 26, married to Maria Benites, native of Los Adaes, 26, one daughter.
FRANCISCO SANTA CRUZ, native of Los Adaes, 49, married to Maria Gertrudis Padilla, 32, one daughter.
JOSE ANTONIO SANTA CRUZ, native of Los Adaes, 26, married to Joaquina Rineon,

---

[29] The term Nacogdoches as it appears in Spanish colonial records before the 1819 Adams-Onis Treaty was applied to a vaguely defined area lying between the Arroyo Honda in present-day Louisiana on the east and either the Trinity or Brazos Rivers on the west, and from the Gulf Coast on the south to the Red River on the north; although it could was used to refer to the village of Nacogdoches alone.

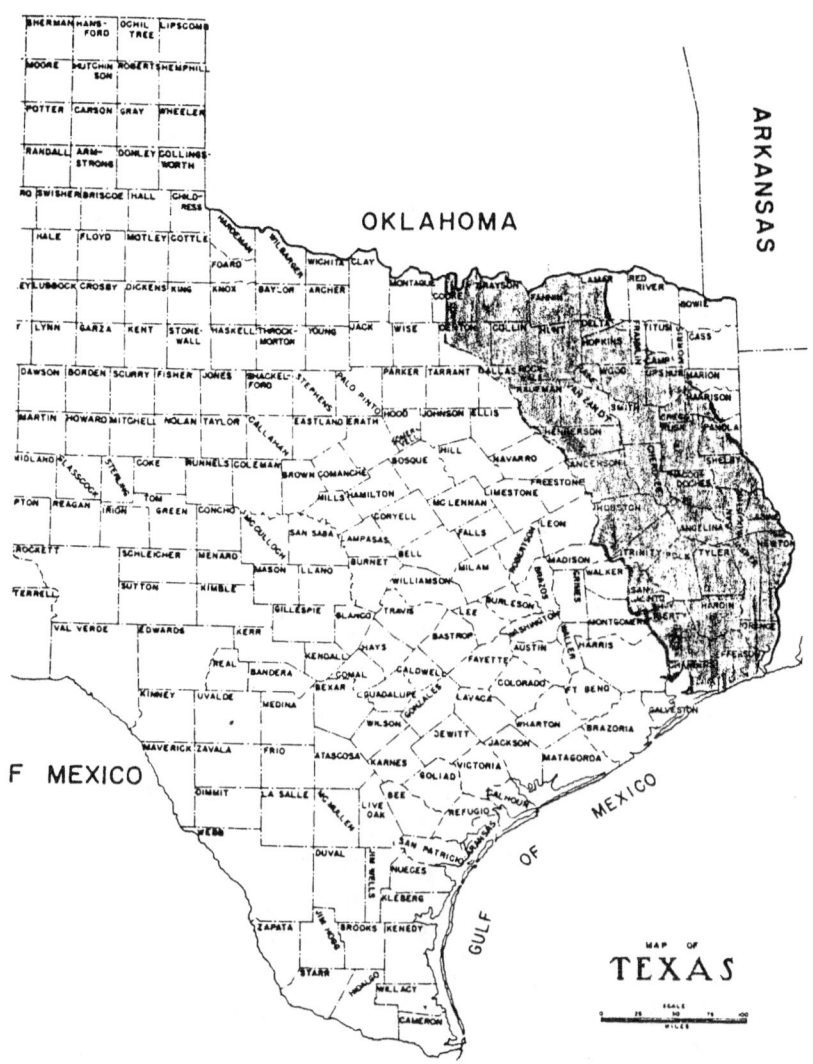

NACOGDOCHES DISTRICT - 1792

[NACOGDOCHES--GATEWAY TO TEXAS 1773-1849]

native of Bucarelli, 19.
ENGLE, native of New Orleans, 48, married to Juana Santa Cruz, native of Los Adaes.
JOSE TOARVE, native of Los Adaes, 29, married to Anastacia Mansole Leva, native of Los Adaes, 23, two sons and two daughters.
MARTIN IBARVO, native of Los Adaes, 25, married to Josefa Arriola, half-caste widow, native of Los Adaes, 26, four sons and one daughter.
PENCIANE IBARVO, native of Los Adaes, 20, unmarried.
MANUEL IBARVO, half-caste, native of San Saba, married to Luisa Sanchez, widow, native of Los Adaes, 38, two daughters.
SERNAQUE, Frenchman, native of Paris, 66, married to Maria Cortinas, half-caste, 32, four sons and one daughter.
JUAN ANTONIO FLORES, native of Los Adaes, 46, married to Gertrudis Martinez, half-caste, 34, two children.
FRANCISCO PEREZ, native of San Antonio de Bexar, 36, married to Martina Grande, native of Los Adaes, 32.
JUAN RIVERA, half-caste, native of Mexico, 38.
MIGUEL de CORDOVA, native of Los Adaes, 56, widower, one son.
JOSE SEPULVEDA FLORES, native of Monterrey, 49, married to Melchora del Rio, native of Los Adaes, two children.
LUIS GRANDE, native of Orcoquisas, 30, married to Trinidad Sanchez, half-caste, native of Bucarelli, 19, two daughters.
MARIA ANTONIA IBARVO, widow, native of Los Adaes, married to Maria Andrea Chirino, native of Los Adaes, 42.
MARIA del PILAR PRESELA, mulatto, widow, native of Los Adaes, 35, four sons and two daughters.
JOSE JUAQUIN de CASTILLE, native of Real of Mategula, 42.
JUAN JOSE MARTINEZ, native of Monterrey, 36, married to Maria de los Santos, native of San Antonio de Bexar, 25.
JOSE de los SANTOS, half-caste, native of San Antonio de Bexar, 22, unmarried.
BARON DE CORDOVA, native of Los Adaes, 30, married to Theresa Reolo, native of Los Adaes, 24, three sons and one daughter.
PEDRO PRESELA, half-caste, native of Los Adaes, 30, married to Josefa de Cordova, half-caste, native of Los Adaes, 24, two sons.
BARTOLEME de SOTO, native of Los Adaes, 63, married to Maria Antonia Sierra, mulatto, native of Los Adaes, 59, one son, 30, unmarried.
MANUEL FLORES, Indian, native of Los Adaes, 32, married to Paula Soto, half-caste, native of Los Adaes, 25.
GREGORIO SOTA, half-caste, native of Los Adaes, 39, married to Juana de los Reyes, native of Los Adaes, 30, two sons, 23 and 12, and two daughters, 11 and 7.
PEDRO GONZALES, Native of Havana, 39, married to Maria de Jesus del Rio, 13, one daughter, 11.
MARCOS SANTA CRUZ, native of Los Adaes, 31, married to Maria de la Trinidad Gonsales, half-caste, native of Los Adaes, 16.
CHRISTOVAL GRACIA, Indian, native of Candela, 38, married to Maria Lucia Ramirez,

Indian, 26, three sons, 10, 7 and 3, and one daughter, 14.

XAVIER PADILLA, native of Los Adaes, 52, married to Juana Guiros, Indian, native of Oquisa, 27, one son, 14.

JOSE MANUEL DE ACOSTA, Indian, native of Los Adaes, married to Juana Quiros, native of Orcoquisa, 27, one son 14.

JUAN de ACOSTA, Indian, native of Los Adaes, 25, married to Maria Sanchez, half-caste, native of Los Adaes, 19, one daughter, 19.

ANNA MARIA VILLALPANDE, native of New Mexico, 45, widow, one daughter 14.

ANDROS de ACOSTA, half-caste, native of Los Adaes, 30, married to Maria de la Concepcion, half-caste, 25, one son, 9.

MARIANE GARZA, Indian, native of Nacogdoches, 21, married to Maria del Pilar, Indian, native of Los Adaes, 20, two daughters, 5 and 3.

VICENTE SAN MIGUEL, native of Los Adaes, 38, married to Maria de la Ara, Indian, native of Los Adaes, 20, one son 5, and one daughter, 2.

MELCHOR PROCELA, half-caste, native of Los Adaes, 30, married to Antonia de la Ara, half-caste, native of Los Adaes, 24, three sons, 11, 9, and 7, and four daughters, 12, 8, 4, and 2.

OCASIA FLORES, widow, native of Los Adaes, 40, one son 10.

PEDRO de la ARA, Indian, native of Los Adaes, 62, married to Maria Rosales, half-caste, native of Los Adaes, 38, one son, 16.

STEPHEN GOUGUET, French, native of New Orleans, 37, married to Juana de la Ara, half-caste, 23, one daughter 11.

VICENTE MAJOR, colored, native of Saltillo, 26, unmarried.

JOSE CERVATES, native of Mexico City, 36, married to Manuela Aragon, Indian, native of Los Adaes, 17.

CLEMENTE GONSALES, Indian, native of La Bahia, 46, married to Beatris Pena, native of Los Adaes, 57.

XAVIER CORTINAS, native of Los Adaes, 57.

FRANCISCO de los SANTOS, 39, married to Ria de Luna, colored, native of the Presidio Rio Grande, 28, four sons, 16, 12, 9, and 8, one daughter 11.

PEDRO MENCHACA, native of the Presidio Rio Grande, 51, married Manuela Areola, colored, native of San Antonio de Bexar, 35, one son, 22.

JACINTE RAMON, colored, native of San Antonio de Bexar, 37.

MANUEL SANTA CRUZ, native of Los Adaes, 38, married to Magdalena Padilla, native of Los Adaes, 20, one son, 17, and one daughter, 12.

ANTONIO CORDOVA, half-caste, native of New Mexico, 33, married Juana Bega, Indian, native of Los Adaes, 49, two sons, 17 and 12, and two daughters, 14 and 12.

JOSE CARO, Indian, native of Los Adaes, 28, married to Micaela Equis, Indian, native of Bucarelli, 16, one son 13, and one daughter 2.

POLICIANO SANDOVAL, Indian, native of New Mexico, 30, married to Josefa Caro, colored, native of Nacogdoches, 16, two daughters, 4 and 2.

ANTONIO ROSALES, half-caste, native of Los Adaes, 35, married to Maria Neives, colored, native of Los Adaes, 21, one son, 14, one daughter, 10.

JULIAN ROSALES, Indian, native of the San Antonio de Bexar, 21, married to Maria

Alamillo, Indian, native of Bucarelli, 16, one daughter 2.
FRANCISCO GARCIA, native of the City of Cadis, 40, married to Ignacia Rosales, half-caste, native of Bucarelli, 18.
GERONIMO EQUIS, colored, native of Los Adaes, 26, married to Micaela Caro, Indian, native of Los Adaes, 25, two sons, 9 and 7, one daughter 3.
JOSE ANTONIO CORTINAS, native of Coahuila, 40, unmarried.
MICAELA MEDINA, Mulatto, 26, native of San Antonio de Bexar.
BISENTA MEDINA, Mulatto, 26, native of San Antonio de Bexar, one son 8, and one daughter 6.
MARIANO SANTA CRUZ, native of Los Adaes, 38, married to Josefa Bargas, half-caste, native of San Antonio de Bexar, 20, two sons, 12 and 9, one daughter 10.
PHELIPA LONGORIA, widow, native of San Antonio de Bexar, 60, one son 10.
JOSE GUADALUPE RAMIRES, Indian, native of San Antonio de Bexar, 30, married to Maria Benites, half-caste, native of San Antonio de Bexar, 20, one son 3, one daughter 2.
JOSE MARIA SIERRA, Indian, native of Los Adaes, 41, married to Rosa del Rio, colored, native of Los Adaes, 23, one son 12.
LOUIS DOAR, French, native of Paris, 58.
JOSE del RIO, native of Los Adaes, 26, married to Juan Caro, Indian, native of Los Adaes, 22, four sons, 10, 9, 8, 7, and two daughters, 6 and 5.
NICHOAS ANTONIO CHAVEZ, Indian, native of New Mexico, with Josefa Benero, half-caste, native of Los Adaes, 31, one daughter 7.
GAYITANO VILLAFRANCA, Indian, native of Los Adaes, 32, married to Juana de la Ara, half-caste, native of Los Adaes, 24.
AUGUSTIN SAN MIGUEL, half-caste, native of Los Adaes, 25, one daughter 4.
JUAN de MORA, colored, 38, married to Maria Morin, 20, three children, 10, 8, 6.
JETOMAS ESPARZA, colored, native of Los Adaes, 23, married to Barbara Morin, half-caste, native of Los Adaes, 21.
JUAN JOSE MEDINA, mulatto, married to Maria Antonia Ruis, 57, one son 7 and one daughter 3.
LUIS SANCHEZ, native of Los Adaes, 27, married to Maria Bersole, half-caste, native of Orcoquisa, 19, one son 6 and one daughter 3.
LUIS BELANSHE, native if Canada, 42, widower, two sons 6 and 3.
JUAN JUARES, half-caste, native of Louisiana, 39, unmarried.
MIGUEL del RIO, colored, native of Los Adaes, 61, married to Maria Serafino Benites, half-caste, native of La Bahia, 58, two sons 26 and 5.
PEDRO JOSE ESPARZA, native of Los Adaes, 49, married to Antonia del Rio, half-caste, native of Los Adaes, 28.
NEPOMUCENO de la CERDA, native of Los Adaes, 49, married to Maria Seledina Flores, half-caste, native of Los Adaes, 32, two sons, 7 and 4, four daughters, 12, 11, 9, and 8.
JUANA RODRIGUES, widow, native of Los Adaes, 88.
AUGUSTINA ALBARDO, half-caste, widow, native of Los Adaes, 60.
FRANCISCO PADILLA, native of Los Adaes, 26, married to Josefa de la Cerda, native of Los Adaes, 18, one daughter, 4.

ANTONIO PADILLA, native of Los Adaes, 29, married to Maria de la Cerda, native of Los Adaes, 20, two daughters, 4 and 2.

DIMAS GUILLERMO DE MOYA, native of Monterrey, 25, married to Maria Sanchez, half-caste, native of Los Adaes, his age 59 [?].

MANUEL SANCHEZ, Lobo, native of Los Adaes, 59, widower, one son 7, and two daughters, 11 and 9.

JOSE de la BEGA, native of San Miguel el Grande, 27, married to Maria de Aro, native of Los Adaes, 20.

MAGDALENA del RIO, native of Los Adaes, 32, widow, one daughter 7.

PEDRO CORDOVA, native of Orcoquisa, 27, married to Catarina Prieto, Indian, native of Bucarelli, 14.

MANUEL QUINNONES, half-caste, native of San Antonio de Bexar, married to Josefa Barrera, native of Los Adaes, 21.

GABRIEL GURBELO, colored, native of San Antonio de Bexar, 52, married to Juana Maria Dorvan, colored, native Los Adaes, 21.

MARIANE BASQUES, half-caste, native of Los Adaes, married with Maria de la Censousion Morin, native of Los Adaes, 20, two daughters, 6 and 2.

GREGORIO MORA, native of Los Adaes, 21, married to Josefa Caro, native of Los Adaes, 20.

JUAN DOMINGO DOMINQUES, native of New Mexico, 36, married to Maria Santa Cruz, native of Los Adaes, 20.

JUAN JOSE SANCHEZ, half-caste, native of Los Adaes, 48, married with Barbara Cordova, native of Los Adaes, 50, one son, 25, one daughter 11.

NICOLAS de la COMPANIA ESPANOLA, native of Cadis, 36, married to Santa Sanchez, native of Los Adaes, 19, on daughter 2.

MARIANO SANCHEZ, native of Los Adaes, 22, married to Paula Ruis, Indian, native of Los Adaes, 19, one daughter 3.

JUANA de TREJO, mulatto, native of San Antonio de Bexar, 38, widow, one son, 9, three daughters, 8, 7, 5.

JOSE ILDEFONSO INQJOSA, native of Monterrey, 40.

FRANCISCO GONSALES, Negro, native of Guatemala, 49.

MELCHOR MORIN, native of Los Adaes, 62, married to Isabela Padilla, 43.

JOSE MORIN, native of Los Adaes, 26, married to Feliciana Ibarvo, native of Los Adaes, 19, one daughter 2.

ESTEVAN MORIN, native of Los Adaes, 20, married to Maria de la Zerda, native of los Adaes, 13.

CHRISTOBAL PADILLA, native of Los Adaes, 90, unmarried.

PRUDENCIO BARRON, colored, native of San Antonio de Bexar, 30, married to Isabel Leiba, Indian, native of San Antonio de Bexar, 14.

JOSE LUIS MALDONADO, native of San Antonio de Bexar, 30, married to Juana Barron, Indian, native of Los Adaes, 14.

BALTASAR de la GARZA, native of Los Adaes, 26, married to Rita Peralta, native of New Mexico, 38, two sons, 10 and 9, and two daughters, 7 and 4.

ASENSIO de ARREOLA, colored, native of San Antonio de Bexar, 21, married to Maria de la Consencion Gallego, native of Nacogdoches, 13.

JOSE ANTONIO CONEJO, native of Parral, 50, married to Juana Palacio, native of Monterrey, 42.

MATIAS PENA, colored, native of Laredo, 31, married to Bernalda Arriola, half-caste, native of San Antonio de Bexar, 19.

ANTONIO AURIDA, native of Los Adaes, 35, married to Anna Coba Equiz, native of Bucarelli, 13, one son, 1.

BALTASAR ESPARSA, native of Los Adaes, 56, married to Juana Basquez, colored, native of Los Adaes, 22, one son, 6, and one daughter, 4.

MANUEL de MORA, broken color, native of Los Adaes, 57, married to Isabel de Esparza, colored, native of Los Adaes, 36, one son, 8, and two daughters 9 and 6.

JUAN BENITES, Indian, native of Orcoquisa, 29, married to Maria Refugia Mora, broken color, native of Los Adaes, 19, one son, 5, and one daughter 6.

ESPARRAGO, JUAN, native of Catalonia, 46.

TERESA de MORA, widow, native of Los Adaes, 38, six sons, 19, 12, 12, 8, 7, and 6, and three daughters, 14, 12, and 7.

JOSE ANTONIO CHIRINO, half-caste, native of Los Adaes, 37, married to Maria Antonio de Mora, half-caste, native of Los Adaes, 28, two sons, 7 and 4.

ANTONIO MORA, native of Los Adaes, 26.

LUCIANO GARCIA, Indian, native of San Nicolas, 30, married to Juana de Acosta, Indian, 29.

JOSE MARIA de LUNA, broken color, native of Los Adaes, 23, unmarried.

FRANCISCO VILLALPANDO, broken color, native of Los Adaes, 29, married to Gertrudis Rosales, Negress, native of Los Adaes, 30.

JUAQUIN de CORDOVA, native of Coahuila, 47, married to Juana Maria Sierra, native of Los Adaes, 33, four sons, 19, 12, 10, and 2, and one daughter 4.

JOSE de CORDOVA, native of San Antonio de Bexar, 21, married to Tiburcia Ybarvo, native of Los Adaes, 23.

JUAN JUAREZ, native of Camargo, 34, unmarried.

SAMUEL LEONE, French, native of Leon, France, 76, married to Anna Maria, Apache Indian, 37, four sons, 19, 7, 3, and 3.

CHRISTOVAL CHONCA, native of Canada, 47, married to Mariana, Apache Indian, 39.

PEDRO PADILLA, native of Los Adaes, 26, married to Josefa de Torres, half-caste, native of Los Adaes, 49.

MIGUELA CARO, Indian, native of Los Adaes, 40, widow, three daughters, 14, 9, and 7.

RIAS ESPARZA, native of Los Adaes, 21, unmarried.

MANUEL ARAGON, Indian, native of Los Adaes, 22, married to Josefa Perez, native of San Antonio de Bexar, 43.

JOSE INOJOSA, native of Santa Rosa, 50, unmarried.

ALENZO de LEON, native of Coahuila, 43, widower, two sons, 31 and 14.

PHILIP NOLAN, Irishman, 30, unmarried.

PEDRO LOBO, Frenchman, unmarried, native of Canada.

PEDRO BRUNO, broken color, 27.

GASPAR RUIZ, Indian, native of Mexico, 62, married to Rosalia Camacho, broken color,

native of Los Adaes, 40, two sons, 21 and 18, two daughters, 12 and 9.
ANDRES RUIS, broken color, native of Los Adaes, 37, married to Maria Sanchez, half-caste, native of Los Adaes, 19, three daughters, 4, 3, and 2.
JOSE MENDOSA, native of Santa Rosa, 50.
MIGUEL IBARVO, Apache Indian, 32, married to Serafina Rosales, mulatto, native of Los Adaes, 29.
JOSE NAVARRO, broken color, native of Los Adaes, 36, unmarried.
ANDRES RODRIQUES, broken color, native of San Antonio de Bexar, 25.
JOSE de TORRES, broken color, native of Los Adaes, 19, unmarried.
JUANA SANTA CRUZ, native of Los Adaes, widow, 19.
MANUEL TALAMANTES, half-caste, native of Durango, 39, married to Polonia Aragon, colored, native of Los Adaes, 22, one daughter, 2.
SANTOS ARAGON, colored, native of Los Adaes, 40, married to Clara Solis, Indian, native of San Antonio de Bexar, 34, four sons, 10, 8, 7, 6, and two daughters, 4 and 2.
JUAN TENELOTE, French, 49, unmarried.
SANTIAGO MENDOSA, native of Santa Rosa, 30.
NEGRO MALE SLAVES, 7 in number, 30, 24, 21, 20, 23, 12, and 10; 6 female slaves, 40, 26, 20, 11, 8, and 5.

Legend: Half-caste=Spanish-Indian; mulatto=Spanish-Negro; lobo=Indian-mulatto or Indian-Negro; colored=Negro; broken color=unknown.
Note: Unless otherwise designated, all individuals are classed as Spanish or Spaniard.
Source: Census of Our Lady of Pilar de Nacogdoches, 1792, Bexar Archives, reprinted in Institute of Texan Cultures, The University of Texas, Residents of Texas: 1782-1836 (3 vols. 1984), Vol I, pp. 104-114.

After ten years of governing the Nacogdoches District, Y'Barbo was charged with illegally granting land, and smuggling. He tendered his resignation as Civil Governor and was removed to San Antonio. Gil Y'Barbo had been a strong leader, replacing him proved a difficult task. Don Christoval de Cordova was placed in temporary command, and finally, in 1795, Lieutenant Bernado Fernandez was given the permanent assignment. In a few months, however, Fernandez was reassigned, and Don Jose Maria Guadiana became his successor. Guadiana was replaced by Don Jose Miguel del Moral in 1799. During these times of changes in leadership, the population of the Nacogdoches Pueblo increased to 609 in 1795, to 614 in 1796, to 679 in 1797, remaining at just over 600 the rest of the century.

In 1800, Nacogdoches was the second largest Spanish settlement in Texas and a center for the eastern Indian trade. It was situated on the eastern frontier of the province and lying directly on the Camino Real (King's Highway), the major road from Nacogdoches to the provincial capital, San Antonio de Bexar, and on beyond to Saltillo in northern Mexico.

American Louisiana. France again acquired sovereignty over Louisiana in 1800, and three years later Emperor Napoleon Bonaparte sold the Territory to the United States. These events presented Spanish officials in Mexico City and Madrid with the specter of foreign invasion. They were no longer confronted with the lethargic French in Louisiana but with the energetic, land-hungry, westward-moving Americans.

Early Foreign Settlers. People of other than Spanish descent were not uncommon on the eastern frontier. In 1792, for example, eighty-six of the 125 foreigners living in Texas lived in Nacogdoches. (See Table V below.)

Table V

List of Foreigners in Nacogdoches (1796)

RICHARD SIMS, English, native of New England, living here 4.5 years.
VICENTE MICHELLI, Italian, unmarried, living here 3.5 years.
JOSEPH WALES, Virginia, living here 12.5 years.
JAMES WALES, Virginia, living here 12.5 years.
JOHN KORNEGY, native of Flanders, living here 10.5 years.
ANTONIO BOUGACIER, Philadelphia, living here 5.5. years.
EDWARD DILL, Philadelphia, married, living here 12.5 years.
CHRISTOPHER DILL, Philadelphia, married, living here 12.5 years.
JAMES DILL, Philadelphia, married, widower, living here 12.5 years.
WILLIAM SNODDY, married, living here one month.
THOMAS BLAIN, native of Ireland, single, living here 4 months.
ESTEVAN ROGET, Arkansas, married, living here 19 years.
PEDRO DOLET, native of Natchitoches, married, living here 16 years.
FRANCISCO PRUDOMME, native of Natchitoches, married, living here 11 years.
ANDREW VALENTINE, native of Natchitoches, married, living here 4 years.
ANTONIO DUBOIS, native of Natchitoches, married, living here 3 years.
BAPTISTE PIFERMO, native of Natchitoches, married, living here 4 years.
PIERRE ENGLE, native of New Orleans, living here 20 years.
NICHOLAS PON, native of New Orleans, single, living here 20 years.
LOUIS BELANCHE, native of Canada, widower.
FRANCOIS MORVAN, native of Natchitoches, unmarried, living here 11 years.

Source: Nacogdoches Archives, Vol. VIII, pp. 199-200.

The Early Americans. The Spanish commandant reported that in 1796 only twelve persons other than Spanish or French ancestry resided in Nacogdoches and that the average length of their residence was less than eight years. Eight of those persons were from the United States, but neither his report nor any other official document attempted to estimate the number of foreigners who had entered Texas illegally. In reality, Anglo-Americans began to trickle into Spanish Texas as early as 1789.

Among those entering legally, as indicated in Table V above, was Richard Sims. Sims had been born about 1765 in Bristol, England, son of John and Marguerite (Chisley) Sims. He left England at age sixteen following the death of his father, joined the British navy, and was imprisoned for more than a year in Cuba as a prisoner of war. Sims married Maria Concepcion Perez September 22, 1789, arriving in Nacogdoches in 1793 with his wife and eight children. Sims was dead by 1830.[30]

Another, Vicente Michelli, was born about 1760 in Italy, son of Vicente and Maria (Lengeven) Michelli. Michelli married first Helena Robleau July 8, 1793 in Natchitoches, Louisiana and second Maria S. Maro by 1811 in Nacogdoches. He died after 1820.[31]

Also, Joseph Wales born about 1748 in Virginia (Maryland?), married Mary Ann Berry in 1795, but was a widower in 1804. James Wallace, born in Virginia about 1773, son of Joseph Wallace and Denee Bertrand, married Marie Jacinta Gane November 16, 1795, Natchitoches, Louisiana, died by 1806.[32]

Also, Antonio Bougacier, was born about 1745 in Philadelphia, Pennsylvania, married Mary North. Edward Dill, was born about 1735 in Philadelphia, Pennsylvania, married Elizabeth ----. Christopher Dill was born about 1764 in Philadelphia, Pennsylvania, married Maria Leconte. James (Santiago) Dill was born about 1766 in Lancaster, Pennsylvania, married Helena Kimble (Gimlech) September 14, 1791 in Arkansas. He died 21 November 1825 after

---

[30] Carolyn Reeves Ericson, Nacogdoches: Gateway to Texas (Nacogdoches: Ericson Books, 1991), Vol.I, p. 347.

[31] Ibid., p. 248.

[32] Ibid, p. 395.

a fall from a horse. He was buried Natchitoches, Louisiana.[33]

Also, Francisco Prudhomme, born about 1738 in Natchitoches, Louisiana, was the son of Jean Phillipe and Catherine (Meiller) Prudhomme, married Maria Barbara Rambin in 1778, daughter of Louis and Marie Francoise Clairmont Rambin.[34] Andres (Andrew) Francois Valentine was born about 1770 at Natchitoches, Louisiana, son of Francois and Maria Louisa (Totin) Valentine. He married first Maria Louise Angelica Malisse (Malige) November 22, 1790 and second Marie Loucouviche July 11, 1820.[35]

Also, Antoine Phillippe Dubois was born August 20, 1766 in Natchitoches, Louisiana, son of Jean Baptiste and Marie Josepha (Cleremont) Dubois. Antoine married Maria Josefa Malige January 19, 1795, Natchitoches.[36] Juan Baptiste Pifermo was born about 1745 at Natchitoches, Louisiana, and in time married Maria Clemencia Larnodier.[37] Pierre Engle was born 1754, died August 1809, native of New Orleans, Louisiana, married first Juana Santa Cruz and second Maria Delores Rio.[38]

Also, Nichoas Pon(t), born about 1752 in France, "[a] native of New Orleans," who was single.[39] Louis Belanche was born about 1750 in Canada, widower.[40] And Francois Morvan who was born about 1733 in Natchitoches, Louisiana, was an unmarried laborer who received a tract of land lying within the "late Neutral Territory."[41]

Two of the earliest and most important Anglo immigrants were William Barr and Peter

---

[33] Ibid, pp. 37 and 102.

[34] Ibid., p. 298.

[35] Ibid, p. 387.

[36] Ibid., p. 107.

[37] Ibid., p. 288.

[38] Ibid., p. 115.

[39] Ibid., p. 292.

[40] Ibid, p. 26.

[41] Ibid, p. 261.

Samuel Davenport. Barr was a native of Ireland born in Londonderry, Ulster County, about 1762. At age twelve with his parents he immigrated to Pennsylvania in 1774, resided for a time in Philadelphia, but thereafter moved westward settling in Pittsburgh. After serving an enlistment in the United States Army, in 1786 he moved to Louisiana, then a Spanish possession, where the following year he became a Spanish subject. He engaged in the mercantile business in Natchitoches until 1793 when he immigrated to Nacogdoches and entered the mercantile business there. Barr died in about 1810 leaving most of his considerable estate to his partner Davenport.

Although christened Peter Samuel Davenport, early in life Barr's partner abandoned the Peter and thereafter was known only as Samuel Davenport. Born February 4, 1764, in Carlisle, Cumberland County, Pennsylvania, the son of William and Ann (Davidson) Davenport, but early in life he moved with his family to the Natchez District of Georgia, now Mississippi.

In an affidavit dated June 16, 1809, Davenport stated that he left his "native county" when sixteen years of age and went to Louisiana about 1785. In any case, sometime between 1787 and 1809, probably about 1794 his parents both died, and he determined to immigrate to Spanish Texas, arriving in Nacogdoches soon thereafter where he immediately entered the mercantile business.

He returned to Louisiana in 1802 where he married Marie Louisa Gagnon, daughter of Pierre and Marie Thereza (Valentine) Gagnon, both reputed to be French-Canadians. Before her death in 1812, the Davenports had four children: Juan Benigno Bernardino, born about 1803 who later married Jane Beall Edwards, daughter of Empresario Haden Edwards; Theresa Eliza, born about 1808 who married Dr. Samuel Price Russell, May 20, 1824; Marie Azalie, born December 30, 1807; and a daughter who died young.[42]

In 1798, Barr and Davenport entered into partnership with Luther Smith and Edward Murphy to form a trading firm under the name Barr and Davenport destined to become the major mercantile establishment in East Texas for more than a decade (1798-1812). The firm supplied the friendly East Texas Indians with articles of merchandise and the quartermaster's

---

[42] Joe E. and Carolyn R. Ericson, <u>Personalities on the East Texas Frontier: Brief Narratives of their Lives and Times</u> Nacogdoches: Ericson Books, 1998), pp. 13-22.

department of Nacogdoches with flour, beef, salt, soap, and chili. During those years, European and American settlers, most without legal authorization, moved into the area; while traders, filibusterers, and fugitive slaves used it as a "Gateway" to Texas.

One of those entering the province without authorization was a young horse trader, Philip Nolan. In September 1794 Nolan had been issued a passport authorizing him to capture horses in Texas to supply Spanish troops stationed in Louisiana. This document averred that Nolan had been living in Nacogdoches for the previous four years. He may, indeed, have made his first entry as early as 1785. By 1800, however, Nolan was still in Texas and without, at this time, official approval.

Nolan had been born about 1762, a native of Belfast, Ireland, married Frances Lintot, December 19, 1799, daughter of Bernard Lintot of Natchez in the Mississippi Territory. Nolan was slain March 21, 1801, by Lieutenant Miguel Musquiz in the vicinity of present-day Waco, McLennan County, Texas.[43]

Neutral Ground. Almost as soon as the United States acquired the Louisiana Territory in 1803, disagreement over the boundary between the new American Territory and the Spanish Province of Texas surfaced. It was not settled until 1806 when a compromise was forthcoming by which the territory between the Arroyo Hondo in western Louisiana and the Sabine River was set aside as a "neutral ground" between the two nations. The final boundary settlement was not agreed upon until 1819 when the Sabine River was established in the Adams-Onis Treaty.

Filibusters. Following the Neutral Ground agreement, tensions along the eastern frontier of Texas relaxed, although smuggling and illegal entry continued apace. In 1812, however, filibustering expeditions began entering Texas, crossing the Sabine River, and driving the Spanish troops from East Texas. Led by Bernardo Gutierrez de Lara and Augustus William Magee planned to seize Texas and create either a Mexican State or a Mexican Republic. The expedition was turned back the next year, and its participants driven from Texas.

Jose Bernardo Maximiliano Gutierrez de Lara, son of Santiago Gutierrez de Lara and

---

[43] Ericson, Gateway to Texas, Vol. I., p. 269; Partin, Ericson, Ericson, and McDonald, Nacogdoches, pp. 45-46.

Marie Urbide, was born at Revilla (today's Guerrero), Tamaulipas, Mexico, August 20, 1774. He married his cousin Maria Josefa Urbide. Bernardo died May 13, 1841, at the home of his daughter in Santiago, Mexico. His co-leader, Augustus William Magee, was born in 1789 in Boston, Massachusetts, attended West Point and upon graduation was commissioned a lieutenant in the United states Army. In 1812, he contracted a serious illness while camped near the Trinity River, and died February 6, 1813, at the presidio of Neustra Señora de Loreto.

Another filibustering expedition entered Texas in 1819 under the command of Dr. James Long, which quickly organized a new civil government for Texas and declared the province a free and independent nation. In less that one year, Long and his party were driven from Texas and the expedition crushed. Filibustering into Texas came to an end by 1821 when the Mexicans rose up in successful rebellion against the Spanish government.

James Long was born Culpeper County, Virginia, about 1793, moved first to Kentucky and then to Tennessee, became a United states Army surgeon in the War of 1812, and set up practice in Natchez, Mississippi. He married Jane Herbert Wilkinson, daughter of William W. M. and Anne (Herbert) Wilkinson, May 14, 1815. Long was killed by a Mexican guard in Mexico City April 8, 1822.

Although the Nolan excursions had little adverse effect on the growing European community gathered around Nacogdoches, the subsequent filibustering expeditions wrecked havoc in the area. Population for the area stood at 791 in 1804, rose to 811 in 1805, to 891 in 1806, and approximately 900 in 1810; but in 1823 it had been reduced to a scant 200.

A Spanish census conducted in 1805, for example, listed 51 foreign heads of household. (See Table VI below.) A second Spanish census conducted in 1809 for the first time provided the names of not only the heads of household but also wives and children. (See Appendix I below.)

Ayish Bayou Settlers. In 1779, as Gil Y'Barbo led his band of refugees back to Nacogdoches, new and former residents of Texas moved into the area they called the Ayish Bayou. The bayou headed up in northern San Augustine County some five miles north of the town of San Augustine and flowed south out of the county. The area was well within the twenty league strip east of Nacogdoches where settlement was not allowed by colonial regulations. Nevertheless, for more than thirty years thereafter both Spanish and Anglo-

American immigrants settled in the area. "Most of the American immigrants, including Indians, came from Mississippi, Alabama, Georgia, Tennessee, and Kentucky."[44]

About 1794 Antonio Leal and wife Gertrudis de los Santos settled at the site of present-day San Augustine and built a small house. In 1801, Leal transferred his title to Edmund Quirk, and in the next few years Anglo-Americans began to settle on lands in the area which they assumed were vacant.

Anglo-American settlement in Sabine County to the south of Ayish Bayou began with the construction of ferries, first by Michael Crow in 1797 and later, in 1812, by James Gaines. Still later, in 1819, Isaac Lindsey settled near today's Pineland and began farming operations to become the first Anglo-American settler in Sabine County.

Just across the Sabine River from the Neutral Ground and just north east of Nacogdoches was present-day Shelby County on a direct path to the interior of Texas. Tradition says that the first permanent settler in the county was John Latham who in 1818 settled in its southeastern section.

Table VI

Census of Foreigners in Nacogdoches (1805)

WILLIAM BARR, Munster, Ireland, unmarried, living here 10 years.
SAMUEL DAVENPORT, Pennsylvania, married, 40, living here 9 years.
JAMES McNULTY, Munster, Ireland, unmarried, 45, living here 9 years.
RICHARD SIMMS, Englishman, native of New England, married, 38, living here 13 years.
JOSE LUCOBICHE, native of Corsica, Italy, 37, married, living here 10 years.
STEVEN GOGUET, Frenchman, native of the Post of Arkansas, Louisiana, 44, married, living here 26 years.
JAMES DILL, Pennsylvania, 43, married, living here 5 years.
FRANCOIS MORVAN, Frenchman, native of Natchitoches, married, 39, living here 13 years.
PIERRE ENGLE, Frenchman, native of New Orleans, married, 54, living here 27 years.
PIERRE LAVIGNE, Frenchman, native of Natchitoches, 36, married, living here 9 years.
JEAN IGNACIO PIFERMO, alias Chichi, Frenchman, native of Natchitoches, 65, married, living here 13 years.
BARDINO GANE, native of Natchitoches, 29, married, living here 4 years.

---

[44] Joe Ellis Ericson, Early East Texas: A History from Indian Settlement to Statehood (Bowie, Maryland: Heritage Books, 2002), p, 93.

LOUIS RELIQUET, Frenchman, native of Bayonnes, 44, married, living here 9 years.
JEAN FONTENO, Frenchman, native of Rochelle, 43, married, living here 7 years.
JEAN SARNAC, native of Rochelle, 73, widower, living here 26 years.
JEAN ROSALES, Frenchman, native of Bordeaux, 34, married, living here 8 years.
JOHN McFARLAND, American, native of Virginia, married, 37, living here 7 years.
JULIAN SANDERS, Scotch, 55, living here 3 years.
JAMES QUINELTY, native of Natchitoches, 25, living here 19 years, with two brothers 22 and 19.
JOSE CAPUTAN, Frenchman, native of Bayonne, widower, 48, living here 10 years.
BERNARD d'ORTOLANDT, Frenchman, native of Bordeaux, widower, 61, living here 9 years.
JOSE de la BAUM, Frenchman, native of Languedoc, 57, widower, living here 3 years.
PIERRE DOLET, native of Natchitoches, 39, married, living here 24 years.
MICHEL RAMBIN, native of Louisiana, married, 26, living here 24 years.
VINCENT MICHEL BENSAN, native of Louisiana, married, 26, living here 7 years.
PIERRE ROBLEAU, native of Natchitoches, 39, married, living here 9 years.
LOUIS FORTUNE, native of Louisiana, 65, living here 12 years.
FRANCOIS PRUDHOMME, native of Natchitoches, married, 61, living here 10 years.
ANTOINE DUBOIS, native of Natchitoches, married, 39, living here 12 years.
ANDRES VALENTINE, native of Natchitoches, 44, married, living here 12 years.
JAQUES CHRISTIAN, Frenchman, native of Piedmont, 19, married, living here 7 years.
MICHAEL CROW, Englishman, native of South Carolina, 39, married, living here 8 years.
JOSE TECIER, Frenchman, native of Canada, unmarried, 52, living here 9 years.
ANTONIO BOUGUER, American, native of Virginia, 46, married, living here 8 years.
EDMUND QUIRK, American, native of Virginia, 46, married, living here 4 years, born 1759. formed a partnership with Edward Murphy and established a trading post in San Augustine.
JAMES LEPINE, native of Louisiana, married, 56, living here 8 years.
WILLIAM BEBE, native of Louisiana, married, 32, living here 7 years.
CHRISOSTOMO CHONCA, native of Canada, 66, married, living here 22 years.
PIERRE BOSQUE, Frenchman, native of Bordeaux. 66, married, living here 10 years.
JOSE WALLET, native of Canada, 41, unmarried, living here 10 years.
JAMES ISIDRO, German, 38, married, living here 3 years.
JOSEPH PAILLAR, Frenchman, native of St. Malo, 37, unmarried, living here 2 years.
JOHN O'CONNOR, Irishman, native of Connaught, 37, unmarried, living here 7 years.
JOHN BROWN, American, native of Virginia, 47, unmarried, living here 4 years.
JOSEPH JOHNSTON, American, native of Virginia, 45, unmarried, living here 3 years.
JOSEPH REESE, American, native of Pennsylvania, 42, unmarried, living here 6 years.
JOHN DAVIS, American, native of Virginia, 32, unmarried, living here 7 years.
WEMBLE, American, native of South Carolina, 37, unmarried, living here 12 years.

Source: Bexar Archives.

Other "newcomers" who did not appear on the 1792 census of foreigners included

Edmund Quirk who had been born about 1759 in Philadelphia, Pennsylvania, son of John and Rebecca Quirk. He married Anna Marie Alsop, and was slain by John Bodine in 1835 in San Augustine. Henry Quirk was born about 1760 in Virginia. [45] Lattney Anthony Parrot, who was born about 1768 in North Carolina, died in Nacogdoches before August 31, 1847. He married first Martha Maria Quirk, daughter of Edmund Quirk, and second Elizabeth Sheridan.[46]

Also, William Johnston, who was born about 1758 in Virginia, married Marie Constancia by 1806.[47] Joshua Reese, born in Pennsylvania about 1763, was an unmarried man in 1804 living in the town of Trinidad del Salcedo.[48] Joseph Michael Crow, born in South Carolina about 1766, married first Marguerite LaFleur by 1804 and second a widow Chabineau.[49] James Quinelty (Santiago Conelte) was a bachelor in 1804 born about 1781, a native of Ireland. Another James Quinelty, who had been born about 1774, married first Maria Manuela Eshbete (Chelette) and second Josefa Perez about 1804. He was "reared in the Post of Piedras Creek."[50]

Also, John O'Connor, born about 1762 in Connaught, Ireland, was a single man in 1804.[51] John O'Connor, who married Feliciana Torres, was also a native of Ireland (same man?). Jean Fonteno was born about 1762 in France and married Maria Concepcion Avila by 1804.[52] Bernardo Dortolan, a native of Brodeaux, France, was born about 1739, son of Raimundo de Ortoland and Maria Juana Labatut, and died about 1822. He married first Marie

---

[45] Ericson, Gateway to Texas, Vol. I, p. 300.

[46] Ibid., p. 282.

[47] Ibid., p. 191.

[48] Ibid., p. 308.

[49] Ibid., p. 90.

[50] Ibid., p. 299.

[51] Ibid,. p. 273.

[52] Ibid., p. 127.

Anne Grappe, October 9, 1776 and second Catherine Bardon, daughter of Raymundo and Mariana (Verneuil) Bardon, native of New Orleans. Left Texas in 1813.[53]

Also, John Joseph de la Baume, born about 1730 in Montpelier, France, son of Count de la Baume and Marie Isabella D'Alton, died in 1834 at San Antonio de Bexar age 104. He married first Feliciana ---- and second Maria Louisa Courturier. He was a veteran of the Revolutionary War and the Texas Revolution.[54] Louis Reliquet was born in France about 1761 and married Maria Candida Grande by 1804.[55]

Also, Pierre (Peter) Bosques, born in France about 1752, married Juana Tijerina.[56] Joseph Capuran, native of Bayonne, France, was born about 1754 and married Carlotta Mecia, who died by 1806.[57] Steven (Estevan) Goguet, native of New Orleans born there about 1755, moved as a young boy to the Post of Arkansas where he lived until about 1767 when his father died and the family returned to New Orleans. He came to Texas in 1775.[58]

In 1810, a list of foreigners and their children living on the Bayou Pierre in the far western limits of Spanish Texas, now in Louisiana, was prepared for officials in Mexico City and Madrid. Among the persons listed were:

> Mickle Rambin, his wife, 3 sons, 3 daughters, 1 nephew.
> Louis Bertrand, his wife, 2 daughters.
> Francois Prudhomme, his wife, 2 sons, 2 daughters.
> Andres Valentine, his wife, 1 son.
> Pierre Lafitte, his wife, 3 sons, 2 daughters.
> Baptiste Prudhomme, his wife, two sons.
> Juan Supuvadore, his wife, 2 sons.
> Marie De Soto, 1 son.
> Mickle Vanviente, his wife.
> Charles Grillet, his wife.

---

[53] Ibid., p. 105.

[54] Ibid., p. 23.

[55] Ibid., p. 309.

[56] Ibid., p. 36.

[57] Ibid., p. 56.

[58] Ibid., p. 143.

Baptiste Colet, his wife, 5 sons, 2 daughters and their husbands, 4 sons.
Anthony Dubois, his wife, 4 sons.
Santiago (James) Wallace, his wife, 3 adult sons.
Remi Christian, his mother, 2 brothers, 3 sisters.
Pierre Roubeaux, his wife, 1 son, 2 daughters.
Vicente Rolan, his wife, 1 son, 2 daughters.
Louis Marley, his wife, 1 son, 2 daughters.
Jose Morvan and Pedro Morvan, their mother, 1 brother, 1 sister.
Bela Bouquire, his mother.[59]

August 1, 1810, Spanish and American troops began a program of eviction for those living in the Neutral Strip who were not qualified to remain. They began eviction at Gaines Ferry on the Sabine River. They reported:

> Mickle (Michael) Crow, married to the widow Isabel Chabineax, with daughter Isabel married to an American--allowed to remain since they were there before January 1, 1806.
> John MacClanahan. House burned and MacClanahan made to depart.
> James Cunningham and Robertson, houses burned and men ordered to leave.
> Jose Miguel de Barneas (Joseph Mickle Barnes), married to Marie Isabelle Poissot, one child, Marie's father, William Poissot, lives with them with his son Thomas, and daughters Marie and Sousan--made to leave and house burned.
> Louis Laithum and Finnemore, houses burned, men sent to Natchitoches.
> Franklin, Burger, and Denny, houses burned and ordered to leave.
> John L. Petit, house burned, man sent to Natchitoches.[60]

> At the Town of Bayou Pierre: The widow Bouquier was not disturbed, but Evans and John Davis working for her were driven out.
> Edward Bolen and Charles Craig, house burned and driven out.
> Home of widow Morban (Morvan) and her family not disturbed; neither was the house of Prudhomme disturbed.
> At the home of Christian on Tierra Blancas Creek were John Kirkham and his wife, evicted and sent to Natchitoches.
> Benjamin Collier, his wife, and 8 year old son, made to vacate and house burned.
> Widow Tontin now married to Louis Bisson and Bisson's two sons not disturbed, had proof the land had been granted to Julian and Pierre Bisson in 1779.

---

[59] Louis R. Nardini, <u>My Historic Natchitoches, Louisiana, and Its Environment</u> (Natchitoches: Nardini Publishing Company, 1963), p. 123.

[60] <u>Ibid.</u>, pp. 124-125.

Vicente Rolan and wife Melani Vascocu, a Frenchwoman, not disturbed.[61]

Between 1813 and 1818, new settlers moved into the Neutral Ground. Among them were: Peter Parker and four brothers built a large tavern in 1813 which became "a notorious hangout for the shady characters of the Neutral Ground."

Also in the "Strip" at this time were: William Black, Henry Tully, John Doe, Frank and Jim Copeland, William Jennings, the Yocum clan, Raynond Daley, Latney Parrot, and John Ayers. Each of them married a daughter of Edmund Quirk. Daley and Ayers later settled in the San Augustine area. Quirk and his wife, Anna Alsop, lived in Natchitoches with Edward Murphy for a time during this period.

The "Yocum clan included John, Thomas D., Jesse, Mathias (Matthew), one-time residents of Natchitoches, who claimed land on Ewany Prairie.

James Gaines, who was born in Culpeper, Virginia in 1779, brother of General Edward Pendleton Gaines of the United States Army, living in Natchitoches in 1805, in 1806 established a mercantile business and ferry across the Sabine River at the crossing on the King's Highway (El Camino Real). He later founded the town of Pendleton, Texas.

Settlement in Northeast Texas. Meanwhile, about 1804-1805, Anglo-Americans began infiltrating the area of northeast Texas along the Red River. As early as 1700, however, the river had been regarded as the dividing line between the possessions of France and those of Spain. Indeed, a royal decree in 1805 proclaimed the Red River as the northern and eastern Boundary of the Spanish province of Texas. Soon after the United States acquired the Louisiana Territory, an American, William Dunbar, explored up the river in 1804 and 1805; and Dr. John Sibley supplied the United States with a description of the area. In 1819, the river was again set forth as the northern boundary of Texas in the Adams-Onis Treaty. At the same time, illegal immigrants continued to cross the river until 1821 when Texas was opened to American colonization.

Thus, before the Battle of New Orleans (1815) was fought Anglo-Americans were already crossing the Red River and settling in what is now northeast Texas. "Three of the

---

[61] Ibid., p. 125.

earliest settlements in this area were Jonesboro, Pecan Point, and Burkham."[62] Prior to that time, however. perhaps the first Europeans to enter the area in 1718 or 1719 were Frenchmen. Shortly thereafter, the French established Le Poste des Cadodaquious in present-day Bowie County.[63]

In 1814, American immigrants moved into the eastern section of what is now Red River County. Among these Anglos were Charles Burkham, Posey Benningfield, a Bankston, and a Bateman. At that time, Red River County was "an indefinitely described area that reached far beyond present-day Grayson County.[64] Charles Burkham had been born in Virginia before 1790, but moved to Madison County, Kentucky in 1804 where he married Nancy Ann Abbet September 30, 1804, This couple had a son they named James and five other children. Charles Burkham founded Burkham's Settlement on Mill Creek near the boundary between Red River and Bowie Counties of today. In 1837, Charles was "murdered by a man named Page."[65]

Among the earliest Anglo inhabitants of Pecan Point in northeastern Red River County were the Wetmore brothers who arrived in 1815 and Claiborne Wright who arrived in 1816 with his family along with Walter Pool. Pecan Point was the site of Caddo village called Natchitosh located on a peninsula formed by a loop of the Red River. The first Americans who settled there were a dozen or more fugitives who arrived in the summer of 1811 and remained there until 1815.

In 1815, George and Alex Wetmore established a trading post, and soon thereafter William Mabbit set up a rival post in the area. George Wetmore was born in England and married Mary Levins after immigrating to the United States. The following year Wright arrived after a six-month journey from Tennessee. Claiborne was born January 5, 1779,

---

[62] Martha Sue Stroud, Gateway to Texas: A History of Red River County (Austin: Nortex Press, 1997), p. 23.

[63] Cecil Harper, Jr., "Red River County," The New Handbook of Texas, Vol. 5, p. 495.

[64] A. W. Neville, The Red River Valley: Then and Now, (Paris: North Texas Publishing Co., 1948, p. 13..

[65] Christopher Long, "Charles Burkham," The New Handbook of Texas, Vol. 1, p. 835.

probably in Surry County, North Carolina, son of William and Henrietta (Claiborne) Wright, married first Elizabeth Travis in 1804 and settled with her on the Cumberland River east of Carthage, Tennessee; after her death in 1823 he married Harriet Brown. From his first marriage, Claiborne had a son, Travis, a daughter Henrietta, and three other children; from his second marriage he had two sons. In early 1816, he moved his family to the Red River and settled in southwestern Arkansas, but soon moved west to northeast Red River County. In 1828, he moved to a site between Jonesboro and Pecan Point. Wright died November 21, 1829 in Jonesboro.[66]

The shifting course of the Red River destroyed the Pecan Point settlement after the Civil War. A larger early settlement during the early years of the Nineteenth Century was Jonesboro, located on the south bank of the Red River, about thirty miles northwest of Pecan Point. Today, it too has been abandoned.

In the years immediately preceding the Mexican Revolution (1821), although two distinct area of settlement had developed in East Texas, there was little or no communication between them. The Indian villages north of Nacogdoches, the distance between the areas, and the difficulties presented by travel between them all contributed to their relative isolation.

Mexican Colonization. As a result of the furor caused by filibustering expeditions and growing unsettled conditions leading up to the Mexican Revolution, in 1820, the Nacogdoches settlement was virtually abandoned. An American traveler passing through that year described the village as a desolate place with a population of less than 100 persons; and a year later Stephen F. Austin was able to assemble no more than thirty-six inhabitants for a town meeting.[67] By 1828, however, its inhabitants numbered about 1000 and 3500 by 1834 on the eve of Texas independence.

Mexican Departments. Following Mexican independence, Texas and Coahuila were

---

[66] Skipper Steely, Six Months from Tennessee (Wolfe City: Hennington Publishing Company, 1983) and Skipper Steely, "Claiborne Wright," The New Handbook of Texas, Vol. 6, p. 1089.

[67] Eugene C. Barker, The Life of Stephen F. Austin, Founder of Texas (Nashville and Dallas: Cokesburry Press, 1925), p.31.

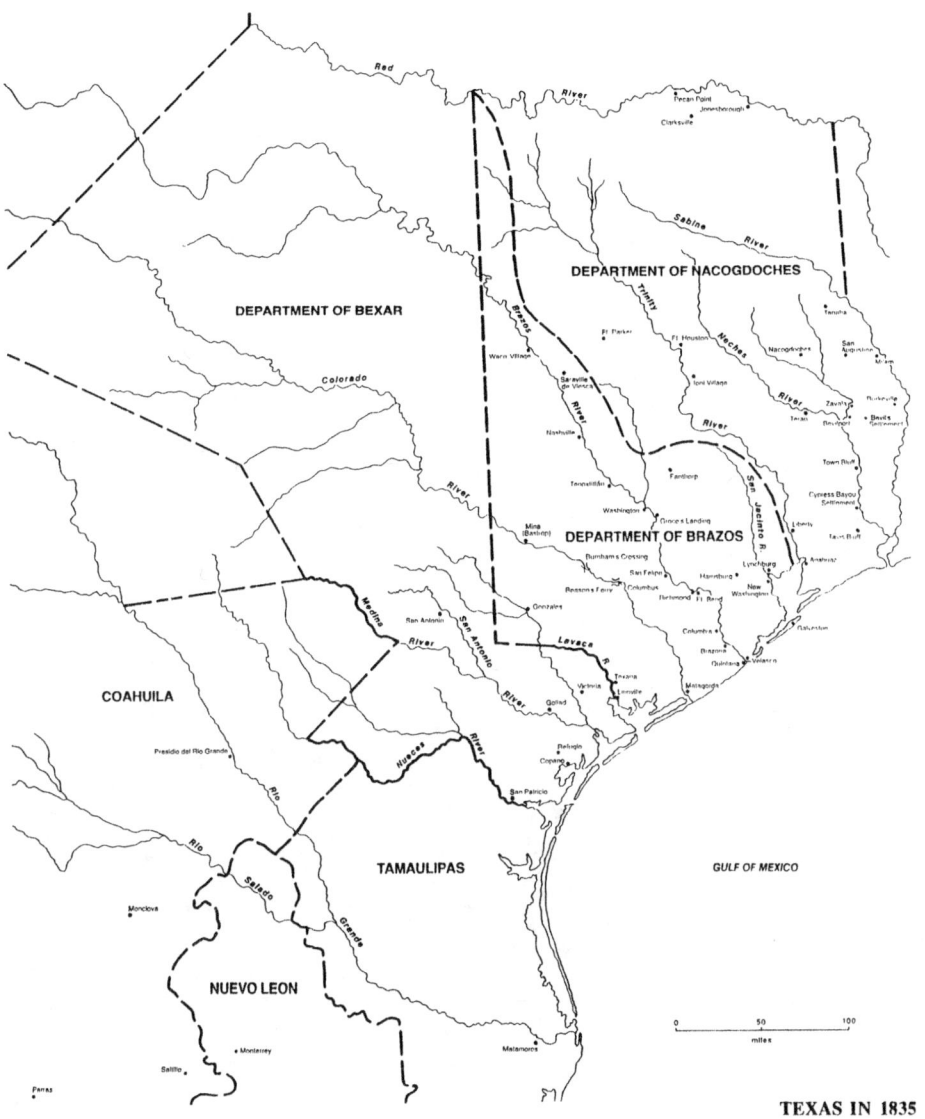

TEXAS IN 1835

© 1988 University of Oklahoma Press

joined to form a state in the Mexican federation, and Texas was included in the newly created Department of Bexar. The department was further subdivided into a number of Municipalities, of which Nacogdoches was one with jurisdiction over a wide area between the Neches and Sabine Rivers.

In 1831, the Department of Nacogdoches was created and given authority over all of Texas east of the Trinity River. (See Map IV.) During this period of Mexican rule (1821-1836) Nacogdoches residents saw a tide of American settlers begin flowing into Texas and the town became a center of political activities that culminated in the Texas Revolution. In 1821, however, still suffering from the effects of the filibustering expeditions, the town lay in ruins. Only the church, the Stone House, and six other dwellings remained.

During the 1820s increasing numbers of Americans crossed the Sabine and settled between the Attoyac Bayou and the Sabine River. Most entered illegally. In 1824, Juan Seguin, <u>alcalde</u> of Nacogdoches, directed that every inhabitant of the Nacogdoches District wishing to reside in Texas and become a Mexican citizen come to Nacogdoches and take an oath of allegiance to the Mexican Constitution of 1824. Few of those settled east of the Attoyac responded.

Mexican Colonization Efforts. Recognizing the need to populate the vast area of the former Spanish province of Texas if it was not to be lost to American and European penetration, in 1824, the Mexican national congress enacted a national colonization law. That statute surrendered to the various Mexican states the authority to create regulations to dispose of any unappropriated lands within their borders for colonization. The statute further provided that all state regulations must conform to the national law and the national constitution; no lands within twenty leagues of an international boundary or within ten leagues of the sea coast could be claimed; and titles to land were to be restricted to residents and could not exceed eleven leagues.

The following year, the Congress of the State of Coahuila and Texas enacted a state colonization law providing that all who entered provide satisfactory evidence of their Christian beliefs, morality, and good habits. Titles to land could be obtained by individual families or through the action of an empresario. Families, after payment of some small fees, could obtain a league of land; they were required to cultivate or occupy the land within six years; native-born Mexican citizens might purchase as much as eleven leagues of land; and colonists were exempt from taxation for a period of ten years.

In 1825, two men were granted empresario contracts in 1825 to settle colonists in East Texas: Frost Thorn and Haden Edwards. Thorn's contract called for the settlement of 400 families and that of Edwards for 800 families. Neither man fulfilled the obligations of his contract. The Edwards contract included the area surrounding Nacogdoches, an area that had been inhabited by European settlers since 1716.

Since 1779, when Gil Y'Barbo returned to the area with the displaced Adaesanos, Europeans had inhabited their lands continuously, so that by the time Edwards received his contract two generations of settlers had grown to adulthood in East Texas. To be sure, most of them did not hold legal title to the land they called their own, but their roots were deeply imbedded in the soil of the area. Mingled with the Spanish settlers, were French creoles, outlaws from the Neutral Ground, American frontiersmen, Southern planters, and the fragments of several Indian tribes.

Disputes between Haden, his brother Benjamin Edwards, and the old settlers broke out almost as soon as Haden and his family arrived in Nacogdoches in September 1825, and they escalated over the next several months. Conditions worsened to the point that after persistent complaints from the old settlers and local Mexican officials, the President of the Republic of Mexico ordered Edwards' contract nullified and his expulsion from the colony.

Between April and October 1826, disputes over land titles multiplied and became increasingly critical. Disagreements over ownership were regularly resolved in favor of the older settlers by Mexican alcalde, Samuel Norris, while at the same time a band of "Regulators" under the leadership of James Gaines opened a campaign of harassment directed toward those who opposed Alcalde Norris. When Haden Edwards was informed that his contract had been cancelled and that he was ordered to leave Texas, he determined to retain his lands by detaching East Texas from Mexican rule. This determination launched an armed revolt that came to be known as the Fredonian Rebellion.[68]

---

[68] Joe Ellis Ericson, Early East Texas, A History from Indian Settlement to Statehood (Bowie Maryland: Heritage Books, 2002), pp. 86-87; Joe E. Ericson, The Nacogdoches Story, An

Fredonian Rebellion. The uprising began when a band of men lead by Colonel Martin Parmer and Major John S. Roberts rode into Nacogdoches, arrested Alcalde Norris and Sindico Jose Antonio Sepulveda, placed the empresario and his brother on parole on their word of honor, and convened a court martial to deal with Norris and Sepulveda. The court found both men guilty, removed them from office, and declared them ineligible to hold office ever again.

When news of the capture of Nacogdoches reached San Antonio de Bexar, on December 11, a detachment of Mexican troops numbering some 110 infantry left the provincial capital. They were reinforced by 250 militiamen from Stephen F. Austin's colony. and the combined force reached Nacogdoches February 8, 1827, along with 150 more volunteers from the Ayish Bayou area. By the time the Mexican troops and their allies reached Nacogdoches, the rebellion had collapsed, and the Edwards brothers and their allies had fled eastward across the Sabine River into the United States and safety. Those settlers who remained were fairly treated by the Mexican authorities. Local government, peace, and order were soon reestablished.[69]

(A Mexican Census taken in 1826 listed the individuals shown in Table VII below.)

Table VII
Nacogdoches Census (1826)

JOSE ANTONIO CHIRINO, 77
  wife, 55
MANUEL CHIRINO, 33
  wife, Martina Y'Barbo, 28
  child, Polonio, 14
  Antonio Herculiano 12
  Maria Faustina 10
  Anastacio, 6
  Maria Gorgonia, 4
JOSE MARIA CHIRINO, 25
  wife, Maria Rafaela de Jesus, 18
  dau., Maria Bencelada de Jesus, 8 mos.
FRANCISCO MORA, 60
UCEBIO y SUR, 24
  wife, Maria Eme Bascoqui, 20
  dau., Narua Glee y Sur, 4
  niece, Maria Modesta Toten, 9
JOSE LUTERIO LOPES, 26
  wife, Maria Consecion Arriola, 21
  son, Jose Angel Lopes, 4.
MARIA BERNARDINE de CENA, 1
PEDRO Y'BARBO, 43.
  wife, Juana de la Garza, 37
  son, Jose Remigio de Jesus
  Maria Josefa Lionicia, 16
  Maria Cantu, 14
  Manuel Monetre, 10
  Jose Luciano, 8

Informal History (Bowie, Maryland: Heritage Books, 200), pp. 35-45.

[69] Ibid., pp. 89-90.

Juana Bautista, 5
Maria Feliciana, 1
JUAN JOSE Y'BARBO, 36
   wife, Maria Garcia, 29
   son, Jose Gregorio
   son, Juan Pablo
JUAN ANTONIO Y'BARBO, 25
ANASTACIO Y'BARBO, 40
   wife, Manuela Sanches, 26
   dau., Encarnacion
   niece, Anastasia Maria Petra Cordova
JOSE de JESUS GAMES, 28
   wife, Maria Gregoria Sanches, 25
   dau., Maria Godonia, 1
MANUEL Y'barbo, 33
   wife, Maria Gertrudes Calderon
   son, Jose Maria, 8
   dau., Candelario, 6
   son, Jesus, 4
   dau., Maria Brijida, 7 mos.
MARIA GARCIA, 13
FRANCISCO GUERRERO, 55
JOSE IGNACIO Y'BARBO, 50
   son, Benino, 20
   son, Manuel, 18
   son, Maximilano, 7
   son, Juan Antonio, 24
   dau., Maria Carmel, 16
   dau., Maria Teresa, 2
JUAN PALVADOR, 56
   wife, Lenora Tesie, 55
   son, Jose, 20
   dau., Anastacia Tesie, 7
VICENTE DIAS, 35
   dau., Maria, 12
   dau., Maria Asensia, 6
   dau., Juana Maria, 2
   Maria Gertrudis
JUAN ALBARDO, 47
   wife, Maria Ygnasia Garcia, 28
   son, Santos Garcia, 12
   son, Jose Gil, 1
DAMASIO Y'BARBO, 43
JUAN BAUTISTA GANE, 32

JOSE CARO, 54
   wife, Michela Exis, 46
   son, Jose Agaton, 30
   son, Juan, 25
   son, Pilar, 18
   dau., Felician, 16
   son, Jose Sabastian, 14
   dau., Maria antonia, 12
   dau., Cleta, 9
   son, Jose Torbido, 7
   dau., Maria Jesusa, 4
TOMAS CARO, 37
   wife, Gertrudis Texada, 30
   dau., Maria Basilia, 9
   dau., Maria Ygnasia, 5
   dau., Leonisa, 5
   son, Jose Justo, 3
   dau., Marselina
   son, Jose Alexandro, 3
NORIN Y'BARBO, ?
JOSE Y'BARBO, 40
   wife, Maria Caro, 28
   son, Jose Antonio, 10
   son, Francisco, 8
   son, Vicente, 4
   son, Leonisio, 2
JOSE ANTONIO SEPULVEDA, 45
   wife, Guadalupe Chavana, 21
   son, Felice Segumendo, 7
   dau., Maria Antonia, 6
   dau., Maria Rernave, 4
   dau., Maria Torivia, 1
RAMON CHAVANA, 53
   wife, Maria Josefa Sanches, 42
   son, Antonio, 26
   son, Santiago, 17
   son, Faustino, 12
   son, Guillermo, 8
   dau., Maria de los Remedios, 4
   son, Jose Fermin, 1
SANTIAGO ERIE, 22
   wife, Maria Enselma Chevana, 14
JOSE MARIANO ACOSTA, 35
   wife, Maria Josefa Delgado, 29

    son, Francisco, 7
    dau., Juana Francisca, 5
    son, Juan Jose, 3
    dau., Maria de la Paz, 1
MANUEL SANTOS, 37
    wife, Guadalupe Chirino, 30
    son, Juan, 13
    son, Bernino, 11
    dau., Maria Antonia, 7
    dau., Maria Carmel, 5
SIPRIAN del TORO, 48
RICARDO SANCHES, 40
    son, Bentura, 17
TRINIDAD GARCIA, 40
DELORES MARTINES, 44
JUAN YGNACIO ZOTO, 47
    wife, Jesusa Maldonado, 44

YGNACIA SANTOS, 51
    wife, Gertrudis Chirino, 36
ESIDUO de la GARZA, 24
VICENTE CORDOVA, 29
    wife, Maria Antonia Cordova
    ?, Juan Nepomuseno Cordova
ANDRE TORRES, 30
    wife, Jesusa de Lone, 22
    dau., Maria Anna, 8
    ?, Jose Natavio Torres
FRANCISCO PERES, 25
    wife, Carmel Trevino, 20
    dau., Maria Sultana
CLETO TORRES, 20
    wife, Pilar Acosta, 22
    dau., Carmel, 3
MARIA ANTONIA CRUS, 60.

Source: <u>Residents of Texas</u>, Vol. 2, pp. 210-214.

No Anglo-American or other foreign names appear on this 1826 Mexican Census. Since this enumeration was taken during the turbulent times leading up to or in the midst of the Fredonian Rebellion, perhaps all such persons had fled the settlement, crossing the Sabine River to safety in the United States or fleeing westward beyond the reach of the warring factions and possible retaliation on the part of Mexican authorities. In any case, an 1828 census covering the area from the Attoyac to the Loco Creek does include the following individuals:

    Joseph Durst, unmarried, 35
    Delilah Dill, married, 32 with son James, 9
    Henry Stockman, 36, married, wife Dorcas Trebite, 35, son Henry Samuel, 7, daughters
        Tabitha, 5 and Harriet, 1.
    Anthony Stockman, unmarried, 21
    Peter Stockman, unmarried, 26, and mother, Catherine Desponete, 57
    Joseph Robinson, unmarried, 37, brother Moses Robinson, 26, married, wife Barbara
        Frederick, 36, daughter Helen, 7, and son James, 4
    Helen Kimble, widow, 58, and niece Maria Louisa, 6
    Joaquin Chiver, widower, 54.[1]

Also, residents of the "town proper:"
    John S. Roberts, married, 30, wife Harriet, 30, son John, 4
    Leonardo Duboy, unmarried, 27, with Maria Luisa Rechar, 26.

John Durst, married, 27, wife Henrietta M. Thomason (sic.), 20, son Luis, 0, and Mme. McFarland, widow, 50.

Frost Thorn, married, 42, wife Susan Edwards, 26, and Haden [H.] Edwards, unmarried, 17.

Jacob Garrett, widower, 46 and daughter, unnamed

Nathaniel Norris, married, 39, wife Juana Puario, 33, son Maria Priscilla, 10, son Maria Glorendia, 8, and son Jose Augustin, 7

James Gaines, married, 47, wife Jesusa Norris, 29, son Ramon Gaines, 13, son John Baptist, 10, and son James, Jr, 1

Robert Casey, unmarried, 30

Ysur Pantaleon, married, 26, wife Ame Andres, 19. daughter Agraye, 6 and daughter Chrisanta, 4

Ceasar Lafitte, married, 40, wife, Isabel Layton, 37, son Jose Maria, 19, son Feliciana Rublo, 17, son Juan Jose Fulgencio, 15, son Luis, 7, Pedro, 4, son Ylario, 1

Bernardo Pantaleon, married, 31, wife Maria Delilah Meziers, 21, son David, 3, and son Moriel, 0.²

Also, residents from the Attoyac and Ayish Bayou west to Trinity River:

Elias Lloyd, married, 53, wife Maria, 46 [born about 1773, Maryland]

Raymondo Norris, married, 61, wife Maria Seleste Gega, 58

Thomas Norris, married, 32, wife Maria Paurie, 20, son William, 0

John Norris, married, 28, wife Celeste Stockman, 17, Maria Juliana, 0

Jose Franco. Anto. Lafour, married, 47, wife Celestina [Buran], 38, daughter Maria Loreta, 17, daughter Maria Magdalena, 15, daughter Maria, 12, daughter Maria Margarita, 10, son Jose Antonio, 8, son Jose Eugenio, 6, son Jose Salestino, 4, and daughter Maria Celestine, 1

Eduardo Arreola, married, 42, wife Candelaria Simms, 36

William Goyens (free man of color), unmarried, 43, with Jesusa Linse, 20, Maria Linse, 26, and her son Manuel, 10

Julian Taylor, married, 38, wife Maria, 26

Thomas F. McKinney, married, 27, wife Melson Watts, 30, and brother Politico, 0

Phillip Sublett, married, 31, wife Catherine, 20

William Bebe, married, 56, wife Maria Gualteman, 47

William Bebe, married, 24, wife Maria Josefa Sarnac, 30, son Jose, 7, daughter Maria, 5, son Santiago, 3, and son Marselino, 1[70]

Also, west of Nacogdoches to the Trinity River:

Daniel Clark, married, 51, wife Maria Floque, 58[71]

---

[70] Ibid., pp. 222-229.

[71] Ibid., p. 229.

Also, from Attoyac to Nacogdoches:
   David McQueen, unmarried, 28
   Baptiste Puarie (Porrier), married, 26, wife Juliana Norris, her son Jose Anto. Quirk, 19, her son Henry Quirk, 18, and her daughter Maria Losoya, 12[72]

JOSEPH DURST was born April 8, 1789, son of Jacob and Ann (Schesser) Durst, married Delilah Dill about 1818 (remarried by priest August 3, 1839).[73]

HENRY STOCKMAN, native of Natchez, Mississippi, was born about 1792 and died February 2, 1852 in Rusk County, Texas. He was the son of C. C. F. and Catherine (des Bonnet) Stockman. He married Dorcas Trebite and came to Texas about 1806.[74] JOSEPH ANTHONY STOCKMAN was born about 1806 at Atascocita on the Trinity River and died by February 1834 in Nacogdoches County, son of Frederick and Catherine (des Bonnet) Stockman.[75] PETER STOCKMAN was born about 1802 in Alabama and died about 1865 in McLennan County, Texas. He was another son of Frederick and Catherine (des Bonnet) Stockman.[76]

JOSEPH ROBINSON was born about 1790. MOSES ROBINSON, who was born about 1802, married Barbara Frederick and settled on west bank of Red River.[77]

HELENA (HELEN) [Gimelech or Chamleich] KIMBLE was born about 1770 in Maryland and died about 1848 near Alto, Cherokee County, Texas. She was the daughter of John and Catherine Chamleich and married first James Dill September 14, 1791 in Arkansas and second William Nelson.[78]

JOHN S. ROBERTS was born July 13, 1796 in Virginia, son of John S. Roberts, Sr.,

---

[72] Ibid.

[73] Ericson, Gateway to Texas, Vol. I, p. 110.

[74] Ibid., p. 365.

[75] Ibid.

[76] Ibid.

[77] Ibid., p. 319.

[78] Ibid., p. 198.

and died August 9, 1871 in Nacogdoches, buried in Oak Grove Cemetery. He married Harriet (Fenley) Callier December 26, 1826, adopted her son John F. (Callier) Roberts and had one son Lycurgus. Roberts came to the Sabine District of Texas in 1826 and the following year to San Augustine and finally to Nacogdoches[79]

JOHN DURST was born February 4, 1797 at Arkansas Post, Arkansas Territory and died February 9, 1851 Leon County, Texas, son of Jacob and Anna (Schesser) Durst and Godson of Samuel Davenport. He married Harriet Matilda Jamison, daughter of Colonel John Jamison February 15, 1821.[80]

FROST THORN, native of Glen Cove, New York, born there about 1793 and died December 3, 1854 Nacogdoches, buried in Oak Grove Cemetery. He married Susan Edwards, daughter of empresario Haden Edwards,[81]

JACOB GARRETT was born about 1776 in Virginia and died at Hot Springs, Arkansas, about 1842. He was the son of John and Jane Garrett and was married to Charity Taylor March 12, 1802.[82] He came to Texas in 1824 from Arkansas, a widower.

NATHANIEL NORRIS, who was born about 1791 and died prior to 1854, was the son of Edmund and Sarah Norris. He married Juana Puerie (Poirier) about 1817 in Natchitoches, Louisiana.[83]

JAMES TAYLOR GAINES was born about 1776 in Virginia, son of Richard and Jemima (Pendleton) Gaines, and died November 1856 in California. He married twice, name of first wife unknown but second wife was Susanna (Jesusa) Norris, daughter of Edmund and

---

[79] Ericson and Ericson, Personalities on the East Texas Frontier, p. 75; Joe E. Ericson and Carolyn R. Ericson, Spoiling for a Fight, The Life of John S. Roberts and Early Nacogdoches (Waco: Texian Press, 1989).

[80] Ericson, Gateway to Texas, Vol. I, p. 110.

[81] Ibid., p. 379.

[82] Ibid., p. 137.

[83] Ibid., p. 270.

Sarah Norris.[84]

EUSEBIO YSUR PANTALION, native of Natchitoches, Louisiana, was born there May 14, 1802, son of Bernard and Margueritte (Detchou) Pantalion, and died in Nacogdoches, probably buried in Vital Flores Cemetery. He married first Ame Andres, second Maria Esne Bascoqui February 2, 1822, and third Eduvijen Flores. BERNARD (BERNARDO) PANTALION was born October 7, 1797 at Natchitoches, Louisiana, son of Bernard and Margueritte Grillet (Torin) Pantalion. He married Maria Delilah Meziers March 1, 1821.[85]

JOSEPH MARIE CESAR LAFITTE was born August 9, 1787, son of Paul Bouet and Marianne (de Soto) Lafitte in Bayou Pierre, Louisiana. He married Mary Elizabeth [Isabel] about 1817.[86]

THOMAS NORRIS, who was born about 1796 in Maryland, was the son of Edmund and Sarah Norris. He married Maria Pueres [Poirier] October 11, 1826 and came to Texas by 1828 with wife and four children. JOHN NORRIS was born November 22, 1800 in Rapides Parish, Louisiana, son of Edmund and Sarah (Rogers) Norris. He married Celeste Stockman November 6, 1826.[87]

EDWARDO ARRIOLA was born about 1789 and died 1850 in California. He was the son of Jose Antonio and Anna Maria (Equis) Arriola. He married Maria Candelaria Sims, daughter of Richard Sims.[88]

WILLIAM GOYENS, born 1794 in Moore County, North Carolina, a free man of color, son of William Goins and his wife Elizabeth. He married a widow, Mary (Pate) Sibley. He died June 20, 1856 in Nacogdoches.[89]

THOMAS FREEMAN McKINNEY, son of Abraham and Eleanor (Prather) McKinney,

---

[84] Ibid., p. 133.

[85] Ibid., p. 278.

[86] Ibid., p. 203.

[87] Ibid., p. 270.

[88] Ibid., p. 12.

[89] Ibid, p. 147; Ericson and Ericson, Personalities on the East Texas Frontier, p. 91.

was born November 1, 1801 in Lincoln County, Kentucky and died October 2, 1836. He married first Melson Watts, second Nancy Wilson, a widow, and third Anna G. Gibbs September 23, 1842 in Galveston, Texas.[90]

PHILLIP A. SUBLETT, born May 22, 1802 in Green County, Kentucky, died February 22, 1850 in San Augustine County, Texas, buried in Sublett Cemetery. He married Ester Jane Roberts, daughter of Elisha Roberts.

WILLIAM BEBE, SR. was born about 1770 and married Mary Whitman. WILLIAM BEBE, JR. was born about 1804 in Nacogdoches, son of William amd Mary (Whitman) Bebe. He married Maria Josefa Sarnac.[91]

DANIEL CLARK was born about 1777 and died by 1832. He was married to Maria Floque in 1828 and to Maria Elena Van Sickle in 1831.[92]

By 1779, "[m]ost of these early setters, especially those determined to make their homes within the forbidden twenty league strip east of Nacogdoches, came and went without leaving a record of their presence."[93] A fair number of both Spanish and Anglo-American settlers, however, made homes in the area, the Americans coming primarily from Mississippi, Alabama, Georgia, Tennessee, and Kentucky. The Ayish Bayou district of the time included today's San Augustine, Sabine, and Shelby Counties.

Attoyac Settlers. Records from 1821 indicate that at least sixteen male persons lived east of the Attoyac River, while three years later a petition from the area contained thirty-six signatures. Another petition circulated about the same time contains the names of more than 1,000 persons settled between the Sabine and Attoyac Rivers in East Texas.[94] A list of free males of the Ayish Bayou District provides the names of some ninety-seven men. (See Table VIII below.)

---

[90] Ibid,. p. 228.

[91] Ibid., p. 25.

[92] Ibid., p. 74.

[93] Ericson, Early East Texas, p. 93.

[94] Ibid, p. 95.

Table VIII

Men in Ayish Bayou (1826)

Theodore Dorsett	Thomas F. McKinney
James Bullock	Danniel Elam
William A. Gwin or Irwin	Lemuel Hopkins
Edwin Hendrick	----- Campbell
Adam Robards	----- Ausbourn
Obedia Hendricks	James Fulcher
Stephen Prather	Baly Anderson, Snr.
Moses Wooton	Baly Anderson, Jun.
William McDonal	Vincent Anderson
Myrick Davis	David Erles
Robert Wiseman	----- Tele
Thomas W. Spencer	----- Lankford
Benjamin Thomas	James Quinlety
Samuel Horton	John Cartwright
John M. Taylor	----- Fruth
William Johnston	James Allin
Amos Tims	John Inglish
Charles Dorsett	Thomas Inglish
M. S. Brake	William Inglish
William H. Howester	Jacob Shannon
Shadrick D. Thomas	Owen Shannon
Wiley S. Thomas	Henry Goff
G. F. Thomas	Lewis Hallaway
John Buckley	James Williams
Thomas Cartwright	Thomas Shote
William H. Hodges	Lewis Noggin
Elisha Roberts	----- Noggin, Sr.
Henry Hendrick	Mason G. Coal
Isaack Lyndsy	Francis Murphy
Aaron Colvin	James Bridges
Thomas Slaughter	John Scritchfield
John Burdine	John Coal
Stephen Johnson	Stephen Lynch
Benjamin Lyndsy	----- Blackburn
James Morton	Nathin Davis
Jacob Fulsher	John A. Williams
Leonard Marshel	----- Millspaugh
Joseph Sims	Josiah Sims

Antoner Revo	John McWilliams
Henry Leny	Bateast Guire
----- Howard	Bateast Boda
John Sanders	John Magrue
John Creepin	James Inglish
Basett Basett	Bateast Boye
John Sprowl	----- Bassett
----- Williams	
----- Lofton	
Jesse Simes	

Source: Nacogdoches Archives

Settlers in the Red Lands. The first great infiltration of immigrants into the Ayish Bayou settlement came following news of the Mexican Colonization Law of 1824. In little more than a decade some 2,500 immigrants had settled in the San Augustine Municipality which included today's San Augustine, Sabine, and Shelby Counties. The early settlers in the area known later as the Red Lands virtually all settled in the redland belt on either side of the King's Highway (El Camino Real). As more and more people came to the Red Lands, they began locating along the various water courses: Ayish Bayou, Palo Gacho, Patroon Creek, and Ironosa. The main body of settlers, however, remained rather evenly distributed along a strip about ten miles wide running east and west through the region.

A scattering of area settlements ultimately became known as the Ayish Bayou District, gaining its name from the fact that a stream of that name runs north to south through it. The settlements in the northern half of present San Augustine County, together with those down the Attoyac River and a few along the Angelina River, the northern part of Sabine County, and the eastern part of Shelby County, even then were beginning to be known as the Tenehaw District. Although it was legally a part of the Municipality of Nacogdoches, it was regarded as a separate district because of its distance from the town of Nacogdoches and because nearly all of its inhabitants were Anglo-Americans, while the majority of those in Nacogdoches were Mexicans.

Among the early Anglo-American immigrants in the area "all authorities concur in naming Nathan Davis as the first settler" within modern San Augustine County.[95] Davis, who had been born in South Carolina about 1779, later moved to Kentucky and then Illinois, came to Texas in 1818 with slaves. He settled on the Ayish Bayou near the King's Highway crossing. Davis suffered from a case of crippled feet, but he "took a lively interest in the affairs of the settlement." He married a Jane ---- and died probably in San Augustine County, date unknown.[96]

About the same time, "the Anderson family came from Indiana, crossing the Sabine River near the site of Logansport, January 1, 1819, and settled on the Ayish Bayou" south of Nathan Davis. Its head, Bailey Anderson, Sr., was the son of John Anderson, a native of Scotland. Bailey went to Kentucky about 1795 and fifteen years later moved to Indiana. On the journey from Indiana to Texas his wife, Mary Wyatt Anderson, died on the Mississippi River.[97]

His son, Bailey, Jr., came to Texas with him. The younger Anderson was born February 25, 1788 and died about 1865 in McLennan County, Texas. He had married Elizabeth McFadden June 4, 1811, in Warren County, Kentucky.[98] Jonathan Anderson, grandson of Bailey, Sr. and nephew of Bailey, Jr., also came in 1819. He located about ten miles south of the town of San Augustine. He soon moved to the Patroon neighborhood and settled near Nathan Davis.[99]

In 1820 or 1821, Warren Davis settled in the district. He was a Virginian of English descent. With him came his sons, Elias K. and Edward B. Davis. They located their homesites a short distance from the Milton Garrett place. Warren was born about 1766 and died about 1838 near Chireno, Texas. Elias K. was born about 1797 and married Martha -----. Edward B.

---

[95] George L. Crocket, Tow Centuries in East Texas: A History of San Augustine County and Surrounding Territory (Austin: Hart Graphics reprint ed., 1982), p. 82.

[96] Ibid.

[97] Ibid., p. 82.

[98] Ericson, Gateway to Texas, Vol. I., p. 7.

[99] Ibid.

was born November 4, 1804, in Virginia and died in Grimes County. He married Mary Lawrence.[100]

In 1824, Benjamin Thomas, Sr., came to the Ayish Bayou area from Alabama. He had been born April 16, 1778 in Edgecombe County, North Carolina, died about 1834 probably buried in Thomas Cemetery, San Augustine County, and married Mary Ann Dickinson. He was the son of Major Theophilus and Mary Rogers Thomas. Three of Benjamin's sons, Shadrick D., Iredel D., and Theophilus, and his two daughters, Mrs. E. K. Davis and Mrs. Noel G. Roberts "left numerous descendants." Shadrack Dickinson Thomas was born September 1799 in Edgecombe County, North Carolina and died after 1874 in San Augustine County, Texas, probably buried in the Thomas Cemetery. He married first Sarah ----, second in 1827, Mrs. Lucretia Brown, and third November 15, 1855, Mary Brown. His brother, Iredell Dickinson Thomas, was born January 6, 1805, and died February 29, 1866, He married first Penelope Thomas, daughter of Amos and Penelope (Ashmore) Thomas, and second Elizabeth Holman Campbell February 23, 1845. Theophilus Thomas was born August 13, 1813, Madison County, Alabama, and died May 1, 1881 in San Augustine County. He married Susan Winn, daughter of Robert Winn, September 12, 1837.[101]

In 1823, Jonas Harrison came from New Jersey and settled north of the present town of Patroon. Although born in New Jersey, he was educated in Buffalo, New York. Jonas was born October 11, 1777, in Woodbridge Township, New Jersey, son of William and Elizabeth Harrison, and died August 6, 1836 on his farm in Shelby County, buried near Patroon. Married, name unknown, in Georgia before coming to Texas.[102] A neighbor of Jonas Harrison was George English, who became the first sheriff of San Augustine County in 1827.[103]

---

[100] Ericson, Gateway to Texas, Vol. I., 95.

[101] Ibid., pp. 375-376.

[102] Ibid., p. 165.

[103] Crocket, Two Centuries in East Texas, p. 84.

In 1824 and 1825 "the first great influx immigrants came into the country." Alexander Horton, then a young man, came to Ayish Bayou District with his mother Susanna Horton and her younger children, in the company of Elisha Roberts. Alexander had been born April 18, 1810, in Halifax County, North Carolina, son of Julius and Susannah (Purnell) Horton, and died January 11, 1894 in San Augustine County. Alexander married Mary Elizabeth Harrell December 30, 1847. He came to Texas in 1824[104]. Elisha Roberts was born in 1774 in Watauga Settlement, Tennessee, son of William Roberts. He married Martha "Patsy" Gill about 1800 and the couple had nine children. Roberts came to Texas in 1824 from Kentucky and St. Tammany Parish, Louisiana. He died October 3, 1844 in San Augustine County and was buried near his farm home.[105]

In his memoirs, published late in his life, Horton identified persons living in the county in 1824 when his mother moved to Texas:

> I found James Gaines keeping a ferry on the Sabine River. The next house was Maximillian's. At the Polygoch [Palo Gacho], Macon G. Cole. The next settler was Bryan Daugherty, living at the place where Elisha Roberts formerly lived. The next place was Nathan Davis, living at the crossing of the Ayish Bayou. The next place. . .lived John A. Williams. [Next was] the place where Milton Garrett lived. There a man named Fulcher lived. At or near the Attoyac lived Thomas Spencer. That was about the number of inhabitants living in the country January 1, 1824.[106]

According to Horton, the country thereafter began to fill up rapidly. Among these early settlers, he named: David and Isaac Renfro, Elisha Roberts, Donald McDonald, John Cartwright, Willis Murphy, Phillip A. Sublett, John Chumly, Nathan Davis, Obadiah Hendricks, John Bodine, John A. Lout, Bailey Anderson, Benjamin Thomas, Wiley Thomas, Shadrack Thomas, Thomas Cartwright, Isaac Lindsey, John G. Love, Martha Lewis, George

---

[104] Ericson, Gateway to Texas, Vol. I, p. 177.

[105] Ibid., p. 316; The New Handbook of Texas, Vol. 5, p.609.

[106] Crocket, Two Centuries in East Texas, p. 85.

Jones, Achilles Johnson, Elias K. Davis, Theodore Dorset, John Dorset, Benjamin Lindsey, Stephen Prather, Wyatt Hanks, James and Horatio Hanks, Solomon Miller, Hyram Brown, William Lace, George Teal, Edward Teal, John Sprowl, James Bridges, Ross Bridges, Peter Galloway, and John McGinnis.[107]

Juan Ignacio Maximillian Arze y Larenodiere, son of Juan de Arze and Francesca Larenodiere, was born July 1, 1782 in Natchitoches, Louisiana and died 1866 in Texas. He married Anastacia Sims, daughter of Richard Sims and Concession Perez about 1809.

Another list of early settlers published by Horton in 1888 provides these additional names: William and Thomas English, Neal McNeal, Jacob, William and Milton Garrett, James W. Bullock, Squire Brown, John, Garry, and Iredell Thomas, Henry and Edmund Hendrick, William and Dr. S. P. Wilson, Samuel S. Davis, Jonas Hale, John S. and Reuben D. Wood, Henry Augustine, Isaac Thacker, William Loyd, Thomas Malone, James Perkins, Boyd Irvine, and Claiborne Garrett.[108]

Others who settled in the area between 1833 and 1835 included: Chichester Chaplin, L. H. Mabbit, James Carter, Harrison E. Watson, Samuel Stedham, David Brown, Abram Zuber, Augustus Hotchkiss, Emery Raines, Blassingame W. Harvey, S. W. Blount, J. C. Lawhorn, Samuel Sexton, John Sanders, Nathaniel Hunt, Charles S. Hunt, Andrew Caddell, A. G. Kellog, John C. Brooke, R. H. Foote, William Kimbro, A. M. Davis, John P. Border, John Gillespie, Samuel Stivers, Burwell J. Thompson, Isaac W. Burton, Samuel D. McMahon, and John W. Bradley.[109]

East Texas historian George Crocket commented regarding early settlement in the area: "As the country was explored, settlements were made and farms opened along the various water courses, whose fertile valleys attracted home seekers. From the first, the Ayish Bayou and the Palo Gacho proved to be attractive. A few years later a number of persons. . .moved to the Patroon Creek in the edge of Shelby." Yet another settlement grew up around the

---

[107] Ibid, p. 85.

[108] Ibid., pp. 85-86.

[109] Ibid., p. 86.

southern headwaters of Ironosa Creek twenty-two miles west of San Augustine.[110]

Colonization Law of 1830. During this same period, after the Fredonian Rebellion had been quashed in 1827, Colonel Jose de las Piedras and the Twelfth Permanent Battalion of Mexican troops were stationed in Nacogdoches and a measure of relative quiet and prosperity descended on the Nacogdoches district. From a low of approximately 200 persons in 1823, by 1828, the population had grown to some 1,000 and was still growing. The overwhelming number of the new inhabitants was made up of foreigners who had entered Texas illegally. The illegal immigrants, for the most part, refused to present themselves to seek permission to settle, they simply "squatted" on the land of their choice. They questioned the government's authority to compel them to seek permission and steadfastly maintained that they had every right to settle wherever they pleased.

In 1830, confronted with the ever increasing volume of illegal immigrants entering Texas from the United States, Mexican officials discerned a threat to the nation's control over the region. Whereupon, the National Congress issued a decree on April 6, 1830, forbidding nationals from foreign countries adjacent to Mexican territory from settling in Texas and other parts of Mexico adjoining its territory.

The ban on further American immigration led to an order by Colonel Piedras requiring all Anglo-Americans in the Nacogdoches area to surrender their weapons to him in Nacogdoches. He hinted that failure might well result in a war of extermination waged by Mexican troops and local Indians. The East Texans reacted promptly by organizing a militia with which to defend themselves. Soon after the militia began organizing, many local residents again chose to move to the east as they had done many times in the past. The Nacogdoches militia was then consolidated with the militias organized in Ayish Bayou, Tenaha (Tenahaw), the Sabine District, and the Bevil (Jasper) Settlement to form a "National Militia" under the command of Colonel James Whitis Bullock, a native of North Carolina and a veteran of the War of 1812 and an Ayish Bayou resident. Bullock had been born about 1795 and died about 1856 at Millwood, Collin County, Texas. He had married Nancy Horton, daughter of Julius

---

[110] Ibid., p. 89.

and Susanna (Purnell) Horton.[111]

Battle of Nacogdoches. In August the National Militia issued an ultimatum to Colonel Piedras who replied by asserting that he would remain loyal to the constitution and laws of his country. Whereupon the militia began a march on the town square. They ultimately seized the Stone House and other buildings on the square while other units of the militia marched toward the north and from the west. Routed by the attacking forces, the Mexican troops fled the town toward the west. The "Battle of Nacogdoches" cleared the eastern section of Texas of all Mexican military forces, and it remained clear of them up to and during the time of the Texas Revolution (1836).

Leaders of the National Militia, in addition to Colonel Bullock included: Captains Bailey Anderson, Sr., Isaac W. Burton, Vicente Cordova, Wyatt Hanks, and Frederick Moz; Lieutenant Nathaniel Norris; and Ensigns Mallhead D. Doya, Juan Lazarin, Antonio Manchaca, Juan Mora, and Adolphus Sterne.

Isaac Watts Burton was born about 1805 in Clarke County, Georgia, and died January 1843 in Crockett, Houston County, Texas. He married Martha Lacy, daughter of Martin Lacy. He came to Texas January 14, 1832.[112] Vicente Cordova, son of Ramon Cordova, was born 1798, killed in the Battle of Salado (1813). He married his cousin, Maria Antonia Cordova.[113] N. Wyatt Hanks, son of Peter and Isabella Hanks, was born November 27, 1795 and died about 1862, probably in Jasper County. He married Hannah Gates. With his brothers James and Horatio and his mother, he came to Texas from the Kentucky-Indiana country.[114]

Juan Maria Lazarin, son of Joseph and Juana Maria (Rivas) Lazarin, was born about 1796 and died by 1838, probably in Nacogdoches County. He married Maria Josefa de la Vega, daughter of Antonia Flores April 28, 1819 in Natchitoches, Louisiana.[115] Nicholas

---

[111] Ericson, <u>Gateway to Texas</u>, Vol. I, p. 49.

[112] Ericson <u>Gateway to Texas</u>, Vol. I, p. 51.

[113] <u>Ibid</u>., p. 84.

[114] <u>Ibid</u>., p. 161; Crockett, <u>Two Centuries in East Texas</u>, p. 125.

[115] <u>Ibid</u>., p. 208.

Aolphus Sterne, son of Emmanuel and Helen Sterne, was born April 15, 1801, Cologne, Germany, and died March 27, 1852, New Orleans, Louisiana, buried Oak Grove Cemetery, Nacogdoches, Texas. He married Eva Catherine Rosine Ruoff June 2, 1828.[116] (Table IX, below, lists all known participants in the Battle of Nacogdoches. In fact, 239 men were known, exclusive of officers who took part, but the names of many others have not been recorded.)

Table IX
Participants: Battle of Nacogdoches (1832)

Bailey Anderson, Jr., Shelby County
Bailey Anderson, Sr. Shelby County (Captain)
Henry William Augustine (Lieutenant)
John Batey
John M. Bradley, Tenaha (Captain)
James Bradshaw, Neches District (Captain)
Henry Mitchell Brewer, Nacogdoches
John Brewer, Nacogdoches
Hiram Brown, Ayish Bayou (Lieutenant)
James Whitis Bullock, San Augustine (Colonel)
Isaac Watts Burton, Ayish Bayou (Captain, Adjutant)
Samuel Burress, Nacogdoches (Major)
James Carter
George Cartwright
Mican Chamirma (Chamiroro)
Francisco Encarnacion Chireno, Nacogdoches
Vincente Cordova, Nacogdoches (Captain)
Daniel Davis
George Davis
E. K. Davis, Ayish Bayou?
Samuel S. Davis, Sabine County (Captain)
Malldred (Mallhed) D. Doya (Ensign)
John M. Durst, Nacogdoches (Interpreter and Scout)
Asa M. Edwards, Nacogdoches
William E. Garrett

James Gaines, Sabine County
John Harvey Hamby
Horatio Hanks
---- Hart
W. Hathaway
Edwin Hendrick, San Augustine (Ensign)
Simal P. Hopkins, Ayish Bayou District
Alexander Horton, San Augustine
Augustus Hotchkiss, Nacogdoches
Almanzon Huston, San Augustine
W. (William?) Irvin, Ayish Bayou (Lieutenant)
Asa Jarman
A. E. C. Johnson
George Jones
Martin Lacey
William Young Lacy
Juan Lazarine (Ensign)
George Lewis
Martin B. Lewis
Samuel Lewis (Lieutenant Colonel)
Benjamin Lindsey, Ayish Bayou
William Lloyd
Samuel Looney, Neches District (Lieutenant Colonel, Adjutant Major)
Barry Low
Neil Martin
John Maximillian
Antonio Manchaca, Nacogdoches (Ensign)
James Mora

---

[116] Ibid., p. 363.

Juan Maria Mora, Nacogdoches (Ensign)
Frederick Moz (Captain)
Donald McDonald, Ayish Bayou
Thomas S. McFarland, Ayish Bayou
James B. McMahan (Lieutenant Colonel)
Samuel D. McMahan (Major)
John Noilin
Nathaniel Norris, Nacogdoches (Lieutenant)
Stephen Prather, Bevil (Captain)
John S. Roberts, Nacogdoches

---- Smith
William Sneed
Samuel Steadham
Adolphus Sterne, Nacogdoches (Ensign)
Philip A. Sublett, Ayish Bayou
Charles S. Taylor, Nacogdoches
George Teal
Iredell Thomas
Theophilus Thomas
Jack Thompson
Daniel M. Vancel
Samuel Williams

Source: Linda Ericson Devereaux, <u>Tales from the Old Stone Fort</u> (Lufkin: Piney Woods Press, 1976), pp. 65-69.

Henry William Augustine was born about 1795, came to Texas in 1827 from Augusta County, Alabama. He married Eliza ----, date unknown. Henry Mitchell Brewer, son of Henry and Susanna (Mitchell) Brewer, a native of Georgia, was born June 3, 1807 and died March 1849, buried Brewer Cemetery, Nacogdoches County. He married Sarah Windsor October 9, 1836. John Brewer, son of Henry and Sarah (Windsor) Brewer, was born January 23, 1819 in Mississippi, and died February 23, 1909, buried Brewer Cemetery, Nacogdoches County. He married first Nancy Octavia Taylor April 14, 1839 and second Sarah Johnson September 15, 1871.[117]

Hiram Brown, a native of Washington County, New York, was born there about 1813 and came to Texas October 1821. He married Kate Blackburn and was living in Angelina County, Texas in 1879.[118] George W. Cartwright was born August 12, 1812, Smith County, Tennessee, son of John and Mary (Crutchfield) Cartwright, and died June 25, 1881, buried Sabine County, Texas. He came to Texas in 1826 where he married Anne Oliver February 14, 1844.[119]

---

[117] Ericson, <u>Gateway to Texas,</u> Vol. I, pp. 14; 41.

[118] Ibid., p. 45.

[119] Ibid., p. 60.

Elias K. Davis, born about 1797, was the son of Warren Davis. He married Martha Thomas. He arrived in Texas in 1826 with wife and four children.[120] John M. Durst was born February 4, 1797 at Arkansas Post, Arkansas Territory and died February 9, 1851 in Leon County, Texas. He was the son of Jacob and Anna (Schesser) Durst and God-son of Samuel Davenport. He married Harriet Matilda Jamison, daughter of Colonel John Jamison, February 15, 1821.[121]

William E. Garrett, son of Jacob and Charity (Taylor) Garrett, was a native of Davidson County, Tennessee, born there about 1808 and died January 12, 1884 in San Augustine County, buried in Garrett Cemetery. He came to Texas in 1828 and married first Mary Cartwright November 14, 1833 and second Lucette Teal November 18, 1847.[122] John Harvey Hamby, son of John and Rhoda Hamby, was born May 5, 1812 in Tennessee and died April 11, 1852. He came to Texas August 1, 1837 with his wife, Elizabeth Hickman.[123]

N. Wyatt Hanks was born in Kentucky November 27, 1795, son of Peter and Isabella Hanks, and died about 1862 in Liberty County, Texas.[124] Archibald Hotchkiss, son of Christopher and Cynthia (Dickinson) Hotchkiss, ws born February 1, 1795 in Washington County, New York and died January 20, 1882, Anderson County, Texas. He married first Polly Crampton January 13, 1818 in New York and second Emily Packard.[125]

Almanzon Huston, son of Thomas and Susannah (Campbell) Huston, was born October 22, 1799, in Madison County, New York and died August 16, 1861, San Augustine County. He arrived in Texas about 1825-1826 with wife, Elizabeth Newton, whom he married

---

[120] Ibid., p. 95.

[121] Ibid., p. 110.

[122] Ibid., p. 138,

[123] Ibid., p. 158.

[124] Ibid., p. 161.

[125] Ibid., p. 177.

April 16, 1819.[126] Martin Lacy (Lacey), son of William Hughes Lacy, was born May 20, 1794 in the Pendleton District of South Carolina and died about 1847. He came to Texas in 1831 with his wife, Dorothy "Dolly" Young, whom he had married April 22, 1813, in Caldwell County, Kentucky.[127] William Young Lacy (Lacey) was born in Caldwell County, Kentucky, son of Martin and Dolly (Young) Lacy on March 20, 1814. Lacy was living in Anderson County, Texas, in 1874. He married first Louisa J. Bean (Beene), daughter of Peter Ellis Bean, January 10, 1841, and second on July 30, 1845, Eliza Lindsay.[128]

Jose Encarnacion Chireno, son of Bartolo and Maria Josefa (Arriola) Chireno, was born about 1789 but was killed in the Battle of Nacogdoches August 1832. He married Maria Josefa Candida Delgado at Natchitoches, Louisiana, January 20, 1820. Town of Chireno in Nacogdoches County was named for him.[129] Juan Maria Lazarine was born about 1796, son of Joseph and Juana Maria (Rivas) Lazarine and died before 1838. He married Maria Josefa de la Vega, daughter of Maria Antonia Flores.[130]

Martin Baty Lewis, son of Samuel S. and Sarah (LeMaster) Lewis, was born January 13, 1806, Clark County, Indiana. He married Nancy Moore October 25, 1825 and with her came to Texas in 1830 with wife and five children. Lewis died in 1840.[131] Samuel S. Lewis was born July 4, 1784 in Virginia and died February 14, 1838, in Jasper County, Texas. Lewis married Sarah Lemaster August 7, 1804, in Henry County, Kentucky.[132]

Antonio Menchaca was born about 1797. He married Feliciana de los Santos Sanches,

---

[126] Ibid., p. 183.

[127] Ibid., p. 202.

[128] (b9d.,p. 202.

[129] Ibid., p. 70.

[130] Ibid., p. 208.

[131] Ibid., p. 213.

[132] Ibid., p. 213.

probably August 1, 1825.¹³³ Jose Maria Mora was born about 1772 and died November 17, 1853. Jose Mora married Maria Theresa Procella.¹³⁴ Juan Mora was born about 1800 and died June 1850. Juan married Maria Carmel Y'Barbo.¹³⁵

Donald McDonald was born near Niagra Falls, Ontario, Canada, January 23, 1789, and died May 2, 1884 in San Augustine County. He married first Maria Luisa Maximillian by 1825, second Maria Lomax in 1843, and third Elizabeth Hightower January 30, 1854, in San Augustine County.¹³⁶ James B. McMahan, son of Samuel Doak and Phoebe (Young) McMahan, was born October 1, 1814, Maury County, Tennessee and died July 25, 1882, Bell County, Texas. James married Matilda F. Mackey, daughter of Charles and Naomi Mackey. He came to Texas in 1831 to Sabine County.¹³⁷ Samuel Doak McMahan was born either March 5 or November 5, 1789, in Tennessee and came to Sabine County, Texas in 1831. He died in 1854 in Sabine County and was buried in McMahan's Chapel Cemetery. He married first Phoebe Young about 1812 in Tennessee and later Tabitha ---- after coming to Texas.¹³⁸

Stephen Prather, son of Thomas and Mary (Phillips) Prather, was born June 18, 1782, in Lincoln County, Virginia (now Mercer County, Kentucky) and died December 19, 1833, San Augustine County, buried Wood-Snell Cemetery. Prather married Tamora Elizabeth Plowden in December, 1804. He came to Texas by 1821.¹³⁹ Phillip A. Sublett was born May 22, 1802 in Green County, Kentucky. Sublett married Ester Jane Roberts, daughter of Elisha Roberts, March 6, 1828. He died February 25, 1850, San Augustine County, buried Sublett

---

¹³³ Ibid., p. 145.

¹³⁴ Ibid., p. 257.

¹³⁵ Ibid., p. 257.

¹³⁶ Ibid., p. 225.

¹³⁷ Ibid., p. 230.

¹³⁸ Joe E. Ericson, Judges of the Republic of Texas (Dallas: Taylor Publishing Company, 1980), p. 188.

¹³⁹ Ibid., p. 295.

cemetery.[140].

Charles Stanfield Taylor was born about 1808 in London, England and died November 1, 1865, in Nacogdoches, buried in Oak Grove Cemetery, Nacogdoches. Taylor married Anna Maria Ruoff May 28, 1831.[141] John H. Thompson, son of Dr. Samuel and Precious (Wofford) Thompson, was born about 1810 in South Carolina. Thompson settled in San Augustine County.

Mexican Municipalities. Between 1731 and 1836, first the Spanish and then the Mexican governments created political subdivisions known as municipalities (municio; municipalidad). Some twenty-nine such local governments with territory wholly or partially in Texas were established. Each of them included one or more villages and the surrounding agricultural land. Only two of these, Nacogdoches and Liberty, had been created by 1831: the Nacogdoches Municipality from 1831 to 1834 was an immense region stretching from the Sabine and Red Rivers on the east to the Trinity River on the west and from the Red River on the north to the southern extremes of today's Houston, Angelina, Sabine, and San Augustine Counties on the south; while Liberty Municipality lay south of the Nacogdoches line to the Gulf of Mexico and from the Sabine River on the east to the Trinity River to the west.[142] (See Map V below.)

During 1834 and 1835, authorities in Saltillo began carving the vast territory known for many years as the Nacogdoches Municipality into additional municipalities. By 1835, at least six of these smaller local governments were in existence: San Augustine (1834), Shelby (Tenahaw, 1835), Red River (1835), Jasper (1835), and Sabine (1835).

Liberty Municipality. The new Liberty Municipality was "bounded on the east by the Sabine River, on the west by the San Jacinto [River], by Nacogdoches Municipality on the north, and by the Gulf of Mexico on the south. . . .[A] new seat of government, called Liberty

---

[140] Ibid., p. 369

[141] Ibid., p. 372; Ericson and Ericson, Personalities on the East Texas Frontier, pp. 129-132.

[142] See: Imogene K. Kennedy and J. Leon Kennedy, Genealogical Records in Texas (Baltimore: Genealogical Publishing Company, 1987), pp. 3-5.

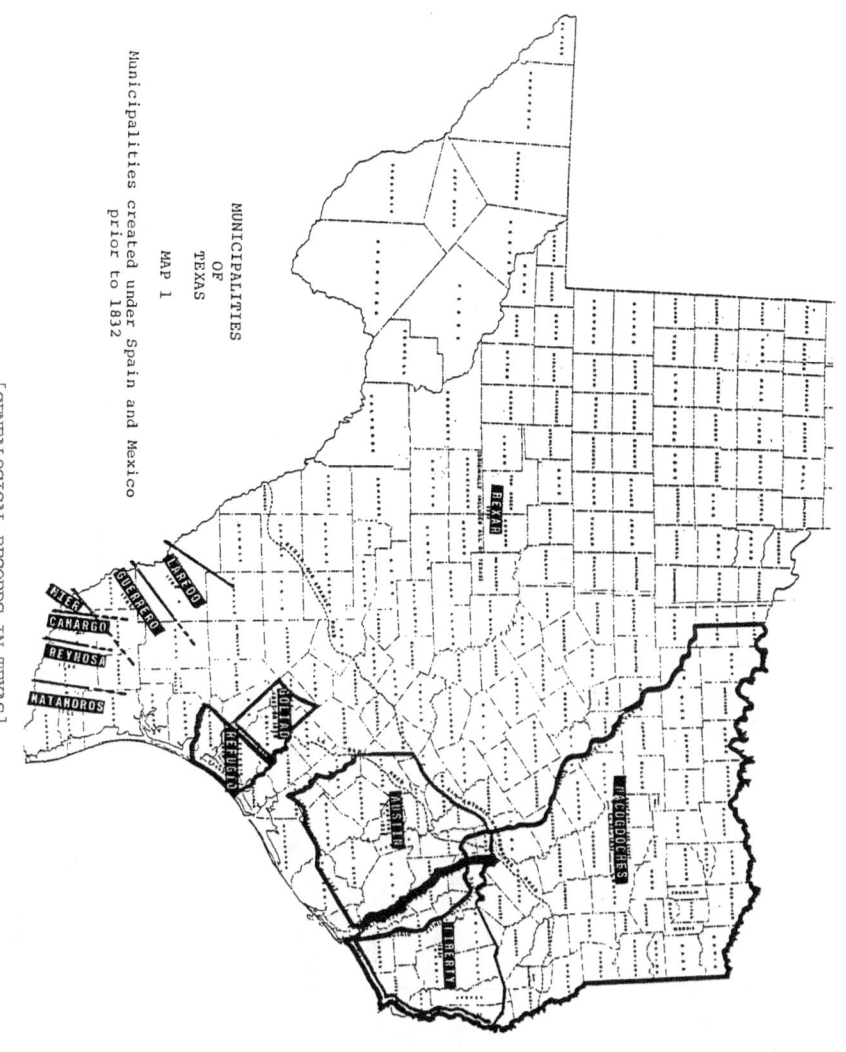

by the Anglo-Americans, was located about three miles southwest of old Atascosito."[143] (Table X below provides the name of some of the earliest settlers in the Liberty Municipality.)

Table X
Some Early Settlers of Liberty Municipality

Name	Year	Name	Year
James W. Allen	1827	Benjamin M. Green	1827
Alexander Burton	1827	B. W. Hardin	1827
Benjamin Barrow, Sr.	1827	A. B. Hardin	1825
Solomon Barrow	1824	Matthew Hubert	1828
Levi Barrow	1830	James Jarney	1826
Reuben Barrow, Sr.	1824	Jarusha Hardin	1828
Vincent Barrow	1830	Hugh B. Johnston	1825
Robert Burrell	1828	Hugh Jackson	1823
Benjamin Barrow, Jr.	1830	William Johns	1830
George Clark	1830	Samuel Jermain	1830
Jose Coronado	1825	S. Kirkham	1830
William Cherry	1825	James Knight	1828
Thomas Cope	1828	Benjamin Lanier	1829
Aaron Choate, Jr.	1825	Alfred Lani	1830
David Choate, Sr.	1825	Frederick K. Louis	1830
John Choate	1825	N. D. Labadie	1830
M. A. Carroll	1828	William Moore	1829
M. Chavence	1828	Jesse Preutt	1824
Aaron Cherry, Sr.	1825	James Rogers	1823
Henry Dunman	1828	Robert Rogers	1823
Jas. T. Dunman	1828	William Smith	1830
Thos. Dever	1825	Amy Swail	1824
P. P. Dever	1825	Silas Smith	1830
John C. Devers	1825	Elisha Stephenson	1829
William Dunman	1825	Samuel Strang	1825
Meredith Duncan	1825	Taylor B. Self	1823
Charles Dorsett	1829	Jacob E. Self	1823
Burrell Franks	1826	Thomas Stubblefield	1830
Richard Green	1830	Stephen Smith	1830
W. R. Griffin	1830	William M. Smith	1830
J. H. Griger	1829	Rozelia Scott	1830
Presly Gill	1824	James Shaw	1829
Nancy Gowan	1827	Edward Tanner	1827
Amos Green	1828	Burden Targenter	1827

---

[143] Don A. J. Kleiner, "Liberty County," The New Handbook of Texas, Vol. 4, p. 188.

James R. Tanner	1829		William Heron	1829
Jane Taylor	1830		Felix Newman	1828
William Thompson	1830		Moses H. Carroll	1828
Polly Tier	1828		Charles Tilton	1829
Robert Whitlock	1827		William Everett	1827
Mary Whitlock	1827		James Robinson	1825
E. H. R. Wallis	1824		Ansen Taylor	1828
N. Whitcher	1829		Edward Dorr	1825
James T. White	1828		James San Germain	1830
A. B. J. Winfrie	1827		James M. Rankin	1827
Charles Wilcox	1830		Amos Barber	1829
William Walles	1825		Esther Clark	1829
Hezekiah Williams	1828		Rebecca Coleman	1825
C. P. Welch	1829		William Dobie	1830
T. J. Williams	1827		B. M. Spinks	1825
William H. White	1825		Jos. Laurence	1824
Samuel Whitting	1827		Jno. Saul	1825
<u>Additional Names</u>			John Watts	1825
Clayton Harper	1826		Robert Woseman	1827
James Humphreys	1827		George Orr	1824
Nancy Gowen	1827			

Source: Records of the Texas General Land Office, Austin, Texas, transcribed in Gifford White, <u>1830 Citizens of Texas</u> (Austin: Eakin Press, 1983.)

San Augustine Municipality. On March 6, 1834, the Municipality of San Augustine was established with these limits defined: beginning at the junction of Little Cow Creek and the Sabine River, thence in a straight line to the mouth of the Ayish Bayou ascending the Bayou to its principal headwaters, thence north to the Sabine River, descending that river to the place of beginning. With those boundaries it included all of San Augustine, Sabine, and Shelby Counties, more than half of Panola County, the northern section of Newton County, and a small part of Jasper County. (See Map VI below.)

Earlier, on the eve of the Battle of Nacogdoches, a mass meeting of then people living in the old San Augustine District met and decided to create a new town as the home of their local government. A committee of fifteen men was selected to determine the location of the new town: William McFarland, Shadrack Thomas, Henry W. Augustine, David Huffman, Wyatt Hanks, James Hanks, John G. Love, William Garrett, Alexander Horton, David Renfro, Achilles E. C. Johnson, Elisha Roberts, David O. Warren, Mathew Cartwright, and Philip A.

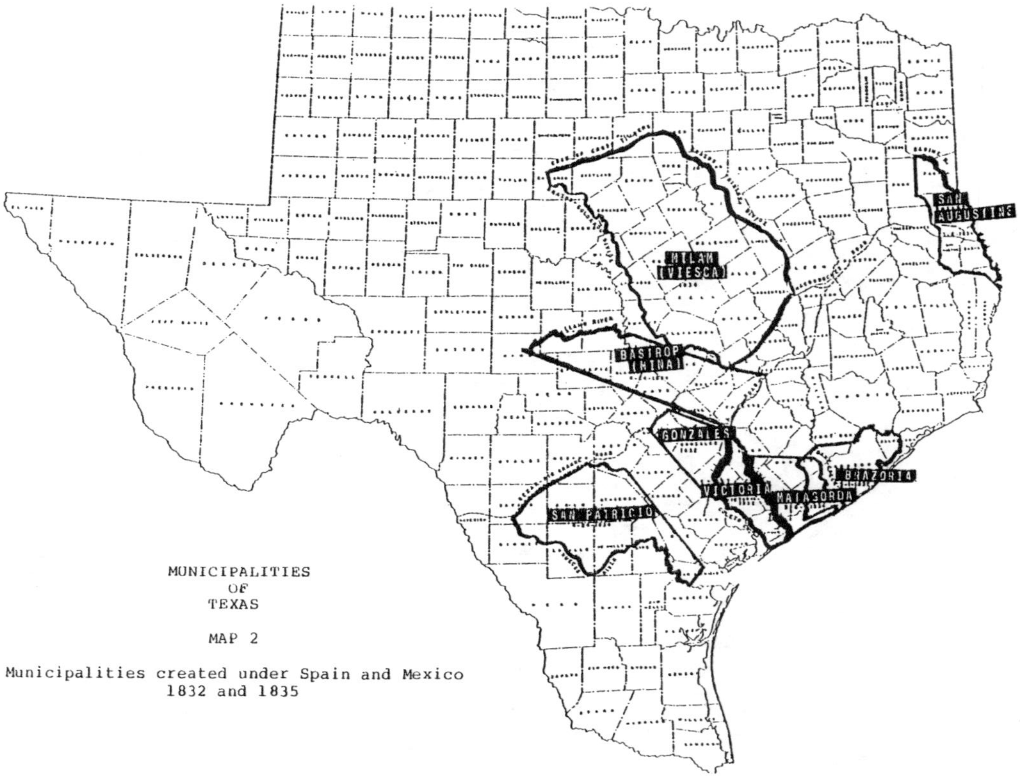

MUNICIPALITIES
OF
TEXAS
MAP 2

Municipalities created under Spain and Mexico
1832 and 1835

Sublett.

William McFarland was born May 8, 1774 in Lancaster, Pennsylvania and died August 6, 1840 in Newton County, Texas. William married in 1798 in Cincinnati, Ohio to a woman whose name is not recorded. He came to Texas as a widower with children.[3] David A. Huffman, native of Viginia, was born there April 24, 1819, and died January 25, 1884. David married Elvira McLaurin December 10, 1839. The couple had at least three children.[4]

Table XI

Some Early Settlers of San Augustine Municipality

Name	Year	Name	Year
Vincent Anderson	1825	Donald McDonald	1830
Bailey Anderson	1822	William Montgomery	1822
John Bodine	1825	Archibald Ruddle	1824
James Bridges	1821	Samuel Stiddum	1828
George E. Brownrigg	1830	Francis Sythe	1828
James W. Bullock	1824	James Simms	1830
Julius W. Bullock	1827	Shadrac D. Thomas	1826
Henry B. Blackwell	1828	Edward J. Teal	1828
Thomas Chumley	1828	Henry Teal	1828
W. G. Cartwright	1825	Jackson Thomas	1823
Anna Davis	1821	Theophilus Thomas	1825
Edward B. Davis	1828	Samuel Moss	1826
Robert H. Foote	1830	John Holloway	1821
Christian Groce	1830	John Cartwright	1825
William Garrett	1830	Martin V. Lout	1830
Thomas D. Hendricks	1825	Charity Sanders	1830
Alexander Horton	1824	David Earl	1824
H. P. Horton	1825	William Quirk	1824
Isabella Hanks	1829	Andrew Spears	1826
Wyatt Hanks	1828	David Harris	1827
Edwin Hendricks	1824	A. A. Lewis	1828
George W. Jones	1829	Martha Renfro	1830
William Johnson	1822	Isaac W. Linn	1830
W. D. Irvine	1830	Theo Vaughn	1827
Josephus Irvine	1830	Michel Thaya	1830
John G. Love	1826	James Mooney	1829
George W. Lewis	1826	Thomas Tipps	1829
Wm. M. Loyd	1828	Elisha Roberts	1830
Daniel T. D. Moore	1826	S. S. Matthews	1829
John McGinnes	1830	P. L. Carney	1829

Davis Warren	1824		Claiborn Rice	1830
Andrew McHenry	1827		Reuben H. Smith	1830
Willie Morse	1828		Lucas Browning	1830
Philo K. Cole	1827		Jackson D. Lang	1830
Jno. S. King	1829		William E. Lang	1829
Elijah Preston	1826		Noel Manning	1830
Ambrose Bass	1828		Silas Whetstone	1829
White Littleton	1830		Jackson C. Allen	1830
Gains Simpson	1829		James Passing	1830
Nathaniel B. Moore	1829		Lawrence Masters	1830
Lewis Y. Patterson	1827		Minos Graves	1830
Jno. M. Allen	1828		Cesar Pope	1829
James Jones	1830		Charles S. Purnell	1830
Samuel Dumas	1829		William S. Purnell	1830
John Jowers	1829		Levi H. Carroll	1829
Nathaniel Tinsley	1826		Dennis C. Carroll	1829
John W. Baker	1830		Jos. W. Brightman	1830
Cary W. Williams	1829		John Snyder	1830
Silas Moss	1830		R. Boyd Irvine	1830
Holloway Simpson	1826		Robert H. Willson	1828
Jacob Garrett	1824		William Lakey	1829
Benjamin Lindsey	1824		Daniel Thompson	1829
Leonard Walker	1830		William E. Parron	1829
Martin T. Reed	1830		William McDonough	1827
Elias Stephen	1830		Hezikiah Graves	1829
Aaron Sparks	1830		Edmond Turner	1826
Ellis Dewees	1830		David Lagow	1826
Felix Smith	1830		Robert Manna	1828
Rufus Pearce	1830		Johnson Malvin	1827
Andrew Carter	1830		David L. Moore	1830
James Tyres	1830		John S. Mason	1828
Moses Starks	1830		Jacob Newton	1828
Nathaniel B. Moore	1829		Richard C. Lumpkin	1827
Charles Moring	1829		Samuel T. Moore	1829
Sewall Collins	1829		John Newton	1829
Cary W. Dunham	1829		William McElroy	1828
Norris H. Jones	1829		Thomas R. Graham	1827
Dayton Beckett	1829		Peter Monroe	1826
Ezekiel Harrell	1829		James McLain	1830
Philip Sutton	1830		Richard Malvin	1830
James Sutton	1830		John Monroe	1826
Elias Fury	1830		John McRe	1829
William Worrell	1829		William T. Monroe	1828
Asa Knap	1829		Edmond Allbright	1828

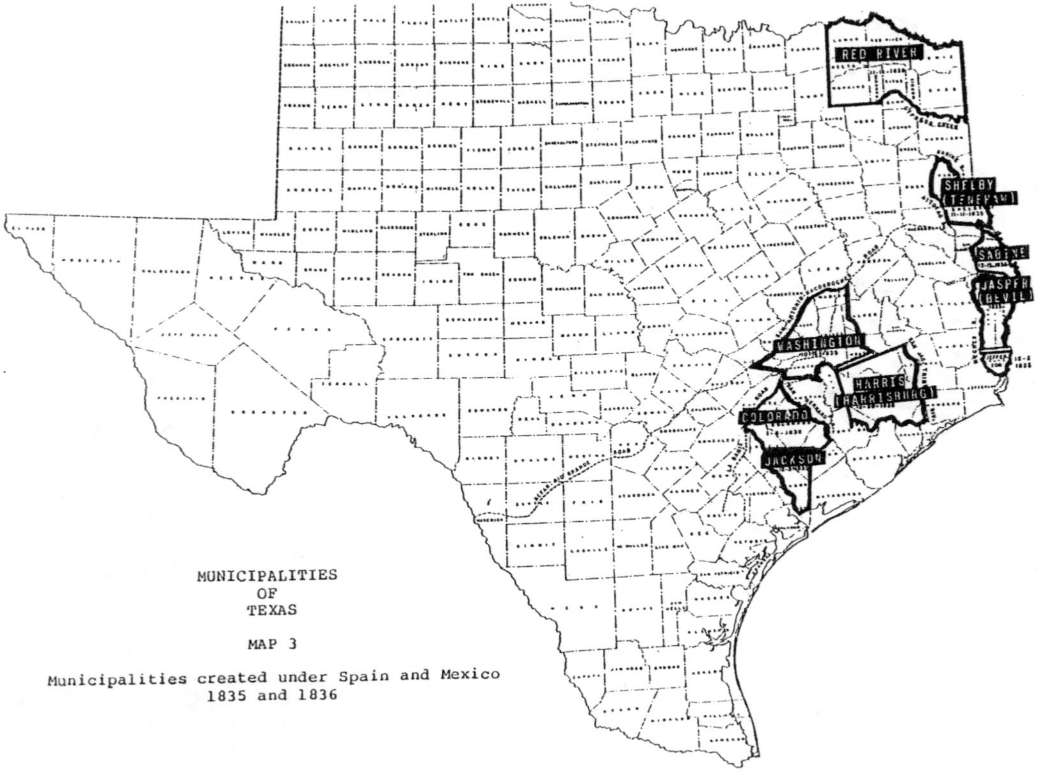

MUNICIPALITIES
OF
TEXAS

MAP 3

Municipalities created under Spain and Mexico
1835 and 1836

Jas. T. Calvertson	1828	James Rogers	1829
Phillip Caloway	1826	Richard Bacon	1830
Henry Calvertson	1828	Thomas Lee	1828
David Newell	1829	Tilmon Williams	1829
Peter Larkin	1829	Henry W. Estes	1829
Edward McBride	1829	Abel Burney	1826
Elisha Eldridge	1829	Abner Gorman	1830
Elisha Allsup	1830	George W. Childs	1826
Thomas Duvaul	1828	John Nobles	1826
Jas. C. Hundley	1826	John McDavid	1830
Zachary Woodruff	1828	William Leroy	1828
Joseph McMullen	1826	James Morton	1827
Charles McMullen	1828	Peter Morton	1827
M. Sowell	1826	Wm. S. Tomlinson	1825
Alfred Watkins	1825	James Perdue	1828
Jno. T. Ashton	1830	Lemuel Collins	1827
Jno. T. Sowell	1830	Frances Hambleton	1828
Edwin R. Cravens	1829	Edmund Ziegler	1826
Archiblad Ballard	1827	Samuel Comb	1830
Allen S. Ray	1826	Adam Goodall	1826
Dickson Burgess	1828	Jas. S. Andrew	1828
Jas. T. Bridgeman	1826	Jas. V. Mask	1830
Seth W. Fuller	1826	Susanna Horton	1825
Richard V. Parker	1826	Josephus S. Irvine	1820
Selwin L. Brown	1828		

Source: Records Texas General Land Office transcribed in White, <u>1830 Citizens of Texas</u>.

Sabine Municipality. El Camino Real was the determining factor in the selection of land by the first settlers in the Piney Woods of East Texas. Land along its route contained the best soil and was along a well-traveled road. Early in the Eighteenth Century the French frontiersman Louis Juchereau de St. Denis had led an expedition into the area that took him through what is now northern Sabine County along the Old San Antonio Road, but not until late in the century did the Spanish authorities begin issuing land grants.

Jack Cedars, an Anglo male who married the daughter of the captain of the Spanish garrison at the Borreagas Crossing of Borreagas Creek in the northern part of the Sabine County of today, was the first Anglo-American settler in the region. Prior to 1832 the area was a part of the Municipality of Nacogdoches and from 1832 to 1835 a part of the Municipality of San Augustine. In 1835, it was finally established as the Municipality of Sabine.

James Gaines, a native of Virginia, was a cousin of Lieutenant Edmund P. Gaines of the Army of the United States. He accompanied his cousin in making a survey of the waterway from Nashville, Tennessee down the Cumberland River to the Ohio River, then down the Ohio to the Mississippi River, then on to New Orleans. In 1805 he traveled with American soldiers to Fort Jessup near Natchitoches, Louisiana. In 1824, Gaines married Susanna Norris, sister of Samuel Norris of Nacogdoches. The couple established a home just across the Sabine River from the Neutral Territory. He soon acquired ownership of a ferry service and opened a tavern at what became known as Gaines Ferry which was situated at a major entry point for immigrants entering Texas.

Incoming Anglo-American settlers in 1828 established a settlement in the northern section of the region along the old road to San Antonio. The Geneva settlement originally known as Shawnee Village, however, had grown up as well in the same part of the area. Local tradition maintains that the village is the oldest continuously occupied community in East Texas. By far the greatest number of early Anglo-Americans entered the Spanish province via the ferries across the Sabine River into what became the Sabine Municipality.

The earliest crossing employed by the Spanish was at a shoal in the river located above the Gaines Ferry crossing. The area was then known as the Las Borreagas by local Indians, but the early American settlers called it Red Mound. When the town of Milam was first surveyed in 1828, it was named Red Mound, but the name was changed at the insistence of John S. Roberts to honor Texas hero Ben Milam.

For a time therefore the Milam settlement was the first village encountered along El Camino Real. In 1835, however, the town of Sabine, known today as Sabinetown, with its ferry replaced Milam. The newer town soon became the largest village in the area having the advantage of being both a river port and a location along the King's Highway.

Table XII below provides a list of some of the early settlers of the Municipality of Sabine.

Table XII
Some Early Settlers of Sabine Municipality

Joseph Brown	1817	Matthew Earl	1824

William Earl	1824	Charles Delass	1829
Joseph Eastep	1821	Abraham Johnson	1829
James Easley	1828	Edmond French	1829
E. P. Gaines	1822	William F. White	1829
Larkin Gross	1828	John W. Lake	1828
John B. Gaines	1824	Aaron L. Day	1830
Burgess Hall	1828	George T. Burke	1829
Moses Hill	1822	Horatio Young	1829
William Isaacs	1824	Henry Summers	1830
John McKean	1829	Richard Roberts	1829
Henry Martin	1822	B. T. Forbes	1830
John Maxamillan	1822	H. Flint	1830
James Mason	1830	G. Pool	1830
Willis Murphy	1828	T. W. Scott	1830
James McKim	1825	A. Powe	1830
William McKim	1825	L. P. Gray	1830
Charles McKim	1825	William L. Lee	1828
William Mason	1830	S. P. Gray	1828
Elizabeth Melton	1822	James B. Saul	1827
Washington Oment	1824	John Little	1830
Matthew Parker	1822	Eli Penn	1828
John Pace	1826	S. Duncan	1828
Isac Renfro	1825	J. S. Richey	1828
James Rains	1829	Jas. E. Kean	1828
Francis Richards	1830	K. Rowson	1827
William Robert	1822	J. Goodley	1827
Major Smith	1828	G. L. White	1830
Philip Smith	1830	Davis Allen	1820
Joan Ferrian Johan	1822	Daniel Tanner	1826
Jacob Walker	1829	James Gaines	1812
Elizabeth Warren	1825	Frederick Jones	1929
Martin D. White	1822	Ira D. Jones	1828
Benjamin White	1823	Damion Trew	1829
Corene Chapple	1822	Johnson Williams	1830
John M. Neely	1830	Samuel Gray	1829
Thomas Harden	1830	Everett Jones	1830
Charles McKay	1825	Lisabel Cieders	1828
Prissa Wood	1830	Emory Jackson	1830
Samuel Daverson	1830	James R. Reeve	1829
William Pace	1826	James G. Porter	1830
Tebosha Marshak	1826	M. K. Lacy	1830
James McKim	1828	E. M. Nobles	1830
John Smith	1830	Thomas M. Rariden	1830
John Crowder	1828	Simpson F. Flinn	1830

Elizabeth Lowe	1828		Nehemiah Warren	1830
Joseph Evans			David W. Love	1830
Jas. H. Irion	1830		Jackson P. Stewart	1830
Elbort Hines	1823		A. Walthington	1829
Davis Hines	1823		Jesse Denton	1830
Robert Nicholas	1828		Frederick Sargent	1830
John D MacAdams			Thomas Sargent	1830
Daniel Easly	1830		Ralph Sargent	1830
Thomas C. Holt			Jarvis Phillips	1830
David Renfro	1828		Nathaniel Phillips	1830
J. F. Pace	1828		John C. Sewell	1830
John Taylor	1823		William D. Irving	1830
Ransom Hines	1829		George W. Prentiss	1830
Truman Taylor	1829		Franses Graves	1830
Abram Coulter	1829		Steven Hartwell	1830
Nathan Gescom(?)	1830		S. Mourhouse	1830
Benjamin Story	1830		Jared P. Ellison	1830
Philip Yates	1830		J. Francis Thomas	1830
Benjamin Stibbens	1830		Grason Doone	1830
Wilson Foote	1830		P. T. Laurence	1830
Nathan Davis, Jr.	1830		T. T. Truworthy	1830
Andrew Hoffman	1830		Orvill Northrop	1829
Benjamin Atherton	1830		Jose Anto. Prese	1830
Isaac D. Harper	1830		Joseph Irion	1830
Samuel W. Newell	1830		John W. Stearn	1830
Ira Singleton	1830		Epps G. Stockton	1830
Reubin Graves	1830		Reubin Manson	1828
Truman Richmond	1830		Jacob Richards	1829
John R. Richmond	1830		Lemuel Richardson	1830
Steven Porter	1830		William J. Stone	1830
Jesse Warren	1830		Gerry Dennis[on]	1830

Source: Records, Texas General Land Office, transcribed in White, <u>1830 Citizens of Texas.</u>

Adam Jackson Bennett was born January 27, 1815 at Laurel Hill, West Felicianna Parish, Louisiana, the son of Henry and Mary (Palmer) Bennett. He died in 1833, leaving minor children. John Cartwright was living on the Ayish Bayou before 1826. His wife Mary Crtuchfield and seven children survived him. He died in San Augustine County July 18, 1841.

Tenahaw (Teneja, Tenaha) later known as the Shelby Municipality. The Mexican regulation prohibiting setlements within twenty leagues of the any boundary with a foriegn government curtailed legitimate settlement in the region immediately west of the Sabine River. As a result, the strip attracted persons given to violence and lawlessness and discouraged permanent residents. However, the portion of this territory lying just north of the Nacogdoches Municipality was organized in 1827 as the Tenahaw District with Nashville (now known as Shelbyville), as its principal settlement. It included territory now located within the present-day Shelby, Panola, Harrison, Rusk, Upshur, and Marion Counties. In 1835, this area was organized as the Tenahaw Municipality with Nashville as the seat of its government. The following year the name of the municipality was changed to Shelby Municipality.

Table XIII provides the names of some of the early settlers of the Tenahaw-Shelby Municipality.

Table XIII

Some Early Settlers of Tenahaw-Shelby Municipality

Name	Year	Name	Year
John English	1825	James Forsythe	1821
Stephen English	1825	E. Rains	1822
Dortrick McDavid	1829	David Strickland	1826
Henry Assabranner	1830	Richard Haley	1825
Nathan Davis	1822	James Bowling	18276
John Forsythe	1821	E. A. Merchant	1825
Silby Forsythe	1822	Mason M. Van	1825
George Butler	1830	Jose Santos	1830
Elizabeth Lewis	1822	Domingo Gonzales	1830
Harrison Davis	1822	David Wilkason	1823
Samuel McFaddin	1821	Elizabeth Choate	1821
Jonathan McFaddin	1825	Mary Strickland	1821
William T. English	1827	Amos Strickland	1821
Moses Wooten	1823	Peter Stockman	1830
Sarah English	1825	Elizabeth Rogers	1823
Monair Smyth	1824	Elizabeth Graves	1823
Bailey Anderson	1825	Pierre Murvoir	1816
Jesse McCelvey	1824	Antoine Duboise	1818
Joseph English	1829	Susan Brewno	1823
George English	1829	Anastasha Carr	1830
Lewis Latham	1824	Joseph S. Palvadore	1825
Alva R. Johnson	1830	A. Whetstone	1830
Jonathan Anderson	1819	Peter Whetstone	1830
Rachel Story	1827	Hiram Thompson	1825
John C. Payne	1825	Samuel Strickland	1826

Thomas Haley	1821		Antoin Bard	1826
Susannah McCelvey	1826		Clement Tutt	1824
Nancy Smyth	1830		John McGrew	1824
William Humphrys	1828		Marela Algese	1830
James English	1822		Samuel Strickland	1824
Matthew Dayne	1825		Alfred Lout	1823
Wiet Anderson	1822		Richard Haley, Jr.	1824
Elenor Harrison	1825		Daniel Farmer	1824
Mary Haley	1825		Mary Alexander	1824
Asa Lankford	1830		James Forsythe	1819
Mary Arocha	1827		Amos Strickland	1826
Elizabeth Nail	1824		Samuel Norris	1806
Nancy Mays	1828		Edward Irons	1823
Baley McFaddin	1821		Catharine Stockman	1824
Hannah Dayne	1827		Joseph S. Good	1824
John Little	1827		Jose Ben Aldsevata	1828
Richard Haley, Sr.	1824		William King	1828
Archibald Smyth	1826		Jno. M. Boadly	1825
John R. Haley	182-		A. D. Martinas	1827
Lucy Maragre	1830		G. T. Assabranner	1830
Andrew McFaddin	1830		William Van	1829
Antonio Carr	1826		George Glass	1827
Marsele Carr	1826		Henry T. Stockman	1827
Beniete Alderata	1828		William F. Allen	1830
Stephen Holmes	1826		Joseph Butler	1830
John Applegate	1826		Antonio Barbose	1815
Hampton Anderson	1825		Joseph Valentine	1823
Gemedey Anderson	1821		Susan Latham	1820
John Latham, Jr.	1821			

Source: Records, Texas General Land Office transcribed in White, <u>1830 Citizens of Texas.</u>

Jasper Municipality. Settlement in the area that became the Jasper Municipality began in 1824 when John Bevil established a homestead at the present site of the City of Jasper. By 1830 some thirty families were living at Bevil Settlement between the Neches and Sabine Rivers. John R. Bevil was born August 24, 1784 in Mecklenburg County, Virginia, son of John Randolph and Laodicae (Burton) Bevil. John married first Frances Boynton, a native of New York and second Mrs. Charles Miles about 1826/7 in Texas. He died November 10, 1862 in Newton County, Texas, buried in Jasper County.

Table XIV provides the names of some of the early settlers of the Jasper Municipality.

Table XIV
Some Early Settlers of the Jasper Municipality

James Conn	1830	Seaborn Berry	1830
Antonia J. Gilchrist	1830	Samuel Isaacs	1825
Michael Daily	1830	Elizabeth Bridges	1830
Mordechi Howard	1830	Mrs. Matilda Cherry	1830
William Jordon	1830	John B. Robinson	1830
William Lewis, Sr.	1828	Thomas Watts	1825
James Lewis	1828	Mrs. Margaret Swift	1830
Peter B. Pry	1829	John R. Swainsbury	1813
William Wilson	1830	John Slaydon	1825
John Dickinson	1830	Mrs. Sarah Winfrey	1829
Jacob Becker	1830	Alexander Wright	1823
James Chessher, Sr.	1829	Joel Robinson	1829
Thomas Williams	1830	Daniel McNeal	1826
Harman Lewis	1830	John Wright	1823
Mrs. Polly Ryan	1830/1	Charles Gilchrist	1830
Eliza Isaacs	1830	Rebecca Beley	1830
Benjamin Burke	1830	A. E. Winfrey	1830
Hiram Watts	1827	Stephen Williams	1830
Benj. Richardson	1830	Joseph McGee	Native
Joseph E. Thompson	1829	Spicy Taylor	1829
Stephen Williams, Jr.	1830	John W. Taylor	1826
George W. Smyth	1830	Alexander Lamb	1830
James B. Wilson	1829	Lawrence Humphry	1830
William Lewis, Jr.	1828	Emily Brown	1830
Andrew Richardson	1830	Allen Goodridge	1830
William Richardson	1830	Franklin Baton	1830
Rachel Sawl	1827	Jane Moore	1830
Gardi West	1828	J. Becker	1830

Source: Records, Texas General Land Office, transcribed in White, <u>1830 Citizens of Texas.</u>

Red River Municipality. American hunters and traders were active in the northeastern segment of Texas by 1815 and permanent settlement was underway at Jonesborough and Burkham's Settlement by 1818. At the time Red River district was a vaguely defined area encompassing all or part of the land of thirty-nine present-day counties. In 1835, when created a municipality by Mexican authorities, its boundaries were the Red River on the north, the

Sabine River on the east, the never clearly defined northern boundary of the Nacogdoches Municipality on the south and the werstern limits of today's Fannin, Delta, and Hopkins Counties.

Table XV below provides the names of some of the early settlers of Red River Municipality.

Table XV
Some Early Settlers of Red River Municipality

Collin M. Aken	1827		Nicholas Levins	1820
James Aken	1827		Josiah D. Lawson	1823
William Akens	1827		Benjamin Lankford	1825
George Brinlee	1824		Eleanor Landford	1825
Charles Burkham	1820		Jas. Levins, Sr.	1819
John Bird	1830		Jas Levins, Jr.	1818
Westly Byers	1824		Blackly McKinney	1824
James Burkham	1820		H. C. McKinney	1826
James Clark	1830		Lee Morris	1824
Charles Collum	1822		Daniel McKinney	1824
Jonathan Collum	1827		Robert Morris	1824
George Collum	1822		G. Y. McKinney	1824
William Clapp	1820		Jefferson Milam	1826
Collin Collum	1820		Ashley McKinney	1824
Isaac Fishback	1828		Collin McKinney	1824
Bradford C. Fowler	1830		Y. S. McKinney	1824
John Fizer	1830		Reuben Mitchell	1824
John Greenwood	1818		James McDaniel	1820
Jacob Gragg	1820		William McKinney	1824
Samuel Gragg	1820		Gabriel Martin	1828
William Gragg	1820		Squire Mays	1826
Milton Gragg	1820		Jas. McKinney	1824
Rich. M. Hopkins	1824		Martin G. Nall	1820
Jas. E. Hopkins	1824		John Nall	1820
Edward Hughart	1830		John Nugert	1826
Adam Hampton	1824		Sarah Pendergrass	1825
John Humphreys	1818		John Ross	1820
Asa Hickman	1825		William Slingland	1820
Aaron Hansoame	1825		James Ward	1820
Andrew Hampton	1826		William B. Ward	1820
Pedro Hendrez	Native		George W. Wright	1830
Joseph James	1824		William Wilson	1830
Joseph Levins	1818		Jas. J. Ward	1830

Jas. J. Ward, Sr.	1830		Massack H. Janes	1825
Francis G. Wright	1828		Sherrod Dunman	1825
William F. Wright	1828		William Collum	1824
Geo. W. Whitmore	1820		John Barkham	1824
Andrew Willett	1819		Samuel Barnam	1830
Joseph Wood	1820		Preston Kitchens	1827
Levi M. Rice	1824		Joseph Stricklen	1825
John Hampton	1818		John Davis	1824
Francis Hopkins	1824		Jacob Buzzard	1826
Aaron Hansome	1825		Richard Rhodes	1827
Henry S. Janes	1826		Henry Vincent	1822
Jacob Barkman	1824		James R. Nyro	1824
Barkley Nall	1819		Lewis Dayton	1824
Hugh B. Shaw	1823		John Edmonson	1825
Henry Stout	1823		David Stricklin	1824
James Stout	1823		Francisco Longordia	Native
Jarrel James	1822		Lewis Richardson	1830
Bryant Homes	1822		James Holland	1822
Robert Hall	1822		Alex. W. Wright	Native
Daniel Cornelius	1820		James Wimbly	Native
Benage Loyd	1821		Johnson Bowers	1820
Hirom Loyd	1821		James Barker	1828
David Clapp	1820/1826		Adam Wright	1828
John Lick, Sr.	1820		Samuel Bush	1830
Jonathan Cochran	1824		Hugh McCelay	1824
Isaac Murfy	1824		Abraham Ogden	1825
James Rodes	1826		Travis G. Wright	1828
Isaac Clover	1822		John Askins	1818
William Shaw, Jr.	1823		Alex. O. Whitmore	1825
W. H. H. Hopkins	1824		Luke Roberts	1820
Hugh B. Shaw	1824		John Levins	Native
John Hanks	1824		Emanuel Grubbs	1829
John Walker	1822		Joseph J. Ward	1830
Eldridge Hopkins	1824		Joseph Ferguson	1825
John E. Janes	1826		Daniel Thompson	1830
James Osgood	1826		James Rhodes, Jr.	Native
William Burnside	1824		Thomas Thombison	1825
Samuel Burnside	1820		Francis Rousseau	1830
John Daniel	1820		Nelson Roubdoux	1830
Richard H. Finn	1822		<u>Fannin County Area</u>	
Jacob Blair	1824		Wm. H. Anderson	1830
Isaac Taylor	1824		Jacob Black	1825
Abijah Burkham	Native		Ancil Peck	1830
William McFarland	1825		David C. Strickland	1825

Source: Records, Texas General Land Office, transcribed in White, <u>1830 Citizens of Texas</u>.

Texas 1832-1835

Texas Revolution. Following the Battle of Nacogdoches in 1832, a brief period of peace and tranquility ensued, but a chain of events that would lead to rebellion and independence in some four years began to unfold. What developed was a deep-seated cultural conflict in which Anglos and Mexicans clashed again and again. The Mexicans failed to comprehend or understand the fact that frontier Americans such as the Anglo-Americans in East Texas were content only so long as they were left virtually free from governmental interference in their lives.

During the period from 1830 to 1835 Mexican authorites sought to exercise control over their East Texas citizens by sending customs collectors to Texas along with a contingent of soldiers to enforce the customs regulations of the nation. Those inspectors, notably Colonel John Davis Bradburn, aroused bitter resentment by their high-handed tactics. For example, he was over zealous in collecting tariff duties; he interfered with the process of granting land titles to Anglo-Anmerican settlers; and he encouraged slaves to run away and refused to return those captured to their owners.

Although the collection of customs was suspended in 1832, colonists were reluctant to leave matters as they stood. They demanded a constructive reform program that was hammered out in a series of consultations and congresses initiated in 1832.

Convention of 1832. In August 1832, the governing body of Austin's Colony at San Felipe issued a call for a meeting of delegates in October at San Felipe to formulate their demands. Fifty-eight delegates assembled to answer the call.

Representatives from the Nacogdoches District were Charles Stanfield Taylor, Thomas Hastings, and Hyman Hertz. Taylor, a native of London, England, arrived in Nacogdoches in 1828. Born about 1808, he died November 1, 1865, buried Oak Grove Cemetery,

Nacogdoches. He married Anna Marie Ruoff May 28, 1831 in Nacogdoches.[144] Thomas Hastings, a native of New York, came to Nacogdoches about 1826. Born about 1805, he was an unmarried man in 1832.[145] Hyman Hertz, a native of Hanover, Germany, was born about 1807 and burned to death on the Steamer Lioness on the way to New Orleans in 1833. He came to Texas with his brother Joseph in 1829 and was still a single man in 1832.

Representatives from the Sabine District were Benjamin Holt, Absalom Hyer, and Jesse Parker. Holt was born April 1, 1795 in the Natchez District, Mississippi and died January 16, 1867, in Brazoria County, Texas. Benjamin married first Charity Ann Wrinkle, and second Nancy Sternes January 21, 1858. He came to the Sabine District in 1825 from Avoyelles Parish, Louisiana, returned to Louisiana in 1837, but reentered Texas going to Brazoria County in 1852.[146] Hyer was born about 1785. He came to Texas in 1831 from Natchitoches, Louisiana and settled in Sabine County in 1840. Hyer married Nancy Vasherry.[147] Parker was born about 1776 in North Carolina and died May 27, 1849, buried at Huntsville, Walker County, Texas. He came to Texas in 1822 with a wife and family.[148] Jesse Parker was born about 1776 in North Carolina and died May 27, 1849, buried Oakwood Cemetery, Huntsville, Walker County, Texas. He went first to Georgia about 1798 then to St. Tammany Parish, Louisiana in 1809 before coming to Texas in 1822, settling in present-day Walker County. Parker married first Sarah ---- about 1798 and second Elizabeth Barker January 1829. Sarah Parker had seven children before her death and Elizabeth Parker seven children.[149]

---

[144] Ericson, Gateway to Texas, Vol. I, p. 372; Ericson and Ericson, Personalities on the East Texas Frontier, pp. 129-132; Biographical Directory of the Texan Conventions and Congresses (Austin: Book Exchange, 1941), p. 179.

[145] Ibid., p. 166, Biographcal Directory, p. 99.

[146] Ibid., p. 176; Biographical Directory, p. 106; Gifford White, Character Certificates in the General Land Office of Texas (Baltimore: Clearfield Co., 1993), p. 91; The New Handbook of Texas, Vol. 3, p. 674.

[147] Biographical Directory, p. 110.

[148] Ericson, Gateway to Texas, Vol. I., p. 280; Biographical Directory, p.149.

[149] The New Handbook of Texas, Vol. 5, p. 60.

Representatives from the Ayish Bayou (San Augustine) District were Phillip A. Sublett, Donald McDonald, William McFarland, Wyatt Hanks, and Jacob Garrett.

Representatives from the Tenahaw (Shelby) District were George Butler, William K. English, Frederick Foy, Jonas Harrison, and John M. Bradley. George Butler was a native of Georgia and came to Texas by 1830 with a family of five persons.[150] English, a native of New River, Virginia, was born about 1790 and died about 1843, son of Captain James and Elizabeth (Denton) English. He married first Elizabeth Tittle and second Myra Anderson in 1824.[151] Foy was born about 1778 in South Carolina and died in Caldwell County, Texas in 1854. He came to the Tenahaw District as a married man in 1828 from Monroe, Louisiana. He moved to San Augustine County, Texas by 1837, to Sabine County in 1845, and to the Prairie Lea area, Caldwell County, in 1851 or 1853 as a married man.[152] John M. Bradley was born about 1800 in North Carolina, and assassinated in San Augustine, Texas in 1844 and buried in the Old Texan Cemetery between San Augustine and Shelbyville, Texas. He came to Texas in 1832 a widower with four children.[153]

Representatives of the Snow River (Tyler County) District were Thomas D. Beauchamp, Elijah Isaacks, James Looney, and Samuel Looney. Beauchamp came to Texas in 1832 as an unmarried man.[154] Isaacks was born February 22, 1775 in South Carolina, son of Samuel and Mary (Wallace) Isaacks, and died November 1, 1859, in Jasper County, Texas. Isaacks came to Texas in 1822 from Pike County, Mississippi and settled in Bevil's Colony.[155] Isaacks married Esther (Hester) Donaho in 1797 and the couple had ten children. James

---

[150] Biographical Directory, p. 61.

[151] Ericson, Gateway to Texas., p. 116.

[152] Biographical Directory, p. 86; The New Handbook of Texcas, Vol. 2, p. 1147.

[153] The New Handbook of Texas, Vol. I, p. 694.

[154] Ibid., p. 51.

[155] Ibid., p. 111.

Looney, born about 1800, came to Texas from Kentucky in 1828 as a single man.[156] Samuel Looney was hanged for accessory to murder April 8, 1834. [157]

Representatrives of the Liberty District were Warren DeWitt Clinton Hall, Patrick Churchill Jack, James Morgan, and Claiborne West. Hall was born 1788 in Guilford County, North Carolina and died in 1867 on Galveston Island, buried the Episcopal Cemetery. He married first Julietta ---- and second Mary A. Moore May 23, 1843. He came to Texas in 1828 from Natchitoches, Louisiana. In 1854 Hall was living in Harris County, Texas.[158] Jack was born in Wilkes County, Georgia about 1809 and died in Houston, Texas of yellow fever August 4, 1844 and buried in the City Cemetery. He came to Texas in 1830 from Jefferson County, Alabama, settling first at Liberty and by 1837 at Brazoria.[159] Morgan was born October 13, 1787 in Philadelphia, Pennsylvania, son of James and Martha (Prudun) Morgan and died March 1, 1866. He came to Texas from North Carolina in 1828 and resided at Anahuac and Morgan's Point by 1836. Morgan married Celia Harrell in North Carolina and the couple had two daughters and one son.[160] West was born in November 1800 in Tennessee and died September 10, 1866, in Guadalupe County, Texas. He went to Louisiana by 1824 and came to Texas from Louisiana in 1831 and settled in the Liberty Municipality (now Jefferson County), then moved to Montgomery County about 1838 and to Guadalupe County about 1850. West married first Anna Garner in 1824 in Louisiana with whom he had nine children, second Mrs. Prudence Kimbell about 1847, Montgomery County, Texas, and third Mrs. Florinda McCulloch Day about 1861 in Guadalupe County.[161]

The delegates to the 1832 Convention asked officials at Saltillo in Coahuila to supply land titles to those persons living east of Austin's Colony, to establish local governments in

---

[156] Ibid., p. 126.

[157] Ibid., p. 126.

[158] Ericson, Gateway to Texas, Vol. I, p. 157; Biographical Directory, pp. 94-95.

[159] Biographical Directory, p. 111; The New Handbook of Texas, Vol. 3, p. 888.

[160] Ibid., p. 143. The New Handbook of Texas, Vol. 4, p. 835.

[161] Ibid., p. 187; The New Handbook of Texas, Vol. 6, p. 886.

the region, to set aside land for school purposes, to exempt East Texans from customs duties on necessities for three years, and to approve a plan for organizing local militia units. For some reason their petitions were never presented to Mexican national or state governments.

Convention of 1833. Expressions of disapproval of their actions from Mexican authorities prompted the call for a second meeting at San Felipe the following year. Delegates were chosen in the same manner as had been the case in 1832, and fifty-three delegates took part in the convention's deliberations.

Thomas Hastings, Nicholas Adolphus Sterne, and Sam Houston represented the Nacogdoches Municipality.

Representing the Liberty Municipality were David Gouverneur Burnet, William Hardin, Patrick C. Jack, Samuel Whiting, and Jesse Woodbury. Burnet was born April 14, 1788 in Newark, New Jersey, son of Dr. William and Gertrude (Gouvernor) Rutgers Butler Burnet, and died December 5, 1870 in Galveston. He went to Ohio as an orphaned child before immigrating to Natchitoches, Louisiana in 1817, returned to Ohio in 1819, and returned to Texas in 1826 obtaining a colonization contract. He was elected President <u>ad interim</u> in 1836 and Vice President of the Republic in 1838.[162] Burnet married Hannah Este in Morristown, New Jersey December 8, 1830, and they had four children. Hardin was born March 25, 1801 in Franklin County, Georgia, son of Swan and Jerusha (Blackburn) Hardin and died of yellow fever January 28, 1839, in Galveston and was buried in Hardin Cemetery, Liberty County. He came to Texas in 1825 from Maury County, Tennessee, with his wife, Sarah Looney, and two children.[163] Whiting was born in Hartford, Connecticut. He came to Texas in 1825 settling at Liberty, later moving to Houston about 1837 and to Austin about 1842. He died in California about 1855 or perhaps New York in 1862.[164] Woodbury came to Texas in 1831 and settled at Liberty. He died in 1837.[165]

---

[162] <u>Ibid.</u>, p. 80; <u>The New Handbook of Texas</u>, Vol. I, pp. 848-849.

[163] <u>Ibid.</u>, p. 97; Ericson, <u>Gateway to Texas</u>, Vol. I, pp. 162-163.

[164] <u>Ibid.</u>, p. 190; <u>The New Handbook of Texas</u>, Vol. 6, p. 946.

[165] <u>Ibid.</u>, pp. 194-195.

Representing the Tenahaw (Shelby) District were John and William English. John English was born July 5, 1793 in New River, Virginia, son of James and Elizabeth (Denton) English, and died December 30, 1868 in Houston County, Texas, and was buried Hicks Cemetery. He married Elizabeth Choate February 24, 1824. English came to Texas in 1825.[166] William English was born about 1786 in North Carolina or Tennessee, son of James and Elizabeth (Denton) English. William married Eliabeth Tittle, daughter of George and Mary (Cooper) Tittle with whom he had three children. The couple separated in 1813 and were granted a divorce by the state legislature. He married second Myra Anderson, daughter of Wyatt and Nancy (McFadden) Anderson with whom he had ten children. English died in the winter of 1836-1837 in Shelby County.[167]

Representing the Ayish Bayou (San Augustine) District were Achilles Edmond Johnson, Elisha Roberts, and Philip A. Sublett. Johnson, a native of Virginia, came to Texas from Missouri about 1824, settling in the San Augustine District. Roberts was born in 1774, son of William Roberts, in Watauga Settlement, Tennessee and died October 3, 1844, San Augustine County. Roberts came to Texas in 1824 settling in San Augustine County, having first immigrated to Kentucky and St. Tammany Parish, Louisiana earlier. He married Martha "Patsy" Gill about 1800.[168]

Petitions addressed by this assembly to Mexican national and state governments set forth the same grievances as those prepared by the 1832 delegates. Again emphasis was placed on repeal of the Immigration Law of 1830 closing the territory to foreign settlement and separation of Texas from the State of Coahuila. Assuming that their request for separate statehood, the delegates drafted a proposed constitution for the new state. Empresario Stephen F. Austin was dispatched to Mexico City to present their petitions. Austin was ultimately arrested and placed in prison and the 1833 petitions ignored.

While Texans awaited news that their petitions had been approved a series of natural

---

[166] Ibid., p. 80; Ericson, Gateway to Texas, Vol. I, p. 116.

[167] The New Handbook of Texas, Vol. 2, pp. 871-872.

[168] Ericson, Gateway to Texas., p. 316; Biographical Directory, p. 159.

disasters focused their attention on survival rather than political activity. An outbreak of floods, a cholera epidemic, and the onset of malignant malaria occupied their attention for the next two years. Despite some favorable responses from the state government, the undercurrents of revolution gathered momentum. Ultimately, on August 15, 1835, a committee of fifteen men issued a call for a convention or consultation to meet at Washington-on-the-Brazos. Settlers responded to the call by electing fifty-five delegates, representing some thirteen municipalities.

Consultation of 1835. Representing the San Augustine District were Henry W. Augustine, Jacob Garrett, Alexander Horton, Samuel Houston, Almanzon Huston, Achilles Edmond Johnson, Albert Gallatin Kellog, and William N. Sigler. Augustine was born 1806, South Carolina. He came to Texas in 1827 from Autauga County, Alabama and settled in the Ayish Bayou District with wife Cynthia -----.[169] Sigler was born 1798 in North Carolina. He came to Texas in 1834 locating in the Bevil Settlement. A Mexican census taken in 1835 describes him as married to Julian Ann with five children all born in Alabama.[170] Johnson was born July 17, 1806 in Virginia and was killed in Fort Bend County, Texas in 1845. He came to Texas from Missouri about 1824 settling in the Ayish Bayou District.[171]

Representing the Bevil (Jasper County) District were John R. Bevil, James H. Blount, Wyatt Hanks, Thomas Holmes, Samuel S. Lewis, Stephen Hendrickson Everitt, and John Allen Veatch. Blount was born about 1797 and disappeared from history in 1836. He came to Texas about 1830 from Louisiana and settled in Jasper County. In 1835, he married Penelope Williams in Jasper County.[172] Holmes came from Mississippi to the Bevil District October 8, 1834. He was born in 1800 in South Carolina, son of Thomas C. and Elizabeth (Jourdan)

---

[169] Ericson, Gateway to Texas, Vol. I, p. 14; The New Handbook of Texas, Vol. 1, p. 188.

[170] Ibid., p. 344; Biographical Directory, pp. 171-172; The New Handbook of Texas, Vol. 5, p.1045.

[171] The New Handbook of Texas, Vol. 3, pp. 950-951.

[172] Ibid., pp. 52-53; Ericson, Gateway to Texas, Vol. I, p. 33; The New Handbook of Texas, Vol. 1, p. 599.

Holmes. Holmes was farming in Newton County in 1850.¹⁷³ Veatch, a physician, was born March 5, 1808 in Knox County, Kentucky and died April 24, 1870, and buried in Lone Fir Cemetery, Portland, Oregon. He was the son of Reverend Isaac and Lucinda (Ramsey) Veatch. Veatch married first Charlotte Sheridan (or Edwards) about 1834, and they had two children in Louisiana and one in Texas before her death. Second he married Mrs. Ann M. Bradley in San Antonio (later divorced), and they had two children. He married third Smantha Brisbae in 1865. Veatch lived in Indiana 1827-1829, came to Texas about 1834, went to California about 1849/50, and finally to Oregon by 1869.¹⁷⁴ Everitt was born November 26, 1806 in Poughkeepsie, New York and died July 12, 1844 in New Orleans. He came to Texas in 1834 and settled in Nacogdoches but was living in the Bevil Settlement in 1835. Everitt married Alta Zera Williams in 1835 and they had four children.¹⁷⁵

Representing the Liberty District were David G. Burnet, Augustine Blackburn Hardin, Hugh Blair Johnson, Pierre (Patrick) J. Mennard, Henry Millard, George Moffit Patrick, Claiborne West, and James B. Woods. Hardin was born July 13, 1797 in Franklin County, Georgia, son of Swan and Jerusha (Blackburn) Hardin and died July 22, 1871, in Liberty County. He married first Mary Garner and second Mariah Dever February 9, 1829. Hardin moved to Maury County, Tennessee, in 1807 with his family and came to Texas in 1825, settling in Liberty County.¹⁷⁶ Johnston was born in 1794 in Georgia but moved to Mississippi before migrating to the Liberty District, Texas, in 1825. He married Martha White, daughter of Matthew G. White about 1823, and the couple had nine children. Johnston died in 1850 in Liberty County and was buried in the family cemetery.¹⁷⁷ Menard was born about

---

¹⁷³ Ibid., p. 105; The New Handbook of Texas, Vol. 3, p. 673.

¹⁷⁴ Ibid., p. 184; Ericson, Gateway to Texas, Vol. I, pp. 390-391; The New Handbook of Texas, Vol. 6, p. 717.

¹⁷⁵ Ibid., p. 82; Ericson, Gateway to Texas, Vol. I, p. 119; The New Handbook of Texas, Vol. 2, p. 910.

¹⁷⁶ Ibid., p. 97; Ericson, Gateway to Texas, Vol. I, p. 162.

¹⁷⁷ Ibid., p. 115; The New Handbook of Texas, Vol. 3, p. 971.

1808 in Canada, the son of Hypolite Menard. He went from there to Illinois before settling in present-day Polk County near the Liberty County line, but by 1839 was living in Galveston. He married first Rosine LeClere January 20, 1834. He married second to Catherine Maxwell; third to Mary Jane Riddle and fourth to Mrs. Rebecca Mary Bass. Menard died after September 28, 1861 in Galveston.[178] Millard was born in Mississippi in 1807, son of Josiah and Nancy Millard of Sarasota County, New York and died in August 1844 in Galveston. He came to Texas in 1835 and settled in the Liberty Municipality. He moved to Calhoun County by 1839 and to Galveston in 1841. He married Mary Dewburliegh Borlance Warren Beaumont August 24, 1826 in Natchez, Mississippi.[179] Patrick was born September 30, 1801, in Albermarle County, Virginia and died at his home at Anderson in Grimes County, Texas, June 28, 1889, now buried in the Texas State Cemetery in Austin. He immigrated to Lafayette County, Kentucky in 1803 with his family and came to Texas by sea in 1827. He was living in Harris County, Texas by 1837.[180] Woods was born about 1802 in Mercer County, Kentucky and died in 1851, buried in the Waelder Ranch Cemetery near Liberty. He came to Texas in 1832 settling in the Liberty Municipality and later lived at Harrisburg, Harris County, Texas. He married first Martha Scaife, native of Maryport, England in 1840 and second Augusta ---- before 1860.[181]

Representing Tenahaw (Shelby) District were Martin Parmer (Palmer). Parmer was born June 4, 1778 in Charlotte County, Virginia, son of Martin and Milly (Hardwick) Parmer. He died March 2, 1850 in Jasper County, Texas, and was buried twelve miles southeast of Jasper and later interred in the Texas State Cemetery in Austin. About 1797 with his family Martin moved to Madison County, Kentucky where in 1800 he married his first wife, Sarah Hardwick, and they ultimately had ten children. Parmer married second Margaret (Griffin)

---

[178] Ibid., pp. 137-138; Ericson, Gateway to Texas, Vol. I., p. 244; The New Handbook of Texas, Vol. 4, pp. 613-614.

[179] Ibid., p. 139; Ericson, Gateway to Texas, Vol. I., p. 249.

[180] Ibid., p. 150.

[181] Ibid., p. 195; The New Handbook of Texas, Vol. 5, pp. 89-90.

Neal in Nacogdoches, Texas, who bore him a daughter before her death. Third, he married Levisa (Anderson) Lout, daughter of Bailey and Mary (Wyatt) Anderson in the Tenahaw District, and this couple had one son. Parmer married fourth Zina Kelly in 1840 in Jasper County, and they had five children. From Kentucky Parmer moved to Tennessee and from there to Missouri before coming to Texas about 1826.[182]

Representing the Nacogdoches Municipality were David A. Hoffman, Daniel Parker, Nathaniel Robbins, James W. Robinson, Thomas J. Rusk, and William Whitaker. Hoffman died by 1838. He married Mary ----. Hoffman came to Texas before 1832, settling first in San Augustine County and later moving to Nacogdoches.[183] Parker was born April 6, 1781 in Culpeper County, Virginia, son of John and Sarah (White) Parker, and died December 3, 1844, buried Pilgrim Cemetery near Elkhart, Texas. Parker came to Texas from Illinois in 1831 settling at Elkhart in Anderson County. Parker married Martha (Patsy) Dickson March 11, 1802.[184] Robbins came to Texas in 1819 and settled at Pecan Point, Red River District and in 1834 in Milam's Colony. He died before 1837. He was the son of Rebecca Robbins and married Lucy ----. This couple had six children.[185] Robinson was born in 1790 in Hamilton County, Indiana, probably the son of Samuel and Margaret (Newell) Robinson, and died October 1857 in San Diego, California. He went to Arkansas in 1828 and on to Texas in 1833 settling in Nacogdoches District and later by 1836 to Gonzales County, Texas and still later in 1840 to Travis County, Texas. Robinson married first Mary Isdell in 1820 in Indiana with whom he had five children before the couple divorced in 1828 and second Sarah Snider whom

---

[182] Ibid., pp. 149-150; Ericson, Gateway to Texas, Vol. I, p. 281; Ericson and Ericson, Personalities on the East Texas Frontier, pp. 59-74; Joe E. Ericson and Carolyn R. Ericson, Martin Parmer: The Man and the Legend (Nacogdoches: Ericson Books, 1999).

[183] Ibid., p. 104; Ericson, Gateway to Texas, Vol. I, p. 173.

[184] Ibid., p. 148; Ericson, Gateway to Texas, Vol. I, p. 179.

[185] Ibid., p. 159; Ericson, Gateway to Texas, Vol. I, p. 315; The New Handbook of Texas, Vol. 5, p. 605.

he married in Arkansas, and she bore him one son. He immigrated to California in 1850.[186] Rusk was born December 5, 1803 in Pendleton District, South Carolina, son of John and Mary (Sterritt) Rusk, and died July 29, 1857 in Nacogdoches, buried Oak Grove Cemetery. Rusk came to Texas in 1834, settling in Nacogdoches. He married Mary Francis Cleveland January 4, 1827.[187] Whitaker was born about 1784 in North Carolina or Kentucky, son of John and Martha Wilcoxson (Wilson) Whitaker, and died 1835, in Nacogdoches, buried in Old North Church Cemetery, Nacogdoches County. Whitaker married Elizabeth Hammond in 1805, Mason County, Kentucky, and she bore him seven children. He immigrated first to Lincoln County, Tennessee about 1809, to Limestone County, Alabama before 1820, to Hardeman County, Tennessee about 1825, and to Texas about 1833 from Louisiana.[188]

The 1835 Consultation adopted a "Declaration of Causes" which proclaimed their allegiance to the Federal Constitution of Mexico and declared that the Texans were no longer bound to the compact creating the United States of Mexico and that they were establishing an independent government. Thereafter, the delegates adopted a plan for a Provision Government for the new political entity.

Mexican Census of 1835. In that same year on the eve of the Texas Revolution, officials in Mexico City mandated that a census be taken throughout the realm. Included were all but one of the municipalites that had been established in Texas: Bevil (Jasper), Liberty, Nacogdoches, Sabine, Shelby (Tenahaw), and San Augustine. The Red River Municipality was not included, and census takers did not include the names of Indians and slaves. Table XVI below provides the names of all adult immigrants listed. The name of those living in the Red River Municipalty have been obtained from the land records in the General Land Office of the State of Texas. Many of these persons, however, may never have become permanent residents of Texas. Some of them claimed land but returned to the United States before patenting it,

---

[186] Ibid., pp. 160-161; Ericson Gateway to Texas, Vol. I, p. 319; The New Handbook of Texas, Vol. 5, pp. 625-626.

[187] Ibid., pp. 165-166; Ericson, Gateway to Texas, Vol. I, p. 328.

[188] Ibid., p. 189; Ericson, Gateway to Texas, Vol. I, p. 409; The New Handbook of Texas, Vol. 6, p. 925.

others claimed the land and sold or otherwise alienated their claim to another person, while still others moved on further into the interior of Texas to establish homesteads.

TABLE XVI
IMMIGRANTS (1835)

Legend: m=married; w=widow or widower; unk=unknown; wives' names indented.

Nacogdoches Municipality
Henry Rueg 39 m Switzerland
Louis Rueg 35 s(?) Switzerland
Nicholas Adolphus Sterne 33 m Germany
  Eva Catherine Rosine Ruoff Sterne 23 m Germany
Jacob Roth 43 s unk
Frost Thorn 38 m New York
  Susan Wroe Edwards Thorn 23 m
Haden H. Edwards 21 s Virginia
John S. Thorn 21 s New York
Washington Tivis 46 w unk
Wilham Sneed 29 s unk
John Moss 24 s unk
John C. Morrison 35 s North Carolina
Jacob Duncan 24 s unk
Moses L. Choate 35 m unk
  Maria Ursula Choate 28 m unk
William Nels 25 s unk
Thomas Grubbs 25 s La(?)
Henry Raguet 39 m Pennsylvania
  Marcia Ann Towers Raguet 35 m Penn
Christina Garling 65 w Del/Penn
James Boulter 37 m unk
  Maria Lisana m unk
Augustus Chapman Allen s New York
C. M. Allen 29 s(?) New York(?)
John Kirby Allen 26 s New York
Samuel L. Allen 26 s(?) New York
John S. Roberts 37 m Virginia
  Harriet F. Callier Roberts
Thomas J. Rusk 28 m South Carolina
  Mary F. Cleveland Rusk 23 m
Charles S. Taylor 27 m. England

  Anna Maria Ruoff Taylor
John Hertz 26 s unk
John M. Dor 35 s France
John C. Leplicher 37 s France
Solomon Rice Peck 35 s unk
Isaac Parker 32 s Georgia
William G. Logan 24 m Kentucky
  Maria (Mary) Bell Logan 20 m unk
Francis Milhomme 68 m unk
  Maria Prudence Milhomme 60 m unk
James Grant 28 s unk
Joseph M. Igelson 45 w unk
David Fanchers 43 s unk
Philip Martin 27 m unk
  Mary Coffee Martin 29 m unk
Henry Jackson 42 m unk
  Betesh Jackson 35 m unk
John Adams 40 m unk
  Bessie 32 unk
George Parker Dikes 57 m Md/Ga
  Julia s. Beacham Dikes 15 m unk
Lovick P. Dikes 27 m unk
  Rodea V. Maddox Dikes 24 m unk
Levi B. Dikes 35 m Georgia
  Lydean Duvall Dikes 20 m unk
John Durst 37 m Arkansas
  Harriett Matilda Jamison Durst m Va
John Roark 62 m unk
  Nancy Chambliss Roark 54 m unk
Sarah Landers 64 w unk
William Johnson 55 m unk
  Polly Dodson Johnson 40 m unk
William Nelson 52 m unk
James Lions 34 m unk

Polly Miller Lions 27 m unk
Nathan G. Allen 61 m New York
  Margaret Quin Allen 32 m unk
William Skinner 60 m unk
  Jinny Webb Skinner 40 m unk
Thomas Skinner 48 w unk
James B. Mitchell 39 m Virginia
  Calphurina Franklin Mitchell m Va
Henry Brewer 59 m N. Carolina/Georgia
  Susannah Mitchell Brewer 58 m NC
Greenberry Brewer 25 m Mississippi
  Sarah Brewer Brewer 28 m unk
William T. Brewer 30 m unk
  Bethany Brewer Brewer 27 m Ga
Durham Avent 30 m N. Carolina
  Susan Winset Avent 28 m Ala
Michael Costly 26 m Illinois
  Elizabeth Reed Costly 22 m unk
Thomas C. Snailum 23 s England
Thomas Hughes 23 m Louisiana
  Missipsa Hughes 21 m unk
James Cobb 24 s unk
Luther Smith 26 w unk
John Skelton 44 m South Carolina
  Jane Alexander Skelton 28 m unk
Joseph Weeks 23 m unk
  Gracy Owens Weeks 23 m unk
Silas Morris 36 m unk
  Harriet Alexander Morris 20 m unk
Isaac J. Midkiff 25 s Tennessee
  Latha Jones Midkiff 18 m unk
Candis Midkiff 32 w unk
Isaac Hicks 25 s unk
Helena G. Kimble 68 w Maryland
Joseph Durst 45 m Arkansas
  Delilah Dill Durst 35 m Arkansas
Alfred Sims 23 s Tennessee
John Bush 35 s unk
John Little 35 w unk
Moses Herrin 31 m Georgia
  Louisa Herrin 22 m Tenn(?)
Isaac H. Reed 22 m Tennessee
  Pervilla Herrin Reed 23 m unk
William Roark 29 m Tennessee
  Margaret Reed Roark 25 m Tenn
Richard Sparks 42 m Mississippi
  Elizabeth Cooper Sparks 39 m Miss
William F. Sparks 21 s Mississippi
James Hawkins Sparks 20 m Mississippi
  Massey C. Wadlington Sparks m S.C.
Sarah Sparks McAnulty 38 w Georgia
Samuel Rogers 20 m Mississippi
  Elizabeth C. Sparks Rogers 16 m unk
Henry C. Cook 23 m unk
  Mary Goodson Cook 16 m unk
Henry Bailey 49 m Virginia
  Sarah Bailey (Sally) 43 m N. Carolina
Howard Bailey 23 s Virginia(?)
John Bailey 21 s Virginia(?)
Benjamin F. Whitaker 29 m Kentucky
  Saletha W. Easter Whitaker 28 m Ky
William Whitaker 52 m Kentucky
  Elizabeth Hammond Whitaker 48 m Ky
Daniel Wilburn 45 m unk
  Elizabeth Wilburn 40 m N Carolina
Milly Berry 23 w Virginia(?)
John Caughram 30 s unk
William Barnhill 60 m South Carolina
  Cynthia Hedge Barnhill 55 m Tenn
Samuel Brimberry 50 m North Carolina
  Mary Jones Brimberry 42 m unk
Creed S. Engledow 21 m Virginia
  Elvira Randolph Engledow 23 m unk
Radford Berry 34 m unk
  Sarah Berry 34 m unkn
John Daugherty 33 m Ireland
Alse Garrett 28 n unk
Patrick Daugherty 22 m unk
Hellena Bradley 45 w unk
John Engledow 54 m. Virginia
  Elizabeth Simpson Engledow 45 m Va
William Smith 53 m unk
John Criss 30 m. unk
Neil Martin, Sr. 45 m Kentucky
  Elizabeth Brown Martin 36 m unk
Isaac Simpson 70 s Virginia
Hiram P. Walker 28 m Tennessee
  Judah George Walker 24 m. unk

Stephen George 22 s Virginia
John Walling 35 m Virginia
  Ann Chisum Walling 30 m unk
William Chisum 30 s Tennessee
John Chisum 35 s Tennessee
John Jordan Simpson 38 m South Carolina
  Jane M. Brooks Simpson 35 m Tenn
John E. Mayfield 38 m Kentucky
  Mary Mayfield 35 m unk
Jacob Mast 45 m North Carolina
  Rebecca Robbins Mast m Ill(?)
Joshua Fulcher 20 m unk
  Rebecca Dimmaux Brooks Fulcher 20 m unk
Thomas Norris 29 m Maryland
  Maria Puarie Norris 28 m unk
John Norris 35 m Louisiana
  Celeste Stockman Norris m unk
Vicente Michelli 44 m Italy
James Quinelty 62 m unk
  Maria Manuela Flett Quinelty 43 unk
William Goyens 44 m North Carolina
  Mary Pate Sibley Goyens m unk
Jesse Korn 31 m unk
  Mary Korn 22 m unk

<u>Bevil (Jasper) Municipality</u>

William Williams 49 m North Carolina
  Sittina Southern Williams 47 m S.C.
Gadi West 35 m Mississippi
  Polly Bivins West 33 m unk
William Baker 20 m unk
  Caroline Mann Baker 19 m unk
Isaac Winfree 31 m unk
  Isabella Guthrie Winfree 21 m unk
Stephen Williams 22 s Louisiana
John Brown 30 m unk
  Rebecca Good Brown 22 m Alabama
James D. Good 22 s Missouri
Mordica Howard 26 s unk
Robert Griffin 38 s Mississippi(?)
Berry West 37 m Mississippi
  Sarah (Sally) Holden West 33 m Ohio/Mo

Thomas C. Holmes 75 w North Carolina
Elizabeth Jourdan West 60 m unk
Edmond Morrison 44 m Maryland
  Patsy Devore Morrison 25 m unk
James F. Blount 38 s North Carolina
Joseph McGhee 35 m unk
  Hulda Ford McGhee 35 m unk
Richard Williams 20 m Louisiana
  Rebecca Wilson Williams 19 m Ala/La
William Guthrie 60 m Virginia
  Nancy Bradberry Guthrie 55 m N. C.
Nathaniel Grigsby 27 s Alabama
Squire Cruse (Crews) 37 m Kentucky
  Piety Hoover Prewitt Cruse 30 m Va
Richard Simmons 34 m South Carolina
  Susan Guthrie Simmons 28 m Miss(?)
Alfred Bevil 22 s Georgia
John Pharish 35 w s South Carolina
Samuel Pharish 28 m South Carolina(?)
  Orpey Smith Pharish 23 m unk
William Pharish 40 m South Carolina
  Polly Squires Pharish 18 m unk
Squire Pharish 26 s South Carolina(?)
Samuel T. Belt 32 m unk
  Helen Taylor Belt 20 m unk
Argalus Parker 26 m North Carolina
  Elzira Taylor Parker m unk
John Saul 40 m Georgia
  Drey Methreana Sutherland Saul 36 m Ga
John McGee 21 m Mexico
  Sally Winfrey McGee 21 m unk
Stephen Hendrickson Everett 29 m N. Y.
  Alta Zera Williams Everett 21 m Tex
Joseph Grigsby 64 m Virginia
  Sally Graham Grigsby 45 m Virginia
Sally Grigsby 26 w Kentucky
John Bevil 51 m North Carolina
  Frances Boynton Bevil 48 m New York
Jehu Bevil 26 m Georgia
  Ann Jane Taylor Bevil 17 m Tennessee
Edward Good 54 m Virginia
  Nancy Daughty Good 45 m Virginia
Caleb Baker 48 m unk
  Hulda Jones Baker 35 m unk

John Anthony Gilchrist 52 m Louisiana
Sally Milholm Gilchrist 41 m Louisiana
James Conn 60 w S. Carolina
Thomas C. Holmes 35 m North Carolina
Elizabeth Odom Holmes 25 m unk
Elizabeth Williams Dailey 28 w La.
Joseph W. Turner 21 m Georgia
Mary Jane Gilchrist Turner 21 m La.
James Lane 65 m unk
Martha Miles Lane 32 m unk
Herman Lewis 27 s unk
Thomas Gray 21 m unk
Martha Winfree Gray 15 m unk
John Droddy 45 m Virginia
Sarah Hays Droddy 53 m unk
John Miller, Sr. 35 m Tennessee
Betsy Barnett Miller 36 m unk
Charles Gilchrist 38 m unk
Jane Chessher Gilchrist 20 m unk
Thomas Tanner 38 m South Carolina
Charlotte Guthrie Tanner 29 m Ky
B. Franklin Jones 36 m Georgia
Latitia Guthrie Jones 24 m Miss.
Britton Hall 34 m. Georgia
Harriet Pool Hall 29 m Georgia
Peter P. Pry 27 m Maryland
Elizabeth Berry Pry 22 m Louisiana
Ephriam Thompson, Sr. 43 m Kentucky
Susan Susannah Grigsby Thompson 36 m Virginia
George W. Smith 31 m North Carolina
Frances Grigsby Smith 24 m Kentucky(?)
Elijah Isaacs 62 m South Carolina
Ester Donoho Isaacs 59 m unk
Nathaniel Allen 51 w Georgia
Delilah Allen 27 w unk
William Allen 39 s Louisiana
William Pamplin 39 m Virginia
Dorcus Coleman Pamplin 43 m Kentucky
Obadiah Denman 23 s Louisiana
James Denman 23 s Louisiana
Owen Taylor 50 m unk
Spicey McQueen Taylor 42 unk
John M. Taylor 22 s Tennessee

John Schrivers 32 m Louisiana
Matilda Isaacs Schriver 28 m unk
Lourany Taylor Lewis 25 w unk
Andersen Barclay 27 m Tennessee
Sarah Ann Prather Barclay 19 m unk
William Wilson, Sr. 45 m. Ireland(?)
Mary Lee Wilson 40 m unk
Joel Roberson 51 s unk
James Chessher 48 m Georgia
Thirza Morgan Chesser 24 m unk
Daniel Chesser 22 s Georgia
Martin Bierly 70 w unk
Adam Bierly 30 s unk
William Bierly 25 s unk
Thomas Bierly 30 m unk
Matilda Hagood Bierly 20 m unk
Henry Hagood 21 s Mississippi
Thomas Watts, Sr. 70 m Ireland
Susan Hutchins Watts 46 m Georgia
Hardy Pace 27 m Georgia
Mahaly Isaacs Pace 22 m Mississippi
John Watts 30 m Mississippi
Mary Netherland Watts 22 m La.(?)
Rachel Farmer 55 w unk
William Addison, Sr. 50 m unk
Mary Cabiere Addison 40 m unk
Richard West 45 w Louisiana
Jesse Dickerson 22 m Kentucky
Presilla West Dickerson 25 m Mississippi
Jefferson West 22 m Mississippi(?)
Nancy Sudduth West 15 m unk
Barney Lowe 46 m South Carolina
Margaret Carelock Lowe 46 m unk
Lewis Lethey 37 m Tennessee
Polly Lowe Letney 25 m Kentucky
Thomas McGallin 59 m Virginia
Elizabeth Strother McGallin 47 m unk
Lemuel Walters, Sr. 39 m North Carolina
Sally Turner Walters 37 m unk
Sebern Berry 21 m Louisiana
Adaline Glass Berry m Louisiana
Chester Rockwell (Rockwall) 22 s N. Y.
Marvin Bill 30 s unk
B. Franklin Mott 21 s Alabama

Willis Donoho 23 s Mississippi
John T. Ballard 26 s unk
William Hays 25 s unk
Calvin C. Robinett 28 m unk
  Mary Donoho Robinett 20 m Miss.(?)
Charles Delaney 26 m Mississippi
  Frances Van Clive Delaney 20 m unk
F. H. Pollard 36 m unk
  Nancy Parrish Pollard 36 m unk
John T. Lewis 27 m Louisiana
  Mariah Stark Lewis 23 m New York
John Humble 34 w unk
Daniel Donoho 66 m South Carolina
  Nancy Larrimore Donoho 45 S. C.
Amos Smith 66 m Virginia
  Frances Rutledge Smith 45 m unk
William Jourdan 38 m South Carolina
  Mahulda Isaacs Jourdan 25 m Mississippi
Nathaniel Addison 23 s Louisiana
Thomas Williams 33 m Louisiana
  Lucinda Isaacs Williams 21 m unk
Isaac Conover, Sr. 40 m unk
Alexander Porter 39 m Virginia
  Mary Smith Porter 18 m unk
Joseph Mott 60 m South Carolina
  Zelpha Wiggins Mott 55 m unk
B. H. Mudd 43 m Maryland
  Elizabeth Robuck Mudd 36 m unk
Sophia Waller Pridgon Dean 36 w unk
William Pridgon M. Dean 35 m Miss
John A. Veatch 27 m unk
  Charlotte Sheridan Dean 25 m Miss
Samuel Ralph 42 m Ireland
  Sophia W. P. Dean Ralph m unk
Thomas B. Huling 30 m Pennsylvania
Henry G. Morgan 30 s New York
Lovick (Lewis) P. Dykes 24 s unk
Samuel S. Lewis 50 m Tennessee
  Sarah (Sally) Lemasters Lewis 50 m Va.
Henry Cochran 25 s Indiana
Murid Gross 68 m unk
  Patsy Goodin Gross 65 m unk
Martin B. Lewis 27 m Indiana
  Nancy Moore Lewis 25 m Indiana

Henry Suddeth 45 m North Carolina
  Sally Golden Suddeth 38 m Georgia
John Dickerson 30 m unk
  Mary Ann Coleman Dickerson 26 m unk
Mary (Polly) Williams 40 w unk
Andrew J. Youngblood 40 s unk
Henry Stagner 33 m North Carolina
  Sarah Pennington Stagner 33 m unk
John Nowland 29 m unk
  Milla Teal Nowland 26 m unk
Robert Conn 35 w South Carolina
John Mires 27 s unk
Edwin Smith 29 m unk
  Rachel Roberts Smith 22 m unk
Joseph Dykes 34 m unk
  Elizabeth Lewis Dykes 15 m unk
William Lewis 56 m unk
  Elizabeth Noland Lewis 46 unk
Westley Dykes 25 m unk
  Harriet Dykes 24 m unk
Sherod Wright, Sr. 40 m Georgia
  Anna Clark Wright 35 m Georgia
Alexander Wright 36 m Georgia
  Polly Winfree Wright 24 unk
Elisha Morris 36 m Alabama
  Susannah Dunn Morris 24 m unk
William Williams 35 m unk
  Barbary Hooter Williams 33 m unk
Jerry Goin 35 m. unk
  Sarafine Drake Goin 28 unk
Parthena Mott 33 w unk
Stephen Williams, Sr. 76 w Louisiana
Horatio McMullen Hanks 27 s Kentucky
Samuel Hanks 22 s Indiana
William Jones 64 w Georgia
Benjamin Burk 43 m Kentucky
  Susannah Ogden Burk 27 m unk
Samuel Isaacks 31 m Ohio
  Martha Patsy Richardson Isaacks m La.
Benjamin Richardson 59 m Georgia
  Rebecca Richardson 27 m Georgia
Timothy Devore 56 w unk
John J. Pemberton 32 m unk
N. Wyatt Hanks, Sr. 40 m Kentucky

Hannah Gates Hanks 40 m unk
H. Good 26 s Tennessee
J. Becker 50 w unk

Sabine Municipality

John McAdams, Sr. 55 m Ire./Alabama
　Martha McAdams 49 unk
James McAdams 30 m North Carolina
　Elizabeth McAdams 22 m unk
William Taylor 42 m England
　Pamela Taylor 38 m unk
Alfred W. Morris 25 m Georgia
　Sarah Ann Taylor Morris 18 m Georgia
Lewis H. Adams 30 s Georgia
Sarah Rugg 27 w Georgia
William Farris 30 m Virginia
　Amanda Farris 23 m unk
Harris Vicker(s) 23 s(?) Georgia
John Horton 39 m North Carolina
　Winnie Horton 38 m North Carolina
Margaret Russell 61 w Virginia
Jonathan Russell 32 m Tennessee
　Emily Russell 26 m unk
Jesse Russell 23 m North Carolina
　Jane Russell 17 m South Carolina
William Gaffee (Gaffene) 47 m. Ireland
　Nancy Gaffee (Gaffene) 40 m unk
Jesse McGee 18 m Arkansas
　Malinda McGee 18 m unk
Jane Junkin 45 w unk
Richard Slaughter 50 m unk
　Elizabeth Slaughter 48 m unk
Eli N. Smith 32 m South Carolina
　Rachel Smith 32 m unk
William T. Slaughter 40 w Kentucky
John Mason 40 m South Carolina
　Fannie Mason 35 m unk
Joseph Smith 38 m South Carolina
　Nancy Smith 22 m unk
Thomas Horsly (Hassely) 47 m unk
　Sarah Horsly (Hassely) 43 m unk
David Harris 50 m unk
　Sarah Harris 45 m unk

John Grisset 22 m unk
　Catherine Grisset 22 m unk
Absalom Hire 45 m unk
　Nancy Hire 50 m Mississippi
James Mason 35 m South Carolina
　Elizabeth Mason 35 m South Carolina
William Mason 20 m South Carolina
　Judith R. (Judy) Mason 25 m S. Carolina
Isaac Powell 27 m North Carolina
　Elizabeth Powell 21 m North Carolina
Elbert Hinds (Hines) 38 m. Georgia
　Mahana Hinds (Hines) 33 m Georgia
John Smith 73 m Virginia(?)
　Mary Smith 63 m unk
S. J. Robertson 39 m unk
　Elizabeth Robertson 46 m unk
Samuel Robertson 25 s unk
Thomas Irvin 24 m unk
　Clarecy Irvin 19 m unk
James Irvin 19 m Tennessee
　Susan Irvin 18 m North Carolina
William Hiram Little 28 m Illinois
　Mary (Polly) Little 22 m unk
William Little 30 m unk
　Nancy Little 28 m unk
John Taylor 36 m unk
　Louisiana Taylor 28 m unk
Susanna Jackson 42 w North Carolina
Henry Martin 52 m Alabama
　Mary Martin 34 m unk
Moses Hill 66 m unk
　Hannah Hill 53 m unk
Mills Whitley 43 m Va./N. C.
　Elizabeth Little Whitley 41 m unk
George Lavanie 25 m unk
　Sarah Lavanie 20 m unk
George Carter 50 m North Carolina
　Priscilla Carter 30 m unk
W. K. Melton 40 m Alabama(?)
　Levanna Melton 20 m unk
Elizabeth Melton 63 w unk
Pleasant Young 26 m Georgia
　Carolina Young 17 m Geolrgia
William Hinds (Hines) 40 m Georgia(?)

Mary Hinds Speights Hix 40 m Ga.
Miranda Nofsen 23 w unk
Drewery Anglin 45 m unk
  Mary Anglin 40 m unk
Sion Smith 44 m Mississippi(?)
  Sarah Smith 46 m Miss. (?)
Alexander Cloud 50 m unk
  Sarah Cloud 45 m unk
Isaac Low 50 m Tennessee
  Elizabeth Parsons Low 50 m Va.
Right Cala 42 m unk
  Rebecca Cala 41 m unk
Shadrac Morris 42 m Kentucky
  Mary Morris 28 m unk
Samuel Nelson 26 m Tennessee
  Sarah Nelson 20 m unk
Elizabeth Nelson 21 s unk
Greenway Cook 26 m Mississippi
  Rebecca Cook 20 m Tennessee
John Law 45 s unk
J. Johnson 35 m unk
  Margaret Johnson 35 m unk
Daniel Easley 40 m Georgia
  Jane (Fanny) Hornbeck Easley 40 m Ga.
John Moore 40 m North Carolina
  Lucy Moore 25 m unk
John C. Gallion 35 m Kentucky
  Susan Gallion 25 m unk
Walter Hughes 36 m Kentucky
  Christine Hughes 32 m unk
Eli Low 27 m Tennessee
  Drusela Cook Low 40 m Georgia
Jesse Low 24 s Tennessee(?)
Henry Necklis (Nichols) 30 m Miss.
  Nancy Necklis (Nichols) 25 m Miss.
John Williams 40 m unk
  Eliza Williams 35 m unk
James Lesley 27 s New York
Maston (Mastin) Latham 38 m Kentucky
  Sarah Latham 35 m unk
Matthew Parker 32 m Kentucky
  Mary Isaacs Parker 29 m unk
William Clark 45 m Connecticut/S. C.
  Elizabeth Isaacs Clark 36 m Miss.

John Clark 18 m Mississippi
  Abbi Clark 23 m Mississippi
Allen Hinds (Hines) 21 m. unk
  Rebecca Hinds (Hines) 24 m unk
Charles Roberts 51 w Georgia
James Thomas 30 m North Carolina
  Mary Thomas 22 m unk
Lewis Latham 45 w unk
William I. Pace 51 m N. C./Louisiana
  Elizabeth Pace 50 m North Carolina(?)
Isaac Caradine (Carridine) 24 m unk
  Margaret Carradine 21 m unk
James Clark 30 m Mississippi
  Elizabeth Clark 27 m unk
William Webb 50 s Virginia
Benjamin Breant 35 m unk
  Roxanna Breant 32 m unk
Rebecca Parker 30 s unk
John Laws 35 s unk
Sharp Whittley 36 m Ill./Missouri
  Sarah Little Whittley 28 m Illinois
Jackson Crouch 38 s Kentucky
James Hazle 25 m unk
  Adaline Hazle 22 m unk
Johnson Newlin 38 s unk
Jonathan Warmsky 45 s unk
Daniel Brown 33 m Ohio
John Pain 50 m unk
William Isaacs 35 m South Carolina
  Sarah Mary Glass Isaacs 34 m Georgia
Benjamin Anderson 70 m South Carolina
  Jane Williams Anderson 42 m S. Carolina
Caldwell Davis 52 m Virginia(?)
  Amelia Davis 35 m unk
Joseph Walker 45 m unk
  Elizabeth Walker 40 m unk
James B. McMahan 21 m Tennessee
  Matilda McMahan 20 m Alabama
Edmund Gaines 20 m Texas
  Mahaly Gaines 17 m Louisiana
Naoma Mackey 45 w unk
James Gaines 53 m. Virginia
  Susannah Norris Gaines 36 m. Louisiana
Francis Mayhon 34 m unk

Lettis Mayhon 34 m unk
David Anding 28 s Mississippi
Cornelius Crainshaw (Crenshaw) 52 m SC
  Permelia Crainshaw 52 m N. Carolina
Thomas Yalis 50 m. unk
  Caintha Yalis 45 m unk
John Maxamilion 50 m. France
  Claire Maxamilion 50 m unk
Rama Crislia 45 m unk
  Laliltt Crislia 45 m unk
David Huffman 40+ m unk
  Eliza Huffman ? m unk
Jonathan Real 35 m unk
  Sarah Real 42 m unk
John Lane 36 s unk
Matthew Earl 53 m Louisiana
  Nancy Earl 43 m unk
Elizabeth White 65 w unk
Burgess Howl 27 s unk
Willis Landrum 29 s unk
James White 37 m unk
  Nancy White 54 m unk
Larken Gross 30 m Kentucky
  Belinda Gross 30 m unk
Benjamin Holt 39 m Mississippi
  Charity Ann Wrinkle Holt 29 m Miss.
Dennis Dykes 25 s unk
Elisha Madison Collins 35 m Tennessee
  Eliza Ann McGrew Collins 20 m Miss.
Jacob Lewis 25 s Georgia
Lewis Warren 55 s Virginia
John Randolph 25 m Tennessee
  Elizabeth Randolph 22 m N. Carolina(?)
Bretain Odom 35 m. Georgia
  Margaret Odom 25 m Georgia
Robert Childers 20 m unk
  Milla Childers 25 m Alabama
William Means 25 m Georgia
  Frances Amelia Blackburn Means 22 m Miss.(?)
James Conly 30 s unk
Hugh Means 40 m unk
  Martha Means 40 m unk
Willis Murfree 40 m Mississippi
  Priscilla Dickson Murfree 40 m Georgia
Isaac Renfro 55 m Virginia
  Priscilla Renfro 56 m unk
Samuel Doak McMahan 49 m Tennessee
  Phoeba R. McMahan 45 m Virginia
William F. Clark 36 m North Carolina
  Martha Clark 33 m Virginia
William W. Baren 44 m unk
  Catherine Baren 35 m unk
William A. Thompson 40 m unk
  Phenats Thompson 33 m unk
Donald McDonald 30 m Canada
  Maria Louisa Maximillian McDonald 22 m Louisiana(?)
William S. Mussett 29 s unk
M. C. Smith 26 s unk
A. T. Baitman 28 m unk
  Nancy Baitman 26 m unk
James Mitchell 19 s unk
John Stinson 36 m unk
  Milla Stinson 27 m unk
Samuel Thompson 70 m North Carolina
  Precous Wofford Thompson 68 m unk
Precious Seats (Seets) 22 w Tennessee
Benjamin Odell 18 s unk
George Fissett 35 s unk
A. E. C. Johnson 28 m Virginia
  Margaret Lewis Johnson 22 m unk
Redin (Redeen) A. Jourdon 30 s Tennessee
John Lee 30 s unk
Martha (Patsy) Lewis 58 w Missori(?)
George Jones 23 m Georgia
  Mary Jones 19 m Alabama
John C. Pain (Payne) 20 s Tennessee
Washington Davis 23 s unk
John McGowan 40 m unk
  Mary Thompson Floyd McGowan 38 m unk
John S. Johnson 45 w unk
William N, Sigler 37 m North Carolina
  Julian Sigler 37 m unk
David O. Warren 27 m South Carolina
  Eliza Warren 19 m Tennessee
Joseph Shackleford 21 s unk

Matison Fuller 29 s unk
Sarah Odell 26 w Tennessee
Peter Teal 28 s Tennessee
Solomon Johnson 27 s unk
Matthew S. Miller 22 s Alabama
Solomon Miller 26 s North Carolina
Leroy Miller 26 s Alabama(?)
Shelby Corzine 41 m N. C. or Tennessee
  Sarah Corzine 41 m North Carolina
Robert C. McDaniel 33 m Virginia
  Eliza Ann McDaniel 23 m unk
John McDaniel 25 s Virginia(?)
Iredell Divisor Thomas 26 m N. Carolina
  Penelope (Penny) Thomas 22 m Kentucky
Augustus (Augustine)Hotchkiss 33 m Ohio
  Anna Hotchkiss 28 m unk
Charles Horatio Gates 38 m Kentucky
  Minerva Fletcher Hanks Gates 25 m unk
Roderic(k) Wiggins 23 m Kentucky
  Julian Wiggins 22 m unk
John Bodine 54 m France/N. Carolina
  Nancy A. Gunnels Bodine 43 m unk
John Riddle 21 s unk
Pinkney Lout 23 m Indiana
  Elizabeth Lout 20 m unk
Joseph Butler 35 m Georgia
  Juriah Butler 30 m unk
Mary Langford (Lankford) 53 w(?) Virginia
Enoch Frier 32 m Kentucky
  Jane Frier 28 m unk
Jeremia Latham 61 w unk
William Harness 32 s unk
Isaac Holmon 59 m North Carolina
  Anna Wigglesworth Holman 51 m Va.
Nancy Davis 45 w Georgia
Samuel Davis 25 s Georgia(?)
Stephen P. Wilson 45 m New York
  Mary Wilson 30 m Georgia
Mary Thomas 65 w North Carolina
Lewis Knight 26 m North Carolina
  Emily Knight 20 m Tennessee
Elzy Keeling 28 s unk
David Griggs Green 21 s Tennessee
Allen Kimbro 22 s unk

Joseph Howe 22 s Ohio
Bailey Anderson 46 m South Carolina
  Elizabeth McFadden Anderson 45 m Ky.
Hazard Anderson 21 m unk
  Elizabeth Webster Anderson 19 m unk
Peter Whetstone 45 m unk
  Edica Whetstone 44 m unk
Bailey Anderson, Sr. 82 w Virginia
Joshua J. Hennas 43 m unk
  Purity Hennas 37 m unk
John Williams 27 s unk
Senaca Legg 30 s unk
John Carvell 22 s unk
William Watson 30 s Kentucky
Ambrose Crain 46 m Georgia
  Mary Burdett Crain 43 m S. Carolina
Patrick McDavid 39 s unk
Jesse Burdett 47 m South Carolina
  Milla Burdett 40 m Georgia(?)
Isaac Clark 21 s unk
Allen Kimbro 22 s unk
William B. Burdett 24 m Tennessee
  Caroline Crain Burdett 24 m Tenn.
Archibald Yancy 38 s unk
Bethany Rogers 34 w South Carolina
Joseph Nations 28 s Georgia
John Kirby 31 m unk
  Sarah Kirby 24 m unk
William Lumpkins 33 m Virginia
  Pauline Lumpkins 26 m Kentucky
Elias M. Eubanks 54 m Virginia
  Elizabeth W. Thompson Eubanks 43 m Virginia
James A. Skillern 45 s Kentucky
Nancy Alcorn Skillern 65 w(?) Va.
Bartlett T. Thompson 54 s Virginia
Isaac C. Skillern 30 m Kentucky
  Lucinda White Skillern 22 m Tenn.
Jesse Warden 30 w unk
Mary Amy Earl 42 w North Carolina
Robert McCombs 27 s unk
John Patterson 35 m Virginia
Joseph Neely 45 s unk
Dinsmore Thompson 40 m unk

Nancy Thompson 30 m unk
Lewis Holloway 53 m unk
  Mary Holloway 55 m unk
Matthew Doyle 34 m unk
  Parmelia Doyle 30 m unk
Simpson Holloway 25 m South Carolina
  Charlotte Holloway 19 m Louisiana
Daniel Holloway 33 s South Carolina
Elizabeth Fulcher 33 w Kentucky
Jane Patton Irvine 46 w North Carolina
David Steele 35 s unk
Frances Richmond 60 w unk
Thomas Spencer 49 m unk
  Margaret Spencer 33 m unk
Stephen Eaton 50 m Illinois(?)
  Charity Arnold Eaton 46 m Ill.
Jacob Garrett 59 w Tennessee
Thomas Malone 35 m unk
  Eliza Malone 26 m unk
James Thomas 47 m unk
  Nancy Thomas 43 m unk
Wesley Currey 45 m unk
  Elifain (Ellifaire) Currey 36 m unk
Thomas Curry 36 m unk
  Matilda Curry 28 m unk
Isaac Lindsey 49 m South Carolina
  Easter Lindsey 51 m South Carolina
William D. Ratcliff 24 m Louisiana
  Evelina (Eveline) Ratcliff 17 m Missouri
Hiram Brown 22 m New York
  Catherine Brown 20 m unk
Lucretia Brown 55 w Canada
Shadrac(k) Dickson Thomas 34 m N. C.
Sarah Holman Thomas 30 m Canada
Richard Sims 35 m Georgia
  Rebecca Sims 30 m Georgia
William C. Bullock 31 m Georgia
  Martha Anderson Bullock 28 m S.C.
Richard Limboy 50 w unk
Andrew Spears 70 m unk
  Marya Spears 46 m unk
Jesse Terry 35 m unk
  Elizabeth Terry 26 m unk
James Johnson 65 w Virginia

Thomas Lawhorn 22 m unk
  Nancy Lawhorn 16 m unk
Green Reeves 28 m Kentucky
  Sarah Jane Johnson Reeves 25 m unk
Carbet Stephens 38 s unk
Zachariah Redman (Redmond) 70 m S. C.
  Frances Redman 60 m unk
Charity Sanders 58 w South Carolina
Thomas J. Hagerty 28 Georgia
  Melinda Bowie Hagarty 21 m Louisiana
Joseph Squires 21 m South Carolina
  Sarah Carroll Squires 30 m La.
William Gregory 35 m unk
  Patsy Gregory 31 m unk
Lavica Linney 23 s unk
Henry Linney 22 s unk
John Howard 43 m South Carolina
  Kiziah Howard 31 m unk
Danniel Pharris 32 m Mississippi
  Kiziah Pharris 30 m unk
Thomas Paine (Payne) 48 m Tennessee
  Esther Paine 22 m unk
Jose Sims 40 m unk
  Susan Sims 30 m unk
Nathaniel Hunt 47 m Tennessee
  Elizabeth Hunt 44 m Georgia
John M. Neeley (Neely) 32 m S. Carolina
  Charity Neeley 22 m Tennessee
Blasingame W. Harvey 40 m S. Carolina
  Eliza M. Prather Harvey 25 m unk
Sarah Wyche 80 w unk
Thomas Freeman Prator 24 s Louisiana
William Caldwell 50 m N. Carolina/Ala.
  Maria Caldwell 50 m unk
Andrew Caddel 40 m North Carolina
  Rhoda (Rodey) Daugherty Caddel 35 m Alabama
Peter Galloway 40 s(?) South Carolina
James Bridges 67 m North Carolina
  Elizabeth Harvey Bridges 45 m N. C.
Matilda Cherry 23 w(?) unk
Elizabeth Rhodes 27 w unk
John McGinnis 33 m unk
  Anna McGinnis 19 m unk

James W. J. Bridges 21 m unk
 Elizabeth Bridges 19 m unk
Ross M. Bridges 26 s(?) Georgia
John Harman 30 m Louisiana
 Elizabeth Clark Harman 22 m La.
John Lookan 35 m unk
 Sarah Lookan 30 m unk
Armstead Chumly 25 m unk
 Harriet Chumly 26 m unk
William Lakey 40 m North Carolina
 Sarah Lakey 35 m North Carolina
John Cartwright 48 m Tennessee
 Mary Crutchfield Cartwright 47 m Tenn.
Peter Teal (Teel) 28 s unk
 Sarah Brooks Teel 31 m Tennessee
Solomon Johnson 25 s Kentucky
Matthew S. Miller 28 s Alabama
Solomon Miller 28 s Alabama
Leroy Miller 26 s Alabama
William S. Kennard 29 m unk
 Elizabeth Kennard 26 m unk
Francis L, Green 26 m Alabama
 Mary Green 18 m Alabama
David O. Warren 27 m South Carolina
 Elizabeth Warren 19 m Tennessee
Sarah Odell 27 w Tennessee
Joseph Shackleford 21 s unk
Matison Fuller 22 s unk
Thomas McDonald 35 m unk
 Elizabeth McDonald 25 m Missouri
Joseph Ship 50 m South Carolina
 Sophia Thompson Ship 49 m Georgia
William Ship 27 m Kentucky
 Minerva Ship 20 m Alabama
Henry Williams 45 m North Carolina
 Maria Williams 40 m North Carolina
Nathaniel Hintons 22 s(?) unk
Jesse Hardy 30 m unk
 Eliza Hardy 31 m unk
George T. W. Collins 22 s(?) Louisiana
Benjamin Lindsay 55 m Tennessee
 Mary Ammy Lindsay 45 m N. Carolina
Nolan Anderson 25 m unk
 Delila Anderson 24 m unk

Thomas Lindsey 22 m Louisiana
 Mariah Lindsey 17 m Louisiana
William Williams 21 m Louisiana
 Elizabeth Williams 17 m La.(?)
Martin White 40 m Louisiana
 Sarah White 30 m unk
Umphries Chappell 45 m unk
 Sarena Chappell 28 m unk
Stephen Jones 45 s Virginia
Thomas Wright 33 m unk
 Mary Wright 31 m unk
Abraham Large 30 m Tennessee
 Drucilla Latham (Zady) Large 25 m Ark.
Isaac Large 23 m Tennessee(?)
 Rebecca Large 14 m unk
Jacob Large 50 m Tennessee(?)
 Deborah Large 41 m unk
Alca Large Latham 21 w unk

Tenahaw (Shelby) Municipality

William English 45 m Tennessee
 Myra Anderson English 35 m Kentucky
Jonas Harrison 50 m New Jersey
 Ellender Shannon (Nelly) Harrison 35 m
 Georgia
Emory Rains (Raines) 35 m Tennessee
 Mareener Raines 30 m Kentucky
Jonathan Anderson 36 m Kentuky
 Hannah English Payne Anderson 36 m
 Tennessee
John Buckley 47 m Virginia
 Elizabeth Buckley 45 m Kentucky
----- Elsey 50 w unk
Stephen English 25 m Tennessee
 Mary English 21 m unk
Joseph English 35 m Tennessee
 Leander English 34 m Tennessee(?)
John Choate 34 m Tennessee
 Mary Choate 24 m Tennessee
Moses (Moss) Wooten 50 South Carolina
 Margartet Wooten 40 m Kentucky
Nathan Davis, Jr. 25 m Illinolis
 Mary Davis 22 m unk

Harrison Davis 2? m Illinois
  Elizabeth Davis 17 m Tennessee
Nathan Davis, Sr. 56 South Carolina
  Jane Davis 55 m South Carolina
John Applegate 35 m unk
  Nancy Applegate 30 m unk
James English 45 m Tennessee
  Susan English 42 m unk
John English 34 m South Carolina/Tenn.
  Elizabeth Choate Blair English 30 m unk
Isaac Roberts 40 m Tennessee
  Rhoda Roberts 38 m unk
Robert Foot(e) 25 s South Carolina
John Bradley 35 w Georgia
Ann Gray 25 s unk
John Latham 45 m North Carolina
  Marguerite Rosalie Sims (Rosey) Latham 42 m Louisiana
John Forsyth(e) 29 m Kentucky
  Martha Forsyth 26 m unk
King H. Latham 27 m Louisiana
  Mary Latham 25 m Tennessee
John Critchfield 41 m unk
  Sarah Critchfield 35 m unk
----- Critchefield 35 w unk
Elanson (Alanson) Barr 35 m Vermont
  Mahaly Barr 27 m unk
Jonas English 30 m Tennessee
  Martha English 20 m Georgia
John Haley 45 m North Carolina
  Susan Haley 45 m unk
Lewis Thompson 27 m unk
  Molly Thompson 25 m unk
Thomas English 40 m Virginia/Tennessee
  Sarah English 27 m North Carolina
Jerry Boling 57 m unk
  Elizabeth Boling 50 m unk
James Boling 25 m Tennessee
  Eliza Nail Boling 20 m Tennessee
Samuel Porter 40 m Virginia
  Mary Porter 38 m Tennessee
Richard Haley, Jr. 27 m Tenn./N.C.
  Susan Haley 28 m unk
Samuel McFaddin 37 m Kentucky

  Margaret McFaddin 35 m unk
James Forsyth 28 m Kentucky
  Darius Forsyth 28 m unk
Charles Askends (Askins) w Tennessee
William Parmer 25 n Kentucky
  Malindy Parmer 24 m Tennessee(?)
Robert Goodwin 25 m Tennessee
  Sarah Goodwin 23 m unk
----- Haley 50 m w unk
Archbald Smith 28 m Louisiana
  Malinda Smith 23 m unk
Joseph Davis 50 m unk
  Mary Davis 45 m unk
Manaem Turnbull Smith 31 m Georgia
  Matilda Haley Smith 23 m Tennessee
Willis B. Watson 40 m Tennessee
  Nancy Watson 40 m unk
----- Dark 21 w unk
John Walker 29 s(?) unk
Levi Gillian 25 s unk
Edward Robertson 55 s Virginia
John Mebble 27 m unk
  Eliza Mebble 17 m unk
Shirley Gooden (Goodwin) 35 m unk
  Elizabeth Gooden 35 m unk
John C. Burk 27 s South Carolina
Henry Goodwin 55 m Georgia
  Sarah Goodwin 54 m South Carolina
Joshua English 25 m Tennessee
  Candas English 20 m unk
William Todd 48 m Georgia
  Martha Todd 47 m unk
John Beauchamp 45 m Delaware
  Susan Beauchamp m unk
Elizabeth English 60 w unk
Jerry Baum (Jeroboam) R. Beauchamp 25 s Kentucky
John Gates 47 m unk
  Jane Gates 27 m unk
John McGee 25 m Mexico
  Susan McGee 25 m unk
James Watkins 50 m unk
  Minerva Watkins 48 m unk
Richard Crawford 27 m unk

Susan Crawford 26 m unk
Richard Haley 50 m North Carolina
  Cyrena McCreary Haley 30 m Miss.
King Latham 25 m Louisiana
  Mary Latham 24 m Tennessee
----- Latham 65 w unk
James Latham 40 m unk
  Sarah Ann Latham 22 m unk
William King, Sr. 45 m Georgia
  Nancy King 35 m Kentucky
Riten Everett 30 m unk
  Anna Everett 27 m unk
Robert Smith 30 m unk
  Sarah Ann Smith 27 m unk
Joseph Jewell 40 m unk
  Winna Jewell 47 m North Carolina
J. Miller 40 m unk
  Jane Miller 37 m unk
James B. Tucker 40 w Virginia
Evin (Evan) Shoemaker 30 m Ala/Tenn
  Matilda Shoemaker 22 m Tennessee
Charles Lindsey 57 m South Carolina
  Polly Lindsey 55 m unk
L. H. Wiggins 36 m unk
  Mary Wiggins 22 m unk
M. Pettett 28 m unk
  Kizeah Pettett 27 m South Carolina
Micager (Micajah) Lindsey 31 m S. C.
  Nancy Lindsey 21 m unk
Pennington Lindsey 25 m South Carolina
  Sarah Lindsey 16 m unk
Isaac Lindsey 50 m South Carolina
  Sarah Lindsey 45 m unk
George Scott 30 s unk
John Hammona 28 m unk
  Malinda Hammona 28 m unk
Newell Hogg 20 m unk
  Dashe Hogg 17 m unk
John Hogg 70 m unk
  Mary Hogg 69 m unk
Bartlett H. Simpson 30 m Va./Tenn.
  Mary Simpson 29 m Virginia(?)
Jackson Crane 40 m unk
  Lydia Crane 35 m unk

Abraham Smith 25 m Tennessee
  Jane Smith 24 m unk
David Smith 27 s unk
George Butler 58 m Georgia
  Elizabeth Butler 59 m unk
William Henry Ashbranner 45 m NC
  Mary (Polly) Butler Ashbranner 40 m Ga.
William Carnwell 27 m unk
  Elizabeth Carnwell 27 m unk
James L. Gibson 25 s Kentucky
Juan Batiste Polvedore 31 m Loouisiana
  Luiza Polvedore 30 m Louisiana(?)
John (Juan) Polvedore 60 m, France
  Louisa Tessier Polvedore 59 m Louisiana(?)
Joseph Polvedore 28 m Texas
  Susan de los Santos Coy Polvedore 30 m Texas
David Strickland 34 m Kentucky
  Rachel Strickland 29 m unk
Edward A. Merchant 45 m South Carolina
  Elizabeth Merchant 40 m unk
John Heath 27 m unk
  Marelda Heath 23 m unk
Claborn Walker 24 s Tennessee
Nancy Galway 60 w unk
William A. Nail 47 w N. C/Tennessee.
Elizabeth Wade 48 w unk
Hardin Wright 27 m Tennessee
  Mary Nail Wright 28 m Tennessee
Andrew Jackson Nail 20 s Tennessee
Abner Nail 25 s Tennessee
Eliza Nail 25 s Tennessee
Solomon Boling 32 m Tennessee
  Lucinda Boling 25 m unk
John D. Merchant 35 m South Carolina
  Sarah Walker Merchant 28 m unk
Mason Van 47 m South Carolina
  Jane Van 45 m unk
James Alford 25 m Georgia
  Anesha Alford 20 m unk
Andrew McFadden 50 m unk
  Jane McFadden 50 m unk
Swanson Zanberry 50 m unk

Cinthe Zanberry 30 m unk
John Wicks 30 m unk
  Sarah Wicks 40 m unk
Ezekiel McCelvy 30 m unk
  Sarah McCelvy 28 m unk
John Inman 33 m South Carolina
  Prudence Inman 28 m unk
Jonathan Biddic 36 m unk
  Jane Biddic 30 m un k
Alexander C. Thornberry 55 m N.C.
  Elizabeth Thornberry 35 m unk
George Grounds 32 m Penn./Missouri
  Catherine Rice Grounds 23 m Tenn.
Christian Gross 40 w unk
Joseph Rice 27 m S.C./Tennessee
  Willie Masters Rice 25 m Ky./La.
Lemuel Rice 32 m Tennessee
  Mary Rice 30 m North Carolina
Clinton Rice 24 m Tennessee
Jane Rice 24 m Tennessee
Sarah Chappell 45 w Tennessee
Hartwell Howard 35 m Virginia
  Mary Howard 35 m unk
John Grigsby 40 m unk
  Eliza Grigsby 21 m unk
Clement Tutt 35 m South Carolina
  Milla Tutt 32 m unk
Robert Irwin 66 m unk
  Sarah Irwin 54 m unk
William McFadden 27 m Louisiana
  Clary McFadden 26 m Louisiana(?)
Isaac Dunegan 45 w unk
Samuel Strickland 40 m Kentucky
  Mary Strickland 42 m unk
Mary McCelvy 60 w unk
John Woodliff 30 s unk
John Johnson Hamons 44 m Ky.
  Malinda Hamons 22 m Tenn.
Newell Hogg 24 m unk
  Doshe Hogg 22 m unk
Joseph Hogg 54 m unk
  Rachel Hogg 53 m unk
Henry Binam 25 s unk
David Wilkenson 33 m South Carolina

  Malinda Wilkenson 29 m unk
Jose Marino 40 m unk
  Mary Marino 41 m unk
Peter Vollentine 41 m unk
  Susan Volentine 37 m unk
John Gilbert 27 m South Carolina
John Pear 29 m unk
  Martha Pear 27 m unk

Choctaw Indians 165
Males 79
Females 85
Huonnas (Caddo) Indians 53
Males 25
Females 28

<u>San Augustine Municipality</u>

Augustus Hotchkiss 35 m unk
  Anna Hotchkiss 29 m unk
Robert B. Irvine 21 s Tennessee
Almanzon Huston 36 m New York
  Elizabeth Newton Huston 30 m Pa.
Elizabeth Newton 21 s unk
Samuel Stivers 37 m New Jersey
  Sarah Stivers 27 m unk
William Scurlock 25 s North Carolina
Joseph Rowe 32 m North Carolina
  Livinia Burditt Rowe 22 m Tennessee
William M. Coot 22 s Ireland
Albert G. Kellog 25 s unk
Isabelle Hanks 61 w unk
Iredell D. Thomas 26 m North Carolina
  Penelope Edwards Thomas 25 m N. C.
Edward D. (C.?) Harris 35 m N. Carolina
  Eely S. Harris 20 m unk
Ely A. Bowen 24 m unk
  Mary Ann Bowen 35 m unk
Harman Frazier 44 m South Carolina
  Martha Wallace Frazier 35 m Tenn.
Robert C. McDaniel 32 m Virginia
  Eliza Ann McDaniel 26 m unk
James W. Bullock 40 m North Carolina
  Nancy Horton Bullock 32 m N.C.

Thomas H. Garner 39 m North Carolina
  Sarah J. Garner 32 m unk
James Gerish 36 m England
  Mary Ann Gerish 32 m unk
James Gerish Sr. 65 s unk
Thomas H. Breas 30 m unk
  Ann Mariah Breas 24 m unk
Ira Parker 41 m North Carolina
  Ann Parker 29 m unk
John Thomas 43 m Georgia
  Elizabeth E. Thomas 34 m unk
W. L. Scott 30 m unk
  Margaret Scott 16 m unk
T. (L.?) H. Mabbit 32 s Arkansas
Henry H. Lockridge 24 s unk
Charlton Thompson 26 s unk
Archibald McLaughlin 26 s unk
Stephen McLaughlin 22 s unk
James Smith 39 m unk
Benjamin Thomas 25 s unk
Obadiah Hendrick 20 s Kentucky
Edwin O. LeGrand 28 s. North Carolina
F. Swetenburg 43 s unk
Joseph Bayliss 27 s unk
William Harness 32 s unk
Calloway Deen 23 s Tennessee
William Melton 40 s Alabama
John Roland (Rolland) 22 s unk
William H. Watts 19 s unk
William A. Irvine 35 s unk
John W. Bryant 26 s Georgia
John E. Winn 33 s unk
Thomas Maxwell 36 s unk
Joel D. Raines 24 s Tennessee
Samuel Cromwell 24 s unk
Joseph Barns 25 s unk
Samuel Wick 32 s unk
David Bullock 38 s North Carolina
Samuel Edmonson 20 s unk
W. R. D. Spain 19 s unk
Elias McMullin 25 s unk
Rice McCollister 25 s unk
Sebastian Francois (Francis) 20 s S. C.
John McCoy Patton 44 s Virginia

Prosper Gular 22 s unk
Manston Sheid 25 s unk
Samuel C. Belden 29 s unk
Isom D. Sledge 25 s unk
James Pattison 21 s unk
James C. Cain 26 s Louisiana
Redmon (Reden) Gainer 27 m Ala.
  Permelia Taylor Gainer 23 m Ala.
Shelby Corzine 42 m NC/Tennessee
  Sarah Kennard Corzine 25 m N.C.
Martin Parmer 50 m Virginia
  Levinia Anderson Parmer 43 m unk
Thomas Parker 29 m unk
  Rachel Parker 19 m unk
Chichester Chaplin 34 m Ireland
  Emily Edwards Chaplin 22 m unk
S. D. Moore 30 m unk
  Nancy Moore 25 m unk
William Garrett 25 m Tennessee
  Maria Cartwright Garrett 20 m unk
John B. Dillard 43 m North Carolina
  Jane Dillard 38 m unk
Harrison E. Watson 27 m Virginia
  Mary Cooper Watson 31 m unk
Elizabeth Gross 40 w South Carolina
A. D. Latten 27 m Vermont
  Elizabeth Cooper Latten 26 m unk
Edmund Quirk 77 m Virginia
Samuel Kindall 35 m unk
  Lucy Kendall 28 m unk
Thomas Cartwright 37 m Georgia
  Ann Cartwright 34 m unk
James Kimbro 27 m unk
  Jane Kimbro 20 m unk
John (Juan) Creed Lawhorn 27 m N. C.
  Elizabeth Rebecca Arnett Lawhorn 25 m Miss.(?)
William McFarlandelizabeth ro 40 w Pennsylvania
John Gilbert Love 46 m Virginia/Tennessee
  Rebecca Exum Love 40 m Tennessee
James Marshall Love 42 m Tennessee
  Elizabeth B. Love 32 m Tennessee(?)
George Teal 45 m Maryland

Rebecca Johnson Teal 30 m Missouri
James Moss 25 m Virginia
Henry W. Augustine 30 m South Carolina
  Eliza Augustine 28 m unk
Elijah Anderson 28 m South Carolina
  Ruth Anderson 27 m Tennessee
George B. Brownrigg 42 m North Carolina
  Theresa Thomas Brownrigg 32 m N. C.
Thomas B. Garrett 35 m unk
  Lavecy Garrett 30 m unk
Susan Purnell Horton 45 w unk
Alexander Horton 25 s North Carolina
Samuel Ranier 25 m unk
  Mary Horton Ranier 17 m unk
Matthew Kuykendall 20 s unk
Edward Teal 40 m unk
Fanny Teal 35 m unk
Nathaniel Hamilton 15 s unk
Elias K. Davis 39 m unk
  Martha Thomas Davis 22 m unk
Jacob Anthony 22 m unk
  Phoebe Anthony 21 m unk
John Gilbert 43 m South Carolina
  Mary Gilbert 46 m unk
Joseph Hall 22 s unk
Nimrod Anthony 28 m unk
  Cynthia Brown Anthony 28 m unk
Lemuel Kimbro 25 s Tennessee
Edley Ewing 58 m Tennessee
  Elizabeth Love Ewing 54 m Georgia
Jonas Hale 25 m unk
  Amanda Ewing Hale 25 m unk
Wilson Ewing 36 m Tennessee
  Hannah DeSpain Ewing 32 m Kentucky
Elijah F. Hanks 27 m unk
  Eliza A. Davis Hanks 24 m unk
Robert Wyres 25 m Virginia/Penn.
  Harriet Ship Wyres 19 m Ala.
Wesley W. Hanks 20 s unk
John Husband 24 s unk

Red River Municipality
  Red River District

Daniel Morris
Albert Hamilton Latimer 32 Tennessee
  Elizabeth Richey Latimer 22 Kentucky
Richard Gideons
Edward M. Dean 36 m Kentucky
Barkley Moreman Ballard m. Virginia
Mary Gillentine Ballard m Virginia
Samuel Lemmons
Samuel F. Moore
Joshua B. Hill 25, m. Tennessee
  Synthia Hill, 22 m Georgia
Edward T. Jackson
Blackly McKinny
Talefore (Toliver) C. Chaflin 25 m N.C.
  Aginot Chaflin 21 m Tennessee
Jacob Collum 23 m Tennessee
Mary W. Collum 28 m Louisiana
James Clark
Jason Watson
Caleb Woods
Richard Peters
Isaac Cruse
Coleman Watson 35 m Kentucky
  Lucy Watson 32 m Kentucky
John H. Fowler
Hiram C. McKinney
George H. Bagby 34 m Virginia
Margaret Bagby 22 m Tennessee
Eli Barnet
Lee Morris
Daniel McKinney 30 m Kentucky
  Dorothy McKinney 14 m
Collen M. Aiken Ala
Samuel Riche
John C. Byers 21 m Texas
  Sarah Byers 19 m Texas
James Lattemer 52 m Connecticut
Jane Hamilton Lattemer 52 m N. C.
Charles Collum 38 m Tennessee
Elizabeth Katherine Hyder Collum
Jonathan Collum
John Greenwood 47 m Virginia
Hiram Brinlee Kentucky/Tennessee
Elizabeth Ann McKinney Brinlee

Charles Lewis
Levi M. Rice
Robert Morris
James Aken (Aiken) 20 m Kentucky
  Brenette Aken (Aiken) 14 m Ark.
George Y. McKenny 17 m Kentucky
  Nancy McKinney 12 m Kentucky
Henry Beven
Samuel Peters
Wilkenson Shearwood
John H. Cherry
William Watts
John W. Weaver
Mark Epperson 40 m Tennessee
  Margaret Epperson 25 m Tennessee
John C. Gahagin
Allen McClelan 19 m Kentucky
  M. G. McClelan 15 m Kentucky
John A. Reed
Jacob Gragg
George Brinlee 27 m Kentucky
  Amy McKinney Brinlee 29 m Ky.(?)
John M. Richey
George Collum
James Abraham
Samuel Richee
David West
David Clark
Ashly McKinny 40 m Kentucky
  Sally McKinney Kentucky
Alexander McAnica
James Ward
Benjamin F. Lynn 31 m Tennessee
  Julietta F. Lynn 28 m Kentucky
William Richee
Wade H. Vining
Gilbert Clark
Collin McKinney 69 m New Jersey
  Elizabeth Lee Coleman McKinney Ky.
Samuel Gragg
Younger S. McKinny 15 s Kentucky
Howard Baines
Abel Bland
Benjamin Bland

Andrew S. Beard
John Gragg
Charles Burkham
Richard M. Hopkins 26 m Kentucky
  Nancy Hopkins 20 m Tennessee
James E. Hopkins
Thomas L. Cowen
John Ware 47 m Virginia
  Anne Ware 25 m Alabama
Francis Hopkins
Robert Tramel
Henry Buckner
Curtis Jurnigin
John B. McInear
Edward Hughart 35 m unk
  Alderena Hughart 17 m unk
William Wheat 45 m Kentucky
  Ester Wheat 41 m Alabama
William B. Ward
Samuel Wilson
Dennis Hardy Sen.
John T. Smith
John Hardy Jun.
James M. Hamilton
George W. Wright 24, m, Tennessee
  Sarah Jane (Membane) Wright 13, m,
  Tennessee
Robert Ragsdale Tennessee(?)
Sherrod Rowland 15 s Alabama
Mitchell (Michael) Keller
George Bason
Thomas Ragsdale 22 m Tennessee
  Amanda M. Ragsdale 13 m N. Carolina
George W. McKirly
John R. Boon
Ambrose Douthit
John Bird
William C. Ward
Noel Arrington
Josiah Wheat 56 m Virginia
  Martha Fletcher Wheat 44 m N. C.
William King
Joseph Reid 66 w Kentucky
John Guest

Thomas D. Mitcalf
Reuben Mitchell
Robert S. Hamilton 52 w Tennessee
  Elizabeth Bethany Hamilton 37 m S. C.
William Wilson
Abner H. McKinzy
William Slingland
Ebenezer Frazier 40 m Tennessee
  J. Frazier 31 m Tennessee
Jonas Bruton
David D. Bruton 23 m Tennessee
  Marium Bruton 13 m Kentucky
Miles Reed 21 m Alabama
  Sarah Reed m. Alabama
Preston Bland
John Becknal
Benjamin Bruton
Andrew G. Milton
William A. Bucknal
Andrew G. Minton
William A. Bucknel
Robert H. Wheat
Thomas Satterwhite
Elisha Bruton 29 m South Carolina
William Becknel
Isaac H. Fishback 30 m Kentucky
  Elizabeth Fishback 23 m Illinois
Joseph J. Ward
James McDaniel
Bradford C. Fowler 24 m Kentucky
  Mary A. Fowler m Tennessee
John H. Dyer
James M. Sadler
James C. Sadler
Hiram Sadler
Felix G. Sadler
Adam Hampton
George Park
Peter Miller
Robert Maxwell
Leander W. Hancock
John Vandine (Vandyne)
Thomas Askins
Westly Askens

Sally Reid
Mathias Click 49 m Tennessee
  Lucy Click 45, m Arkansas
Stephen Peters 21 m Tennessee
  Margaret Peters 16 m Tennessee
Absalom Gidens
John Pew
Garland Geer
James J. Ward Sen.
Etheldred Peters 15 s Tennessee
Minerva Boren
Calvin M. Click 20, m, Tennessee
  Sally Click 19, m, Tennessee
David Waggoner
Joshua W. Crow
Benjamin Clark
John Morton 45 m Kentucky
  Cythia Wilson Morton 37 m Tennessee
James Richee (Richey) m Alabama
  Sarah Ann Truit Richee m Tennessee
John Tisdale 35 m North Carolina
  Ann Tisdale 19 m North Carolina
Marshal D. G. Godley
John Robbins
Joseph Levins
Hansford L. Paxton
John Humphres
Martin Crow
Balda C. Johnson
John Paxton
John Levens
William J. Paxton
Martin Binge
Robert Jones
Jesse M. C. Paxton
Francis Godly
Dickson Dyer
Joseph Hownshell
Wily W. Langham
Ira (Asa) Dean
Middleton Scarbery
John B. Styles 38 m Kentucky
  Sally Styles 28 m Kentucky
Jesse Dean

Felix Scarborough
John E. Dorse
Philip Duty
Sewell Hancock
James W. Hancock
William Johnson
James Gambell
Alexander Johnson
Asa Hickman
Ulysis Agar (Aguire)
William Stanham
Benjamin H. Dorse
Moses D. Wright
Joseph Leach
Evand Leach
William Gragg
Daniel Holbrooks
William Clapp
Martin Sitzer
Martin G. Nall
William B. Akens (Aiken) 30 m N. C.
  Aramenta Akens 32 m North Carolina
William M. Williams 26 m Virginia
  Eliza Emberson Williams 13 Arkansas
Ralph Davis
Thomas King
William Edmonson 27 South Carolina
George S. Young
John Wagly
John Emberson
Edward Wideman
Thomas G. Wright 30 m Tennessee
  Mary Wright 29 m North Carolina
James Stonham
Nicholas Levins Louisiana(?)
John Land 45 m South Carolina
  Matilda Land 31 m Mi.
John R. Cradock 27 m South Carolina
  Louisa E. Cradock 12 m Tennessee
George W. Cox
James Hofflefinger
John Nall
Westly Byers
Josiah D. Lawson

Isaac Wilson
Henry Proctor
William Coleman McKinney m Kentucky
  Margaret (Polly) Dooley McKinney m
William R. Revier
Wilson McCrenry
William Brunton
Meredith Hart
James Barkman
John M. Nugent
Joseph Deck
John Rowland
Francis Hopkins
Alexander Bell
John Fizer
John Ragsdale
William Ragsdale
William Fowler Wright
Aaron Hanscome
Gabriel Martin
George C. Witmore
  Henrietta Wright Whitmore
George F. Keller
Adam R. Tabler
Sarah Pendergrass
Bennet T. Logan
Randolph C. Harris
Hatton P. Benningfield
Allen P. Douthit
Thomas Talbott
John S. Downee
Joseph J. Dew
George W. Dyer 25 m North Carolina
  Caroline Dyer 22 m North Carolina
John Nugent
Andrew Hampton
Benjamin Lankford
Harrison Brummet
John S. Porter
Squire Mays
Ira S. Poor
Samuel Moore Fulton 35 m Virginia
  Clara Roberts Fulton m
Nathaniel Dandridge Ellis 27 m Va.

Frances Claughton Routt Wyatt 15 m Va.
Joseph James
Ellenor Lankford
James McKinny 38 m Kentucky(?)
   Mary McKinney McKinney 31 m Ky.
Andrew Willett
James Levins
Elizabeth Poor
Margaret Talbot
Wesly Talbot
Elijah W. Talbot
Durant H. White
Joseph Wood
John Barkman 50 m Indiana
   Hannah Davis Barkman 42 m Kentucky
James Levins, Jr.
Henry Russell Lattemer 18 m Tennessee
   Elikzabeth Gattes Lattemer
Comodore Collier
John H. Kernal
Collen M. Collen (Collin)
Bushrod W. Osborne
Lavinia Mornen
Samuel J. Burress
Robert Cravens
Elijah Young
James H. King
Wily Thompson 37 m South Carolina
   Cynthia Thompson 23 m Georgia
Wily Weatherspoon
Thomas Bromly
Jonathan Hopkins
Richard Ellis 54 m Virginia
   Cherry Dandridge R. Smith m Va.
Henry S. Jones
Sampson Moss
William R. Brown
Farrow Rachon
Henry Shockey 26 m Virginia
   Rachel Shockey 22 m Kentucky
Selvester Williams
Elbert Matthews
Jacob Barkman
Barkley Nall

Elisha Simmons
William Murry 21 s Tennessee
Samuel W. French 42 m Kentucky
   Sarah French 43 m North Carolina
Hugh B. Shaw
Henry Stout
James Stout
Robert Dyer
Jarret Janes
William Heath
Bryant Homes
Robert Nall
Isaac Reid
Daniel Cornelius 55 m S.C./Md./Ark.
   Mary (Polly) Hathorn/Stallings m Ill.
Benage Loyd
Hiramm Loyd
William Watson 20 s(?) Tennessee
Martha Ingram
John H. Nall
John Lick, Sr.
Jonathan Cockram
Isaac Murfy
James Rodes 24 m North Carolina
   Sarah Rodes 28 m South Carolina
Joseph Woods
John Onstatt 35 m North Carolina
   Mary Onstatt 29 m South Carolina
Clark Simmons
Isaac Clover
William Shaw, Jr Tennessee(?)
Abraham Wagly 68
Mathias Mowery 21 m North Carolina
   Malinda Giddens 16 m Kentucky
John Jackson
William Henry Harrison Hopkins 50 m Va.
   Elizabeth Hopkins
William Shaw, Sr. 51 m Tennessee
   Susanna Shaw m
Richard M. Hopkins
John Price 28 m Kentucky
   Mary Price 27 m North Carolina
John Hanks
Lewis C. Dennison

John Walker
Martin Ragsdale 21 s Tennessee
George W. Smith 33 m Tennessee
   Mary Smith 31 m Kentucky
William Browning 32 m Georgia
   Hardena Browning 26 m Georgia
Asa Jarman
Eldridge Hopkins 28 m Illinois
   Harriet Hopkins 26 m Kentucky
Nancy Dicas
Benjamin S. Clark 46 m South Carolina
John Watkins
Elijah McDaniel
Jacob Lacy
James Osgood
William Byrnsides
J. W. Steward
Samuel Byrnsides
John Daniel 44 m Germany
   Rhoda Daniel 29 m Tennessee
Isaac H. Jones 45 m North Carolina
   Rosiania Jones 34 m N. Carolina
Richard H. Finn
James Peace
Jacob Black
James N. Smith 33 w North Carolina
Robert Hamilton
John Sanders
William Creager
Daniel McKinney 65 m New Jersey
   Peggy McClure McKinney
James Graham
Precious Seats
Josph Wagly 31 m North Carolina
   Martha Wagly 26 m Germany
Phillip Cornelius 25 m Arkansas
   Margaret McCowan Corneius 17 m Ill.
Isaac Tyler
Needham Boon(e) 45 m North Carolina
   Elizabeth Robertson Boon(e) 44 m Ga.
William McFarland
Philip Jackson
Massaak H. Janes
Matthew McCabe

Evan Watson
Evan Watson, Jr.
William Collum 37 m North Carolina
   Martha (Patsy) McKinny 34 m
John Barkman 50 m Indiana
   Hannah Barkman 45 m Kentucky
Standly Williams
William F. Morris
Abner Azkey
Fielding Azkey
Hezekiah Walter
Jesse Kitchens
Preston Kitchens
Mary Hays
Joseph Strickland
Jesse Watson
Joseph Bowman 24 m Illinois
   Martha Bowman m Arkansas
Aaron Vanwinkle
John Davis
Noel Scarbrough
Samuel Worthington 35 m Tennessee
   Mary (Polly) Barnes 30 m Tennessee
William Bartee
Christopher Roland
Erasmus Tidwell
Samuel S. Hervy
Leven Hampton
Jacob Buzzard
Richard F. Sullivan
Philip Trammell
David T. Jones
James McMahon
Richard Rhodes
Henry Vincent
William Christopher Ingram 23 S. Carolina
   Rachel Luray Fields Ingram
James R. Myers
John A. Bryant
Morgan Mott
Josiah Garland
Samuel S. Alsop
Joseph Wagly 31 m North Carolina
   Martha Starks Wagly 26 m Germany

Philip Cornelius 25 m Arkansas
   Margaret McCowan Cornelius 17 m Ark.
Isaac Tyler
William Boyes
Elizabeth Ann Forbes w
Patsy Kitchens
Morris Ward
William Cribb
Joseph Watkins
Rebecca McGowan w
Jeffry Brown
Lewis Dayton
John Edmonson
Hugh Fitzpatrick
David Strickland
Edward Owen
Robert Hill
James Holland 30 m Kentucky
   Malinda Holland 28 m Kentucky
John Ball
David Andrews
William Knight 30 s South Carolina
Mary Ann Hampton w
Aquilla Davis
John Irons
Joseph W. Davis
Johnson Bowers
Abner Lee
Moses Williams
James H. Johnson
James Barker
Robert Gamble
Thomas Wilson
Alexander Smith
Adam Wright
Richard Graham
Thomas Barns
Samuel Bush
Hugh McCelby
Granville Morris
John Prophet
Abraham Ogden
Travis G. Wright 30 m Tennessee
   Mary Wright 24 m North Carolina

Mary Johnson w
John Jackson
John Atkins
John H. Dyer
Ensign B. Smith
Zachariah Boltons
Alexander O. Witmore
Luke Roberts
Hugh Smith
William Bartee
John Levins
James W. Boon
Emanuel Grubbs
Sylvester Williams
Hodge Adams
William Adams
Daniel Thompson
Dixon Noble
William C. Carithers
Thomas Tomlinson
Francis Rousseau
Nelson Roubdaux

<u>Fannin District</u>

John Russle
James M. Garner
Jacob Black
Nathaniel Thomas Journey 25 m Tenn.
   Vasti Langford Journey m Arkansas
Thomas Mahurin Illinois(?)
John L. Dillingham
Davis Cunningham
William H. Anderson
Sarah Cross w
Joseph Murphy
Joseph Swagerty
Charles Quellen
William Onstatt 59 m North Carolina
   Elizabeth Onstatt 49 m Kentucky
William Martin
James Garland
William M. Williams
Elender Spencer

William McBee
Daniel Davis
Ancil C. Peck
Bushnel Garner
Fred L. Hart 18 m Arkansas
  Martha Hart 19 m Arkansas
Martin Hart
  Mary Green m
John Hart 45 m North Carolina
  Pryor Hart 20 m North Carolina
Thomas S. Smith
David C. Strickland
William Mason
Robert B. Fowler
Gabriel Chenoeth
William Lankford
Jesse Wallace
Levi Russle
Jefferson Ivey
George Dameron
James Fisher

Sources: Residents of Texas: 1782-1836, Vol. 3; Ericson, Gateway to Texas, Vol. I; Gifford White, First Settlers of Red River County, Texas (Nacogdoches: Ericson Books, 1981); Gifford White, First Settlers of Fannin County, Texas (Nacogdoches: Ericson Books, 1981); Gifford White, Character Certificates in the General Land Office (St. Louis and Nacogdoches: Ingmire Publications and Ericson Books, 1985).

In September 1835, a detachment of Mexican troops arrived in Gonzales determined to commandeer a small six-pound cannon in the posession of Empresario Green DeWitt. A group of Texas volunteers equal in numbers to the Mexican force, on October 2, 1835, launced an attack on the Mexicans and sent them in full retreat toward San Antonio. Without fanfare, the Texas Revolution had begun.

PART IV

THE TEXIANS (TEXANS)

124

THE REVOLUTION YEARS

The following month (October 1835), a large force of Texans under the command of Stephen F. Austin began marching toward San Antonio; while Captain George Collinsworth with a second group of volunteers captured Goliad (La Bahia). In November Austin was replaced as commander by Edward Burleson who continued the march on San Antonio. In early December a force of some 300 volunteers, led by Ben Milam, launched an assault on the old colonial capital, and after five days of battle the Mexican commander surrendered the town. The ease with which the Texans had captured San Antonio led them to believe that the revolution would soon be over.

Convention of 1836. Soon thereafter, an election ordered by the 1835 Consultation was held February 1, 1836, its purpose the selection of delegates to attend a convention to meet March 1 at Washington-on-the-Brazos. Stephen William Blount, Edward Oswald LeGrand, and Martin Parmer represented the San Augustine District; Samuel Price Carson, Richard Ellis, Robert Hamilton, Albert Hamilton Latimer, and Collin McKinney the Red River District; William Clark, Jr.and James Taylor Gaines the Sabine District; William Carroll Crawford and Sydney O. Pennington the Shelby District; Stephen Hendrickson Everitt and George Washington Smyth the Jasper District; Michael Branamour Menard the Liberty District; Robert Potter, John S. Roberts, Thomas J. Rusk, and Charles Stanfield Taylor the Nacogdoches District; and William Bennett Scates and Claiborne West the Jefferson District.

Blount was born in Burke County, Georgia February 13, 1808, son of Stephen William and Elizabeth (Winn) Blount, and died February 7, 1890. He came to Texas in August 1835 settling in San Augustine where he married Mrs. Mary (Landon) Lacy in 1838.[189] LeGrand was born June 28, 1801 in North Carolina, son of John and Margaret (Chambers) LeGrand, and died in 1861 and buried in Macune Cemetery twelve miles south of San Augustine. He came to Texas in 1833 with his wife, Martha McGehee whom he married in North Carolina

---

[189] The New Handbook of Texas, Vol. 1, pp. 599-600; Biographical Directory of Texan Conventions and Congresses, p. 53.

in 1825 from Alabama, settling in the Ayish Bayou community.[190] Potter was born in June 1799 in Granville County, North Carolina and was killed March 2, 1842, and buried at Potter's Point in northeast Texas but reintered in the State Cemetery in 1928. He married first Isabel A. Taylor in April 1828 in North Carolina who divorced him in 1834 and second Harriet A. M. Ames in Texas in 1836. He arrived in Nacogdoches in 1835, then moved first to Harrison County in 1837 and later to Marion County.[191]

Carson was born in Pleasant Grove, North Carolina January 22, 1798, son of John and Mary (Moffit) Carson and died November 2, 1838 in Hot Springs, Arkansas and buried there. He married Catherine Wilson, daughter of James and Rebecca Wilson of Burke Coluntyh, North Carolina May 10, 1831. He immigrated first to Mississippi about 1835 then to Miller County, Arkansas the following year.[192] Ellis was born February 14, 1781 in the Virginia Tidewater section, son of Ambrose and Celia (Stokes) Ellis, and died at home in Bowie County, Texas December 20, 1846, buried in the family cemetery near New Boston, and reintered 1919 in State Cemetery. He married January 9, 1806, Sarah (Watson) Dandridge of Hanover County, Virginia. He immigrated first to Alabama about 1815 then in 1834 to Pecan Point, now located in Miller County, Arkansas.[193] Hamilton was born about 1783 in Scotland, son of William and Euphemia (Alston) Hamilton, and died in Saratoga Springs, New York, August 16, 1843. He came to the United States about 1807, settling in Granville County, North Carolina but moved to Texas in 1834 locating in the Red River community.[194] Latimer was born May 5, 1800 in Huntington, Tennessee, son of James L. and Jane (Hamilton) Latimer, and died January 27, 1877 in Clarksville, Texas. He married first Elritta Smith September 3, 1828 in Tennessee, second Elizabeth Richey 1833 in Tennessee, and third Mary Gattis September 21, 1857, in Texas. He came to Texas in 1833 settling in the Pecan

---

[190] Ibid, Vol. 4, p. 152; Biographical Directory, pp. 122-123.

[191] Ibid., Vol. 5, p. 299; Biographical Directory, p. 156.

[192] Ibid., Vol. 1, p. 994; Biographical Directory, pp., 63-64.

[193] Ibid., Vol. 2, pp. 832-833; Biographical Directory, p. 80.

[194] Ibid., Vol. 3, p. 430; Biographical Directory, p. 95.

Point area.¹⁹⁵ McKinney was born April 17, 1766 in Huntington County, New Jersey, son of Daniel and Massie (Blatchley) McKinney, and died September 9, 1861 in McKinney, Collin County, Texas, buried at Van Alstyne, Texas,¹⁹⁶

Everitt was born November 20, 1806, in Poughkeepsie, New York, and died in New Orleans July 12, 1844. He married Alta Zera Williams and immigrated to Texas in 1834 locating in the Bevil Settlement.¹⁹⁷ Smyth was born May 1803,in North Carolina and died in Austin February 21, 1866, buried in the State Cemetery. He married Frances M. Grigsby in 1834 in Texas. He immigrated first to Alabama then to Tennessee while still a child and finlly to Nacogdoches, Texas, later moving to the Bevil Settlement in 1830.¹⁹⁸

Menard was born December 5, 1805, at LaPrairie, near Montreal, Quebec, Canada, son of Michel and Marguerite (de Noyer) Menard, and died at home in Galveston September 2, 1856, buried in the Catholic Cemetery, Galveston. He married first Marie Diana LeClerc of St. Genevieve, Missouri about 1832, second Adeline Catherine Maxwell in 1837, third Mary Jane Riddle in 1843, and fourth Rebecca Mary Bass about 1848. He immigrated to Minnesota about 1818, to Illinois in 1822, to Missouri about 1825, to the White River area, Arkansas about 1826-1827, and to the Pecan Point community in 1828.¹⁹⁹

Clark was born April 14, 1798 in Bedford County, Virginia or North Carolina and died January 13, 1872 in Nacogdoches, buried in Oak Grove Cemetery in Nacogdoches. He married Martha B. Wall. Clark immigrated first to Georgia, then to Louisiana, then to Sabine County, Texas in 1835, and finally to Nacogdoches County about 1850.²⁰⁰ Gaines was born November 14, 1776, in Culpeper County, Virginia, son of Thomas and Susanah (Strother) Gaines, and died November 12, 1856, buried in Oakland, California. He married first Isabella

---

[195] Ibid., Vol. 4, p. 102; Biographical Directory, pp. 121-122.

[196] Ibid., Vol. 4, p. 419; Biograp;hical Directory, p. 182.

[197] Ibid., Vol. 2, p. 910; Biographical Directory, p. 82.

[198] Ibid., Vol. 5, pp. 1122-1123; Biographical Directory, p. 174.

[199] Ibid., Vol. 4, p. 613; Biographical Directory, p. 137.

[200] Ibid., Vol. 2, p. 138; Biographical Directory, pp. 66-67.

Christian of Tennessee, second Katherine Vincent of Indiana, and third Susanah Norris of the Nacogdoches Municipality. Gaines moved to Bastrop County in 1845 and in 1849 joined in the California Gold Rush.[201]

Crawford was born September 13, 1804 at Fayetteville, North Carolina, son of Archibald and Nancy (Carroll) Crawford, and died September 13, 1895 in Erath County, Texas, buried in Cow Creek Cemetery five miles north of Dublin, Texas. He married Rhoda Jackson Watkins about 1834. He immigrated to Georgia about 1820, then to Alabama about 1830, then to Shelbyville, Shelby County, Texas in 1835. A Methodist minister he moved to Hill County, Texas about 1882 and then to Alvarado, Johnson, County, Texas about 1884.[202] Pennington was born February 27, 1809 in Kentucky and died October 28, 1837 in Shelby County, Texas. He immigrated to Arkansas by 1830 and to the Tenaha community in 1834.[203]

Scates was born June 27, 1802 in Halifax County, Virginia, son of Joseph and Elizabeth Scates, and died October 9, 1863, buried in Osage, Colorado County, Texas, reintered 1929 in the State Cemetery. He married first Theodicia Clardy Smith November 17, 1836 and second Sarah McMillan March 25, 1850. Scates immigrated first to Christian County, Kentucky about 1810, to New Orleans, Louisiana about 1820, to Anahuac, Texas March 2, 1831, and to Washington County, Texas about 1837.[204] West was born about 1800 in Tennessee and died September 10, 1866 in Guadalupe County, Texas. He married first Anna Garner, second Mrs. Prudence Kimbell, widow of George C. Kimble, and third Florinda McCulloch Day. He came to the Liberty District of Texas in 1831, moved to Montgomery County, Texas about 1840, and to Guadalupe County about 1850.[205]

Revoutionary Highlights. Expectations among the Texans in late 1835 and early 1836

---

[201] Ibid., Vol. 3, pp. 42-43; Biographical Directory, p. 87.

[202] Ibid., Vol. 2, p. 396; Biographical Directory, pp. 72-73.

[203] Biographical Directory, pp. 152-153.

[204] The New Handbook of Texas, Vol. 5, p. 912; Biographical Directory, p. 168.

[205] Ibid., Vol. 6, p. 886; Biographical Directory, p. 187.

were dashed beginning in March of the later year. Early that month a Texan force of some 150 men was met and destroyed by Mexican troops; near the middle of the month a Texan force was defeated at a battle near Coleto Creek and subsequently massacred at Goliad; and also early in the month a Mexican army of some 6,000 men besieged the Alamo in San Antonio de Bexar, took it by storm, and slew almost all of its defenders.

The 1836 convention appointed Sam Houston commander-in-chief of Texas forces. Houston proceeded to South Texas where he immediatly assumed command. When Houston learned of the advance toward his smaller army of a much larger Mexican army, he ordered a retreat toward the Brazos River. As the news of the retreat of the Texan Army reached the East Texas settlements brought by fleeing civilians and soldiers, widespread fear developed and the frontier began folding back toward the east.

Runaway Scrape. Loading wagons, oxcarts, sleds, or horses, the frantic settlers, mostly women and children, began a desperate rush to keep ahead of the oncoming Mexican Army. Their flight, known as the "Runaway Scrape," effectively depopulated the western and central parts of the state. The Runaway Scrape became a mass panic wherein horrified Texas civilians fled before Houston's small retreating army that was pursued by thousands of Mexican regulars.

This development was only one of a series of events in the early history of East Texas that produced an ebb and flow of individuals back and forth across the area from the Red River in Western Louisiana to the Angelina and Trinity Rivers in Eastern Texas. At any given moment in the evolution of settlement in the region, as events dictated, an individual or an entire family might be located for a time in a Western Louisiana Parish or in one of the settlements of East Texas.

These almost ceaseless migrations across the Sabine River were prompted by a series of historical circumstances beginning in the last years of the Seventeenth Century when the Spanish first began to penetrate East Texas. By 1719, the French had established a fort at Natchitoches on the Red River causing the Spanish to counter by establishing six missions, five of them in a line from the Neches River to Los Adaes near the Red River in present-day Louisiana (only some thirty miles from Natchitoches). For the next four decades, the Spanish and French continued to stake claim and counterclaim to the territory between the Red River and Sabine River, but the Arroyo Hondo, a small stream in Western Louisiana, was the operative boundary.

In 1762, circumstances changed radically when the French king ceeded the Louisiana Territory to Spain to prevent it falling in the hands of the English. Five years later, a Spanish colonial official reported that this disputed territory was sparsely populated. At the same time adventurous traders began spreading the word of the beauty and fertility of East Texas throughout the United States. Those enticing reports touched off the first wave of a tide of immigration that began easing over the frontier, a wave composed of French settlers from Louisiana, Anglo-Americans from the United States, and immigrants from Europe.

In 1779, when the Spanish began repopulating East Texas, old settlers who had fled as well as newcomers crossed the Sabine from Louisiana into Texas. This migration was further fueled by events in 1800 and 1803. In 1800, Spain transferred the Louisiana Territory back to France, and in 1803, the French sold the territory to the United States bringing the land-hungry and aggressive Anglo-Americans to the eastern boundary of Texas.

Added pressure was created early in the Nineteenth Century by a series of filibustering expeditions into Texas. The Philip Nolan Expedition in 1800-1801, the McGee-Gutierrez Expedition in 1811-1813, and the Long Expedition in 1819-1821 combined to make living conditions in Eastern Texas unacceptable for many settlers caught in the crossfire. Many for a variety of reasons left their homes and sought refuge across the Sabine River. As a result the eastern region of the Texas province became critically depopulated.

Not until 1821 and the successful conclusion of the Mexican Revolution did the settlers who fled in the previous two decades begin gradually returning to their homes. The return of more settled conditions in the 1820s and generous Mexican colonization laws served to bring about a significant resettlement movement.

That movement was slowed in 1826 and 1827 when settlers in the area around Nacogdoches opposed to the Fredonian Rebellion and afraid of a rumored attack by Indians and retaliation from the Mexican government again retreated across the Sabine onto American soil. However, in 1827, when the Fredonian Rebellion collapsed, many, but not all, of the settlers who fled began to trickle back across the Sabine and pick up their lives where they left them before their flight.

East Texas settlers were not destined to be left in peace and safety for long. Within five years, the gathering clouds of the Texas Revolution were once again to produce an ebb and flow. Many, perhaps most of those who fled percipitously in the "Runaway Scrape" of 1836, never returned. Nevertheless, news of the victory at the Battle of San Jacinto and the subsequent creation of the Republic of Texas brought many of them back across the Sabine to their abandoned homes.

Finally, immigration of settlers was significantly influenced by the generous land policies of the Republic of Texas. The new nation literally threw open her doors to settlers with promises of tempting land grants to individuals but expecially to those with families. Those policies tempted old settlers who had fled and newcomers from Europe and the United States to avail themselves of the virtually free land offered by the Republic of Texas in open-handed fashion.

Populating Eastern Texas. In the 1830s all of East Texas remained a frontier area populated for the most part by the rough and ready people usually found in such places. Immigrants from the United States continued to stream through the Sabine River gateways on their journeys to the interior. Many liked the towns or the surrounding countryside and decided to stay. Several hundred Indians: Choctcaws, Seminoles, and others from the Creek Nation likewise crossed the boundary river and alarmed local officials. Other immigrants, deserters from the armies of the United States and Mexico, came in sufficient numbers to cause further unease in the towns of central East Texas. The clouds of impending war failed to dampen the flow of immigrants across the Sabine. In Nacogdoches alone, from January to December 1835, 822 entrance certificates relative to permission to settle were issued. Even after the declaration of war, they kept on coming.

On hearing the news of the victory at San Jacinto and the resumption of civilian governments, many of those who fled in to "Runaway Scrape" began returning swelling the number of settlers incoming. After the revolution the settlements on the Eastern frontier of Texas underwent a new period of development.

From 1836 to 1838-1839, Nacogdoches, along with other communities in central East Texas, experienced a period of relative calm. But that period of tranquility was destined to endure for little more than two years. Under the surface calm was the fact that most citizens of Mexico did not recognize the independence of Texas considered the defeat at San Jacinto only a temporary loss, and formulated plans to reclaim the errant province. Moreover, many former Mexican nationals living in Texas were dissatisied with the outcome of the Revolution and resented having to become citizens of the new predominately Anglo-American nation.

As early as March 1837, rumours of a projected attack on the towns of Nacogdoches and San Augustine by a combination of Mexicans in the vicinity and Indians to the north began circulating but were generally ignored. In central East Texas the principal one of the unhappy Mexicans was Vicente Cordova. He had settled in Nacogdoches as early as 1826 and became active in community affairs.[206] In the summer of 1838, he organized a group of dissatisfied Mexicans and some Indian allies in an effort to recapture Texas for then Mexican nation. Known as the Cordovan Rebellion, the outbreak was put down by a force of some 600 volunteers under the leadership of General Thomas J. Rusk, causing Cordova and a part of his rebels to flee westward managing to reach Mexico in the spring 1839. Fearing an outbreak of hostile actions against them, many of the Spanish-speaking residents of the area fled, some westward toward San Antonio de Bexar and others eastward across the Sabine. Thereafter, the numbers of Spanish-speaking individuals and families were sharply reduced. In the Nacogdoches Municipality, for example, census takers in 1834 found some 688 Spanish-surnamed persons in the municipality down from over 890 in 1806, but 1850 federal census takers located only some 276 such persons.

TABLE XVII

PARTICIPANTS: CORDOVAN REBELLION

Juan Jose Acosta	Andres Bermea
Jose Maria Arocha	Juan Batista Bodan
Eligio Alvarado	Juan Lorenzo Bodan
Juan Francisco de Arriola	Nicholas Bodan
Alfred Bandyham	Pierre (Pedro) Bodan
Thomas Bandyham	Juan Francisco Calderon
---- Bartolo	Antonio Calderon
Jose de la Baume	Daniel Carter

---

[206] Ericson, Gateway to Texas, Vol. I., p. 84.

Juan Carro	Francisco Manuel Morris
Antonio de la Cerda	Jacob Musgrove
Petit de la Cerda	Lorenzo Navarro
Domingo Cervantes	Jose Neyetto
Francisco Cordova	Nathaniel Norris
Juan Manuel Cordova, Sr.	Candelario Perez
Jose Zeferiano Cordova	Francisco Perez
Telesforo Cordova	Jose Pollonio
Vicente Cordova	Jose Anselmo Prado
Juan de los Santos Coy	Juan Prado
Juan Cruz, Jr.	James Quinilty
Guillermo Cruz	John Quinilty
Napoleon DeWaltz	Jinio Rameras (Ginio Ramirez)
Obadiah Dimery	Antonio de los Reyes
William Donovan	Joshua N. Robertson (Negro)
Baptiste Dortolan	More Rablo
Rafael Dortolan (Negro)	Juan Jose Rodrigues
Jose Maria Durango	Antonio Sanchez
Antonio Flores, Sr.	Sequemundo Sepulveda
Francisco Antonio Flores	Petit (Antonio) de la Serda (Cerda)
Antonio Flores, Jr.	Marfil (Margil) Sharnac
Martin Flores	Ignacio Sims
Jose Maria Games	William Smith
Marcus Garcia, Jr.	Juan Francisco F. Tobar
Thomas Guerrera	Miguel Torres
Manuel Herrera	Francisco Valdez
Miguel Herrera	Andres Vernuella
Pierre Labina	Chisanto Villanova
Julio Lazarin	Estevan Villanova
Juan Babtiste Levan	Anastacio Ybarbo
Juan Longoria	Benigno Ybarbo
Georgie Lopez	Candelario Ybarbo
Juan Lopez	Jose Maria Ybarbo
Encarnacion de Luna	Juan Ybarbo
Juan Luna	Luciano Ybarbo
Cayetano Martines	Manuel de los Santos Ybarbo
Dolores Martines	Manuel Mariana Ybarbo
J. Vicente Micheli	Miguel Barbo
Crecencio (Cresences) Morales	W. M. Robinson
Jose Morin	

Source: Devereaux, Tales from the Old Stone Fort, pp. 89-92.

Indian Troubles. A more serious threat was posed in the meantime by deteriorating relations with the Indians who had settled just to the north and west of the Nacogdoches-San Augustine region. Repeatedly they had been promised land grants in the area by both the Mexican governments and then by the government of the Republic, but none had been forthcoming.

Rejection of their claims added to the slow but steady encroachment on their lands by white settlers created ever increasing friction between the Cherokees, Kickapoos, and Shawnees. More animosity was generated in 1838 when General Thomas J. Rusk and his army of volunteers began a march on the Cherokees culminating in a battle in which the Kickapoo village was destroyed and eleven warriors slain.

Sporadic raids in 1838 and 1839 by Indian bands further enhanced the growing friction between white settlers and the Indians. Believing that the Mexican government intended to enlist the aid of the Indians in an attempt to reclaim their lost Texas lands, President M. B. Lamar determined to expel all Indians from East Texas. Thus, in July 1839, Kelsey H. Douglass was given command of about 500 militiamen under the overall command of Edward Burleson, Willis H. Landrum, and Thomas J. Rusk and ordered to move the Indians into the western section of the Arkansas Territory, a part of present-day Oklahoma. By July the Indians were driven out of the boundaries of Texas and into the Arkansas Territory. The Alabama and Coushatta tribesmen were allowed to remain in Texas, however, but were removed to lands in the Big Thicket of East Texas.

Immigrants in large numbers took advantage of this opportunity and promptly entered the area vacated by the departed Indian bands. In a few years enough of them had settled and the region was organized into counties with prosperous towns springing up throughout it. These new counties included Harrison, Henderson, Rusk, Houston, and Anderson.

The Regulator-Moderator Feud. Removal of the threat of Indian incursions did not rid Central East Texas of all trouble. By 1839 a feud had developed in Shelby County that ultimately involved all of the region. Trouble had been brewing for some ten to twelve years. Its roots were embedded in the easy access to the Shelby County area from the Neutral Ground to the east. During those years, little or no legal authority existed allowing hundreds of desperadoes, outlaws, robbers, and other social outcasts to take up residence and live almost totally unrestricted lives but at the same time in constant fear of each other.

Among the various types of such persons were Americans fleeing from justice seeking asylum, speculators dealing in fraudulent land titles, and members of organized bands of thieves, counterfeiters, robbers, and swindlers. Posing as honest voters, they elected cohorts to local office and thereby gained immunity from prosecution. In sheer numbers, they did not constitute a majority or even a plurality of the citizens of Shelby County, but through trickery they gained control of local government.

In 1839, a dispute between Joseph Goodbread and Sheriff Alfred George erupted that soon involved the whole community and spread to neighboring counties as well. An ex-riverboat captain and fugitive from Louisiana, Charles W. Jackson, quickly joined Sheriff George and organized a band of men which he named the Regulators. Their awowed purpose was to supress crime and other types of violence. Edward Merchant then organized a rival band known as the Moderators to curb the activities of the Regulators.

In mid-year 1841 events led to the eruption of violence: murder, arson, vandalism, kidnapping. The Regulators took possession of Shelbyville, the county seat, and threatened members of the rival Moderators. The feuding groups in 1844 signed a truce but very soon violence again broke out. Both sides then recognized that one of them must achieve a final victory, prompting groups to launch a vigorous recruiting campaign and causing the entire population of the county to join one side or the other. Thereupon, volunteers from nearby Harrison and San Augustine Counties were organized to help bring peace and order. Surviving evidence suggests that nearly all of the men who ultimately actively engaged in this feud were small farmers, recent immigrants, who had been pursuaded to join the fray by unscrupulous men.

Ultimately both bands abandoned Shelbyville, and the Regulators erected a number of fortified camps as did the Moderators setting the stage for a series of bloody encounters. President Sam Houston visited the area after learning of the perilous situation. He immediately issued a proclamation calling on all persons engaged in the feud to lay down their arms and retire to their homes. To reinforce his proclamation, Houston, in August 1844, ordered Travis G. Broocks and Alexander Horton to take command of the militia forces of San Augustine, Sabine, Nacogdoches, and Rusk Counties and restore peace and order.

Leaders from both sides were arrested and brought to trial in San Augustine before District Judge William B. Ochiltree, Isaac Van Zandt, and Senator David S. Kaufman. An agreement disbanded both groups, ordered them to disavow the names Regulators and Moderators, and commanded them to forgive, forget, and to resist any further feuding. Thus, law and order was finally restored in Shelby County.

New Local Governments. In 1837, the Congress of the Republic of Texas began reorganizing local governments. The existing Spanish-Mexican scheme of alcalde, ayuntamiento, sindico, and other local officials was replaced by the typical county officials of the American south: county judge, commissioners court, sheriff, clerk, justices of the peace, and constables. Municipal officers alcalde, regidores, and sindicos were replaced by mayors, aldermen, secretaries, and tax collectors.

In 1837, Houston, Jasper, Jefferson, Liberty, Nacogdoches, Red River, Sabine, San Augustine, and Shelby Counties were organized followed in 1838 by Fannin, in 1841 by Bowie and Lamar, in 1842 by Harrison, and in 1846 by Angelina, Cass, Cherokee, Collin, Grayson, Henderson, Hopkins, Hunt, Newton, Panola, Polk, Smith, Titus, Tyler, and Upshur. Also in 1837, towns began to be incorporated. Among those incorporated in East Texas that year were Nacogdoches, San Augustine, and Milam in Sabine County.

Post Revolution Days

The period from 1836 to 1850 constituted a distinct era in the development of Eastern Texas. Life in most locales was full of vim and vigor. Immigrants from the United States and from a number of foreign nations continued to arrive in ever increasing numbers. At the same time, the demographic composition of some areas, notably in the Nacogdoches vicinity and in the region just north of the Nacogdoches, San Augustine, and Shelby settlements and south of the settlements in the Red River and Fannin areas, changed markedly.

In the years following the end of the war of 1812, the Caddos, Wichitas, and other East Texas Indian bands were faced with new pressures which forced them to move even further west. "Anglo-American settlers flooded into the Red River Valley, displacing Indians settled there, bringing alcohol, depleting game; in addition emigrant Indians moved into the region and by 1830 outnumbered the resident Caddos" and their allies.[207] Since the first mission was established by the Franciscans in 1690, the Caddos, Wichitas, and related bands in Northeast Texas had gradually but steadily had their numbers decline and their lands dimish in area. Epidemics occured "about every generation" after European penetration; and the Osages "bore down [upon them] during the last quarter of the Eighteenth Century." By the last years of the Eighteenth Century their inability to obtain trade goods, coupled with political confusion among them casued primarily by disease caused further decline.[208]

Thereafter, in 1820 the federal government ceded all of present-day Oklahoma and the western part of Arkansas to the Choctaw, Chickasaw, and Cherokee Indians. All American settlers living in the region were driven out by military force--some such as Joseph Reed and William Humphries and their families--returned to Alabama or another American state; Claiborne Wright and family, J. J. Hall, Jim Ward, and others merely crossed the Red River into Texas. "Some went back east, but the biggest part crossed over the Red River." Students of the period estimate that some 5,000 people were forced out of Southeastern Oklahoma.[209]

Northeast Texas Pioneers. Those pioneers who came to the Red River area of Northeastern Texas in the years immediately after 1820 came overland from Missouri and Arkansas riding horses or mules or driving oxen. Some from states east of the Mississippi River came to Little Rock on boats and thence overland, while some trappers and traders came in canoes up the Red River.[210] Settlers coming from the north and northeast to Collin County and other parts of the region found that the area was "more accesible by land. . .than was South or West Texas. The route most frequently used by these new settlers was the Texas Road, which came from St.Louis, Missouri, through Oklahoma to Preston on the Red River, where it joined Preston Road. Preston Road was established in 1841 and completed in 1843.

---

[207] F. Tod Smith, The Caddos, the Wichitas, and the United States, 1846-1901 (College Station: Texas A&M Press, 1996) p. 10.

[208] Ibid., pp. 9-10.

[209] Stroud, Gateway to Texas, pp. 28-29.

[210] A. W. Neville, The Red River Valley, p. 10.

On its way, it passed from Preston through the western part of Collin County to Dallas and on to Austin and San Antonio."[211] Between 1840 and the coming of the railroad some thirty years later, the road was the principal immigrant route into northern Texas.

The Republic of Texas began issuing land certicates to eligible settlers by 1837. Thereafter, hundreds of individuals became holders of land certificates entitling them to various amounts of the nation's public land. Holders of such certificates "frequently gave a surveyor from one-fourth to one-half of the land as a fee for his services. And some. . ., particularly those who obtained their grants as bounties for war service, sold their certificates to surveyors or other second parties, who in turn located land under them and received patents as assignees of the original holder or sold the certificates to third parties who finally became the actual land owners."[212]

Historians Stroud and Neville have identified some of the earliest Anglo-American pioneers who settled in the Red River region. Stroud cites Sally Reed and her son and daughter-in-law, Joseph and Cynthia Ann (Humphries) Reed, an Alabama native, who arrived in 1816, as did Collin J. McKinney, Daniel McKinney, Claiborne Wright, of Tennessee, Jim Ward and J. J. Hall, probably from Alabama, William and Rebecca (Reed) Humphries, Alabama natives. Arriving in 1820 were Jim Clark who married a Hopkins girl, Henry Jones who married Nancy Stiles, and John Stiles. George, William and Travis G. Wright, sons of Claiborne, Col. Robert Jones, Ben Milam, and Jim Clark, son of Benjamin Clark, were also early settlers.[213]

Neville identifies the earliest settlers as: John and Jason Wilson (1816); J. W. F. Pierson (1818), John and Luke Roberts (1820); Richard Ellis, John Hart, Frank Hopkins, and Henry Stout (1823); Collin McKinney, James Clark, John Emberson, and Adam Hampton (1824); William Ragsdale (1825); Squire Mays and James Osgood (1826); Bradford Fowler (1830);

---

[211] J. Lee Stambaugh and Lillian J. Stambaugh, <u>A History of Collin County</u> (Austin: The Texas State Historical Association, 1958), p. 22.

[212] W. Walworth Harrison, <u>History of Greenville and Hunt County, Texas</u> (Waco:Texian Press, 1976), p 10.

[213] Stroud, <u>Gateway to Texas</u>, p. 29.

Mitchell Keller (1832); Henry Shockey, Asa Jarman, John R. Craddock, Sam M. Fulton, Robert Cravens, James Stoneham, M. Hart, Robert Wheat, and William Stout (1833); Wiley Witherspoon, John Rowland, George Bason, Joseph Deck, E. Wideman, Caleb Wood, Matthias Click, Adam Hampton, A. McClennon, B. M. Ballard, Sherrod Rowland, and John C. Bates (1834); John H. Williams, Lawrence W. Tinnin, Thomas King, Ralph Davis, Harrison Brummett, William M. Williams, John A. Rutherford, J. P. Majors, Reddin Russell, Larklin Rattan, Wesley Askins, Isaac Cruse, George W. Cox, John V. Cherry, Joseph Houndsell, Alex McAnier, John Pew, S. R. Cherry, John H. Fowler, William Blundell, Robert Patton, J. H. Mebane, Edward H. Tarrant, T. B. Chaffin, John Harris, and James Graham (1835)[214]

Some of the settlers who came to the Bowie County region followed the old southwest trail, later known as the Military Road, through Arkansas to Texas. While others came down the Red River in keel boats propelled by oars, still others came on pack-horses, following the various existing Indian trails.[215] A few of the hardy pioneers who settled in the Bowie County area were James Reeves, who came from Kentucky in 1818; Nathaniel Robbins, Henry Jones, W. P. Roberts, later killed by Indians, and the Humphries family in 1818 as well; Richard Ellis, born in Virginia but came to Texas from Alabama with his family and his slaves in 1823, settled at Spanish Bluff, and died on his plantation in 1849; Samuel P. Carson and his brother about 1824 from North Carolina; and Collin McKinney who came from Arkansas in 1824, although he had born in New Jersey in 1766, and he died in Collin County in 1861.

Collin M. Aiken who came from Kentucky and settled in 1836, as did Josiah W. Fort and Jane Lane from Tennessee. Howell W., Hardin R., Edmond S. and Hiram Runels arrived from Mississippi in 1840 along with Eli and Thomas Moores from South Carolina. (Eli Moores married Minerva Jones, born 1829, Miller County, Arkansas.)[216]

Chandler and Howe described these Bowie pioneer planters in romantic terms, saying they "had large plantations, and many slaves. They were a happy-go-lucky, contented lot. They

---

[214] See his history of Lamar County.

[215] Barbara Overton Chandler and J. Ed. Howe, History of Texarkana and Bowie and Miller Counties, Texas-Arkansas (Texarkana: J. Ed. Howe, 1939), p. 17.

[216] Ibid., pp. 20-21.

rode hard, fought hard, and sometimes drank hard, but they were courtly, chivalrous, gentlemen. Their word was their bond, and they lived the lives of dignified ease."[217]

A list of the early settlers of Grayson County demonstrates that in 1836 came George C. and Daniel V. Dugan, sons of Daniel Dugan, Sr., Daniel Rowlett from Kentucky, Richard H. Locke from Tennessee, Daniel Slack from Mississippi, John and Edward Stephens from Alabama, and also about 1836 Garrett F. Lankford. Coming somewhat later but before statehood were Jabez Fitzgerald, Mark Roberts, Nat. T. Journey, Charles Smith along with Andy Thomas, Donaldson Davis, James Daugherty, and Colonel Holland Coffee. (Coffee married Sophia Suttonfield, daughter of William and Laura Suttonfield, in 1837 at Old Washington.)[218]

Arriving about 1840 were John B. Denton, William C. Young, Dr. John M. Hansford from Kentucky, W. G. Cooke, John R. Farrett, William R. Baker, Thomas and John G. Jouett, John P. Simpson, and John Hart.[219] In 1838 and 1839 came Micajah Davis, William C. Caruthers, J. T. and Thomas Jouett, Bailey English and David Montague. Also arriving then were James S. Baker, Jesse F. Benton, Amos Merrill, J. B. Craig, W. M. Williams, B. Fowler, and Thomas F. Smith.[220]

A Hopkins County historian has identified the following pioneer settlers: the Hargraves family (Robert, J. P., E. Glen, and W. W.) who settled between 1842 and 1844; Billy Barker, Billy Mathis, and Robert E. Mansell in 1844-1845; Johnson Wren, Captain Merett Brannon, and Nash (Wash.?) Cole about 1845; Francis, Dave, and Eldridge Hopkins families late 1830s; Thomas C. Clark, Abner McKinzie, Sam W. Smith, Henry Barclay, James D. Clifton, Wilshire Bailey, S. G. Coyle, Luther Waggoner, Miller Green, Sam Lindley, Red Collins, Crockett H.

---

[217] Ibid., p. 22.

[218] Mattie Davis Lucas and Mita Hulsapple Hall, <u>A History of Grayson County, Texas</u> (Sherman: Scruggs Printing Co., 1936), p. 25.

[219] Ibid., pp. 34-35.

[220] Ibid., pp. 37-39.

Campbell, and Sealin Stout between 1836 and 1846.[221]

According to W. Walsworth Harrison, no permanent Anglo settlements in Hunt County before 1843 have been verified although there were reports of temporary settlements, like that of B. F. Green and his party, as early as 1839."[222] Known early settlers in the county included Isaac Banta in 1839, Warren and Sterling Williams, Elisha Parival, James Hooker, Lewis W. Moore, James R. Horton, and Levi Moore in 1840; William, John W. and David Lane by 1844; Meridith and John Hart, McQuinney Howell Wright, Col. James Bourland, George W. Dunbar, John D. Williams, George Williams, Godfrey G. Smith, and Isaac Riley also by 1844; John Stewart in 1843 from Fannin County; Rev. Benjamin Watson, Benjamin Oldham, Andrew McDonald, Ben Anderson, Dixon Allen, Parson Wiley J. SoRelle, and Peter Barrow in 1845; and Lindley Johnson and Wiley A. Mattox in 1846.[223]

Anglo-Americans began settling in the Cass County area some seven or eight years before Stephen F. Austin's colony went to Southeast Texas in 1821. "Reliable historians have shown that the first permanent settlements of Anglo-Americans were along Red River east of Clarksville, Texas by 1815. Some of them migrated in to Cass County."[224] An earlier settlement, known as Monterey, had been established about 1812 or 1814 in the southeast part of the original Cass County. Some local historians maintain that it was started as a "hideout and meeting place for rapscallions, thieves, murderers, and other disreputable characters" from the nearby area known as the Neutral Ground or "No Man's Land."[225] Later poor crops and the Panic of 1837 in the United States caused large numbers of immigrants to enter Texas during the late 1830s and throughout the 1840s. As a consequence of this and other factors, by 1850, some 600 families had established homes in Cass County.

---

[221] E. B. Flemming, Early History of Hopkins County (privately published, 1902), pp. 50-90.

[222] History of Greenville and Hunt County, Texas (Waco: Texian Press, 1976), pp. 11-12.

[223] Ibid., pp. 12-18.

[224] Nita Jaynes and Willard G. Jaynes, History of Cass County, Texas (Cass County Historical Society, 1972), p. 5.

[225] Ibid.

In 1965, an East Texas historian observed that "rivers were the highways of America in the early 1800s, and it was along Red River that the first Americans made a permanent settlement in Northeast Texas."[226] By 1830, a well settled community had been established at Pecan Point near the northeast corner of present-day Red River County. When settlers there and close by along the Red River became relatively numerous, immigrants began to spread southward along long-established Indian trails, notably the Cherokee Trail later called the Nacogdoches Road. That road entered Titus County near its southwest corner, and went north along the boundary line between Titus and Franklin Counties. It was used repeatedly by persons traveling to and from Nacogdoches.[227] It was along those Indian trails that the first permanent white settlers in Titus County located.

Some of those early setters were Andrew Jackson Titus with his father in 1832, Kendall Lewis in the late 1820s from Georgia, James F. Box and Isaac Burton in 1836, Joseph Reed in 1834, Tillman Smith in 1837, Benjamin Gooch, Joseph Harris, Joseph Binnion, Alexander Nevill (Nevil/Neville/Nevils), and the W. B. Stout in 1838, as well as the Blundell and Coats families about 1838. Also arriving in the 1830s was Ambrose Ripley, In the 1840s came John B. Stephens, Dunstan Taylor, Robert Andrew Cochran, and John Evans, Jr. Other settlers coming in the 1840s were Henry W. Jones, William, Lee, and John Hall, Ranson Rogers, William C. Batte, James S. Harris, and C. C. Carr, Sr.

According to Doyal T. Loyd, "When the white settlers began to come into Texas from Arkansas, Tennessee, and Kentucky, most of them came by the Cherokee Trace (Trail)."[228] The first white settler in Upshur County, John Cotton, settled near the Trace, as did Isaac Moody and O. T. Boulware. When the Indians were removed from Texas this road became well traveled by thousands of early settlers. That Cherokee Trace "came into Upshur County northwest of Simpsonville [located about fifteen miles south of Pittsburg and fifteen miles north of Gilmer] and crossed the southern border near East Mountain [in the southeast corner

---

[226] Taylor Russell, History of Titus County, Texas (Waco: Texian Press, 1965), p. 2.

[227] Ibid.

[228] A History of Upshur County, Texas (Waco: Texian Press, 1966)., p. 3.

of the county north of Gladewater] and forded the Sabine near Longview's city water plant."[229] It was a well-known route through Camp, Titus, and other northern counties.

Only a few people had settled in the Upshur County area until about 1839 when the Indians were removed. Thereafter, "hundreds of the early settlers from the United States came. . .in covered wagons overland from the old states, and others by boat to Jefferson [Marion County] and left there to settle with friends and relations already there."[230] In 1836-1837, only three white families were living in Upshur County. John Cotton had settled along Lily Creek in 1835. In 1836, he was joined by Isaac Moody who settled near West Mountain on the old Cherokee Trace and in 1838 by O. T. Boulware who located near John Cotton.[231] In 1840, W. Boyd and A. B. Denton, brothers-in-law, settled in the region.

Northeast Texas in 1850. In 1850, Texas was included in the federal census for the first time. That enumeration revealed that some 45,248 freemen and 21,218 slaves lived in the thirteen counties that were a part of the old Red River Municipality. Harrison County with the City of Marshall as its county seat held more than one-fourth (26 percent) of the freemen and nearly one-third (33.1 percent) of its slave population. Four other counties in the region: Cass, Red River, Fannin, and Titus contained an additional 16,332 freemen (36 percent) and 8,848 more slaves (41.7 percent). Those five counties, then, held almost two-thirds of all freemen and almost three-fourths of all its slaves. Table XVIII provides data on 1850 population distribution in Northeast Texas.

TABLE XVIII

1850 CENSUS: NORTHEAST TEXAS

Freemen		Slaves	
County	Number	County	Number
Bowie	2,912	Bowie	1,866
Cass	4,991	Cass	3,518

---

[229] Ibid., p. 9.

[230] Ibid., p. 6.

[231] Ibid., p. 22.

Collin	1,950	Collin	432
Cooke	220	Cooke	123
Fannin	3,788	Fannin	3,788
Grayson	2,008	Grayson	602
Harrison	11,822	Harrison	7,013
Hopkins	2,623	Hopkins	352
Hunt	1,520	Hunt	198
Lamar	3,978	Lamar	1,296
Red River	3,906	Red River	1,807
Titus	3,636	Titus	1,208
Upshur	1,894	Upshur	1,784

An analysis of all the relevant data, including the 1850 federal census, reveals some significant immigration patterns for those persons who came to Northeast Texas before 1850. Two such patterns are particularly prominent. In one of them individuals, families, and sometimes whole communities originated in Virginia or Carolina moved first to Kentucky or Tennessee, then to Arkansas or Missouri, then to Ohio, Indiana, or Illinois after the War of 1812 if the men were veterans of the war, if not then directly to Texas. In another pattern they originated in Carolina or Georgia, moved first to Tennessee or Alabama, then to Arkansas or Mississippi, then to Missouri or Louisiana, and ultimately to Texas.

This northeastern corner of Texas attracted only 295 foreign-born immigrants (approximately 0.6 percent of the total population) from some thirteen nations, but principally from Germany (including Prussia and Saxony), England (including Scotland and Wales), and Ireland. A few Indians remained namely some one dozen members of the Choctaw Nation.

Nine Dixie states furnished more than 12,374 immigrants, with five of them: Tennessee, Alabama, Kentucky, North Carolina, and Georgia accounting for 9,544 individuals. Arkansas and Missouri accounted for 2,952 others. Immigrants from traditionally Southern or border states made up over fifty percent of the inhabitants of seven Northeast Texas counties in 1850:

namely, Titus, Upshur, Fannin, Collin, Cooke, Grayson, and Hunt.

Of the more than 45,000 free settlers of Northeast Texas in 1850, only about 1,775 had been born in a northern state. Some fifteen of those states were represented, but six of them: Illinois, Indiana, Ohio, Iowa, Pennsylvania, and New York contributing over 1,700 of them. Those northern-born settlers were primarily from four states: Illinois, Indiana, Ohio, and Iowa. A considerable number of those may have had southern roots, since rather large numbers of southern men who were veterans of the War of 1812 left their southern homes to take up bounty land grants for their wartime service.

Central East Texas Settlement. After order had been restored following the Fredonian Rebellion, a Mexican garrison commanded by Colonel Jose las Piedras was stationed in Nacogdoches, Samuel Norris was reinstated as its alcalde, and a general amnesty was proclaimed for participants in the uprising except for some of the leaders. A Mexican inspector who visited the community in 1828 reported a significant change in the life of the settlement. He wrote that he was disturbed that here in the old outpost as elsewhere in Texas the Mexican population was being relegated to lesser positions, none owned a mercantile establishment, and few occupied professional status. The Spanish-surnamed residents were being overwhelmed by the flood tide of Anglo-American immigrants.[232] That trend continued in mounting proportions. An 1834 Mexican census reported the European population of Texas stood at 24,000 compared with only 2,000 in 1820, but of those 24,000 persons, some 20,000 (more than 80 percent) were Anglo-Americans.

The illegal entry of foreigners, principally Anglo-Americans, increased steadily after

---

[232] Ericson, Early East Texas, pp. 66-67.

1826. They infiltrated the territory and stubbornly refused to obtain legal permission to become permanent settlers. By 1830, the volume of immigrants caused Mexican authorities to view them as a threat to Mexican control over the area. As a consequence, on April 6, 1830, the Mexican National Congress decreed that citizens of foreign countries adjacent to Mexican territory could no longer enter and settle in Texas. By this action, the government hoped to close the door to further Anglo-American immigration, but it was far too late to achieve that end.

During the brief interim between the Fredonian Rebellion and the outbreak of the Texas Revolution, the residents of the old Ayish Bayou settlement now known as the Municipality of San Augustine determined to find a permanent site for a town to meet their needs for local government, trade, and other community activities. Thus, in 1832, a committee of fifteen men was selected at a mass meeting of the inhabitants to select a site for their new town. The committee ultimately opted for a site between the Ayish Bayou and the Carizzo Creek on the east side of the bayou. They recommended that the town (present-day San Augustine) be located on a spot along the Camino Real where an Indian village had existed and where an early Spanish mission had been established.

Early Shelby County Settlement. The Spanish-Mexican prohibition against settlement within twenty leagues of the boundary prevented legal settlement in the areas immediately west of the Sabine River. As a result, this strip of land tended to attract persons given to violence and lawlessness, thereby discouraging permanent residents. In 1827, however, that part of the territory in the northern portion of the Nacogdoches Municipality was organized as the Tenaha (Teneja, Tenaha, Tenahaw) District with Nashville (now Shelbyville) as its principal settlement. It included territory now comprising Shelby, Panola, Harrison, Rusk, Upshur, and Marion Counties.

Later, in 1835, this district was reorganized as the Tenahaw Municipality, and the next year was renamed the Shelby Municipality. Nashville (Shelbyville) was designated the seat of government in 1837 when Shelby County was formed, remaining as its county seat until 1866 when it was moved to Center. Most Anglo-American settlers in the district came from the states of the Old South and brought with them the institution of slavery in spite of the Spanish-Mexican prohibition against human slavery. Thereafter, slaves made up a substantial portion of its population. In 1847, a state census revealed that the county had contained 763 slaves or twenty-three percent of its 3,318 residents.

Early Sabine County Settlement. About 1803 John James (Jack) Cedar, a German national, became the first European settler in present-day Sabine County. He soon married the daughter of the Captain of the Spanish garrison, Maria Belgarda, at the Borreagas Crossing of Borreagas Creek in the northern part of present-day Sabine County. The area was then a part of the Nacogdoches Municipality, but from 1832 to 1835 became a part of the San Augustine Municipality, before the Municipality of Sabine was created.

In 1828, the Milam settlement was established in the northern section of the Sabine District along the King's Highway, and in 1858 became the first county seat of Sabine County. Also growing up in the northern section of the district was the Geneva Settlement, originally known as Shawnee Village. By far the largest number of early settlers in the district were Anglo-Americans entering Texas via the ferries across the Sabine River. One of the best known and often used ferries was established about 1814 by James Gaines.

The southern portion of the original Nacogdoches Municipality along the Neches River began to be settled by Europeans and Anglo-Americans between 1800 and 1810. There the incoming settlers encountered Cherokee, Alabama, and Cousatta Indians, the later recent immigrants from Louisiana. These early immigrants were predominately from the American South, many of whom determined to resume the slave-holding society with which they were familiar. The thick forests and unfavorable soils, however, were not suited for growing cotton or tobacco, hence many quickly left the area. Most of those who remained became poor white farmers who owned no slaves.

One of the first settlements in the region was known as Fort Teran, located on the Neches River where it crossed the Old Spanish Trail from Nacogdoches to Liberty. Another early community was called Town Bluff in what is now known as Tyler County.

Early Cherokee County Settlement. The first immigrants in the Cherokee County region were Caddo Indians, a part of the Hasinai Confederacy, who settled in villages near and along the Old San Antonio Road. In the winter of 1819-1820 Cherokees fleeing westward "first found refuge in Texas." By 1822, the Mexican governor of Texas reported 100 Cherokee warriors and 200 women and children within the province. "New bands continued to join their kinsmen until the tribe occupied the land north of the Old San Antonio Road between the Neches River on the west and the Angelina River on the east, territory now comprising Cherokee and Smith Counties, together with parts of Gregg, Rusk, and Van Zandt Counties.[233] For a time, they formed thereby a barrier to Anglo-American settlement

---

[233] Hattie Joplin Roach, The Hills of Cherokee (Ft. Worth: News Printing Company, 1976), p. 5.

delaying it until after 1832.

In December 1837 a family of early settlers, the Killough family, arrived from Talladega County, Alabama, composed of Isaac and his four sons: Isaac, Jr., Allen, Samuel, and Nathaniel and two daughters: Mrs. George Wood and Mrs. Owen Williams, with their families. They initially settled five miles west of present-day Mt. Selman in Cherokee County. Less than a year later, October, 1838, most of the family was slain in what became known as the Killough Massacre.

The State of Coahuila and Texas granted a total of fifty-six titles to 65.5 leagues of land within the present boundaries of Cherokee County. Among those receiving grants were: Joseph Durst, James Dill, and Henry Berryman about 1830; Peter Ellis (Ellis P.) Bean and wife Candace Midkiff about 1825; John W. Box, Roland W. Box, William S. Box, Samuel C. Box, and James E. Box in 1826.

Early Settlement in Rusk County. In that part of East Texas that became Rusk County, the Spanish never established any permanent settlements, and it was not until 1829 that the first Anglo-Americans came to establish such communities. The first land grant was issued March 22, 1829, to William Elliott, while other early grantees included the Williams brothers, Thomas and Leonard, Joseph Durst, and Henry Stockman.[234] By 1834 white settlers had arrived in such large numbers that in March of the year some forty-three land grants had been awarded. These new settlers arrived by way of Trammell's Trace, the Nacogdoches Road, and the Green Grass Trail. The Indian trail known as Trammell's Trace began at St. Louis, Missouri, crossed into Texas at Fulton, Arkansas, then meandered in a southwesterly direction

---

[234] The New Handbook of Texas, Vol. 5, p. 724.

to Nacogdoches. In 1824, the Trace was cleared by Trammell and Andrew Davis.[235] The Trace became a permanent route thereafter for much traffic and the main highway for travelers from Harmony Hill to Marshall. Most settled in the eastern portion of the area since the Cherokees and Shawnees occupied the western part of the area until 1838.

Most of the incoming colonists came from the Old South, particularly from Tennessee, Georgia, North and South Carolina. The first three applicants for land grants were: William Elliott in 1829, Thomas Williams and Leonard Williams about 1830. Other early applicants included: James McCune in 1829, Joseph Durst, Henry Stockman, and William Williams in 1834, Robert W. Smith and Mary A. O. Mariotine in 1835, and James Smith in 1838. From May 2, 1835 to November 23, 1835, forty-three land grants were issued in what now comprises Rusk County, at least sixteen of them to Mexicans.[236]

Early Panola County Settlement. Two confederacies of Indians, the Caddos and the Hasinais, lived in the Panola County area, with the Sabine River marking the approximate dividing line between them. They were widely known as the Timber Tribes. They were, of course, a temporary barrier to white settlement. Early white settlers entered the area by traveling on the Red River, or along the trails known as the Old San Antonio Road and Trammel's Trace.[237]

The earliest white settlement was established by Daniel Martin in 1833. The Martins came from Missouri, built a small fort, and set up a trading post on Martin's Creek. Later, a

---

[235] Rusk County Genealogical Society, Remembering Rusk County (Dallas: Curtis Media Corporation, 1992), p. 2.

[236] Dorman Winfrey, A History of Rusk County, Texas (Waco: Texian Press, 1961), p. 13.

[237] The New Handbook of Texas, Vol. 5, p. 46.

second settlement was established near the site of present Clayton by Reverend Isaac Reed and a large group of relatives. Still later, "after the Texas Revolution in 1836, the area experienced a great land rush. In 1837 the LaGrone Settlement was established east of the Sabine River near the Louisiana border. . . .By 1840, at least forty-nine families were living in the area that became Panola County. The majority came from Tennessee, North Carolina, South Carolina, and Alabama."

Increasing Settlement. Even as the clouds of impending war gathered immigrants continued to pour across the Sabine River. In Nacogdoches alone, from January to December 1835, 822 entrance certificates were issued by Mexican officials while untold numbers entered without obtaining official sanction. The 1836 declaration of war did not deter most immigrants. Moreover, during the winter of 1835 and the spring of 1836, volunteers for the Texas army continuously passed through Nacogdoches and other frontier settlements on their way to battle. They persisted in coming in significant numbers for months after war's end.

One of the most troublesome problems that plagued Spanish and Mexican colonial officials was the control of smuggling across the Sabine River. In time, a Smugglers' Road or El Camino del Caballo (Horse or Mule Road) or Contraband Trace became a feature of East Texas life. As early as 1780 this road from Natchitoches in Western Louisiana to San Antonio and beyond was a well-known and well-established alternative to the King's Highway. The Smugglers' Trace and the King's Highway were not the only routes through East Texas. Hundreds of Indian trails and animal trails criss-crossed the forest. These routes continued as roadways for the post Revolutionary settlers.

East Texas Pioneers

Although the names of many of the earliest pioneering settlers of the East Texas area have been lost, a considerable number of them were recorded. They have survived in the form of Spanish and Mexican land records and censuses, muster rolls of Spanish, Mexican, and Anglo-American military units, local and regional histories, and other miscellany. Their names and some account of their lives follow below.

<u>Pioneers of the Nacogdoches District</u>. In 1773, a group of Spanish colonials forced to abandon their homes at Los Adaes and in Eastern Texas petitioned Spanish colonial authorities for permission to return to their homes on the frontier. Led by Gil Antonio Y'Barbo most of them survived to relocate at the site of an ancient Indian village and later Catholic mission in the valley between the Banita and La Nana Creeks today known as Nacogdoches. In 1779, they formed the nucleus of the first permanent European settlement in East Texas. The seventy-five heads of families and single adult men who signed the petition and made the return trek were:

Antonio Gil Y'Barbo	Manuel Mora	Candide San Miguel
Juan Mora	Cristoval Equiz	Francisco Ramirez
Augustin Sanchez	Melchor Morin	Pedro Sanchez
Juan Jose Sanchez	Juan Josef Pacheco	Pedro de Luna
Roribie de la Juente	Antonio del Rio	Manuel Lisonde
Josef Zepeda	Miguel Ramos	Francisco Cruz
Pedro Mansolo	Mariano Padilla	Juan de Tobar
Bernabe del Rio	Gasper Ruiz	Nepemucene de la Cerda
Joaquin Cordova	Diego Herrera	Melchor Benitez
Cristoval Padilla	Francisco Cerda	Manuel Barrela
Juan Manuel Padilla	Juan Martinez	Cristoval Garcia
Manuel Mendez	Juan Ygnacio Guerrero	Joseph Calderon
Cayetene Gomez	Dimas Meya	Manuel Trexe
Matis Sanchez	Ygnacio del Rio	Cristoval Ballexe
Marcos Martinez	Francisco Losoya	Domingo Carmena
Salvador de Esperanza	Juan Chirino	Jose Maria Cambero

Joaquin Mansolo	Pedro Rincos
Ambrosio Vasquez	Patricio Padilla
Vicente Cepeda	Gregorie Soto
Pedro de Sierra	Juan de Torres
Barte Soto	Jacinto Mora
Thomas Gutierrez	Nicolas Mora
Gabriel Padilla	Jose Domingo Barcenas
Francisco de Torres	Victor Mansolo
Gil Flores	Manuel Cruz
Lasare de Torres	Manuel del Rio
Francisco Guerrero	Augustin Morillo
Bernarde Cervantes	Usiderie Egunio
Juan Josef Santa Cruz	Ramos Verero
Thomas Y'Barbo	

[Source: Ericson, Gateway to Texas, Vol. I (first edition), p. 178.]

In addition to William Barr and Samuel Davenport, pioneer traders who were residents of Nacogdoches in 1804, other Europeans who had arrived by that date included Jean Sarnac, French merchant, Jose Lucobiche, Italian farmer, Jean Rosales, French carpenter, Estevan Goguet, French farmer, James Dill, Anglo-American farmer, John McFarland, English farmer, James Quinelty, Irish farmer, Bernardo Dortolant, French soldier, Pierre Dolet, French farmer, Pierre Lafitte, French farmer, Michel Bensan, French farmer, Atanacio Poisson, French farmer, Michel Rambin, French farmer, Jean Salvador, French farmer, Pierre Robleau, French farmer, Louis Fortune, French carpenter, Antonio Duboys, French farmer, Francis Prudomme, French farmer, Andrew Valentine, French farmer, Jacques Chastain, French farmer, Francis Morvanm French farmer, Jose Miguel Crow, English farmer, Jose Tecier, French farmer, Antonio Bouguer, English farmer, Edmund Quirk, Anglo-American farmer, Jacques Lepin, French farmer, Guillermo Bebe, French hat-maker, Jean Ignace Pifermo, French farmer, Christososono Jucante, French farmer, Richard Simms, English farmer, Pierre Bosque, French farmer, Pierre Engel, French farmer, Joseph Wales, Canadian carpentrer, and Santiago Isidro, German farmer.[238] Most of those persons designated as Frenchmen were natives or former residents of the Louisiana Territory.

---

[238] 1804 Spanish Census, Bexar Archives.

Arriving in 1805 were James McNulty, Irishman, Pierre Lavigne, Frenchman, Basilio Nane, Frenchman, Jean Fonteno, Frenchman, Jean Sarnac, Frenchman, Nicholas Pont, Frenchman, Josef Campurano, Frenchman, Bernard D'Ortolant, Frenchman, Josef de la Baume, Frenchman, Miguel Binsan, Frenchman, Anthony Booker, Englishman, John O'Connor, Irishman, and John Davis, Anglo-American from Virginia.

Among those arriving in 1806 were: Louis Reliquet, Frenchman, Robert Renglan, American, Christian Hesser, German, Francois Russet, Canadian, Brown Chata, Irishman, Joseph Pallar, Frenchman, Jose Capuran, Frenchman, David Waltmann, German, Anna Alsop, American, William Johnson, American, Jonnie Rose, American, and James Cedar, German.[239] For those coming in 1809 see Appendix I. No census records exist from 1810 to 1826.

Nacogdoches District Immigrants (1810-1826). Information concerning those adults who immigrated to the district in the years between the last Spanish census and the first Mexican census follow (names of wives are indented; dates are those when the persons are first shown in official records; places indicate where they were born or where they last resided):

John Adle, 1819, Alabama
  Jeannvieve Dubois
Oliver Hazard Anderson, 1817, Indiana
  Elizabeth Webster
John Biens, 1810, Ireland
Seaborn Berry, about 1814, La.
Alfred Monroe Bevil, 1823, Georgia
  Adalia Gilchrest
Jehu Bevil, 1822, Georgia
  Annie Jane Taylor
William Bloodgood, 1824, New Jersey
  Levicy Ballew
Levi Bostic, about 1829, unk
Jabes Bradbury, 1822, U.S.A.
Francis Brown, 1809, Germany
James Whitis Bullock, about 1824, N. C.
William Burgess, 1809, Pennsyvania
Stephen Burnaman. 1821, unk
Samuel Burress, 1824-5, Louisiana

Thomas Burrows, about 1825, unk
John Cotton, 1821, unk
Warren Davis, 1821, Virginia
Abraham Denton, 1824, unk
Mary Earl, 1823, unk
Mathew Earl, 1823, Louisiana
  Nancy Matilda White
William Earl, 1821, Louisiana
  Amanda Earl
William Elliott, 1825, New Hampshire
  Maria "Polly" Williams
John English, 1825, Virginia
  Elizabeth Choate
William K. English, 1824, Virginia
  (1) Elizabeth Tittle
  (2) Myra Anderson
Fitts H. Green, 1825, unk
Jonas Harrison, 1820, New Jersey
Allen Hines, 1823, Mississippi

---

[239] This immigration data was obtained from Spanish censuses, copies of which are available from the Bexar Archives and the Barker Collection, Library, the University of Texas at Austin.

James E. Hopkins, 1824, unk
Jesse T. Jones, about 1822, unk
Micajah Lindsey, 1824, U. S. A.
John McDonald, 1825, unk
James McKinney, 1824, unk
Thomas Freeman McKinney, 1826, Ky.
  (1) Melson Watts
  (2) Mrs. Nancy Wilson
  (3) Anna G. Gibbs
William Coleman McKinney, 1824, Ky.
  Margaret (Peggy) Dooley
Daniel McNeel, 1824, unk
John McNeel, 1824, unk
Pleasant McNeel, 1824, Kentucky
Sterling McNeel, 1824, Kentucky
Nathaniel Moore, 1824, unk
Quintas Cincinatus Nugent, 1825, Miss.
William Organ, 1824, unk
Jon C. Peyton, 1824, unk
John Goodloe Warren Pierson, 1824, Ky.
Moses Plummer, 1827, Scotland
Joseph W. Polly, 1824, unk
Jonathan C. Pool, 1822, Georgia
Stephen Prather, 1821, Virginia
  Tamora Elizabeth Plowden
Emory Rains, 1824, Tennessee
Frederick Harrison Rankin, 1824, Ky.
  Elizabeth Smith

Maria S. Richards, 1826, unk
Elisha Roberts, 1824, Tennessee
Harriet Fenley Roberts, about 1825, Ga.
William Roberts, 1826. South Carolina
Moses Rose, 1827, France
Henry Rueg, 1821, Switzerland
  Marie Louise Flores
John Saul, Jr., 1824, Georgia
Fleming Scrutchfield, about 1824, Tenn.
Jacob Shannon, 1822, Georgia
Abner Smith, 1824, unk
Manaen Turnbull Smith, 1822, Louisiana
John Sprowl, 1824, unk
Jacob Stallings, 1819, Illinois
William Taylor, 1826, U. S. A.
Benjamin Thomas, Sr., 1824, N. Carolina
  Mary Ann Dickinson
Theophilus Thomas, 1824, Alabama
  Susan Winn
Burrell J. Thompson, about 1826, S. C.
James Walker, about 1819, unk
William Whitaker, 1822, Kentucky
Peter White, about 1824, unk
James Williams, about 1824, Louisiana
John Williams, about 1824, Louisiana(?)
John A. Williams, about 1824, unk
Solomon Williams, about 1824, unk

[Source: Ericson, Gateway to Texas, Vol. I].

    Ayish Bayou (San Augustine District) Pioneers. Some of the earliest settlers of the area were the Hasaini Caddos who occupied the region when the Spanish and French came beginning in the mid Sixteenth Century. In the Eighteenth Century the Spanish established a mission just south of present-day San Augustine on Ayish Bayou. The mission was ordered abandoned in 1773, but after 1779 both new and former residents moved into the area they named the Ayish Bayou District. Their numbers slowly increased while disease and threats from enemy Indians forced the Caddos to relocate in the Seventeenth Century.

    Most incoming settlers, including scattered remnants of Cherokee, Kickapoo, Delaware, and Shawnee tribes emigrated from Mississippi, Alabama, Georgia, Tennessee, and Kentucky.

In time, settlers began to move into areas further down the Ayish Bayou and the Attoyac River, but most of them remained in the Redlands, the original area of white settlement.

The earliest enumeration of the free males of the Ayish Settlement was conducted by Mexican authorities in 1826. John Sprowl, the enumerator, found just under one hundred of them. They included the following persons (wives where known were added and indented, date of immigration was also added, as was the place of birth or last residence):

Theodore Dorsett, 1825
James Whitis Bullock, 1824, N. Carolina
   Nancy Horton
William A. Gwin (or Irvin)
Edwin Hendrick
Abram Robarts (Roberts), by 1825
   Lucretia Brown (divorced)
Obedia Hendrick, 1824
Stephen Prather, by 1821, Virginia
   Tamora Elizabeth Plowden
Moses Wooton
William McDonal
Myrick Davis
Robert Wiseman
Thomas W. Spencer, 1824
Benjamin Thomas, 1824, North Carolina
   Mary Ann Dickinson
Samuel Horton
John M. Taylor
William Johnston, by 1806, Virginia
   Marie Constancia
Amos Tims
Charles Dorsett
M. S. Brake
William D. Howester
Shadrick D. Thomas, 1824, North Carolina
   (1) Sarah -----
   (2) Mrs. Lucretia Brown
   (3) Mary Brown
Wiley S. Thomas, by 1826, single
G. F. Thomas
John Buckley
Thomas Cartright, by 1824, Tennessee
   Ann -----
William H. Hodges

Elisha Robarts (Roberts), 1824, Tennessee
   Martha "Patsy" Gill
Henry Hendrick, 1825-1826
Isaac Lyndsy (Lindsey), by 1826
Aaron Colvin, by 1824
Thomas Slaughter
John Burdine
Stephen Johnson
John Shannon, by 1824
Benjamin Lyndsy (Lindsey)
James Morton, 1827
Jacob Fulcher, by 1826
   Isabella Griggs
John Fulcher
Leonard Marshel
Joseph Sims, by 1826
   Jesusa Roble
Thomas F. McKinney, by 1826, Kentucky
   (1) Melson Watts
   (2) Mrs. Nancy Wilson
   (3) Anna G. Gibbs
Daniel Elam
Lemuel P. Hopkins
----- Hopkins
----- Campbell
----- Ausborn
James Fulcher
Bailey Anderson, Sr., 1819, Indiana
Bailey Anderson, Jr., 1818, S. Carolina
   Elizabeth McFadden
Vincent Anderson, by 1824
David A. Earls
----- Tele
----- Lankford
James Quinelty, by 1804, Ireland

John Cartright
----- Fryth
James Allin
John English, 1825, Virginia
   Elizabeth Choate
Thomas English
William English, by 1824, Virginia
   Elizabeth Tittle
Jacob Shannon, by 1824, Georgia
Owen Shannon, by 1824, South Carolina
Henry Goff
Lewis Hollaway, by 1819
James Williams, by 1824, Louisiana
   Delila Palvador
James Shote
Lewis Noggin
Lewis Noggin, Sr.
Mason G. Cole, 1824
Francis Murphy
James Bridges, 1819
John Schrutchfield
John Coal
Stephen Lynch, by 1828

George Lout
----- Blackburn
Nathan Davis, 1818, South Carolina
John A. Williams, by 1824
----- Millspaugh
Josiah Sims
Antone Revo
Henry Leny
----- Howard
John Sanders, Sr., Tennessee
   Rachel Willingham
John Creepin
Bassett Bassett
John Sprowl, by 1824
----- Williams
----- Lofton
Jesse Simes
John McWilliams
----- Whitehead
Bateast Guire
Bateast Boda
John Magrue
James English
Bateast Boye
----- Bassett

(Sources: Residents of Texas, Vol. 2; Ericson, Gateway to Texas, Vol. I; First Settlers of San Augustine County).

     Pioneers of the Sabine District. The first permanent settlers of the area were members of the Ais tribe of Caddo Indians. The first European penetration came in the mid-Sixteenth Century by Spanish explorers, but settlment by non-Indians came only in the 1700s when Spanish land grants were initially issued. Late in the Eighteenth century, in the 1790s Jack Cedars, a native of Hanover in Germany, born about 1758, immigrated to Florida about 1773 and to Texas about 1803. Cedars married Maria Belgarda before 1800. Christobal Concha and David Waltman also arrived before 1800. Concha was a native of Quebec in Canada born there about 1747 who came to Texas about 1768 as a married man with family. Waltman was a German native born about 1763, was in the United States by 1789, came to Texas in 1797. He married Isabel Bebe about 1789 in Louisiana.[240]

With aid of Gaines Ferry, first established before 1796 when it was acquired by Michael Crow but in 1812 purchased by James Gaines, communities began to develop in the area. The first permanent European settlments were situated in the northern part of present-day Sabine County. Mexican land grants were issued to about one hundred heads of families and single males by 1830. The list below provides the names of many of them, indicates the date of arrival in Texas, marital status, and names of wives where known. Wives' names are indented below their husbands.

Jacob Walker, 1829, m
John McKean, 1829, m
William W. Ford, 1828, m
Henry Martin, 1822, m
Burgess Hall, 1828, s
John Maximillan, Sr., 1822, m
  Claire Maximillan
Matthew Parker, 1822, m
  Mary (Isaacks)
James Mason, 1830, m
  Elizabeth Mason
James Clark, 1823, m
  Elizabeth Clark
Willis Murphy, 1825, m
  Priscilla (Dickson)
Henry Clark, 1823, m
Elijah Clark, 1823, m
Matthew Earl, 1824, m
  Nancy Matilda (White)
Edmund P. Gaines, 1822, m.
Corene Chapple, 1822, w
Major Smith, 1828, m
Moses Hill, 1822, m
Charles McKim, 1827, s
Elizabeth White, 1828, w
Isaac Carodine, 1829, m
James Easly, 1828, s
William Mason, 1830, m
  Judith Route Blackaby

Larkin Fross (Groce), 1828, m
  Belinda (Earl)
John B. Gains, 1824, s
William Isaacs, 1824, m
  Sarah Isaacs
John Pace, 1826, S
Isaac F. Pace, 1826, s
Joel Lowe, 1828, s
John Clark, 1825, m
  Abbi Clark
Elizabeth Melton, 1822, w
William Roberts 1822, s
Louis Warren, 1825, m
Isaac Lowe, 1828, m
  Elizabeth (Parsons)
Phillip Smith, 1830, s
Martin D. White, 1822, m
  Sarah White
Joseph Eastep, 1821, m
Jesse Lowe, 1821, s
Joseph Brown, 1817, m
James Riley, 1825, m
Benjamin White, 1823, m
Neely Johnson, 1830, m
Charles McKey, 1825, s
Prissa Hood, 1830, w
Samuel Davesson, 1825, m
William Pace, 1826, m
  Elizabeth Pace

---

[240] <u>Citizens and Foreigners of the Nacogdoches District</u>, Vols. I and II.

Tabashak K. Marshack, 1828, w
James McKim, 1828, m
John Smith, 1830, m
  Mary Smith
John Crowder, 1828, m
Charles Delap, 1829, m
William T. White, 1829, m
John W. Lake, 1828, m
Aron L. Day, 1830, m
George T. Burke, 1829, m
Henry Summers, 1830, m
Richard Roberts, 1829, m
Edmond French, 1829, m
R. G. Hall, 1830, m
H. Flint, 1830, m
G. Pool, 1830, m
T. W. Scott, 1830, m
A. Powe, 1830, m
L. P. Gray, 1830, m
William Lee, 1828, m
S. P. Gray, 1828, m
James B. Saul, 1827, m
John Little, 1830, m
Eli Penn, 1828, m

S. Duncan, 1828, m
J. S. Rickey, 1828, m
Jas. E. Kean, 1828, m
Amos Green, 1830, m
K. Rawson, 1827, m
J. Goodleu, 1829, m
G. L. White, 1830, m
Allen Davis, 1830, m
Daniel Tanner, 1826, m
James Gaines, 1812, m
  Susannah (Norris)
Frederick Jones, 1829, m
Ira D. Jones, 1929, m
Damion Trew, 1829, m
Everrett H. Jones, 1830, m
Lisabel Cieders, 1828, w
Emory Jackson, 1830, m
James R. Reeve(s), 1829, s
Moses M. Dennis, 1830, s
James G. Porter. 1830, s
M. K. Lacy, 1830, m
Thomas M. Raridan, 1830, m
Simpson F. Flinn, 1830, m
Mastin Rodes, 1830, m

(Source: Residents of Texas, Vol. II).

Pioneers of the Tenaha (Shelby County) Area. During historic times the area now comprising Shelby County was inhabitated by Caddo Indians. Earliest penetration of the area by Europeans probably occured in the Eighteenth Century when both French and Spanish explorers discovered and traversed the Hasanai Indian trail which by 1714 was a part of El Camino Real (Old San Antonio Road). Sometime around 1818 John Latham, reputedly the first white settler, established a home in the southeastern part of the county. During Spanish colonial times restrictions on settlement within twenty leagues of the eastern boundary inhibited legitimate settlement and encouraged squatters. The county was first organized under Mexican authority as the Tenahaw Municipality in 1833 with Nashville, founded in 1824, as its most important town.

Mexican land grants were issued by the Mexican government to some eighty-five Anglo settlers. The list below provides the name of most of them and includes the date they first entered Texas, marital status, and name of wife where known indented.

John English, 1825, m
Stephen English, 1825, m
Patrick McDavid, 1829, s
Henry Ashabranner, 1830,m
Nathan Davis, 1822
Silby Forsythe, 1822, m
George Butler, 1830, m
Elizabeth Lewis, 1822, w
Harrison Davis, 1822, m
Samuel McFaddin, 1821, m
Jonathan McFaddin, 1825, s
William T. English, 1827, s
Moses Wooton, 1823, m
Sarah English, 1825, w
Jesse McCelvy, 1824, s
William English, 1825, m
Squire Humphreys, 1823, s
James McCelvey, 1824, m
Joseph English, 1829, m
George English, 1829
Alva R. Johnson, 1830, s
Jonathan Anderson, 1819, m
  Rachel Story, 1827, w
John C. Payne, 1825,m
James Forsythe, 1821, m
Emory Rains, 1822, s
David Strickland, 1826, m
Richard Haley, 1825, m
James Bowling, 1827, m
Edward A. Merchant, 1825, m
Manson M. Vann, 1825, m
David Wilkinson, 1823, m
Amos Strickland, 1822, m
Peter Stockman, 1830, m
Elizabeth Rogers, 1823, w
Elizabeth Graves, 1825, w
Joseph S. Palvadore, 1828, m
Charles Thompson, 1825, m
William Humphreys, 1826, m
Thomas Haley, 1821, m
William Smith. 1830, m

  Nancy Smith
Even Lowery, 1822, m
Matthew Dayne, 1822, m
Wiet Anderson, 1822, s
Elener Harrison, 1825, w
Mark Haley, 1825, m
Asa Lankford, 1830, s
Mary Aroche, 1827, w
George Humphreys, 1824, s
Nancy Mayo, 1828, w
Bailey McFaddin, 1821, s
John Little, 1827, s
Richard Haley, Sr., 1825, m
Archibald Smyth, 1826, m
Lucy Margate, 1830, w
Antonio Carr, 1826, s
Marsele Carr, 1826, s
Andrew McFaddin, 1830, m
Stephen Holmes, 1826, s
John Applegate, 1826, m
Hampton Anderson, 1825, s
Grady Anderson, 1821, s
Bailey Anderson, Jr., 1821, s
Ocela Barb, 1826, m
William King, 1828, m
Ephriam Story, 1825, m
Samuel Strickland, 1824, m
Hazard Anderson, 1824, m
Clement Tutt, 1824, m
John Turner, 1826, s
Mary Alexander, 1825, w
James Forsythe, 1819, m
Benjamin Strickland, 1826, s
Samuel Norris, 1806, m
  Sarah H. Norris
Edward Cranston, 1823, s
John Man, 1830, s
Catherine Stockman, 1824, w
Humphrey C. Hogan, 1821, m
William Van, 1829, s
George Glass, 1827, s

(Source: Gifford White, <u>First Settlers of Shelby-Harrison Counties</u>).

<u>Pioneers of Houston County.</u> The Houston County area in historic times was first settled by Caddo Indians, but in early Nineteenth Century they were joined by the Alabama-Coushattas, the Cherokees, and the Tejas Indians. Although French and Spanish explorers penetrated the area in the Seventeenth Century and a Spanish mission established there in 1690, permanent white settlement did not begin until the early years of the Nineteenth Century. The Old San Antonio Road crossed the county, and travel and trade were carried on over this route for a hundred years or more before any permanent settlements were made in the Houston County region.

Possibly the first permanent settler was Daniel McLean, who crossed the area with the Magee-Gutierrez expedition in 1812 and returned with his brother-in-law, John Sheridan, around 1821. They settled near the site of Augusta. McLean was born in Moore County, North Carolina about 1784, but was killed by Indians near Elkhart, Texas May 10, 1837. Sheridan was born April 5, 1796 and was also slain by indians near Elkhart in July 1837. He married Lucinda McLean before coming to Texas.

Mexican land grants were given as early as 1828 to members of the Joseph Vehlein Colony, among them Jacob Masters, Sr., Elijah Gosset and his three sons, and Joseph Rice. Masters was born about 1780 in North Carolina and died about 1854 in Houston County. He and his wife, Elizabeth Shaw, had at least two children. Gossett was born February 1, 1788, in Tennessee and died November 24, 1848 in Van Zandt County, Texas, buried Old Greenwood Cemetery, Crockett, Houston County, Texas. Gossett married Elizabeth Stone Edwards.

By 1830 some twenty individuals had received Mexican land grants. Their names, their dates of entrance into Texas, and their marital status appear below.

Henry Martin, 1829, s
Mary Ware, 1830, w
George W. Wilson, 1830, s
Elisha (Elijah) Clapp, 1822, s
Reuben R. Russell, 1829, s
Jacob Masters, Sr., 1829, m
Jacob Masters, Jr. 1829, s

Martin Pruett, 1823, s
Thomas Mitchell, 1830, m
Joseph Rice, 1828, m
Edward Tyler, 1823, m
Charles S. Roberts, 1830
William P. Davis, 1829, s
John Sheridan, 1829, m

161

Hannah McLean, 1825, s
Hardy Ware, 1825, m
E. D. Ellis, 1830, m

Luther Smith, 1829, m
John Moore, 1830, s
Jacob Pruett, 1822, s

(Source: Gifford White, First Settlers of Houston County).

Early land grants issued to persons living in what would become Cherokee, Henderson, Panola, Rusk, Smith, and Angelina Counties are listed in the records of the Nacogdoches District; and residents of those counties are listed in the Spanish and Mexican Censuses for the Nacogdoches District.

Pioneers of Cherokee County. The earliest arrivals in the area that now makes up Cherokee County were the Caddos who came about 780 and settled in the northern two-thirds of the county. Spanish and French explorers visited the area in the late Sixteenth and early Seventeenth Centuries. European settlement began in 1716 when a mission was founded by Spanish priests and military; it was temporarily abandoned in 1719; reestablished in 1721; and permanently abandoned in 1730.

The first land grant was issued to Nacogdoches merchants William Barr and Samuel Davenport in 1798, but they did not settle in the area. Thereafter, about 1820, the Cherokees, Delawares, Shawnees, and Kickapoos began settling north of the Camino Real. Anglo-American settlers began moving onto land claimed by the Cherokees in the late 1820s.

Rapid settlement began in 1834 with most of the early settlers coming from the southern states of the United States. The Mexican state of Coahuila y Texas granted a total of fifty-six land titles to sixty-five and one-half leagues of land within the boundaries of present-day Cherokee County. Among those receiving early grants were Peter Ellis Bean who first entered Texas in 1801 and came to Cherokee County with wife, Candace Midkiff about 1825; John M. Box of Alabama and his sons Roland W., William S., Samuel C., and James E. arriving in 1826; Joseph Durst and wife, Delilah Dill, Henry Berryman and wife Helena Dill, and James Bradshaw who came in 1830.

Other early settlers included Zaccheus Gibbs, William Roark, and Absalom Gibson who came in 1834; Sarah Ann Duncan, Barbara C. Lewis, Brooks Williams and Levi Jordan who arrived in 1835. Also arriving in the 1830's were William Hicks, J. W. Adkinson, Daniel

Meredith, and Isaac Killough with sons Isaac, Jr., Allen, Samuel, and Nathaniel, and daughters Mrs. George Wood and Mrs. Owen Williams. The Killoughs and their families arrived in December 1837 and became the victims of an Indian massacre in October 1838.

By 1839, in addition, these persons had settled in the county: Elihu C. Allison, Larkin Baker, William Bartee, Crawford Burnet, James Cobb, John Engledow, Alston and Warwick Ferguson, William Gates, Edson Gee, James Hamilton, John Harrison, Edward W. Hackett, Jesse T. Jones, Isaac Kendrick, John Malone, John McGregor, Uriah Moore, Henry Myers, Kinchin Odom, Beverly Pool, Isaac Reed, George Ruddie, Thomas Timmons, John Vaughn, Edward Baxter Ragsdale, and John Walker.

Pioneers of Rusk County. Earliest settlers in the area that ultimately became Rusk County were Caddos who arrived about 1000. Between 1761 and 1810 the Tejas Indians had also settled in the area. At least four early Spanish expeditions crossed the area between 1691 and 1810, although the Spanish never established any permanent settlements in the region.

The first Anglo-American settlers came as early as 1829, with the earliest land grant issued to William Elliott that year. Other early grantees included Thomas and Leonard Williams, Joseph Durst, and Henry Stockman. Elliott was born about 1800 in New Hampshire. He married Maria "Polly" Williams, daughter of Thomas Williams, before they arrived in Texas about 1825. Stockman was born about 1792, Natchez, Mississippi, son of C. C. F. and Catherine des Bonnet Stockman, and died February 2, 1852 in Rusk County. He married Dorcas Trebite, and they came to Texas about 1806.

By 1834 Anglo settlers began to arrive in large numbers. The Mexican government issued forty-three land grants in the area. After the Revolution population grew rapidly as new settlers arrived by way of Trammel's Trace, the Nacogdoches Road, and the Green Grass trail. Most of the colonists came from the Old South, particularly Tennessee, Georgia, and the Carolinas.

Pioneers of Henderson County. When Europeans first entered the area in the Sixteenth Century they found the Hasinais Caddos living along the upper Neches River. People of European origin did not settle the area until after the Texas Revolution. Although no settlers actually lived in the area more than twelve Mexican land grants were made there. White settlers moved first into the area along the Trinity River and the lands claimed by recently displaced Indians.

Some of the earliest of those settlers were Jane Irvine and Henry Jeffreys. Jane was the widow of Josephus Irvine of Bedford County, Tennessee. Jeffreys was born about 1803, but dead by 1849. He married Mary Ann "Polly" Williams, widow of Brooks Williams. He came to Nacogdoches in 1829.

Early Settlement of Panola County. When the United States acquired the Louisiana Territory in 1803 two groups of Indians, the Caddos and the Hasinais, lived in the Panola County area, with the Sabine River marking the approximate dividing line between them. Early non-Indian settlers entered the area by traveling on the Red River or along the trails known as the Old San Antonio Road or Trammel's Trace.

The earliest known white settlement in the area was established by Daniel Martin in 1833. The Martin family came to Texas from Missouri. A second settlement was established by Reverend Isaac Reed and a large group of relatives. Because Mexican colonization regulations prohibited settlement in the area, it was 1835 before Anglo settlers could receive land titles, and in 1836-1837 a great land rush occurred with population increasing steadily thereafter. By 1840, at least forty-nine families were living in the Panola County area. The majority of them had come from Tennessee, Alabama, and the Carolinas.

Daniel Martin was born about 1781 in South Carolina and died about April 11, 1851, buried probably in Panola County. Martin married Mary Eleanor Ayers. He immigrated to Texas in 1833. Isaac Reed was born June 6, 1776 in Pendleton District, South Carolina and died about 1848 in Shelby County, Texas. He married Elizabeth Harper in September 1797 before coming to Texas.

Pioneers of Smith County. The first known settlers in the area were the Caddo Indians (Anadarko Tribe) who had occupied the area for many years before the first Europeans arrived. Spanish missionaries and explorers first penetrated the area in the Eighteenth and early Nineteenth Centuries. Late in the Eighteenth Century disease and threats from other Indians forced the Caddos to abandon the area; but by 1820, the Cherokees settled in the region after being driven south by hostile tribes entering North Texas.

While these and other Indians were inhabiting the region, the Mexican government began issuing land grants to white settlers. These included grants to David G. Burnet in 1826,

Peter Ellis Bean in 1828, and Vicente Filisola in 1831. George W. Bays who arrived in 1823, became the first non-Indian settler. The Fredonian Rebellion and other unrest delayed any sizeable white settlement, so that in 1836 there were only forty people in the bounds of the present county. After 1840 pioneers began arriving in greater numbers, especially small farmers from Alabama and Tennessee.

Pioneers of Angelina County. The area now known as Angelina County was first settled by Caddo and other Indians of Atakapan stock. The first non-Indian settler to receive land in the area was Vincente Micheli May 10, 1801, conveyed to him from Surdo, a Bedias Indian chief. The first Anglo settlers were members of the Burris family who settled in the northern part of the county near present-day Lufkin. In 1834-1835, Mexican authorities began issuing land grants in the area.

The county was settled predominantly by persons from the American South, some of whom established large plantations. Some of the large plantation owners were the Stearns, Oates, Kalty, Stovall, and Ewing families.

TABLE XIX

1850 CENSUS: CENTRAL EAST TEXAS

FREE PERSONS		SLAVES
Angelina	1,165	291
Cherokee	6,673	2,286
Henderson	1,237	411
Houston	2,721	1,595
Nacogdoches	5,193	1,702
Panola	3,871	1,990
Polk	2.348	1,427
Rusk	8,148	3,620
Sabine	2,498	800
San Augustine	3,648	1,382
Shelby	4,239	775
Smith	4,292	2,414
Total	46,033	18,693

1850 Census Data

An analysis of the 1850 Census data reveals that of the slightly more than 100,000 free persons living in East Texas some 45.5 percent were located in the twelve Central East Texas Counties, while of the almost 40,000 slaves living in East Texas some 46.9 percent of them were located in the same East Texas area. Less than one percent of the free persons were foreign born, seventy-five of them were German nationals, thirty-eight Irish nationals, and forty English nationals. Other nations of origin included: Switzerland, Norway, Denmark, France, Poland, Scotland, Canada, Italy, and Mexico, along with a few from the African continent. Nacogdoches County was the most cosmopolitan with seventy-two foreign born residents, Panola County the least cosmopolitan with only seven foreign born residents.

Nacogdoches County also contained the largest number of Spanish surnamed residents some 276, of which 216 were native born and forty-nine born in Louisiana, only eleven were born in the Republic of Mexico. Some 658 (1.4 percent) had been born or immigrated from American states north of the Mason-Dixon line, the greatest number living in Cherokee, Rusk, and Shelby Counties in the northern-most tier of counties. A considerable percentage of the northern born were from the Old Northwest states of Ohio, Indiana, and Illinois, although significant numbers were from Pennsylvania and New York.

States of the Old South furnished some 18,750 (40.7 percent) of the residents of Central East Texas in 1850. Tennessee, Alabama, Georgia, Mississippi, Louisiana, and the Carolinas supplying the greater percentages. Significant numbers also immigrated from Virginia, Kentucky, Missouri, and Arkansas.

The 1850 Census demonstrates at least three significant migration patterns for settlers entering Central East Texas. Perhaps the most prevalent one had the individuals involved born in the Carolinas or Georgia going from there to Tennessee or Alabama then to Mississippi or Louisiana and finally to Texas. Another pattern had persons born in Virginia or Carolina, migrating to Kentucky or Tennessee, then to Arkansas and Missouri, then on to Texas. As third pattern had the settler born in Tennessee, Alabama, or perhaps Mississippi, then on to Louisiana, then to Texas.

Pioneers of Southeast Texas

Little is known of the history of Southeast Texas from the time the area was known as Arkosia until 1825. The area around present-day Liberty County was originally known by its Spanish name, Atascosito. The Spanish established an outpost there as early as 1756. They also established a military road know as the Atascosito Road which "first extended from Refugio and Goliad to the Atascosito Crossing on the Colorado River, and thence across the Brazos at San Felipe de Austin and the San Jacinto. . .at the west of the present bridge across Lake Houston. . . .From there the road ran eastward near the town of Huffman, in Harris County, . . .to the Atascosito Crossing (later known as Green's Ferry) on the Trinity River in Liberty County" terminating ultimately at Opelousas, Louisiana where it intersected roads leading to New Orleans and Natchez, Mississippi.[241] By 1820, this was one of the most traveled trails in Texas, connecting as it did San Antonio, San Felipe, and Atascosito.

The Spanish mission established in the area around 1756 was abandoned about 1770; but sometime "between 1770 and 1790 another settlement, an isolated trading post called Arkosia or Arkokisa, was made on the Trinity." where a detachment of about fifty men was stationed and where additional troops were dispatched in 1805.[242] However, by 1818, except for Indian tribes, the area was almost completely depopulated, the Spanish having evidently again abandoned their outposts on the Atascosito and Orcoquisac Roads leaving the area relatively free and open to any settlers who dared to flaunt Spanish authority and enter. The Alabama Indians took up residence on the Neches River around 1807 where they joined with the Coushattas who were already residing in the area.[243]

By 1825, many industrious settlers had already crossed the Sabine River boundary and settled in Southeast Texas. Many of them came pioneering from nearby Louisiana, Mississippi,

---

[241] Mirian Partlow, Liberty, Liberty County, and the Atascosito District (Austin: Pemberton Press, 1974), p.20.

[242] Arlene Pickett, Historic Liberty County (n. p.: Tardy Publishing Company, 1936), p. 3.

[243] Partlow, Liberty, Liberty County, and the Atascosito District, p. 45. An 1831 Mexican census enumerated 426 adult Coushattas living on the east bank of the Trinity River,along with some 370 adult Alabama Indians. The two groups formed an alliance by 1830.

and other states carved from the Louisiana Purchase of 1803. They were attracted by the tall grass of the coastal prairies and rich farm lands along the river valleys. "Most of the Atascosito colonists had once been Spanish citizens and were accustomed to Spanish laws in the Louisiana Territory when it was under Spanish sovereignty (November 3, 1762 to October 1, 1800)."[244] The earliest of these permanent settlers crossed the Sabine before 1821.

The Atascosito Settlement for some years was located in the Department of Nacogdoches and included territory which today is in Liberty, Chambers, Galveston, Hardin, Polk, San Jacinto, and Tyler Counties. In 1831, on the eve of Texas Independence, they name of the area was changed from Atascosito to Liberty and the Liberty Municipality was created. Most of the early settlers lived on plantations located on the Trinity River.

Early Settlement of Liberty County. The Atascosito area was first inhabited by prehistoric Indians. In 1526, the Karankawas were sole occupants of the future Liberty County area until the 1740s. Spanish exploration in 1748, a Spanish mission and presidio founded in 1756, and a Spanish military road (known as the Atascosito Road), which crossed the Trinity River near the present site of Liberty, mapped out in 1757, are evidences of Spanish penetration. The Louisiana Purchase in 1803 altered the balance of power between the Spanish and the French, and Spanish efforts to discourage American immigration to Texas increased. Nevertheless, the open land of the region attracted numerous immigrants from Louisiana, Mississippi, and adjoining states.

One of the earliest permanent non-Indian settlers was Aaron Cherry, a native of Virginia, who came up the Trinity River in 1819 and selected a site near the Lower Coushatta Indian settlement. With him came his three sons, John, William, and Aaron, Jr., and two daughters, Hanasa and Rachel, all born in Louisiana. The elder Cherry had been born in 1746. Also arriving in 1819 was James Taylor White who settled on Turtle Bayou west of the Trinity in what is now Chambers County. E. L. Branham arrived in 1816, Reason Boyce in 1817, John J. Bryan in 1818, and Reuben Barrow in 1819.

Settling in 1821 was George Orr, a Pennsylvania native. He was joined by Daniel Lyons, a Virginia native, and Peter Whitaker from Louisiana. Coming in 1822 were John A.

---

[244] Ibid., p. 63.

Williams who settled a few miles below Liberty on the Trinity River; Jose Coronado, and Humphrey Jackson, all from Louisiana; also coming in 1822 were Jacob E. Self and David Minchey from Mississippi.

Noah and Nancy Tevis settled at Tavis bluff on the Neches River in 1823; also arriving in 1823 were Samuel Gibson who settled at Taylor's Bayou, John Clark, Shadrack Burney, William Hines, James McFaddin, Jesse Prewitt, James Martin, Duncan St. Clair, and Hugh Jackson. John Bevil established Bevilport on the upper Neches in 1823, and the following year led in carving from the Atascosito District a separate District of Bevil, later known as the Jasper District.

Immigrating from Louisiana in 1824 were Solomon Barrow, William Bloodgood, Thomas Dever, William Duncan, a native of Scotland and son, William Berry Duncan, a native of Louisiana, Marie Hardin, Richard and William Harris, Joseph Lawrence, Thomas F. McKinney, Josiah C. Martin, Isaac Prater, Beasley Prewitt, George W. Tevis, Reuben White, William Whitlock, and John L. Williams.[245] Matthew G. White and his son-in-law, Hugh Blair Johnston, arrived in 1825 along with Rebecca Coleman, Elias K. Davis, John Dever, Charles and Thomas Dorsett, William Everrett, Burril Franks, Amos Green, A. B. Hardin, James Knight, William Milspaugh, Elizabeth Munson, James Roberson, James Robinson, Baker Spinks, Elisha H. R. Wallis, William Swail, Elisha H. R. Willis, Benjamin Winfree, Robert Wiseman, Matilda Wilburn, William Wallace, James S. Ward, and John York, all coming from Mississippi and Louisiana.[246] The leaders of the group arriving in 1825, or at least the contingent from southwestern Mississippi and western Louisiana, were Matthew W. White of Amite County, Mississippi and his son-in-law, Hugh B. Johnston, of Wilkinson County, Mississippi.

The Mexican census of 1826 "showed a population in the settlement of 407 persons including slaves, but enumerators missed at least sixty-three heads of families and single men, including: James Taylor White, John Berry, the Hardin brothers (Benjamin Watson, Augustine

---

[245] Partlow, Liberty, Liberty County, and the Atascosito District, p. 66.

[246] Ibid.

Blackburn, Milton A., Franklin, and William), William McFaddin, and a number of native Mexicans.[247] "Of the 104 heads of families (or single adults) listed in the 1826 census, only six were born outside the United States, and all but eighteen immigrated from Louisiana or Mississippi. Of the eighteen, five came from Alabama, four from Kentucky, three from Tennessee, and one each from Georgia, Missouri, and Pennsylvania."[248] That same census listed 331 white persons and "people of color" and seventy-six slaves, for a total population of 407 persons.

Jesse De Vore came in 1827 followed in 1831 by John Berry, Robert Booth, Esther Clark, Jose Coronado, John, Philip P., and Thomas Dever, Joseph Dunman, George Orr, Jacob Self, and B. M. Spinks; and in 1832 by Benjamin and Joseph L. Ellis and Robert Orson William McManus; in 1833 by Manuel de los Santos Coy; in 1834 by Aaron Cherry and Thomas Jefferson Chambers of Virginia; and in 1835 by Uriah Anderson, Margarite Buye, Joseph Carriere, John Cherry, John R. Faulk, Sr., William D. Smith, and Edward Thomas Branch.

As late as 1831 the settlers around Atascosito had not received titles to their lands. One of the few patents granted was given to John A. Williams who received a league of land on the west bank of the Trinity River. That year the name of the settlement was changed from Atascosito to Liberty and the Liberty Municipality created.

Twenty-seven settlers petitioned for land grants in 1831:

Solomon Barrow	Hugh B. Johnston
John Berry	James Knight
Jose Coronado	James McFaddin
Philip P. Dever	David Minche (Minchey)
William Duncan	James Morton (Martin)
Joseph Duncan	Elizabeth Munson
William Everett	Henry W. Munson
Amos Green	George Orr
Henry Griffin	James Robinson
William Harris	Jacob E. Self
James Humphrey	B. M. Spinks

---

[247] Ibid, p. 67.

[248] Ibid.

Samuel Strong William Whitlock
William Swail John A. Williams
Matthew G. White

(Source: Partlow, <u>Liberty, Liberty County and the Atascosito District</u>, p. 75).

Perhaps "the most dramatic and unusual immigration processions into Liberty County was the arrival of the Creole families from Louisiana in December of 1845. . . .Most of the eight families in this first immigration were direct descendants of. . .Louis St. Denis and his Spanish wife, Maria Emmanuela Sanchez de Navarre, . . .who lived in New Orleans."[249] One of their kinsmen, Baptiste Gillard, preceded them to Liberty County accompanied by the large families of Dr. Edward Joseph Gillard, Joseph Gillard, Volezar de Blanc, John Gillard, Adolph Gillard, Auger Gillard, and Silvier Gillard.[250] Before the influx of Creoles, other French families had already arrived in the area, among them: the Pierre Blanchettes, the Victor Gaillons, the C. C. Cibereases, the Benjamin Lenears, the A. G. Vanpradelles, and the Joseph Dugats.

Early Settlement of Jefferson County. Even though the Spanish demonstrated some sporadic interest in Southeast Texas throughout the Eighteenth Century, they displayed none in the Jefferson County region. In the early 1800s, the future county was a part of the Atascosito District which was bounded on the west by the colony of San Felipe de Austin, on the north by the District of Nacogdoches, on the south by the Gulf of Mexico.

By 1805, however, Spanish authorities faced a multitude of prospective immigrants to Southeast Texas. They included Spanish, French, Indians, and Anglo-Americans of Louisiana who sought to escape the sovereignty of the United States. "Many Anglo-Americans were adventurers or fleeing from justice. Some Louisiana tribes feared American Indian policy and expected better treatment at the hands of the Spanish."[251]

---

[249] Ibid., p. 189.

[250] Ibid, p. 192.

[251] W. T. Block, <u>A History of Jefferson County, Texas from Wilderness to Reconstruction</u> (Nederland: Nederland Publishing Company, 1976), p 18,

Perhaps the earliest Anglo-American settlers in present-day Jefferson County were James and Elizabeth McFaddin who arrived in 1823 and Noah and Nancy Tevis and their five children who settled at Beaumont (known then as Tevis Bluff) in 1824 where a sixth child was born. They were joined by John and Sarah McGaffey in 1826. A Mexican census taken that year found 331 free citizens and seventy-six slaves living in the area.

In 1831, the area was absorbed into the Department of Nacogdoches as the Municipality of Liberty. At that time, some ten or twelve families lived between Jefferson and the Sabine River. Early Mexican land grants were awarded Jose Maria Mora, Manuelo de los Santos Coy, and John Stephenson about 1830. At the same time Joseph Grigsby became the first permanent settler on the Neches River.

Settlement progressed rapidly east of the Neches River (in today's Orange County). There settled Robert and Elizabeth Johnson at Green's Bluff in 1824 along with David and Jacob Garner (Robert's brothers-in-law) at Cow's Bayou, Claiborne West and John McGaffey (also brothers-in-law), and later in 1828 Bradley Garner, Sr., Elizabeth's father. Others settling in the 1820s were James and Absalom Jett in 1823, William Allen in 1823, John Jett in 1826, John and William Allen in 1827, James, William, and Gilbert Stephenson in 1828, and John and David Cole, and David Burrell in 1829.

In the 1830s John Harman, Stephen Jett, Hiram Bunch, Clark Beach, and George A. Patillo also arrived in the area. Ultimately by late 1835 and early 1836, Jefferson County contained 250 free inhabitants.[252]

Early Settlement of Jasper County (Bevil Settlement). In the Sixteenth century when Spanish explorers first entered the region that now comprises Jasper County, Atakapa Indians lived in the southern sections of the county, and Indians of the Caddo Confederacy dominated the northern sections. The area was also the home and hunting grounds of the Ais Indians, who lived between the Sabine and Neches Rivers. Yet another group, the Biloxi Indians, established three villages east of the Neches River before 1846.

One of the first white settlers was John R. Bevil, who moved to Texas by 1829, and around whose home a settlement arose that became known as Bevilport. In time a loosely

---

[252] Ibid., p. 26.

defined community of pre-1836 settlers grew up there between the Neches and Sabine Rivers on land that eventually was organized as Jasper and Newton Counties. In 1830, George W. Smyth found about thirty families living in the community scattered between the two rivers. a few of them established roots to the east in what became Newton County in 1846. In 1834, the western settlers were organized into a municipality whose name was changed to Jasper the following year.

Early Settlement of Newton County. In 1834-1835, at least twenty-one heads of household or single men received titles to land in Newton County.

Early Settlement of Tyler County. The Tyler County area had for centuries been occupied by agricultural Caddoan, and possibly Atakapa Indians. White settlers arriving there in the early years of the Nineteenth Century encountered both Caddoan and Caddoan-related Cherokees uprooted from the east, and groups of Alabama and Coushatta Indians, recent immigrants from Louisiana.

White settlement began before the Texas Revolution. Three Americans received land grants there from Mexican authorities in 1834, and more men and one woman, Jane Taylor, received grants during 1835. These early settlers came predominantly from the American South.

TABLE XX
1850 CENSUS: SOUTHEAST TEXAS

	Freemen	Slaves
Jasper County	1,767	991
Jefferson County	1,836	216
Liberty County	2,522	922
Newton County	1,689	602
Tyler County	1,894	752
Total	9,708	3,483

An analysis of the 1850 Census data reveals that immigrants to Southeast Texas followed a significantly different migration pattern from those followed by settlers in Central and Northeast Texas. Those immigrating to this southernmost section of East Texas tended to come from Mississippi or Louisiana. A fair number, however, were persons of foreign birth, particularly in today's Liberty and Jefferson Counties. Over 100 foreign-born individuals lived in Liberty County representing more than a dozen nations. Germany, England, Ireland, and France contributing more than ninety of them. England and Germany also contributed more than half of those persons living in Jefferson County. In Tyler County a settlement of three German families: Knuppel, Koch, and Gentz, represented more than two-thirds of all German immigrants. The states of New York, Pennsylvania, and Ohio contributed more than sixty percent of all immigrants from the American north.

Population Analysis

The total population for East Texas as revealed in the 1850 federal census was 105,271 free persons and 45,808 slaves or a total of 151,079 individuals.

Census of 1850. Of the total of free persons, 655 were foreign born with Harrison County (93), Liberty County (73), Nacogdoches County (72) and Cass County (50) accounting for 288 (some 40 percent) of them. Eight counties contained less than ten foreign-born residents each. Those individuals with Spanish surnames were almost exclusively found in Nacogdoches County and the southeastern counties of Liberty and Jefferson. Of the 276 Spanish surnamed individuals in Nacogdoches County, for example, 216 were born in Texas and 49 in Louisiana. Most of them preferred to be known as Spanish Texans, not Mexican Texans.

The German states supplied 232 of the foreign born, England 222, Ireland 109, and Scotland 26 or a total of 589 (90 percent) of them. They were concentrated in Rusk, Harrison, Nacogdoches, and Liberty Counties with two counties (Cooke and Hunt in Northeast Texas) having less than ten each.

Settlers who had immigrated from the northern American states numbered more than 2,300 with the largest percentage of them living in Northeastern Texas and the smallest percentage in Southeastern Texas. Some 1,775 northern-born settlers lived in the tier of northern East Texas counties, the largest number concentrated in Fannin, Collin, Grayson, and Lamar Counties. Some 51.0 percent of them immigrants from Illinois, 20.0 percent from Indiana, 9.2 percent from Ohio, and 5.4 percent from Pennsylvania. Thus, more than four-fifths of them from the states of the Old Northwest Territory.

Slightly more than 625 northern-born settlers lived in Central East Texas. The greatest number of those living in Cherokee (117), Rusk (97), San Augustine (76), Sabine (76), and Nacogdoches (63) Counties. Illinois with 170, Ohio with 103, and Indiana (90) contributing the greater number. Thus, here as well almost three-fifths had immigrated from the Old Northwest.

Not surprisingly, the states of the American South supplied more early Texas settlers than any other region in the Western World. In the northeastern section almost 17,000 immigrants came from the Confederate States with Tennessee (28.9 percent), Missouri (16.4 percent), Alabama (14.7 percent), the Carolinas (12.9 percent), Kentucky (8.7 percent), and Virginia (4.7 percent) supplying more than four-fifths of the total. The greatest number of southern settlers were situated in Harrison, Titus, Upshur, Fannin, Red River, and Collin Counties. Harrison County alone accounted for more than 4,000 making it easy to understand why Marshall, the county seat, was the "last Confederate capital."

In the central section of East Texas almost 19,000 (41.0 percent) inhabitants had immigrated from Southern states. Tennessee (26.8 percent), Alabama (21.2 percent), the Carolinas (13,7 percent), Georgia (11.2 percent), and Mississippi (7.6 percent) contributed slightly more than four-fifths of those individuals. They were concentrated in Rusk, Nacogdoches, Cherokee, Shelby, and Panola Counties, Rusk County alone accounting for more than 4,600.

Population Statistics (1836-1846). After 1836, those East Texas colonists who had survived the war after 1836 gradually returned to reclaim and restore their homes and other property still faced the rigors of a tough, pioneering life in the settlements that had virtually been abandoned in the aftermath of the "Runaway Scrape." At that time in all of Texas there were not more than 30,000 Anglo-Americans. Population figures, however, must be accepted with caution. Those proclaiming the number of Anglo-Americans, native Mexicans, or Indians living in Texas between 1821 and 1835 are quite certainly incomplete and only hint at the population of Texas.[253]

---

[253] The New Handbook of Texas, Vol. 1, p. 190.

During the 1820s an estimated 10,000 Americans migrated to the Spanish frontier province, most of whom settled in East Texas. The two major factors fueling the migration were economic pressures and abundant cheap land. During this first generation of Anglo-American settlement, most of the immigrants were non-slaveholding backwoodsmen and small farmers from the hill country of the trans-Appalachian Southwest. Contemporary Texas historians generally identify some six types of individuals making up the bulk of these early settlers: (1) "half-Indian hunters and traders," (2) "the restless and the shiftless," (3) "the earnest colonist," (4) "the crass speculator," (5) "the whiskey peddler," and (6) "the itinerant preacher."[254]

Thereafter, between 1830 and 1834, the numbers of Anglo-Americans doubled to more than 20,700. When legal restrictions on immigration were lifted in May, 1834, an estimated 1,000 Americans a month crossed the borders of Texas. By mid-1830, the number of them and their slaves had risen to 35,000. The American population of Texas at the time was probably on the order of ten times that of the Tejano (native Mexican) population, and with a few thousand "civilized" tribes of Indians, the total population, as computed by Colonel Juan N. Almonte, by 1836 had reached about 40,000.[255] Other computations placed the total population in 1835 at only 24,700. A highly regarded Texas historian, Rupert N. Richardson, placed the white population of Texas in 1836 at an estimated 34,470, "including Mexicans," and an estimated slave population of 5,000 individuals.[256]

During the period of the republic (1836-1846), the population of Texas increased about 7,000 per year, primarily from immigration. In those years, slaves represented about ten percent of the population, excluding Indians. An indicator of the rate of growth is the creation of new counties and cities. In 1839, for example, three new counties were organized: Fannin, Montgomery, and Robertson; and five new towns incorporated: Shelbyville, La Grange (Red River County), Clarksville, Crockett, and Jonesboro, added to thse previously created:

---

[254] Graham Davis, Land, Irish Pioneers in Mexican and Revolutionary Texas (College Station: Texas A&M Press, 2002), p. 26.

[255] Ibid., p. 33.

[256] Lone Star State, p. 140.

Nacogdoches, San Augustine, Nashville, Bevilport, Harrisburg, Liberty, and Houston.[257]

In 1836, in all of Texas there were not more than 30,000 Anglo-Americans. "Probably less than one-half of whom were in the territory now designated East Texas. Most of the wealth was in the former Department of the Brazos."[258] Poor crops in the United states, the Panic of 1837, and the business stagnation that followed combined to send a flood of immigrants in 1837 and the years immediately following. In the summer and fall of 1837 alone, some 6,000 American immigrants crossed the Sabine River at one ferry. The year 1840 "saw the heaviest immigration Texas had known and that volume was sustained in 1841 and the early part of 1842."[259] This tide of American immigrants added to the practice of Mexican authorities in ignoring Indian rights from prior occupancy meant that the Mexican population became increasingly outnumbered.

Texas historian R. N. Richardson reported that the white population of Texas had reached 102,961 by 1847, the number of slaves to 38,753, and the number of "free Negroes" to 295, creating a total of 142,009 individuals.[260] By 1850, when the first federal census to include Texas was taken, many of the people who were listed in the 1835 Mexican census and the land records for East Texas were no longer residents of Texas. Some had sought refuge in Louisiana, Arkansas, or other states because of the dangerous events surrounding the Texas Revolution; others had fled at the time of the Cordovan Rebellion; some had gone to California to take part in the Gold Rush; and still others had left the region to avoid the economic downturn that resulted from inflation and other depressing conditions in the Republic.

---

[257] T. C. Richardson, East Texas Its History and Its Makers, 4 vols. (New York: Lewis Historical Publishing Company, 1940), p. 102.

[258] Ibid., p. 98.

[259] Richardson, Lone Star, pp. 139-140.

[260] Ibid., p. 140.

1. Residents of Texas, Vol. 2, pp. 214-216.
2. Ibid., pp. 216-222.
3. Ericson, Gateway to Texas, Vol. I, p. 226.
4. Ibid., p. 181.

APPENDIX I

APPENDIX I
NACOGDOCHES CENSUS (1809)

MARIA SANCHES s 10 Nacogdoches
JOSEFA RUIZ Nacogdoches
SOLEDAD RUIZ PADILLA w 47 Los Adaes
MATIAS PADILLA s 14 Nacogdoches
ANDROS PADILLA s 10 Nacogdoches
JOSE ANTONIO PADILLA Nacogdoches
ANTONIO PADILLA Nacogdoches
ESTEFANIA PADILLA Nacogdoches
ANDRES DE ACOSTA m 65 Los Adaes
MARIA CONCEPCION ACOSTA m 47 Los Adaes
JUAN MANUEL ACOSTA s 27 Nacogdoches
JOSE ISIDRO ACOSTA s 16 Nacogdoches
JUAN JOSE de la CRUZ s 13 Nacogdoches
ANTHONY PARROT m 41 North Carolina
MARIA QUIRK PARROT m 24 Kentucky
JAMES PARROT s Nacogdoches
MARIA FRANCISCA PARROT s Nacogdoches
ANTONIO ARRIOLA m 48 Bexar
ANA JACOBA EQUIS ARRIOLA m 42 Los Adaes
EDUARDO ARRIOLA s 19 Nacogdoches
JOSE MOREL w 63 Cuba
D. BERNARDO d'ORTOLAN w 65 Bordeaux
RAMON d'ORTOLAN s 26 Nacogdoches
ATANACIO d'ORTOLAN 23 Nacogdoches 5 slaves: Maximilian, Rafael, Francisco, Gregorio, Jose
FRANCISCA d'ORTOLON 24 Natchitoches
MARIA ENGRACIA d'ORTOLON Nacogdoches
BALTASAR de la GARZA 51 m Los Adaes
RITA PORALTA de la GARZA 51 m New Mexico
MANUEL de la GARZA 29 s Nacogdoches
CLEMENTE ARRIOLA 10 s Nacogdoches
TRINIDAD GONZALES 49 m Los Adaes
CAYETTANO VILLAFRANCA 49 m Los Adaes
JUANA LARA VILLAFRANCA 47 m Los Adaes
PEDRO de LARA POSOS 73 w LOS ADAES
CHRISOTOMO YUCANTE 70 m Canada
MARIANA YUCANTE m 57 Apache
CHRISOTOMO YUCANTE 28 s Canada
MARIA YUCANTE Nacogdoches
JOSE VELANCHE 24 s Nacogdoches
DIONICIO LOPEZ 39 m Parras
GUADALUPE CORDOVA LOPEZ 31 m Nacogdoches
FELIX LOPEZ 11 s Nacogdoches
ATANACIO LOPEZ s Nacogdoches
MARIA LOPEZ s Nacogdoches
FRANCISCA de JESUS s Nacogdoches
DAMASENA BARRERA 38 w Los Adaes
FELIPE RAMIRES m absent
TIBURSIA PERES RAMIRES 17 m Nacogdoches
JOSE MARIA CASTRO 32 s Havana
DAMIAN AROCHA 42 m Bexar
ANTONIA FLORES AROCHA 18 m Nacogdoches
JOSE MARIA AROCHA s Nacogdoches
JUANA AROCHA s Nacogdoches
DOMINGO IBARBO 28 m Tex. Ind.
DELORES SANCHEZ IBARBO 18 m Nacogdoches
DAVID WALTMAN 40 m Mississippi
JOSEFA BEBE WALTMAN 36 m Point Coupe
MIGUEL LARRUA s Nacogdoches
DENIS QUINELTY 24 s Opelousas
DIEGO CASANOVA 29 m Altamira
JUANA PROCELLA CASANOVA 22 m Nacogdoches
JOSE CASANOVA s Nacogdoches
MARIA PAULA CASANOVA s

Nacogdoches
STEPHEN GOGUET 55 m Arkansas
JUANA LARA GOGUET 47 m Los Adaes
ESTAVAN PROCELLA s Nacogdoches
----- SAN MIGUEL 38 m Los Adaes
MICHAELA GOGUET SAN MIGUEL 27 m Nacogdoches
----- MENCHACA w 61 Bexar
----- MORIN m 36 Trinidad
TELESFORA CERDA m 30 Nacogdoches
JOSE CERDA s 13 Nacogdoches
ALEON CERDA s Nacogdoches
RTIN CERDA s Nacogdoches
MARIA GERTRUDIS CERDA s 16 Nacogdoches
JUANA MARIA CERDA s Nacogdoches
BERNARDA CERDA s Nacogdoches
GETRUDIS TRINIDAD CERDA s Nacogdoches
MARIA DE JESUS CERDA s Nacogdoches
ESTEVAN MORA m 24 Nacogdoches
GETRUDIS CERDA MORA m 14 Nacogdoches
JUANA MARIA PADILLA MACEDONIA s Nacogdoches
FRANCISCO VILLA PANDO m 57 New Mexico
GETRUDIS ROSALES VILLA PANDO m 54 Los Adaes
MARIA JOSEFA SIERRA Nacogdoches
FRANCISCO GARCIA w 52 Murcia
JOSE SIMON GARCIA Nacogdoches
JOSE ENCARNACION GARCIA Nacogdoches
MARIA GARCIA Nacogdoches
FRANCISCO de los SANTOS m 47 Sta. Rosa
RITA de LUNA SANTOS m 43 Rio Grande
IGNO de los SANTOS s 30 Nacogdoches
MANL de los SANTOS s 20 Nacogdoches
PEPE JOSE DAVID SANCHES Nacogdoches
FELIS BARELA m 61 New Mexico
JOSEFA CARO BARELA m 36 Los Adaes
ANASTACIO BARELA s 17 Nacogdoches
FRANCISCO ANTONIO BARELA Nacogdoches
FELIX BARELA Nacogdoches
JUANA BTA. BARELA Nacogdoches
MARIA ANTONIA BARELA Nacogdoches
FRANCISCO PADILLA m 47 Los Adaes
JOSEFA CERDA PADILLA m 32 Trinidad
FRANCISCO DEL RIO m 47 Orcoquisa
GERTRUDIS IBARVO DEL RIO m 28 Nacogdoches
FELIX DEL RIO s 11 Nacogdoches
FRANCISCO DEL RIO s Nacogdoches
JOSE RAMON DEL RIO s Nacogdoches
ISIDRO DEL RIO s Nacogdoches
GREGORIO MORA 35 m Los Adaes
JOSEFA CARO 35 m Los Adaes
SERFERINO MORA 13 s Nacogdoches
GERTRUDIS MORA 16 s Nacogdoches
GERONIMO EQUIS 45 m Los Adaes
RUGER TRINIDAD GARCIA EQUIS 23 m Nacogdoches
JOSE CESARIO EQUIS 13 s Nacogdoches
JOSE MARIA EQUIS s Nacogdoches
GRAVIEL TORRES 41 m Bexar
MARIA RACHAL TORRES 39 m Natchitoches
SEFERINA TORRES CONOR 17 w Nacogdoches
SEFERINA CONOR s Nacogdoches
WILLIAM BEBE 36 m Point Coupe
MARIA WALTMAN BEBE 26 m Point Coupe
JAMES BEBE 11 s Point Coupe
FRANCISCA BEBE 10 s Point Coupe
MARIA BEBE s Point Coupe
MARGARITA BEBE s Point Coupe
MARIA LUCIA BEBE s Point Coupe
WILLIAM QUIRK 29 m Natchez
ANN NORRIS QUIRK 16 m Maryland
WILLIAM BARR 47 s Ireland
SAMUEL DAVENPORT 44 m Pennsylvania
LUISA GAÑON DAVENPORT 23 Natchitoches

BENIGNO DAVENPORT s Nacogdoches
TERESA DAVENPORT s Nacogdoches
MARIA CELIN DAVENPORT s Nacogdoches
JOHN DURST 12 s Arkansas
MAURICIO CORTINIAS 10 s La Bahia
MARIA LUISA RICHARDS 11 s Ouchita 12 slaves
----- PATRICIO m 23 Bexar
DOROTEA PATRICIO m 23 Nacogdoches
JOSEFA PATRICIO Nacogdoches
JOSE SANCHES 43 m Los Adaes
MARIA JOSEFA IBARVO SANCHES 34 m Los Adaes
JOUCIANA SANCHES 12 s Nacogdoches
VICENTE SANCHES s Nacogdoches
ANASTACIA SANCHES 14 s Nacogdoches
GERTRUDIA SANCHES 10 s Nacogdoches
GERGORIA SANCHES s Nacogdoches
MARIA ENCARNACION SANCHEZ s Nacogdoches
MARIA JOSEFA s Nacogdoches
JOSE ANTONIO MORA 21 m Nacogdoches
CATARINA VASQUEZ MORA 18 m Nacogdoches
MARIA MORIN 42 w Los Adaes
JOSE GIL MORA 23 s Nacogdoches
JOSE MARIANO MORA 18 s Nacogdoches
LEANDRO MORA 15 s Nacogdoches
JOSE LUCOBICHE 43 m Araguia
MAURICIA MORA LUCOBICHE 29 m Nacogdoches
JOSE DE JESUS LUCOBICHE s Nacogdoches
MARIA TEODORA LUCOBICHE s Nacogdoches
JUAN IBARBO s Nacogdoches
ANTONIA IBARBO 13 s Nacogdoches
EUSEVIA IBARBO 11 s Nacogdoches
JOSE ANTONIO FERNANDEZ 40 m Pesqueriage
LUCIA VARELA FERNANDEZ 21 m Nacogdoches
TORIBIO FERNANDEZ s Nacogdoches
TELESFORA FERNANDEZ s Nacogdoches
JUANA BAUTIA XIMENES 57 w Los Adaes
JUAN IGNACIO SOTO 33 m Trinidad
MARIA de JESUS MALDONADO SOTO 30 m Trinidad
JOSE MARIA SOTO s Nacogdoches
FRANCISCO ANTONIO SOTO s Nacogdoches
JOSE CORDOVA 34 m Bexar
TRIBUCIA IBARBO CORDOVA 31 m Nacogdoches
FRANCISCO CORDOVA 15 s Nacogdoches
JOSE CORDOVA 14 s Nacogdoches
TELESFORO CORDOVA s Nacogdoches
GERTRUDIS CORDOVA s Nacogdoches
JOSE MARIA CORDOVA 28 m Nacogdoches
GERTRUDIS CHIRINO CORDOVA 18 m Nacogdoches
MARIA ANTONIA CORDOVA s Nacogdoches
FRANCISCA PERES 44 w Bexar
SANTIAGO CHICHI 28 m Natchitoches
JOSEFA CHICHI 48 m Bexar
JOSE ANTONIO SANTA CRUZ 47 m Los Adaes
SIMONA RUIZ SANTA CRUZ 18 m Nacogdoches
MARIA ANTONIA SANTA CRUZ s Nacogdoches
GERTRUDIS RUIZ 10 s Nacogdoches
GETRUDIS PADILLA 64 w Los Adaes
MARIA de JESUS SANTA CRUZ 45 w Nacogdoches
JOSE IBARBO 46 m Los Adaes
ANASTIA MANSOLO IBARBO 44 m Los Adaes
JOSE IBARBO 25 s Nacogdoches
MIGUEL IBARBO 22 s Nacogdoches
FRANCO de SALES IBARBO s Nacogdoches
MARIA TELESFORA IBARBO 16 s Nacogdoches

MARTISIA IBARBO 14 s Nacogdoches
JOSE VALENTIN IBARBO s Nacogdoches
JOSE IGNACIO IBARBO 27 m Nacogdoches
CLETA FLORES IBARBO 21 m Nacogdoches
BENIGNO IBARBO s Nacogdoches
MANUEL MARIANO IBARBO s Nacogdoches
1 slave
JOSE MARIANO SANCHES 41 m Laredo
JOSEFA ROSALES SANCHES 28 m Nacogdoches
MARIA BRIGIDA SANCHES 11 s Nacogdoches
JOSE ANTONIO RODRIGUEZ 35 m Monterrey
THOMASA ALAMILLA RODRIGUEZ 33 m Trinidad
TERESA RODRIGUEZ 16 s Nacogdoches
MARIA de la CRUZ RODRIEGUEZ 11 s Nacogdoches
CAFERINO ESTRADA 26 w Nacogdoches
MANUEL ESTRADA 10 s Nacogdoches
JUANA MARIA PADILLA s Nacogdoches
JULIAN ROSALES 37 m Los Adaes
AUGUSTA ALAMILLA ROSALES 32 m Trinidad
GERTRUDIS ROSALES 15 s Nacogdoches
FRANCISCO ROSALES 10 s Nacogdoches
IGNACIA ROSALES s Nacogdoches
TRINIDAD ROSALES s Nacogdoches
RITA BERGARA 78 w Los Adaes
JUAN SEGUIN 47 m Bexar
JOSEFA GOMES SEGUIN 31 m Bexar
MARIA MANUELA SEGUIN s Nacogdoches
JUAN JOSE HERNANDEZ 37 m Bexar
GERTRUDIS ALAMILLA HERNANDEZ 21 m Nacogdoches
MARIA ISABEL HERNANDEZ s Nacogdoches
JOSE FLORES 47 m Los Adaes
ESTEFANIA EQUIS FLORES 27 m Nacogdoches
VITAL FLORES 18 s Nacogdoches
PEDRO FLORES 16 s Nacogdoches
FELIPE FLORES 13 s Nacogdoches
JOSE de JESUS FLORES s Nacogdoches
JUAN GUILLERMO FLORES s Nacogdoches
ANTONIA MARIA FLORES s Nacogdoches
1 slave
MARIA MICHAEL CARO 70 w Los Adaes
JOSEFA EQUIS 23 Nacogdoches
JULIAN CAESIS 28 m Trinidad
TRINIDAD FLORES CAESIS 23 m Nacogdoches
BACILIA CAESIS s Nacogdoches
JOSE ROSALES 24 m Bexar
MARIA ORTIS ROSALES 15 m Bexar
JOAQUIN MONTES 22 m Bexar
ROSALIA RUIZ MONTES 20 m Nacogdoches
MARIA de JESUS RUIZ s Nacogdoches
JOSE MARIA VASQUEZ 40 m Los Adaes
ANTONIA SANCHES VASQUEZ 24 m Nacogdoches
JUAN JOSE SANCHES 67 w Los Adaes
RAMON CHAVANA 40 m Point Lampazos
JOSEFA SANCHES CHAVANA 25 m Nacogdoches
ANTONIO CHABANA 11 s Nacogdoches
ADAUTO CHABANA s Nacogdoches
JOSE MARIA CHABANA s Nacogdoches
FELIPE SANTIAGO CHABANA s Nacogdoches
MARIA GUADALUPE CHABANA s Nacogdoches
JUANA TREJO 53 w Los Adaes
JOSE de la PEÑA 21 s Nacogdoches
MARIA MARTINA PEÑA 23 s Nacogdoches
JACINTA PEÑA 20 s Nacogdoches
JUAN de ACOSTA 42 m Orcoquisa
DOLORES SANCHES ACOSTA 36 m Los Adaes
MARIA del PILAR ACOSTA 10 s

Nacogdoches
JOSE ACOSTA 18 m Nacogdoches
MARIA SANTA CRUZ ACOSTA 15 m Nacogdoches
JOSE MARIA MORA 34 m Bexar
MARCINA GRANDE MORA 46 m Orcoquisa
PEPE ANA JACOBA s Nacogdoches
2 slaves
LUIS CORTINAS 10 s Nacogdoches
2 servants
JOSE ZEPEDA 66 m Bexar
BEATRIS SANCHES ZEPEDA 63 m Los Adaes
JUAN PINEDA s Nacogdoches
JOSE MARIA MEDRANO 26 m San Juan del Rio
MARIA CORTINAS MEDRANO 15 m Nacogdoches
JUAN BELANCHE 24 m Nacogdoches
JUANA RUIZ BELANCHE 25 m Nacogdoches
JUAN BENITES 40 m Orcoquisac
REFUGIA MORA BENITES 36 m Trinidad
JOSE BENITES 12 s Nacogdoches
JUAN MATA MEDINA 47 m Bexar
MARIA RUIZ MEDINA 45 m Los Adaes
JOAQUIN MEDINA 18 s Nacogdoches
JOSE MARIA MEDINA s Nacogdoches
JOSE DOMINGEZ 43 m Mexico
GERTRUDIS MECINA DOMINGEZ 17 m Nacogdoches
JOSE TESSIER 43 s Canada
1 servant; 1 slave
EUGENIA ARAGON 33 m Bexar
JOSE MARIA ARAGON 30 m Bedais
MARCELA ARAGON 13 s Nacogdoches
GERTRUDIS ARAGON s Nacogdoches
MARIA ARAGON s Nacogdoches
JOSE MORILLA 47 m Los Adaes
JUANA BALLANOVA MORILLA 34 m Los Adaes
JUAN MORILLA 26 s San Nicholas
JOSE PROCELA 24 m Nacogdoches
OLIVERA PADILLA PROCELA 22 m Nacogdoches
BENIGNO PROCELA s Nacogdoches
JOSE MARIA PROCELA 33 m Trinidad
MANUELA CERDA PROCELA 23 m Nacogdoches
MARIA ANTONIA PROCELA 10 s Nacogdoches
MARIA GETRUDIS PROCELA s Nacogdoches
MARIA LOUISA PROCELA s Nacogdoches
FRANCISCO ANTONIO PROCELA s Nacogdoches
JOSE NICOLAS PROCELA s Nacogdoches
JUAN IGNACIO PIFERMO 70 m Natchitoches
CLEMENCIA PIFERMO 55 m Natchitoches
MAXIMILIAN ARZE 28 m Natchitoches
ANASTACIA SIMES 21 m Natchitoches
2 servants; 6 slaves
JOSE CARO 38 m Los Adaes
MANUELA EQUIS CARO 38 m Los Adaes
TOMAS CARO 18 s Nacogdoches
ANTONIO CARO 16 s Nacogdoches
AGATON CARO 14 s Nacogdoches
MARIA CARO 12 s Nacogdoches
JOSE de la BEGA 49 m San Miguel
MARIA de AROS de la BEGA 47 m Los Adaes
MARIA JOSEFA de la BEGA s Nacogdoches
JOSE DOMINGO de la BEGA 11 s Nacogdoches
MARIA JACOBA de la BEGA s Nacogdoches
FRANCISCA de la BEGA 32 Guinea
2 slaves
JOSEPH MIGUEL CROW 40 m South Carolina
MARGARET LAFLORE CROW 39 m Ireland
JOHN CROW
LUIS CHARVON s

ANDRES CHARVON s
HENRY CHARVON s
MARGARET CHARVON s
LOUIS CHARVON s
JUAN BAUTISTA MOREL 38 m Arkansas
JUANA MARIA MOREL 46 m Apache
PAUL LEONE MOREL 16 s Nacogdoches
JOAQUIN TREVIÑO 39 w Camargo
CONSEPSION ABILA FONTENO 17 m Carmago
JUAN FONTENO absent
EUSTAQUIA FONTENO s Camargo
JOSE de los SANTOS COY 32 m Bexar
CONCEPSION JUPA de los SANTOS COY 24 m Philadelphia
JOSE ANTONIO de los SANTOS COY s Nacogdoches
MARIA DE JESUS de los SANTOS COY s Nacogdoches
HERNARDA de los SANTOS COY s Nacogdoches
MARIA LUISA de los SANTO COY s Nacogdoches
JOSEFA URRUTIA de los SANTOS COY 57 w Bexar
MARIANO ZEPEDA 15 s Bexar
JUAN JOSE ALAMILLA 28 m Nacogdoches
PAULA MANSOLLA ALAMILLIA 21 m Comanche Bexar
JOSE ANTONIO ALAMILLIA s Nacogdoches
JUANA BAUTISTA ACOSTA 61 m Los Adaes
LUCIANO GARCIA m absent Chihuahua
LINO CHAVANA 39 m Lampazos
BARBARA CHAVES CHAVANA 21 m Nacogdoches
JOSE CHAVANA s Nacogdoches
LOUIS FORTUNE 69 m Canada
MANUELA ARAGON FORTUNE 43 m Bexar
MARTIN IBARBO 42 m Los Adaes
JOSEFA ARRIOLA IBARBO 44 m Bexar
BAUTISTA CHIRENO 23 w Nacogdoches
JOSE ENCARNACION CHIRENO 18 s Nacogdoches
JOSE CONCEPCION IBARBO 15 s Nacogdoches
JOSE ANG. CHIRINO s Nacogdoches
MARTIN SANTA CRUZ 38 m Los Adaes
ROSA PROCELA SANTA CRUZ 28 m Nacogdoches
ANSELMO SANTA CRUZ 10 s Nacogdoches
JUAN BATUISTA SANTA CRUZ s Nacogdoches
JUAN FRANCISCO SANTA CRUZ s Nacogdoches
CRIST. GUILLERMO SANTA CRUZ s Nacogdoches
MARGARITA SANTA CRUZ s Nacogdoches
JOSE ANTONIO MENDOZA 62 s Saltillo
MANUEL SANTA CRUZ 53 m Los Adaes
MAGDALENA PADILLA SANTA CRUZ 51 m Los Adaes
BENANCIAS SANTA CRUZ FEBLE 28 m Nacogdoches
FRANCISCO FEBLE absent Natchitoches
MANUEL FLORES 52 m Los Adaes
JUANA VASQUES FLORES 43 m Los Adaes
ANDRES ESPARSA 19 s Nacogdoches
MARIA GERTRUDIS FLORES s Nacogdoches
MARIANO SANTA CRUZ 54 m Los Adaes
ROSA del RIO SANTA CRUZ 48 m Los Adaes
ANTONIO SIERRA 30 s Nacogdoches
ASENCIO SIERRA s Nacogdoches
JOSE SANTA CRUZ 30 m Nacogdoches
DOMINGO CORDOVA SANTA CRUZ 22 m Nacogdoches
JUAN JOSE SANTA CRUZ s Nacogdoches
MANUEL CORDOVA 25 m Nacogdoches
MARIA JOSEFA EQUIS CORDOVA 19 m Nacogdoches

JOAQUIN CORDOVA s Nacogdoches
MARIA TOMASA CORDOVA s Nacogdoches
ANDRES SOLIS 27 s Nacogdoches
TIBURCIA SOLIS 22 s Nacogdoches
MARIANO MORA 37 m Los Adaes
MARIA TRINIDAD PROCELA MORA 28 m Nacogdoches
JUAN MORA 10 s Nacogdoches
JOSE MORA s Nacogdoches
GUADALUPE ROSALES 12 s Nacogdoches
MICHAELA SANTA CRUZ 60 w Los Adaes
MARIA JUSTA 23 m Natchitoches
IGNACIO COBUS 43 s San Bartolo
MANUEL del RIO 22 m Nacogdoches
LINA PADILLA del RIO 18 m Nacogdoches
JOSE ANTONIO del RIO s Nacogdoches
JOSE VIVIANO del RIO s Nacogdoches
JOAQUINA del RIO s Nacogdoches
MARIA DEL PILAR PROCELA 54 w Los Adaes
PEDRO ALAMILLA 30 s Nacogdoches

ILARIO ALAMILLA 27 s Nacogdoches
SERAFINA ALAMILLA 19 s Nacogdoches
JUANA ALAMILLA 13 s Nacogdoches
MARIANO SANCHES 39 m Los Adaes
PAULA RUIZ SANCHES 41 m Los Adaes
JOSE MARIANO SANCHES 18 s Nacogdoches
JULIAN SANCHES 14 s Nacogdoches
FRANCISCO SANCHES 11 s Nacogdoches
SIMON SANCHES s Nacogdoches
LUIS SANCHES s Nacogdoches
JOSE MARIA SANCHES s Nacogdoches
JOSE ANTONIO SANCHES s Nacogdoches
GETRUDIS SANCHES 13 s Nacogdoches
ALAMULA SANCHES s Nacogdoches
MARIA ANTONIA IBARBO 59 w Los Adaes
FRANCISCO GUERRERO 35 s Los Adaes 3 slaves

MANUEL SANCHES 49 m Los Adaes
APOLONIA SANTOS SANCHES 40 m Bexar
PACIFICA ACOSTA 13 s Nacogdoches
MAZULO GARCIA 28 s Nacogdoches
MANUEL GARCIA 20 s Nacogdoches
NICHOLAS PON 54 s Orleans
WILLIAM PALLAR 46 s St. Malo
MANUEL BUSTAMANTE 37 m Jalapa
LUISA SANCHEZ BUSTAMANTE 22 s Nacogdoches
JOSE GUADALUPE BUSTAMANTE s Nacogdoches
JOSE RAMON BUSTAMANTE s Nacogdoches
SECUNDO SANCHES 10 s Nacogdoches
JUAN JOSE SANCHES s Nacogdoches
MANUEL PROCELA 28 m Nacogdoches
POLINARIA EQUIS PROCELA 22 m Nacogdoches
JOSE PROCELA s Nacogdoches
JOSE IGNACIO PROCELA s Nacogdoches
FELIPE PROCELA s Nacogdoches
MIGUEL IBARBO Apache 49 m
JOSEFA RODRIGUEZ IBARBO 26 m Bexar
MATIAS PEÑA 45 m San Fernando

BERARDA ARRIOLA PEÑA 37 m Bexar
MICHELA MEDINA 40 w Bexar
CLEMENTE BENITES 20 s Nacogdoches
MARIA ANTONIA BENITES 21 m Nacogdoches
PEDRO RODRIGUEZ absent m Louisiana?
MARIA ZARAGOSA SANTA CRUZ 51 w Los Adaes
FRANCISCO ELDE 17 s Nacogdoches
IGNACIO ELDE 15 s Nacogdoches
MARIA JOSEFA ELDE 13 s Nacogdoches
CONCEPSION ELDE 11 s Nacogdoches
MARIA TRIBURCIA REBALCABA 60 w Aguas Calientas
DOMINGO GOMES 25 s Bexar
DOLORES GOMES 11 s Bexar

MARIA de JESUS GOMES s Bexar
MARIANO GARZA Malay Indian 47 m Malay
MARIA del PILAR EQUIZ 43 m Los Adaes
CIPRIANO GARZA 22 s Nacogdoches
NEPOMUCENO CERDA 63 m Los Adaes
MARIA CELESTA FLORES CERDA 50 m Los Adaes
ATANACIO CERDA 24 s Nacogdoches
GREGORIO SERNAC 11 s Nacogdoches
JOSEFA SERNAC s Nacogdoches
MARIA del PILAR SERNAC s Nacogdoches
NARCISO LA BAUME 40 m Ouachita
MARIA CELESTE LA BAUME 27 m Natchitoches
HENRY LA BAUME 13 s Natchitoches
PONCIANO IBARBO 33 m Trinidad
MARIA PETRA PADILLA IBARBO 29 m Nacogdoches
PEDRO PROCELLA 53 m Los Adaes
JOSEFA CORDOVA 47 m Los Adaes
JUAN PROCELA 23 s Nacogdoches
LUIS PROCELA 21 s Nacogdoches
JOSE PROCELA 26 m Nacogdoches
GERTRUDIS IBARBO PROCELA 23 m Nacogdoches
MARIA SALOME PROCELLA s Nacogdoches
PEDRO TESSIER 34 m Canada
MADELINE CEDAR TESSIER 16 m Natchitoches
MARIA TESSIER s Nacogdoches
MARIA LENORE TESSIER s Nacogdoches
PEDRO SILVERIO PADILLA 53 m Los Adaes
JOSEFA ALVARADO PADILLA 68 m Los Adaes
AGUSTINA ALVARADO 63 w Los Adaes
TOMAS ALVARADO 12 s Nacogdoches
PEDRO GONZALES 61 m Havana
JESUSA de RIO GONZALES 56 m Los Adaes

MANUEL GONZALES 17 s Nacogdoches
MARIA DELFINA BENITES 82 w Los Adaes
MARIANO del RIO 37 s Los Adaes
JOSE IGNACIO GONZALES 21 s Nacogdoches
NAVOR MENCHACA 30 s Bexar
PEDRO CORDOVA 41 m Orcoquisac
CATARINA MALDONADO CORDOVA 33 m Los Adaes
MARIA TOMASA CORDOVA 16 s Nacogdoches
RICHARD SIMMES 48 m England
MARIA CONCEPCION PEREZ SIMMES 42 m Bexar
JOSE de JESUS SIMMES 12 s Nacogdoches
JOSE IGNACIO SIMMES s Nacogdoches
CANDELARIA SIMMES 16 s Nacogdoches
ANTONIA ILDEFONSA SIMMES 14 s Nacogdoches
MARIA BENIGNA SIMMES s Nacogdoches
EDMUND NORRIS 55 m Maryland
SARAH SANDERS NORRIS 48 m Maryland
NATHANIEL NORRIS 20 s Maryland
SAMUEL NORRIS 22 s Maryland
TOMASA NORRIS 11 s Maryland
SUSANA NORRIS s Maryland
JANE NORRIS s Maryland
EDMUND QUIRK 22 s Virginia
ANNA ALSOP QUIRK 50 m Virginia
EDMUND QUIRK absent
ANNA QUIRK 15 s Virginia
WILLIAM SUEL 50 s Pennsylvania
ROSALIA CAMACHO 50 w Los Adaes
MARIA RUIZ 31 w(?) Trinadad
NARCIS SANCHES 16 s Nacogdoches
SILVERIO SANCHES 10 s Nacogdoches
MARIA SANCHES 12 s Nacogdoches
LORETA BUENTELLA s La Bahia
MARIA TRINIDAD SANCHES s Nacogdoches
SANTIAGO RUIZ 39 m Los Adaes

JUANA ROSA GONZALES RUIZ 31 m Trinidad
JAMES DILL 36 m Pennsylvania
HELENA GIMLECH DILL 42 m Germany
FRANCES DILL 17 s Arkansas
DELILAH DILL 15 s Arkansas
MARIA CELESTE DILL 12 Nachitoches
MARIA HELEN DILL s Nacogdoches
MARIA CASILDA DILL s Nacogdoches
1 servant
JAMES LEONE 32 m Nacogdoches
MARIA JOSEFA MORA LEONE 28 m Nacogdoches
JOSE LEONE Nacogdoches
SUSANA MORO 39 w Natchitoches
JOSE MORO s Nacogdoches
MARIA JOSEFA MORO 14 s Natchitoches
JAMES CEDAR 42 m Germany
MARIA BELGAR CEDAR 45 m Mexico
JAMES CEDAR 21 s Natchitoches
ISABEL CEDAR 13 s Natchitoches
JAMES LEPINE 50 m New Orleans
MARIA BEBE LEPINE 43 m New Orleans
JULIANA LEPINE 16 s Natchitoches
TOMAS MENCHACA 41 m Monclova
SOLEDAD de los SANTOS MENCHACA 34 m Bexar
TERESA MORA 58 w Los Adaes
ANATASTACIO IBARBO 27 s Nacogdoches
JUAN JOSE IBARBO 20 s Nacogdoches
MANUEL IBARBO 18 s Nacogdoches
JUAN ANTONIO IBARBO 8 s Nacogdoches
PEDRO IBARBO 29 m Nacogdoches
JUANA MARIA de la GARZA IBARBO 27 m Nacogdoches
RAFAELA IBARBO s Nacogdoches
TOMAS MANSOLO 47 m Los Adaes
DOROTEA SARNAC MANSOLO 26 m Nacogdoches
MELCHOR MANSOLO 10 s Nacogdoches
GERTRUDIS MANSOLO s Nacogdoches
FRANCISCA MANSOLO s Nacogdoches
GETRUDIS MANSOLO s Nacogdoches
MARIA de los MANSOLO s Nacogdoches
TRINIDAD MANSOLO 39 w Los Adaes
JOSEFA MANSOLO 12 s Nacogdoches
JUAN SARNAC 76 w Rochelle
VICENTE SARNAC 26 s Nacogdoches
GERONIMA SARNAC 11 s Nacogdoches
VICENTE NAJAR 59 s Saltillo
VICENTE SAN MIGUEL 51 m Los Adaes
MARIA DE LARA SAN MIGUEL 41 m Los Adaes
VICENTE del RIO 39 m Los Adaes
ENCARNACIONA SANTA CRUZ del RIO 29 m Bexar
FECUNDO del RIO s Nacogdoches
JOSEFA del RIO 11 s Nacogdoches
PIERRE ENGLE 58 m New Orleans
DOLORES del RIO ENGLE 50 m Los Adaes
XAVIER PADILLA 62 m Los Adaes
JUANA de MORA PADILLA 58 m Los Adaes
JOSE PADILLA 31 s Trinidad
XAVIER CORTINAS 72 m Los Adaes
BEATRIS PEÑA CORTINAS 61 m Los Adaes
ISABEL ESPARZA 52 w Los Adaes
GETRUDIS MORA 23 w Nacogdoches
PEDRO JOSE ESPARZA 55 w Los Adaes
MARIA PROCELA 15 s Nacogdoches
PEDRO BELA 28 m Carmargo
DELORES GARZA BELA 22 m Nacogdoches

APPENDIX II
NACOGDOCHES CENSUS (1826)

JOSE ANTONIO CHIRINO 77
 WIFE 55
MANUEL CHIRINO 33
MARTINA YBARBO CHIRINO 28
POLONIO CHIRINO 14
ANTONIO HURCULIANO CHIRINO 12
MARIA FAUSTINA CHIRINO 10
ANASTACIO CHIRINO 6
MARIA GORGONIA CHIRINO 4
JOSE MARIA CHIRINO 25
MARIA RAFAELA de JESUS CHIRINO 18
MARIA BENCELADA de JESUS CHIRINO 8
FRANCISCO MORA 60
UCEBIO Y SUR (PANTALLION) 24
MARIA EME BASCONQUI Y SUR 20
MARIA GLEE Y SUR 4
MARIA CRISANTES Y SUR 8 mos.
MARIA MODESTA TOTEN 9
JOSE LUTERIO LOPES 26
MARIA CONSECION ARRIOLA LOPES 21
JOSE ANGEL LOPES 4
MARIA BENARDINA DE CENA 1
PEDRO YBARVO 43
JUANA de la GARZA YBARVO 37
JOSE REMIGIO de JESUS YBARVO 16
MARIA JOSEFA LIONICIA YBARVO 14
MARIA CANUTA YBARVO 12
MANUEL HONOFRE YBARVO 10
JOSE LUCIANO YBARVO 8
JUANA BAUTISTA YBARVO 5
MARIA FELICIANA YBARVO 1
JUAN JOSE YBARVO 36
MARIA GARCIA YBARVO 29
JOSE GREGORIO YBARVO 15
JUAN PABLO YBARVO 11
JUAN ANTONIO YBARVO 25
ANASTACIO YBARVO 40
MANUELA SANCHES YBARVO 26
ENCARNACION YBARVO 1 month

ANASTACIO MARIA PETRA CORDOVA 3
JOSE DE JESUS GOMES 28
MARIA GREGORIA SANCHES GOMES 25
MARIA GODONIA GOMES 1
MANUEL YBARVO 33
MARIA GERTRUDES CALDERON YBARVO 26
JOSE MARIA YBARVO 8
CANDELARIO YBARVO 6
JESUS YBARVO 4
MARIA BRIJIDA YBARVO 7 mos.
MARIA GARCIA 13
FRANCISCO GUERRRERO 55
JOSE YGNACIO YBARBO 50
BENINO YBARBO 20
MANUEL YBARVO 18
MAXIMILIANO YBARVO 7
JUAN ANTONIO YBARVO 24
MARIA CARMEL YBARVO 16
MARIA TERESA YBARVO 2
JUAN PALVADO 56
LEONOR TRESIE PALVADO 55
JOSE PALVADO 20
ANASTASIA TESIE PALVADO 7
VICENTE DIAS 35
MARIA DIAS 12
MARIA ASENSIA DIAS 6
JUANA MARIA DIAS 2
MARIA GERTRUDIS ?
JUAN ALBARADO 47
MARIA YGNASIA GARSIA ALBARADO 28
SANTOS GARCIA ALBARADO 12
JOSE GIL ALBARADO 1
DAMASIO YBARVO 43
JUAN BAPRISTA GAÑE 32
JOSE CARO 54
MICAELO EXIS CARO 46
JOSE AGATON CARO 30

JUAN CARO 25
PILAR CARO 18
FELISIAN CARO 16
JOSE SEBASTIAN CARO 14
MARIA ANTONIA CARO 12
CLETA CARO 9
JOSE TORIBIO CARO 7
MARIA JESUSA CARO 4
TOMAS CARO 37
GERTRUDIS TEXADA CARO 30
MARIA BASILIA CARO 9
MARIA YGNASIA CARO 7
LEONISIA CARO 5
JOSE JUSTO CARO 3
MARSELINA CARO ?
JOSE ALEXANDRO CARO 3
NORIN PALVADO ?
JOSE YBARBO 40
MARIA CARO YBARBO 28
JOSE ANTONIO YBARBO 10
FRANCISCO YBARBO 8
VICENTE YBARBO 4
LEONISIO YABARBO 2
JOSE ANTONIO SEPULVEDA 45
GUADALUPE CHAVANA SEPULVEDA 21
FELIPE SEGUMONDO SEPULVEDA 7
MARIA ANTONIA SEPULVEDA 6
MARIA BERNAVE SEPULVEDA 4
MARIA TORIVIA SEPULVEDA 1
RAMON CHAVANA 53
NARIA JOSEFA SANCHES CHAVANA 42
ANTONIO CHAVANA 26
SANTIAGO CHAVANA 17
FAUSTINO CHAVANA 12
GUILLERMO CHAVANA 8
MARIA de los REMEDIOS CHAVANA 4
JOSE FERMIN CHAVANA 1
SANTIAGO HEVIE 22
MARIA ENSELMA CHAVANA HEVIE 14
JOSE MARIANO ACOSTA 35
MARIA JOSEFA DELGADO ACOSTA 29
FRANCISCO ACOSTA 7
JUANA FRANCISCA ACOSTA 5

JUAN JOSE ACOSTA 3
MARIA de la PAZ ACOSTA 1
MANUEL SANTOS 37
GUADALUPE CHIRINO SANTOS 30
JUAN SANTOS 13
BENINO SANTOS 11
MARIA ANTONIA SANTOS 7
MARIA CARMEL SANTOS 5
SIPRIAN del TORO 48
RICHARDO SANCHES 40
BENTURA SANCHES 17
TRINIDAD GARCIA 40
DELORES MARTINES 44
JUAN YGANCIO ZOTO 47
JESUSA MALDONADO ZOTO 44
YGNACIO SANTOS 51
GERTRUDIS CHIRINO SANTOS 36
ENSIDUO d la GARZA 24
VICENTE CORDOVA 29
MARIA ANTONIA CORDOVA 19
JUAN NEPOMUSENO CORDOVA 1
ANDRES TORRES 30
JESUSA de LEONE TORRES 22
MARIA ANA TORRES 8
JOSE NATAVIO TORRES 1
FRANCISCO PERES 25
CARMEL TREVIÑO TORRES 20
MARIA SULTANA PERES 1
CLETO TORRES 20
PILAR ACOSTA TORRES 22
CARMEL TORRES 3
MARIA ANTONIA CRUS 60
MARIA JOSEFA TORRES 22
MIGUEL TORRES 17
MANUEL SAVALA TUSCANO 30
GERTRUDIS SANCHES TUSCANO
SANTIAGO TUSCANO 5
MARIA ROSELIA TUSCANO ?
TRINIDAD MANSOLO 50
MARIA JOSEFA MANSOLO 23
JOSE MARIA MANSOLO 7
SIMON SANCHES 22
POLONIA SUARES SANCHES 20
SEFERINO SANCHES 4

ANDRES de ACOSTA 72
MANUEL ACOSTA 41
JUAN YSIDRO ACOSTA 30
ENCARNACION ZOTO ACOSTA 24
MARIA DOMINGA ACOSTA 6
MARIA EUSIA ACOSTA 4
JOSE NICHOLAS TOLENTINO
JOSEFA de ZOTO 14
JUAN JOSE ACOSTA 28
MARIA JACINTA CASTRO ACOSTA 20
GUADALUPE ACOSTA 3
JOSE RUMADO ACOSTA 1

INDEX

-A-

ABBET
  Nancy Ann, 49
ABRAHAM
  James, 115
ACOSTA
  Francisco, 55
  Jose Mariano, 54
  Juan Jose, 55, 132
  Juana Francisca, 55
  Maria de la Paz, 55
  Pilar, 55
ADAMS
  Bessie, 99
  Hodge, 119
  John, 99
  Lewis, 104
  William, 119
ADDISON
  Mary Cabiere, 102
  William, Sr., 102
ADKINSON
  J. W., 162
ADLE
  Jeannvieve Dubois, 154
  John, 154
AGAR (AGUIRE)
  Ulysis, 117
AIKEN
  Collen, 114
  Collin M., 139
AKEN
  Collin, 86
  James, 86
AKEN (AIKEN)
  Brenette, 115
  James, 115
AKENS
  William, 86
AKENS (AIKEN)
  Aramenta, 117
  William B., 117
ALAMILLO
  Maria, 33
ALBADRO
  Jose Gil, 54
  Santos Garcia, 54
ALBARDO
  Augustina, 33
  Juan, 54
ALDERATA
  Beiniete, 84
ALDSEVATA
  Jose Ben, 84
ALEXANDER
  Mary, 84, 160
ALFORD
  Anesha, 111
  James, 111
ALGESE
  Marela, 84
ALIN
  James, 157
ALLBRIGHT
  Edmond, 78
ALLEN
  Augustus Chapman, 99
  C. C., 99
  Davis, 81
  Delilah, 102
  Dixon, 141
  Jackson C., 78
  James W., 75
  Jno. M., 78
  John, 172
  John Kirby, 99
  Margaret Quin, 100
  Nathan G., 100
  Nathaniel, 102
  William, 102, 172(2)
  William F., 84
ALLIN
  James, 61
ALLISON
  Elihu C., 163
ALLOVERBIGNESS, 19
ALLSUP
  Elisha, 79
ALSOP
  Anna, 48, 154
  Anna Marie, 45
  Samuel S., 119
ALVARADO
  Eligio, 132
AMES
  Harriet A. M., 126
ANDERSON
  Bailey, 65, 77, 83, 97, 107
  Bailey, Jr., 63, 69, 156, 160
  Bailey, Jun., 61
  Bailey, Snr., 61
  Bailey, Sr., 63, 69, 107, 156
  Ben, 141
  Benjamin, 105
  Captain Bailey, Sr., 68
  Delila, 109
  Elijah, 114
  Elizabeth McFadden, 107, 156
  Elizabeth Webster, 107, 154
  Gemedey, 84
  Grady, 160
  Hampton, 84, 160
  Hannah English Payne, 109
  Hazard, 107, 160
  Jane Williams, 105
  John, 63
  Jonathan, 63, 83, 109, 160
  Mary (Wyatt), 97
  Mary Wyatt, 63
  Myra, 90, 93
  Nancy (McFadden), 93
  Nolan, 109
  Oliver Hazard, 154
  Ruth, 114
  Uriah, 170
  Vincent, 61, 77, 156
  Wiet, 84, 160
  William H., 119

  Wm. H., 87
  Wyatt, 93
ANDING
  David, 106
ANDRES
  Ame, 56, 59
ANDREW
  Jas. S., 79(2)
ANDREWS
  David, 119
ANGLIN
  Drewery, 105
  Mary, 105
ANNA MARIA, 35
ANTHONY
  Cynthia Brown, 114
  Jacob, 114
  Nimrod, 114
  Phoebe, 114
APPLEGATE
  John, 84, 110, 160
  Nancy, 110
ARAGON
  Manuel, 35
  Manuela, 32
  Polonia, 36
  Santos, 36
AREOLA
  Manuela, 32
ARIOLA
  Anna Maria (Equis), 59
  Edwardo, 59
  Jose Antonio, 59
ARNER
  Mary, 95
AROCHA
  Jose Maria, 132
  Mary, 84
AROCHE
  Mary, 160
ARREOLA
  Eduardo, 56
ARRINGTON
  Noel, 115
ARRIOLA
  Bernalda, 35
  Josefa, 31
  Maria Consecion, 53
ARZE Y LARENDOIERE
  Francesca, 66
  Juan, 66
  Juan Ignacio Maximillian, 66
ASHABRANNER
  Henry, 160
ASHBRANNER
  Mary (Polly) Butler, 111
  William Henry, 111
ASHTON
  Jno. T., 79
ASKENS
  Charles, 110
ASKINS
  John, 87
  Thomas, 116
  Wesley, 116, 139
ASSABRANNER
  Henry, 83
ATHERTON
  Benjamin, 82

ATKINS
  Alfred, 79
  John, 119
AUGUSTINE
  Cynthia, 94
  Eliza, 70, 114
  Henry, 66
  Henry W., 76, 94, 114
  Henry William, 69, 70
AURIDA
  Antonio, 35
AUSTIN
  Stephen F., 16, 50, 53, 93, 125, 141
AVENT
  Durham, 100
  Susan Winset, 100
AVILA
  Maria Concepcion, 45
AYERS
  John, 48
AZKEY
  Abner, 119
  Fielding, 119

-B-

BACK BONE, 19
BACON
  Richard, 79
BAGBY
  George H., 114
  Margaret, 114
BAILEY
  Henry, 100
  Howard, 100
  John, 100
  Sarah, 100
  Wilshire, 140
BAINES
  Howard, 115
BAITMAN
  A. T., 106
  Nancy, 106
BAKER
  Caleb, 101
  Caroline Mann, 101
  Hulda Jones, 101
  John W., 78
  Larkin, 163
  William, 101
  William R., 140
BALL
  John, 119
BALLANCE
  Domingo, 152
BALLARD
  Archibald, 79
  B. M., 139
  Barkley Moreman, 114
  John T., 103
  Mary Gillentine, 114
BALLEXE
  Christoval, 28
BANDYHAM
  Alfred, 132
  Thomas, 132
BANTA
  Isaac, 141

INDEX

BARB
  Ocela, 160
BARBER
  Amos, 76
BARBO
  Miguel, 133
BARBOSE
  Antonio, 84
BARCENAS
  Jose Domingo, 28, 153
BARCLAY
  Anderson, 102
  Henry, 140
  Sarah Ann Prather, 102
BARD
  Antoin, 84
BARDON
  Catherine, 46
  Mariana (Verneuil), 46
  Raymundo, 46
BAREN
  Catherine, 106
  William W., 106
BARGAS
  Josefa, 33
BARKER
  Billy, 140
  Elizabeth, 89
  James, 87, 119
  James S., 140
BARKHAM
  John, 87
BARKMAN
  Hannah, 119
  Hannah Davis, 118
  Jacob, 87, 118
  James, 117
  John, 118, 119
BARNES
  Jose Miguel (Joseph Mickle), 47
BARNHILL
  Cynthia Hedge, 100
  William, 100
BARNS
  Joseph, 113
  Thomas, 119
BARR
  Elanson (Alanson), 110
  Mahaly, 110
  William, 39, 153, 162
  William], 43
BARRELA
  Manuel, 152
BARRERA
  Josefa, 34
  Maria, 30(2)
BARRON
  Juana, 34
  Prudencio, 34
BARROW
  Benjamin, Jr., 75
  Benjamin, Sr., 75
  Levi, 75
  Peter, 141
  Reuben, Sr., 75
  Solomon, 75, 169, 170
  Vincent, 75
BARTEE
  William, 119(2), 163
BASON
  George, 115, 139
BASQONQUI
  Maria Esne, 59
BASQUES
  Mariane, 34
BASQUEZ
  Juana, 35
BASS
  Ambrose, 78
  Mrs. Rebecca Mary, 96
  Rebecca Mary, 127
BASSET
  Basset, 62
BASSETT
  Bassett, 157
BATES
  John C., 139
BATEY
  John, 69
BATON
  Franklin, 85
BATTE
  William C., 142
BAYLISS
  Joseph, 113
BAYS
  George W., 165
BEACH
  Clark, 172
BEAN
  Louisa J., 72
  Peter Ellis, 72, 162, 165
  Peter Ellis (Ellis P.), 149
BEARD
  Andrew S., 115
BEAUCHAMP
  Jerry Baum (Jeroboam) R., 110
  John, 110
  Susan, 110
  Thomas D., 90
BEAUMONT
  Mary Dewburlilegh Borlance W., 96
BEBE
  Guillermo, 153
  Jose, 56
  Maria, 56
  Marselino, 56
  Santiago, 56
  William, 44, 56(2)
  William, Jr., 60
  William, Sr., 60
BECKER
  J., 85, 104
  Jacob, 85
BECKETT
  Dayton, 78
BECKNAL
  John, 116
BECKNEL
  William, 116
BEGA
  Juana, 32
BELANCHE
  Louis, 37, 39
BELANSHE
  Luis, 33
BELDEN
  Samuel C., 113
BELEY
  Rebecca, 85
BELGARDA
  Maria, 147
BELL
  Alexander, 117
BELT
  Helen Taylor, 101
  Samuel T., 101
BENERO
  Josefa, 33
BENITES
  Juan, 35
  Maria, 30(2), 33
BENITEZ
  Melchor, 28, 152
BENNETT
  Adam Jackson, 82
  Henry, 82
  Mary (Palmer), 82
BENNINGFIELD
  Harmon P., 117
  Posey, 49
BENSAN
  Vicente Michel, 44
BENSART
  Michel, 153
BENTON
  Jesse F., 140
BERMEA
  Andres, 132
BERMUDEZ
  Phelipe, 25
BERRY
  Adline Glass, 102
  John, 169, 170(2)
  Mary Ann, 38
  Milly, 100
  Radford, 100
  Sarah, 100
  Seaborn, 85, 154
  Sebern, 102
BERRYMAN
  Henry, 149
BERSOLE
  Maria, 33
BERTRAND
  Denee, 38
  Louis, 46
BERYMAN
  Helena Dill, 162
  Henry, 162
BEVIL
  Adalia Gilchrest, 154
  Alfred, 101
  Alfred Monroe, 154
  Ann Jane Taylor, 101
  Annie Jan Taylor, 154
  John, 101, 154, 169
  John R., 84, 94, 172
  John Randolph, 84
  Laodicae (Burton), 84
BIDDIC
  Jane, 112
  Jonathon, 112
BIENS
  John, 154
BIERLY
  Martin, 102
  Matilda Hagood, 102
  Thomas, 102
BIG BONE, 18
BIG FIELD, 19
BIG JOHN, 19
BIG RUMP, 18
BILL
  Marvin, 102
BINAM
  Henry, 112
BINGE
  Martin, 116
BINNION
  Joseph, 142
BIRD
  John, 86, 115
BISSON
  Julian, 47
  Louis, 47
  Pierre, 47
BLACK
  Jacob, 87, 119(2)
  William, 48
BLACKBURN
  Kate, 70
BLACKWELL
  Henry B., 77
BLAIN
  Thomas, 37
BLAIR
  Jacob, 87
BLANCHETTES
  Pierre, 171
BLAND
  Abel, 115
  Benjamin, 115
  Preston, 116
BLOODGOOD
  Levicy Ballew, 154
  William, 154
BLOUNT
  Elizabeth (Winn), 125
  James F., 101
  James H., 94
  S. W., 66
  Stephen William, 125
BLUNDELL
  William, 139
BODA
  Bateast, 62, 157
BODAN
  Juan Batista, 132
  Juan Lorenzo, 132
  Nicholas, 132
  Pierre (Pedro), 132
BODINE
  John, 65, 107
  Nancy A. Gunnels, 107
BOLEN
  Edward, 47
BOLING
  Eliza Nail, 110
  Elizabeth, 110
  James, 110
  Jerry, 110
  Lucinda, 111
  Solomon, 111
BOLTONS
  Zachariah, 119
BOON
  James W., 119
  John R., 115
BOON(E)
  Elizabeth

196

INDEX

BOON(E) (continued)
  Robertson, 119
  Needham, 119
BOOTH
  Robert, 170
BORDER
  John P., 66
BORDINE
  John, 77, 156
BOREN
  Minerva, 116
BOSCOQUI
  Maria Eme, 53
BOSQUE
  Pierre, 44, 153
BOSQUES
  Pierre (Peter), 46
BOSTIC
  Levi, 154
BOUGACIER
  Antonio, 37, 38
BOUGNER
  Antonio, 153
BOUGUER
  Antonio, 44
BOULTER
  James, 99
  Maria Louisa, 99
BOULWARE
  O. T., 142, 143
BOUQUIRE
  Bela, 47
BOURLAND
  Col. James, 141
BOWEN
  Ely A., 112
  Henry, 115
  Many Ann, 112
BOWERS
  Johnson, 87, 119
BOWLES
  Chief, 14, 18
  John (the Bowl), 15
BOWLES (DUWALI)
  Chief, 12, 13, 15
BOWLING
  James, 83, 160
BOWLS
  Stanly, 18
BOWMAN
  Joseph, 119
  Martha, 119
BOX
  James E., 149, 162
  James F., 142
  John M., 162
  John W., 149
  Richard W., 162
  Roland W., 149
  Samuel C., 149, 162
  William S., 149, 162
BOYD
  W., 143
BOYE
  Bateast, 62, 157
BOYLES
  William, 119
BOYNTON
  Frances, 84
BRADBURN
  Colonel John Davis, 88
BRADBURY
  Jabes, 154
BRADLEY
  Hellena, 100
  John, 110
  John M., 69, 90
  John W., 66
  Mrs. Ann M., 95
BRADSHAW
  James, 69, 162
BRAKE
  M. S., 61, 156
BRANCH
  Edward Thomas, 170
BRANHAM
  E. L., 168
BRANNON
  Captain Merett, 140
BRANTON
  David D., 116
  Marium, 116
  William, 117
BREANT
  Benjamin, 105
  Roxanna, 105
BREAS
  Ann Mariah, 113
  Thomas H, 113
BREWER
  Bethany Brewer, 100
  Greenberry, 100
  Henry, 70
  Henry Mitchell, 69, 70
  John, 69, 70
  Sarah Brewer, 100
  Susanna (Mitchell), 70
  William T., 100
BREWNO
  Susan, 83
BRIDGEMAN
  Jas. T., 79
BRIDGES
  Elizabeth, 85, 109
  Elizabeth Harvey, 108
  James, 61, 66, 77, 108
  James W. J., 109
  Ross, 66
  Ross M., 109
BRIGHMAN
  Jos. W., 78
BRIMBERRY
  Mary Jones, 100
  Samuel, 100
BRINLEE
  Amy McKinney, 115
  George, 86, 115
  Hiram, 114
BRISBAE
  Samantha, 95
BROMLY
  Thomas, 118
BROOCKS
  Travis G., 135
BROOKE
  John C., 66
BROWN
  Catherine, 108
  Daniel, 105
  Emily, 85
  Francis, 154
  Harriet, 50

  Hiram, 69, 70, 108
  Hyram, 66
  Jeffry, 119
  John, 44, 101
  Joseph, 80, 158
  Lucretia, 108
  Mary, 64
  Mrs. Lucretia, 64
  Rebecca Good, 101
  Selwin L., 79
  Squire, 66
  William R., 118
BROWNING
  Hardena, 119
  Lucas, 78
  William, 119
BROWNRIGG
  George E., 77
  George W., 114
  Theresa Thomas, 114
BRUMMETT
  Harrison, 139
BRUNO
  Pedro, 35
BRUTON
  Benjamin, 116
  Jonas, 116
BRYAN
  John J., 168
BRYANT
  John A., 119
  John W., 113
BUCKLEY
  Elizabeth, 109
  John, 61, 109, 156
BUCKNAL
  William A., 116
BUCKNER
  Henry, 115
BULLOCK
  Colonel James Whitis, 67
  David, 113
  James, 61
  James W., 66, 77, 111
  James Whitis, 69, 154, 156
  Julius W., 77
  Martha Anderson, 108
  Nancy Horton, 112, 156
  William C., 108
BUNCH
  Hiram, 172
BURAN
  Celistina, 56
BURDEN
  Caroline Crain, 107
  William B., 107
BURDETT
  Jesse, 107
  Milla, 107
BURDINE
  John, 61
BURGESS
  Dickson, 79
  William, 154
BURK
  Benjamin, 103
  Susannah Ogden, 103
BURKE

  Benjamin, 85
  George T., 81, 159
BURKHAM
  Abijah, 87
  Charles, 49, 86, 115
  James, 49, 86
BURLESON
  Edward, 125, 134
BURMAN
  Samuel, 87
BURNAMAN
  Stephen, 154
BURNELL
  Robert, 75
BURNET
  Crawford, 163
  David G., 95, 164
  David Gouverneur, 92
  Dr. William, 92
  Eli, 114
  Gertrude (Gouvernor) Rutgers Butler, 92
BURNEY
  Abel, 79
  Shadrack, 169
BURNSIDE
  William, 87
BURRELL
  David, 172
BURRESS
  Samuel, 69, 154
  Samuel J., 118
BURRIS FAMILY, 162
BURROWS
  Thomas, 154
BURTON
  Alexander, 75
  Captain Isaac W., 68
  Isaac, 142
  Isaac W., 66
  Isaac Watts, 69
BUSH
  John, 100
  Samuel, 87, 119
BUTLER
  David, 111
  Elizabeth, 111
  George, 83, 90, 111, 160
  Joseph, 84, 107
  Juriah, 107
BUYE
  Margaret, 170
BUZZARD, 19
  Jacob, 87, 119
BYERS
  John C., 114
  Sarah, 114
  Wesley, 86
  Westly, 117
BYRNSIDES
  Samuel, 119
  William, 119

-C-

CADDELL
  Andrew, 66, 108
  Rhoda (Rodey) Daugherty, 108
CAIN
  James C., 113

INDEX

CALA
  Rebecca, 105
  Right, 105
CALAWNTALITE, 18
CALDERON
  Josef, 28
  Joseph, 152
  Juan Francisco, 132
CALDWELL
  Maria, 108
  William, 108
CALLIER
  Harriet (Fenley), 58
CALOWAY
  Phillip, 79
CALVERTSON
  Henry, 79
  Jas. T., 79
CAMBERO
  Jose Maria, 152
CAMERON
  John, 17
CAMPBELL
  Crockett H., 140, 141
  Elizabeth Holman, 64
CAMPURANO
  Josef, 154
CAPURAN
  Jose, 154
  Joseph, 46
CAPUTAN
  Jose, 44
CARADINE (CARRIDINE)
  Isaac, 105
  Margaret, 105
CARDOVA
  Antonio, 32
CARITHERS
  William C., 119
CARMENA
  Domingo, 28
CARNEY
  P. L., 77
CARNWELL
  Elizabeth, 111
  William, 111
CARO
  Cleta, 54
  Felicia, 54
  Jose, 32, 54
  Jose Agaton, 54
  Jose Alexandro, 54
  Jose Justo, 54
  Jose Sabastian, 54
  Jose Torbido, 54
  Josefa, 32, 34
  Juan, 54
  Juana, 33
  Leonisa, 54
  Maria, 54
  Maria Antonia, 54
  Maria Basilia, 54
  Maria Jesusa, 54
  Maria Ygnasia, 54
  Marselina, 54
  Micaela, 33
  Miguela, 35
  Pilar, 54
  Tomas, 54
CARODINE
  Isaac, 158
CARR
  Anastasha, 83
  Anotnio, 84
  Antonio, 160
  C. C., Sr., 142
  Marsele, 84, 160
CARRIERE
  Joseph, 170
CARRO
  Juan, 133
CARROLL
  Dennis C., 78
  Levi H., 78
  M. A., 75
  Moses, 76
CARSON
  John, 126
  Mary (Moffit), 126
  Samuel P., 139
  Samuel Price, 125
CARTER
  Andrew, 78
  Daniel, 132
  George, 104
  James, 66, 69
  Priscilla, 104
CARTRIGHT
  Ann, 156
  John, 157
  Thomas, 156
CARTWRIGHT
  Ann, 113
  George, 69
  George W., 70
  John, 61, 65, 70, 77, 82, 109
  Mary, 71
  Mary (Crutchfield), 70
  Mary Crutchfield, 82, 109
  Matthew, 76
  Thomas, 61, 65, 113
  W. G., 77
CARUTHERS
  William C., 140
CARWELL
  John, 107
CASEY
  Robert, 56
CAT FLOATING, 19
CATAWAH, 19
CAUGHRAM
  John, 100
CEDAR
  James, 154
  John James (Jack), 147
CEDARS
  Jack, 79, 157
  Maria Belgarda, 157
CEPEDA
  Vicente, 28, 153
CERDA
  Francisco, 27, 152
CERVANTES
  Bernardo, 153
  Domingo, 133
  Jose, 32
CHAFFIN
  T. B., 139
CHAFLIN
  Aginot, 114
  Talefore (Toliver) C., 114
CHAMBERS
  Thomas Jefferson, 170
CHAMIRMA (CHAMIRORO)
  Mican, 69
CHAMLEICH
  Catherine, 57
  John, 57
CHAPLIN
  Chichester, 66, 113
  Emily Edwards, 113
CHAPPELL
  Hartwell, 112
  Mary, 112
  Sarena, 109
  Umphries, 109
CHAPPLE
  Corene, 81, 158
CHASTAIN
  Jacques, 153
CHATA
  Brown, 154
CHAVANA
  Antonio, 54
  Faustino, 54
  Guadalupe, 54
  Guillermo, 54
  Jose Fermin, 54
  Maria de los Remedios, 54
  Ramon, 54
  Santiago, 54
CHAVENCE
  M., 75
CHAVEZ
  Nicholas Antonio, 33
CHELETTE
  Maria Manuela Eshbete, 45
CHENOETH
  Gabriel, 120
CHERRY
  Aaron, 168, 170
  Aaron, Jr., 168
  Aaron, Sr., 75
  Hanasa, 168
  John, 170
  John A., 168
  John H., 115
  John V., 139
  Matilda, 108
  Mrs. Matilda, 85
  Rachel, 168
  S. R., 139
  William, 75, 168
CHESSHER
  Daniel, 102
  James, 102
  James, Sr., 85
  Thirza Morgan, 102
CHEVANA
  Maria Enselma, 54
CHEWWACKOTAH, 19
CHEWWAH, 19
CHILDERS
  Milla, 106
  Robert, 106
CHILDS
  George W., 79
CHIRENO
  Bartolo, 72
  Francisco, 69
  Francisco Encarnacion, 69
  Jose Encarnacion, 72
  Maria Josefa (Arriola), 72
CHIRINO
  Anastacio, 53
  Antonio Herculiano, 53
  Gertrudis, 55
  Guadalupe, 55
  Jose Antonio, 35, 53
  Jose Maria, 53
  Juan, 28, 152
  Manuel, 53
  Maria Andrea, 31
  Maria Bencelada de Jesus, 53
  Maria Faustina, 53
  Maria Georgonia, 53
  Polonio, 53
CHISUM
  William, 101
CHIVER
  Joaquin, 55
CHOATE
  Aaron, Jr., 75
  David, Sr., 75
  Elizabeth, 83, 93
  John, 109
  Maria Ursula, 99
  Mary, 109
  Moses L., 99
CHONCA
  Christostomo, 44
  Christoval, 35
CHRISTIAN
  Isabella, 127, 128
  Jaques, 44
  Remi, 47
CHUMLEY
  Thomas, 77
CHUMLY
  Armstead, 109
  Harriet, 109
  John, 65
CIBEREASES
  C. C., 171
CIEDERS
  Lisabel, 81, 159
CLAPP
  David, 87
  Elisha (Elijah), 161
  William, 86, 117
CLARK
  Abbi, 105, 158
  Benjamin, 116, 138
  Benjamin S., 119
  Daniel, 56, 60
  David, 115
  Elijah, 158
  Elizabeth, 105, 158
  Elizabeth Isaacs, 105
  Esther, 76, 170
  George, 75, 115
  Henry, 158
  Isaac, 107
  James, 86, 105, 114, 138, 158

INDEX

CLARK (continued)
  Jim, 138(2)
  John, 105, 158, 169
  Martha, 106
  Martha B. Wall, 127
  Thomas C., 140
  William, 105
  William F., 106
  William, Jr., 125
CLEVELAND
  Mary Francis, 98
CLICK
  Calvin M., 116
  Lucy, 116
  Mathias, 116
  Matthias, 139
  Sally, 116
CLIFTON
  James D., 140
CLOUD
  Alexander, 105
  Sarah, 105
CLOVER
  Isaac, 87, 118
COAL
  John, 61
  Mason G., 61
COBB
  James, 100, 163
COCHRAN
  Henry, 103
  Jonathan, 87
  Robert Andrew, 142
COCKRAM
  Jonathan, 118
COFFEE, 18
  Colonel Holland, 140
COLE
  David, 172
  John, 172
  Macon G., 65
  Mason G., 157
  Nash (Wash.?), 140
  Philo K., 78
COLEMAN
  Rebecca, 76, 169
COLET
  Baptiste, 47
COLIER
  Comodore, 118
COLLEN (COLLIN)
  Collen M., 118
COLLIER
  Benjamin, 47
COLLINS
  Elisha Madison, 106
  Eliza Ann McGrew, 106
  George T. W., 109
  Lemuel, 79
  Red, 140
COLLINSWORTH
  Captain Charles, 125
COLLUM
  Charles, 86, 114
  Collin, 86
  Elizabeth
    Katherine Hyder, 114
  George, 86, 115
  Jacob, 114

Jonathan, 114
Jonathon, 86
Martha (Patsy)
  McKinney, 119
Mary W., 114
William, 87, 119
COLVIN
  Aaron, 61, 156
COMACHO
  Rosalia, 35
COMB
  Samuel, 79
CONCHA
  Christobal, 157
CONEJO
  Jose Antonio, 35
CONLY
  James, 106
CONN
  James, 85, 102
  Robert, 103
CONOVER
  Isaac, 103
CONSTANCIA
  Maie, 45
COOK
  Greenway, 105
  Henry C., 100
  Mary Goodson, 100
  Rebecca, 105
COOKE
  W. G., 140
COOT
  William M., 112
COPE
  Thomas, 75
COPELAND
  Frank, 48
  Jim, 48
COPWEN
  Thomas L., 115
CORDERY
  Early, 18
CORDOVA
  Anastacia Maria Petra, 54
  Barbara, 34
  Captain Vicente, 68
  Francisco, 133
  Joaquin, 27
  Jose Zeferiano, 133
  Juan Manuel, Sr., 133
  juan Nepomuseno, 55
  Juaquin, 152
  Maria Antonia, 55
  Maria Antonio, 68
  Pedro, 34
  Ramon, 68
  Telesforo, 133
  Vicente, 55, 69, 133
  Vincente, 132
CORDOVES
  Antonio Gregorio, 25
CORNELIUS
  Daniel, 87, 118
  Margaret McCowan, 119, 120
  Mary (Polly)
    Hathorn/Stallings, 118
  Philip, 119(2)
CORONADO

Jose, 75, 169, 170
CORONODO
  Jose, 170
CORTINAS
  Antonio, 30
  Jose Antonio, 33
  Xavier, 32
CORTINES
  Delores, 18
CORTRINAS
  Gertrudis, 31
CORZINE
  Sarah, 107
  Sarah Kennard, 113
  Shelby, 107, 113
COSHATTA KILLER, 19
COSTLY
  Elizabeth Reed, 100
  Michael, 100
COTTON
  John, 142, 143, 154
COULTER
  Abram, 82
COUTURIER
  Maria Louisa, 46
COX
  George W., 117, 139
COYLE
  S. G., 140
CRADDOCK
  John R., 117
  Louisa E., 117
CRAIG
  Charles, 47
  J. B., 140
CRAIN
  Ambrose, 107
  Mary Burdett, 107
CRAINSHAW
  Cornelius, 106
  Permelia, 106
CRAMPTON
  Polly, 71
CRANE
  Jackson, 111
  Lydia, 111
CRANSTON
  Edward, 160
CRAVENS
  Edwin R., 79
  Robert, 118, 139
CRAWFORD
  Archibald, 128
  Nancy (Carroll), 128
  Richard, 110
  Susan, 111
  William Carroll, 125
CREAGER
  William, 119
CREEPIN
  John, 62, 157
CRIBB
  William, 119
CRISLIA
  Lalitt, 106
  Rama, 106
CRISS
  John, 100
CROCKETT
  George, 66
CRODDOCK

John R., 139
CROMWELL
  Samuel, 113
CROSS
  Sarah, 119
CROUCH
  Jackson, 105
CROW
  John Michael, 45
  Jose Miguel, 153
  Joshua W., 116
  Martin, 116
  Michael, 43, 44, 158
  Mickel (Michael), 47
CROWDER
  John, 81, 159
CROWN
  David, 66
CRUS
  Maria Antonia, 55
CRUSE
  Isaac, 114, 139
CRUSE (CREWS)
  Piety Hoover
    Prewitt, 101
  Squire, 101
CRUTCHFIELD
  John, 110
  Sarah, 110
CRUZ
  Francisco, 28, 152
  Guillermo, 133
  Juan, Jr., 133
  Manuel, 28, 153
CUNNINGHAM
  Davis, 119
CURREY
  Elifain
    (Ellifaire), 108
  Wesley, 108
CURRY
  Nakubda, 108
  Thomas, 108

-D-

DAILEY
  Elizabeth
    Williams, 102
DAILY
  Michael, 85
DALEY
  Raymond, 48
D'ALTON
  Marie Isabella, 46
DAMERON
  George, 120
DANDRIDGE
  Sarah (Watson), 126
DANIEL
  John, 87, 119
  Rhoda, 119
DARDY
  Dennis, Senr., 115
DARVAN
  Maria Antonia, 30(2)
DAUGHERTY
  Bryan, 65
  James, 140
  John, 100
  Patrick, 100

199

INDEX

DAVE
  Francis, 140
DAVENPORT
  Ann (Davidson), 40
  Juan Benigno Bernardino, 40
  Marie Azalie, 40
  Peter Samuel, 40
  Samuel, 40, 43, 58, 71, 153, 162
  Theresa Eliza, 40
  William, 40
DAVERSON
  Samuel, 81
DAVESSON
  Samuel, 158
DAVIS
  A. M., 66
  Allen, 159
  Amelia, 105
  Andrew, 150
  Anna, 77
  Aquilla, 119
  Caldwell, 105
  Daniel, 69, 120
  Donaldson, 140
  E. K., 69
  Edward B., 63, 77
  Elias K., 63, 66, 71, 114, 169
  Elizabeth, 110
  George, 69
  Harrison, 83, 110, 160
  Jane, 63, 110
  John, 44, 47, 87, 119, 154
  Joseph, 110
  Joseph W., 119
  Martha, 63
  Martha Thomas, 114
  Mary, 109, 110
  Micajah, 140
  Mrs. E. K., 64
  Myrick, 61, 156
  Nancy, 107
  Nathan, 63, 65(2), 83, 157, 160
  Nathan, Jr., 82, 109
  Nathan, Sr., 110
  Nathin, 61
  Ralph, 117, 139
  Samuel, 107
  Samuel S., 66, 69
  Warren, 63, 71, 154
  Washington, 106
  William P., 161
DAY
  Aaron L., 81, 159
  Florinda McCulloch, 128
  Mrs. Florinda McCulloch, 91
DAYNE
  Hannah, 84
  Matthew, 84, 160
DAYTON
  Lewis, 87, 119
DE ABILA
  Agustin, 24
DE ACOSTA
  Andros, 32
  Jose Manuel, 32
  Joseph, 25
  Juan, 32
  Juana, 35
DE ACOSTA Y ARIAS
  Joseph Antonio, 25
DE ALBARDO
  Joseph, 24
DE ALCALA
  Joseph Ventura, 25
DE ALVARADO
  Luis de Moscoso, 1
DE AREJO
  Joseph, 24
DE ARMIJO
  Juan, 24
DE ARO
  Maria, 34
DE ARRIOLA
  Asensio, 34
  Juan Francisco, 132
DE BEGARA
  Don Joseph Cayetano, 24
DE BLANC
  Volezar, 171
DE BUSTILLO
  Don Juan Antonio, 24
DE CASTILLE
  Jose Juaquin, 31
DE CENA
  Maria Bernardine, 53
DE CORDOVA
  Baron, 31
  Christoval, 30
  Don Christoval, 36
  Jose, 35
  Josefa, 31
  Juaquin, 35
  Miguel, 31
DE CORVARRABIAS
  Juan Antonio, 25
DE ESPARANZA
  Salvador, 152
DE ESPARZA
  Isabel, 35
DE ESPERANZA
  Marcos, 27
  Salvador, 27
DE ESPINOSA
  Fray Isidro, 10
DE FUENTRES (MONTES?)
  Ypollito, 25
DE GALVEZ
  Viceroy Count, 2
DE JESUS
  Father Antonio Margil, 22, 23
  Maria Rafaela, 53
DE LA ARA
  Antonia, 32
  Juana, 32, 33
  Pedro, 32
DE LA BAUM
  Jose, 44
DE LA BAUME
  Count, 46
  Feliciana, 46
  John Joseph, 46
  Jose, 132
  Josef, 154
DE LA BEGA
  Jose, 34
DE LA CARDONA
  Nicholas Antonio, 25
DE LA CERDA
  Antonio, 133
  Josefa, 33
  Maria, 34
  Nepemucene, 28, 152
  Nepomuceno, 33
  Petit, 133
DE LA CONCEPCION
  Maria, 32
DE LA ENCARNATION
  Juan Joseph, 24
DE LA GARZA
  Baltasar, 34
  Esiduo, 55
  Juana, 53
DE LA JUENTE
  Roribie, 152
  Rorible, 27
DE LA SALLE
  Robert Cavelier, Sieur, 1
DE LA SANTOS COY
  Juan, 133
DE LA SERDA (CERDA)
  Petit (Antonio), 133
DE LA VEGA
  Josefa, 68
  Maria Josefa, 72
DE LA VERA
  Joseph Antonio, 25
DE LA ZERDA
  Francisco, 24
  Maria, 34
DE LARA
  Bernardo Gutierrez, 41
  Santiago Gutierrez, 41
DE LAS PIEDRAS
  Colonel Jose, 67, 68, 145
DE LEON
  Alonzo, 35
  Governor, 2
  Governor Alonso, 1
  Jesusa, 55
DE LOS POSOS
  Manuel Salvador, 25
DE LOS REYES
  Antonio, 133
  Juan, 24
  Julio, 25
  Manuel Luis, 25
  Maria de Jesus, 31
DE LOS SANTOS
  Francisco, 32
  Gertrudis, 43
  Jose, 31
  Maria, 31
DE LOS SANTOS COY
  Manuel, 170, 172
DE LUNA
  Encarnacion, 133
  Jose Maria, 35
  Pascual, 24
  Pedro, 28, 152
  Ria, 32
DE MORA
  Juan, 33
  Manuel, 35
  Maria Antonio, 3
  Nicholas, 30
  Teresa, 35
DE MOYA
  Dimas Guillermo, 34
DE NAPOLES
  Francisco, 24
DE ORTOLLAND
  Raimundo, 45
DE PADILLA
  Juan, 25
DE PANAIGUAN
  Antonio, 24
DE RIO
  Bernabe, 152
  Maria de Jesus, 31
DE RIPPERDA
  Governor Juan Maria Vicencio 28
DE SALCEDO
  Trinidad, 45
DE SAN MIGUEL
  Francisco, 25
DE SANTIAGO
  Cristobal, 24
  Francisco, 25
DE SIERRA
  Pedro, 28, 153
DE SOTO
  Bartoleme, 31
DE SOTO
  Marie, 46
DE TALAMANTEZ
  Francisco Xavier 25
DE TOBAR
  Juan, 28, 152
DE TORRES
  Francisco, 28, 153
  Joachin, 25
  Jose, 36
  Josefa, 35
  Juan, 25, 28, 153
  Lasare, 153
  Lazare, 28
DE TREJO
  Juana, 34
DE VILLAFRANCA
  Diego, 25
DE VILLAREAL
  Blas, 24
  Juan, 25
DEAN
  Edwin M., 114
  Ira (Asa), 116
  Jesse, 116
DECK
  Joseph, 117, 139
DEEN
  Calloway, 113
DEL MORAL
  Don Jose Miguel, 36
DEL PILAR
  Maria, 32
DEL RIO
  Antonia, 33
  Antonio, 27, 152
  Augustin, 28
  Bernabe, 27
  Cristobal, 24

INDEX

DEL RIO (continued)
  Domingo, 24
  Jose, 33
  Magdalena, 34
  Manuel, 28, 153
  Melchora, 31
  Miguel, 33
  Philipe, 24
  Rosa, 33
  Ygnacio, 27, 152
DEL TOTO
  Siprian, 55
DELANEY
  Charles, 103
  Frances Van
    Clive, 103
DELAP
  Charles, 159
DELASS
  Charles, 81
DELGADO
  Maria Josefa, 54
  Maria Josefa
    Candida, 72
DENMAN
  James, 102
  Obadiah, 102
DENNIS
  Moses M., 159
DENNISON
  Lewis C., 118
DENNIS[ON]
  Gerry, 82
DENTON
  A. B., 143
  Abraham, 154
  Jesse, 82
  John B., 140
DESPONETE
  Catherine, 55
DEVER
  John, 169, 170
  Mariah, 95
  P. P., 75
  Philip P., 170(2)
  Thomas, 169, 170
  Thos., 75
DEVERS
  John C., 75
DEVORE
  Jesse, 170
DEVORE
  Timothy, 103
DEW
  Joseph J., 117
DEWALTZ
  Napoleon, 133
DEWEES
  Ellis, 78
DEWITT
  Green, 16, 120
DIAS
  Maria, 54
  Maria Asensia, 54
  Maria Gertrudis, 54
  Vicente, 54
DICAS
  Nancy, 119
DICKERSON
  Jesse, 102
  John, 103
  Mary Ann Coleman, 103
  Prrsilla West, 102
DICKINSON
  John, 85

  Mary Ann, 64
DICKSON
  Martha (Patsy), 97
DIKES
  George Parker, 99
  Julia S. Beacham, 99(2)
  Levi B., 99
  Lovick P., 99
  Lydean Duvall, 99
  Rodea V. Maddox, 99
DILL
  Christopher, 37, 38
  Delilah, 55, 57
  Edward, 37, 38
  Elizabeth, 38
  James, 37, 43, 55, 57, 149, 153
  James (Santiago), 38
DILLARD
  Jane, 113
  John B., 113
DILLINGHAM
  John L., 119
DIMERY
  Obadiah, 133
DOAR
  Louis, 33
DOBIE
  William, 76
DOE
  John, 48
DOLET
  Pedro, 37
  Pierre, 44, 153
DOMINGUES
  Juan Domingo, 34
DONAHO
  Esther (Hester), 90
DONOHO
  Daniel, 103
  Nancy Larrimore, 103
  Willis, 103
DONOVAN
  Baptiste, 133
  William, 133
DOONE
  Grason, 82
DOR
  John M., 99
DORR
  Edward, 76
DORSE
  Benjamin H., 117
  John E., 117
DORSET
  John, 66
  Theodore, 66
DORSETT
  Charles, 61, 75, 156, 169
  Theodore, 61, 156
  Thomas, 169
DORTOLAN
  Bernardo, 45
DORTOLAN (NEGRO)
  Rafael, 133
D'ORTOLANDT
  Bernard, 44
D'ORTOLANT
  Bernard, 154
DORTOLANT

  Bernardo, 153
DORVAN
  Juana Maria, 34
DOUGLASS
  Kelsey H., 134
DOUTHIT
  Allen P., 117
  Ambrose, 115
DOWNEE
  John S., 117
DOYA
  Ensign Mallhead D., 68
  Malldred (Mallhed) D., 69
DOYLE
  Matthew, 108
  Parmelia, 108
DRODDY
  John, 102
  Sarah Hays, 102
DRY, 18
DUBOIS
  Anthony, 47
  Antoine, 44
  Antoine Phillipe, 39
  Antonio, 37
  Jean Baptiste, 39
  Marie Josepha (Claremont), 39
DUBOISE
  Antoine, 83(2)
DUBOY
  Leonardo, 55
DUBOYS
  Antonio, 153
DUGAN
  Daniel V., 140
  Daniel, Sr., 140
  George C., 140
DUGATS
  Joseph, 171
DUMAS
  Samuel, 78
DUNBAR
  George W., 141
  William, 48
DUNCAN
  Jacob, 99
  Joseph, 170
  Meredith, 75
  S., 81, 159
  Sarah Ann, 162
  William, 169, 170
  William Berry, 169
DUNEGAN
  Isaac, 112
DUNHAM
  Cary W., 78
DUNMAN
  Henry, 75
  Jas. T., 75
  Joseph, 170
  Sherrod, 87
  William, 75
DURANGO
  Jose Maria, 133
DURST
  Ann (Schesser), 57
  Anna (Schesser), 58
  Anna (Schlesser), 71
  Delilah Dill, 100, 162

  Harriet Matilda Jamison, 99
  Jacob, 57, 58, 71
  John, 56, 58, 99
  John M., 69, 71
  Joseph, 55, 57, 100, 149(2), 150, 162, 163
  Luis, 56
DUTY
  Philip, 117
DUVAL
  Thomas, 79
DYER
  Caroline, 117
  Dickson, 116
  George W., 117
  John H., 116, 119
  Robert, 118
DYKES
  Dennis, 106
  Elizabeth Lewis, 103
  Harriet, 103
  Joseph, 103
  Lovick (Lewis) P., 103
  Westley, 103

-E-

EARL
  Amanda, 154
  David, 77
  Mary, 154
  Mary Amy, 107
  Matthew, 80, 106, 154, 158
  Nancy, 106
  Nancy Matilda (White), 158
  Nancy Matilda White, 154
  William, 80, 154
EARLS
  David A., 156
EASLEY
  Daniel, 105
  James, 81
  Jane (Fanny) Hornbeck, 105
EASLY
  Daniel, 82
  James, 158
EASTEP
  Joseph, 81, 158
EATON
  Charity Arnold, 108
  Stephen, 108
EDMONSON
  John, 87, 119
  Samuel, 113
  William, 117
EDWARDS
  Asa M., 69
  Benjamin, 52
  Haden, 16, 40, 52, 58
  Haden H., 56, 99
  Jean Beall, 40
  Susan, 56, 58
EGG, 18
EGUNIO
  Usiderie, 153
ELAM
  Daniel, 156
  Danniel, 61

INDEX

ELDRIDGE
  Elisha, 79
ELLIOTT
  Maria "Polly"
    Williams, 154,
    163
  William, 149,
    150, 154, 163
ELLIS, 18
  Ambrose, 126
  Benjamin, 170
  Celia (Stokes),
    126
  Cherry Dandridge
    R. Smith, 118
  E. D., 162
  Frances Claughton
    Routt Wyatt, 117
  Joseph L., 170
  Nathaniel
    Dandridge, 117
  Richard, 118,
    125, 138, 139
ELLISON
  Jared P., 82
EMBERSON
  John, 117, 138
ENGEL
  Pierre, 153
ENGLE, 31
  Pierre, 37, 39,
    43
ENGLEDOW
  Creed S., 100
  Elizabeth
    Simpson, 100
  Elvira Randolph,
    100
  John, 100, 163
ENGLISH
  Bailey, 140
  Candas, 110
  Captain James, 90
  Elizabeth, 110
  Elizabeth
    (Denton), 90, 93
  Elizabeth Choate,
    154
  Elizabeth Choate
    Blair, 110
  Elizabeth Tittle,
    154, 157
  George, 64, 83,
    160
  James, 84, 93,
    110, 157
  John, 83, 93,
    154, 157, 160
  Jonas, 110
  Joseph, 83, 109,
    160
  Joshua, 110
  Leander, 109
  Martha, 110
  Mary, 109
  Myra Anderson,
    109, 154
  Sarah, 83, 110,
    160
  Stephen, 83, 109,
    160
  Thomas, 66, 110
  William, 66, 93,
    109, 157
  William K., 90,
    154
  William T., 83,
    160

EPPERSON
  Margaret, 115
  Mark, 115
EQUIS
  Geromino, 33
  Micaela, 32
EQUIZ
  Anna Coba, 35
  Christoval, 27
  Cristoval, 152
EQUNIO
  Usiderie, 28
ERIE
  Santiago, 54
ERLES
  Davis, 61
ESPANOLA
  Nicholas de la
    Compania, 34
ESPARRAGO
  Juan, 35
ESPARSA
  Baltasar, 35
ESPARZA
  Jetomas, 33
ESTE
  Hannah, 92
ESTES
  Henry W., 79
EUBANKS
  Elias M., 107
  Elizabeth W.
    Thompson, 107
EVANS
  John, Jr., 142
  Joseph, 82
EVERETT
  Alta Zera
    Williams, 101
  Riten, 111
  Stephen
    Hendrickson, 101
  William, 76, 169,
    170
EVERITT
  Alta Zera
    Williams, 127
  Stephen
    Hendrickson, 94,
    125
EWING
  Edley, 114
  Elizabeth Love,
    114
  Hannah DeSpain,
    114
  Wilson, 114
EWING FAMILY, 162
EXIS
  Michela, 54

-F-

FAMES
  Jose Maria, 133
FANCERS
  David, 99
FARMER
  Daniel, 84
  David, 172
  Jacob, 172
  Rachel, 102
FARRETT
  John R., 140
FARRIS
  Amanda, 104
  William, 104
FAULK

  John R., Sr., 170
FERGUSON
  Alston, 163
  Joseph, 87
  Warwick, 163
FERNANDEZ
  Lieutenant
    Bernardo, 36
FIELDS
  Richard, 15, 16
FILISOLA
  Vicente, 165
FINN
  Richard H., 87,
    119
FISHBACK
  Elizabeth, 116
  Isaac, 86
  Isaac H., 116
FISHER
  James, 120
FISSETT
  George, 106
FITZER
  John, 117
FITZPATRICK
  Hugh, 119
  Jabez, 140
FIZER
  John, 86
FLINN
  Simpson F., 81,
    159
FLINT
  H., 81, 159
FLOQUE
  Maria, 56, 60
FLORES
  Antonio, 68
  Antonio, Jr., 133
  Antonio, Sr., 133
  Edubijen, 59
  Francisco
    Antonio, 133
  Gil, 28, 153
  Jose, 30
  Jose Sepulveda,
    31
  Juan Antonio, 31
  Manuel, 31
  Maria Seledina,
    33
  Martin, 133
  Miguel Julian, 25
  Ocasia, 32
FODLEY
  Francis, 116
FONTENO
  Jean, 44, 45, 154
FOOT(E)
  Robert, 110
FOOTE
  R. H., 66
  Robert H., 77
  William, 82
FORBES
  B. T., 81
  Elizabeth Ann,
    119
  John, 17
FORD
  William W., 158
FORSYTH
  Darias, 110
  James, 110
FORSYTH(E)
  John, 110
  Martha, 110

FORSYTHE
  James, 83, 84,
    160(2)
  John, 83
  Silby, 83, 160
FORT
  Josiah W., 139
FORTUNE
  Louis, 44, 153
FOWLER
  B., 140
  Bradford, 138
  Bradford C., 86,
    116
  John H., 114, 139
  Mary A., 116
  Robert B., 120
FOX, 19
FOY
  Frederick, 90
FRANCOIS (FRANCIS)
  Sebastain, 113
FRANKS
  Buril, 169
  Burrell, 75
FRAZIER
  Ebenezer, 116
  Harman, 112
  J., 112
  Martha Wallace,
    112
FREDERICK
  Barbara, 55, 57
FRENCH
  Edmond, 81, 159
  Samuel W., 118
  Sarah, 118
FRIER
  Enoch, 107
  Jane, 107
FROSS (GROCE)
  Belinda (Earl),
    158
  Larkin, 158
FULCHER
  Elizabeth, 108
  Isabella Griggs,
    156
  Jacob, 156
  James, 61, 156
  John, 156
  Joshua, 101
  Rebecca Dimmaux
    Brooks, 101
FULLER
  Matison, 107, 109
  Seth W., 79
FULSHER
  Jacob, 61
FULTON
  Clara Roberts,
    117
  Sam M., 139
  Samuel Moore, 117
FURRY
  Elias, 78

-G-

GAFFEE (GAFFENE)
  Nancy, 104
  William, 104
GAGNON
  Marie Louisa, 40
  Marie Thereza
    (Valentine), 40
  Pierre, 40
GAHAGIN

202

INDEX

GAHAGIN (continued)
  John C., 115
GAILLONS
  Victor, 171
GAINER
  Permelia Taylor, 113
  Redmon (Reden), 113
GAINES
  E. P., 81
  Edmund, 105
  Edmund P., 158
  General Edward Pendleton, 48
  James, 43, 48, 52, 56, 65, 69, 80, 81, 105, 146, 158, 159
  James Taylor, 58, 125
  James, Jr., 56
  Jemima (Pendleton), 58
  John B., 81, 158
  John Baptist, 56
  Lieutenant Edmund P., 80
  Mahaly, 105
  Ramon, 56
  Richard, 58
  Susanna (Struther), 127
  Susanna Norris, 105
  Susannah (Norris), 159
  Thomas, 127
GALLEGO
  Maria de la Consencion, 35
GALLION
  John C., 105
  Susan, 105
GALLOWAY
  Peter, 66, 108
GALWAY
  Nancy, 111
GAMBELL
  James, 117
GAMBLE
  Robert, 119
GAME
  Marie Jacinta, 38
GAMES
  Candelario, 54
  Jesus, 54
  Jose de Jesus, 54
  Jose Maria, 54
  Maria Brijida, 54
GAMEZ
  Juan, 24
GANE
  Bardino, 43
  Juan Bautista, 54
GARCIA
  Christoval, 28, 31
  Cristoval, 152
  Francisco, 33
  Luciano, 35
  Marcus, Jr., 133
  Maria, 54
  Maria Ygnasia, 54
  Trinidad, 55
GARLAND
  James, 119
  Josiah, 119

GARLING
  Christina, 99
GARNER
  Anna, 91, 128
  Bradley, Sr., 172
  Bushnel, 120
  David, 172
  Jacob, 172
  James M., 119
  Sarah J., 113
  Thomas H., 113
GARRET
  Jacob, 56
  Milton, 63
GARRETT
  Alse, 100
  Charity (Taylor), 71
  Claiborne, 66
  Jacob, 58, 66, 71, 78, 90, 94, 108
  Jane, 58
  John, 58
  Lavecy, 114
  Maria Cartwright, 113
  Milton, 65, 66
  Thomas B., 114
  William, 66, 76, 113
  William E., 69, 71
GARZA
  Mariane, 32
GATES
  Charles Horatio, 107
  Hannah, 68
  Horatio, 68
  James, 68
  Jane, 110
  John, 110
  Minerva Fletcher, 107
  Philip, 82
  William, 163
GATTIS
  Mary, 126
GAULTEMAN
  Maria, 56
GEE
  Edson, 163
GEER
  Garland, 116
GEGA
  Maria Seleste, 56
GENTZ FAMILY, 169
GEORGE, 19
  Sheriff Alfred, 135
  Stephen, 101
GERISH
  James, 113
  James, Sr., 113
  Mary Ann, 113
GERRERA
  Thomaso, 133
GESCOM(?)
  Nathan, 82
GIBBS
  Anna G., 60
  Zaccheus, 162
GIBSON
  Absalom, 162
  James L., 111
  Samuel, 169
GIDENS

Absalom, 116
GIDEONS
  Richard, 114
GILBERT
  John, 112, 114
  Mary, 114
GILCHRIST
  Antonia J., 85
  Charles, 85, 102
  Jane Chessher, 102
  John Anthony, 102
  Sally Milholm, 102
GILL
  Martha "Patsy", 65, 93
  Presly, 75
GILLARD
  Adolph, 171
  Auger, 171
  Baptiste, 171
  Dr. Edward Joseph, 171
  John, 171
  Joseph, 171
  Silvier, 171
GILLESPIE
  John, 66
GILLIAN
  John, 110
GIMLECH
  Helena Kimble, 38
GIZZARD, 18
GLASS
  George, 84, 160
GODLEY
  Marshal D. G., 116
GOFF
  Henry, 61, 157
GOGUET
  Estevan, 153
  Stevan (Estevan), 46
  Steven, 43
GOIN
  Jerry, 103
  Sarafine Drake, 103
GOINS
  Elizabeth, 59
  William, 59
GOMEZ
  Cayetene, 27, 152
GONSALES
  Clemente, 32
  Francisco, 34
  Maria de la Trinidad, 31
GONZALES
  Domingo, 83
  Lieutenant Don Joseph, 25, 26
  Pedro, 31
GONZALEZ
  Don Joseph, 24
GOOCH
  Benjamin, 142
GOOD
  Edward, 101
  H., 104
  James D., 101
  Joseph S., 84
  Nancy Daughity, 101
GOODALL
  Adam, 79

GOODBREAD
  Joseph, 135
GOODEN (GOODWIN)
  Elizabeth, 110
  Henry, 110
  Sarah, 110
  Shirley, 110
GOODLEY
  J., 81
GOODRIDGE
  Allen, 85
GOODWIN
  Robert, 110
  Sarah, 110
GORMAN
  Abner, 79
GOSSET
  Elijah, 161
  Elizabeth Stone Edwards, 161
GOUGUET
  Stephen, 32
GOWEN
  Nancy, 76
GOWN
  Nancy, 75
GOYENS
  Mary Pate Sibley, 101
  William, 56, 59, 101
GRACIA
  Maria, 54
GRAGG
  Jacob, 86, 115
  John, 115
  Milton, 86
  Samuel, 86, 115
  William, 86, 117
GRAHAM
  James, 119, 139
  Richard, 119
  Thomas R., 78
GRANCE
  Maria Candida, 46
GRANDE
  Luis, 31
  Martina, 31
GRANT
  James, 99
GRAPPE
  Francois, 15
  Marie Anne, 46
GRAVES
  Elizabeth, 83, 160
  Frances, 82
  Hezekiah, 78
  Minos, 78
  Reubin, 82
GRAY
  L. P., 159
  Martha Winfree, 102
  S. P., 81(2), 159
  Samuel, 81
  Thomas, 102
GREEN
  Amos, 75, 159, 169, 170
  B. F., 141
  Benjamin M., 75
  David Griggs, 107
  Fitts H., 154
  Francis L., 109
  Mary, 109
  Miller, 140
  Richard, 75

INDEX

GREENWOOD
　John, 86, 114
GREGORY
　Patsy, 108
　William, 108
GRIFFIN
　Henry, 170
　Robert, 101
　W. R., 75
GRIGER
　J. H., 75
GRIGSBY
　Eliza, 112
　John, 112
　Joseph, 101(2), 172
　Nathaniel, 101
　Sally Graham, 101
　Sarah, 101
GRILLET
　Charles, 46
GRISSER
　Catherine, 104
　John, 104
GROCE
　Christian, 77
GROSS
　Belinda, 106
　Christian, 112
　Elizabeth, 113
　Larken, 106
　Larkin, 81
　Murid, 103
　Patsy Goodin, 103
GROUND HOG, 19
GROUNDS
　Catherine Rice, 112
　George, 112
GRUBBS
　Emanuel, 87
　Emmanuel, 119
　Thomas, 99
GUADIANA
　Don Jose Maria, 36
GUERRERO
　Anna Maria, 30
　Francisco, 28, 54, 153
　Juan Ignacio, 30
　Juan Ygnacio, 27, 152
GUERRO
　Anna Maria, 30
GUEST
　John, 115
GUIRE
　Bateast, 62, 157
GUIROS
　Juana, 32
GUITIERREZ
　Thomas, 28
GULAR
　Prosper, 113
GURBELO
　Gabriel, 34
GUTHRIE
　Nancy Bradberry, 101
　William, 101
GUTIERREZ
　Thomas, 153
GWIN (IRVIN)
　William A., 156
GWIN (IRWIN)
　William A., 61

-H-

HACKETT
　Edward W., 163
HAGERTY
　Melinda Bowie, 108
　Thomas J., 108
HAGOOD
　Henry, 102
HALE
　Amanda Ewing, 114
　Jonas, 66, 114
HALEY
　John, 110
　John R., 84
　Mark, 160
　Mary, 84
　Richard, 83, 110, 111, 160
　Richard, Jr., 84
　Richard, Sr., 84, 160
　Sarah, 110
　Susan, 110
　Thomas, 84, 160
HALL
　Britton, 102
　Burgess, 81, 158
　Harriet Pool, 102
　J. J., 137, 138
　John, 117, 142
　Joseph, 114
　Julietta, 91
　R. G., 159
　Robert, 87
　Warren DeWitt Clinton, 91
HALLAWAY
　Lewis, 61
HAMBLETON
　Frances, 79
HAMBY
　John, 71
　John Harvey, 69, 71
　Rhoda, 71
HAMILTON
　Elizabeth Bethany, 116
　Euphemia (Alston), 126
　James, 163
　James M., 115
　Nathaniel, 114
　Robert, 119, 125
　Robert S., 116
　William, 126
HAMMOND
　Elizabeth, 98
HAMMONS
　John, 111
　Malinda, 111
HAMONS
　John Johnson, 112
　Malinda, 112
HAMPTON
　Adam, 86, 116, 138, 139
　Andrew, 86
　John, 87
　Leven, 119
　Mary Ann, 119
HANCOCK
　James W., 117
　Leander W., 116
　Sewell, 117
HANKS
　Captain Wyatt, 68
　Elijah F., 114
　Eliza A. Davis, 114
　Hannah Gates, 104
　Horatio, 66, 69
　Isabella, 68, 71, 77, 112
　James, 66, 76
　John, 118
　N. Wyatt, 71
　N. Wyatt, Sr., 103
　Peter, 68, 71
　Samuel, 103
　Wesley W., 114
　Wyatt, 66, 76, 77, 90, 94
HANSCOME
　Aaron, 117
HANSFORD
　Dr. John M., 140
HANSOME
　Aaron, 86, 87
HARDEN
　Thomas, 81
HARDIN
　A. B., 75, 169
　Augustine Blackburn, 95, 169
　B. W., 75
　Benjamin Watson, 169
　Franklin, 170
　Jarusha, 75
　Jerusa (Blackburn), 92
　Jerusha (Blackburn), 95
　Marie, 169
　Milton A., 170
　Swan, 92, 95
　William, 92, 170
HARDWICK
　Sarah, 96
HARDY
　Eliza, 109
　Jesse, 109
　John, Jun., 115
HARGRAVES
　E. Glen, 140
　J. P., 140
　Robert, 140
　W. W., 140
HARMAN
　Elizabeth Clark, 109
　John, 109, 172
HARNESS
　William, 107, 113
HARPER
　Clayton, 76
　Isaac D., 82
HARRELL
　Celia, 91
　Ezekiel, 78
　Mary Elizabeth, 65
HARRIS
　David, 77, 104
　Edward D. (C.?), 112
　Eely S., 112
　James S., 142
　John, 139
　Joseph, 142
　Randolph C., 117
　Richard, 169
　Sarah, 104
　William, 169, 170
HARRISON
　Eleanor, 84
　Elener, 160
　Elizabeth, 64
　Ellender Shannon (Nelly), 109
　James, 109
　John, 163
　Jonas, 64, 90, 154
　W. Walsworth, 141
　William, 64
HART
　Fred L., 120
　John, 120, 138, 140, 141
　M., 139
　Martha, 120
　Martin, 120
　Mary Green, 120
　Meredith, 117
　Meridith, 141
　Pryor, 120
HARTWELL
　Steven, 82
HARVEY
　Blasingame W., 108
　Blassingame W., 66
　Eliza M. Prather, 108
HASTINGS
　Thomas, 88, 89, 92
HATHAWAY
　W., 69
HAYS
　Mary, 119
　William, 103
HAZLE
　Adaline, 105
　James, 105
HE STOPS THEM, 19
HE THROWS THEM DOWN, 19
HEATH
　John, 111
　Marelda, 111
　William, 118
HENDREZ
　Pedro, 86
HENDRICK
　Edmund, 66
　Edwin, 61, 69, 156
　Henry, 61, 66, 156
　Obadiah, 113
　Obedia, 156
HENDRICKS
　Edwin, 77
　Obedia, 61
　Obediah, 65
　Thomas D., 77
HENNAS
　Joshua J., 107
　Purity, 107
HERNANDEZ
　Juana Luzgarda, 26
　Nicholas, 24, 26
HERON
　William, 76
HERRERA

INDEX

HERRERA (continued)
  Diego, 27, 152
  Manuel, 133
  Miguel, 133
HERRIN
  Louisa, 100
  Moses, 100
HERTZ
  Hyman, 88, 89
  John, 99
  Joseph, 89
HERVY
  Samuel S., 119
HESSER
  Christian, 154
HICKMAN
  Asa, 86, 117
  Elizabeth, 71
HICKS
  Issac, 100
  William, 162
HIGHTOWER
  Elizabeth, 73
HILL
  Hannah, 104
  Joshua B., 114
  Moses, 81, 104, 158
  Robert, 119
  Synthia, 114
HINDS (HINES)
  Allen, 105
  Elbert, 104
  Mahana, 104
  Mary Hinds
    Speights Hix, 105
  Rebecca, 105
  William, 104
HINES
  Allen, 154
  Davis, 82
  Elbert, 82
  Ransom, 82
  William, 169
HINTONS
  Nathaniel, 109
HIRE
  Absalom, 104
  Nancy, 104
HODGES
  William H., 61, 156
HOFFLEFINGER
  James, 117
HOFFMAN
  Andrew, 82
  David A., 97
  Mary, 97
HOG STONES, 19
HOGAN
  Humphrey C., 160
HOGG
  Dashe, 111
  Doshe, 112
  John, 111
  Joseph, 112
  Mary, 111
  Newell, 111, 112
  Rachel, 112
HOLBROOKS
  Daniel, 117
HOLLAND
  James, 87, 119
  Malinda, 119
HOLLOWAY
  Charlotte, 108
  Daniel, 108

  John, 77
  Lewis, 108, 157
  Mary, 108
  Simpson, 108
HOLMAN
  Anna
    Wigglesworth, 107
  Isaac, 107
HOLMES
  Bryant, 118
  Elizabeth
    (Jourdan), 94
  Elizabeth Odom, 102
  Stephen, 84, 160
  Thomas, 94, 101
  Thomas C., 94, 102
HOLT
  Benjamin, 89, 106
  Charity Ann
    Wrinkle, 106
  Thomas C., 82
HOMES
  Bryant, 87
HOOD, 19
  Prissa, 158
HOOKER
  James, 141
HOPKINS
  Eldridge, 87, 119, 140
  Elizabeth, 118
  Francis, 87, 115, 117
  Frank, 138
  Harriet, 119
  James E., 115, 155
  Jas. E., 86
  Jonathan, 118
  Lemuel, 61
  Lemuel P., 156
  Nancy, 115
  Ric. M., 86
  Richard M., 115, 118
  Simal P., 69
  W. H. H., 87
  William Henry
    Harrison, 118
HORSLY (HASSELY)
  Sarah, 104
  Thomas, 104
HORTON
  Alexander, 65, 69, 76, 77, 94, 114, 135
  H. P., 77
  James R., 141
  John, 104
  Julius, 65, 67
  Nancy, 67
  Samuel, 61, 156
  Susan Purnell, 114
  Susanna, 65
  Susanna
    (Purnell), 68
  Susannah
    (Purnell), 65
  Winnie, 104
HOT HOUSE, 19
HOTCHKISS
  Anna, 107, 112
  Archibald, 71
  Augustus, 66, 69,

112
  Augustus
    (Augustine), 107
  Christopher, 71
  Cynthia
    (Dickinson), 71
HOUNDSELL
  Joseph, 139
HOUSTON
  Sam, 17, 92, 94, 129
HOWARD
  John, 108
  Kiziah, 108
  Mordechi, 85
  Mordica, 101
HOWE
  Joseph, 107
HOWESTER
  William D., 156
  William H., 61
HOWL
  Burgess, 106
HOWNSHELL
  Joseph, 116
HOWTISKEY, 19
HUBERT
  Matthew, 75
HUFFMAN
  David, 76, 106
  David A., 77
  Eliza, 106
HUGHART
  Alderena, 115
  Edward, 86, 115
HUGHES
  Cristine, 105
  Missipsa, 100
  Thomas, 100
  Walter, 105
HULING
  Thomas B., 103
HUMBLE
  John, 103
HUMPHREY
  James, 170
HUMPHREYS
  George, 160
  James, 76
  John, 86, 116
  William, 160
HUMPHRIES
  Rebecca (Reed), 138
  William, 136
HUMPHRY
  Lawrence, 85
HUMPHRYS
  William, 84
HUNDLEY
  Jas. C., 79
HUNT
  Charles H., 66
  Elizabeth, 108
  Nathaniel, 66, 108
HUNTER
  John Dunn, 16
HUSBAND
  John, 114
HUSTON
  Almanson, 69, 71, 112
  Almanzon, 94
  Elizabeth Newton, 112
  Susannah
    (Campbell), 71

  Thomas, 71
HYER
  Absalom, 89

-I-

IBARVO
  Manuel, 31
  Maria Antonia, 30(2), 31
  Martin, 31
  Miguel, 36
  Penciane, 31
IBRARVO
  Felicina, 34
IGELSON
  Joseph M., 99
INGLISH
  James, 62
  William, 61
INGRAM
  Martha, 118
  Rachel Luray
    Fields, 119
  William
    Christopher, 119
INMAN
  John, 112
  Prudence, 112
INOJOSA
  Jose, 35
  Jose Ildefonso, 34
IRION
  Jas. H., 82
  Joseph, 82
IRONS
  Edward, 84
  John, 119
IRVIN
  Clarency, 104
  James, 104
  Robert, 112
  Sarah, 112
  Susan, 104
  Thomas, 104
  W. (William?), 69
IRVINE
  Boyd, 66
  Jane, 164
  Jane Patton, 108
  Josephus, 77, 164
  Josephus S., 79
  R. Boyd, 78
  Robert B., 112
  W. D., 77
IRVING
  William D., 82
ISAACKS
  Elijah, 90
  Martha Patsy
    Richardson, 103
  Mary (Wallace), 90
  Samuel, 90, 103
ISAACS
  Elijah, 102
  Eliza, 85
  Ester Donoho, 102
  Samuel, 85
  Sarah, 158
  Sarah Mary Glass, 105
  William, 81, 105, 158
ISDELL
  Mary, 97
ISIDRO

INDEX

ISIDRO (continued)
  James, 44
  Santiago, 153
IVEY
  Jefferson, 120

-J-

JACK, 19
  Patrick C., 92
  Patrick
    Churchill, 91
JACKSON, 19
  Betsey, 99
  Charles W., 135
  Edward T., 114
  Emory, 81, 159
  Henry, 99
  Hugh, 75, 169
  Humphrey, 169
  John, 118, 119
  Philip, 119
  President Andrew, 14
  Susanna, 104
JAMES
  Henry S., 87
  Jarnet, 118
  Jarrel, 87
  John E., 87
  Joseph, 86, 118
JAMISON
  Colonel John, 58, 71
  Harriet Matilda, 58, 71
JANES
  Massaak H., 119
  Massack, 87
JARMAN
  Asa, 69, 119, 139
JARNEY
  James, 75
JEFFREYS
  Henry, 164
  Mary Ann "Polly"
    Williams, 164
JENNINGS
  William, 48
JERMAIN
  Samuel, 75
JESSE, 19
JETT
  Absalom, 172
  James, 172
  John, 172
  Stephen, 172
JEWELL
  Joseph, 111
  Winna, 111
JOHAN
  Joan Ferrian, 81
JOHN, 19
JOHNS
  William, 75
JOHNSON
  A. E. C., 69, 106
  Abraham, 81
  Achilles, 66
  Achilles E. C., 76
  Achilles Edmond, 93, 94
  Alexander, 117
  Alva R., 83
  Alvis R., 160
  Balda C., 116
  Elizabeth, 172

Hugh Blair, 95
J., 105
James, 108
James H., 119
John S., 106
Lindley, 141
Margaet, 105
Margaret Lewis, 106
Mary, 119
Neely, 158
Polly Dodson, 99
Robert, 172
Sarah, 70
Solomon, 107, 109
Stephen, 61, 156
William, 77, 99, 117, 154
JOHNSTON
  Blair, 169
  Hugh B., 75, 169, 170
  Joseph, 44
  Maria Constancia, 156
  William, 45, 61, 156
JONES
  B. Franklin, 102
  Col. Robert, 138
  David J., 119
  Everett, 81
  Everett H., 159
  Frederick, 81, 159
  George, 66, 69, 106
  George W., 77
  Henry, 138, 139
  Henry S., 118
  Henry W., 142
  Ira D., 81, 159
  Isaac H., 119
  James, 78
  Jesse T., 155, 163
  Latitia Gutherie, 102
  Mary, 106
  Minerva, 139
  Norris H., 78
  Robert, 116
  Rosiania, 119
  Stephen, 109
  William, 103
JORDAN
  Levi, 162
  William, 85
JOUETT
  J. T., 140
  John G., 140
  Thomas, 140(2)
JOURDAN
  Mahulda Isaacs, 103
  William, 103
JOURDON
  Redin (Redeen), 106
JOURNEY
  Nat. T., 140
  Nathaniel Thomas, 119
  Visti Langford, 119
JOUTEL
  Henri, 1
JOWERS

John, 78
JUARES
  Juan, 33
JUAREZ
  Juan, 35
JUCANTE
  Christosono, 153
JUNKIN
  Jane, 104
JURNINGAN
  Curtis, 115

-K-

KALTY FAMILY, 162
KAUFMAN
  Senator David S., 136
KEAN
  Jas. E., 81
KEELING
  Elzy, 107
KEEN
  Jas. E., 159
KELLER
  George F., 117
  Mitchell, 139
  Mitchell (Michael), 115
KELLOG
  A. G., 66
  Albert G., 112
  Albert Gallatin, 94
KELLY
  Zina, 97
KENDRICK
  Isaac, 163
KENNARD
  Elizabeth, 109
  William S., 109
KERNAL
  John H., 118
KILLOUGH
  Allen, 149, 163
  Isaac, 149, 163
  Isaac, Jr., 149, 163
  Nathaniel, 149, 163
  Samuel, 149, 163
KIMBELL
  George C., 128
  Mrs. Prudence, 91, 128
KIMBLE
  Helen, 55
  Helena (Helen) Gimelech, 57
  Helena G., 100
KIMBRO
  Allen, 107(2)
  James, 113
  Jane, 113
  Lemuel, 114
  William, 66
KINDALL
  Lucy, 113
  Samuel, 113
KING
  James H., 118
  Jno S., 78
  Nancy, 111
  Thomas, 117, 139
  William, 115, 160
  William, Sr., 111
KIRBY
  John, 107

Sarah, 107
KIRKHAM
  John, 47
  S., 75
KISHESCAW, 19
KITCHENS
  Jesse, 119
  Patsy, 119
  Preston, 87, 119
KNAP
  Asa, 78
KNIGHT
  Emily, 107
  James, 75, 169, 170
  Lewis, 107
  William, 119
KNUPPEL FAMILY, 169
KOCH FAMILY, 169
KORN
  Jesse, 101
  Mary, 101
KORNEGY
  John, 37
KRAK KILLER, 19
KUYKENDALL
  Matthew, 114

-L-

LABADIE
  N. D., 75
LABATUT
  Maria Juana, 45
LABINA
  Pierre, 133
LACE
  William, 66
LACEY
  William Young, 72
LACY
  Jacob, 119
  M. K., 81, 150
  Martha, 68
  Martin, 68, 69
  Mrs. Mary (Landon), 125
  William Young, 69
LACY (LACEY)
  Martin, 72
  William Hughes, 72
LAFITTE
  Cesar, 56
  Felicina Rublo, 56
  Jose Maria, 56
  Joseph Marie Cesar, 59
  Juan Jose, 56
  Luis, 56
  Marianne (de Soto), 59
  Mary Elizabeth [Isabel], 59
  Paul Bouet, 59
  Pedro, 56
  Pierre, 46, 153
  Ylario, 56
LAFLEUR
  Marguerite, 45
LAFOUR
  Jose Antonio, 56
  Jose Eugenio, 56
  Jose Franco Antonio, 56
  Jose Salestino, 56

206

INDEX

LAFOUR (continued)
  Maria, 56(2)
  Maria Celestine, 56
  Maria Loreta, 56
  Maria Magdalena, 56
  Maria Margarita, 56
LAGOW
  David, 78
LAITHUM
  Louis, 47
LAKE
  John W., 81, 159
LAKEY
  Sarah, 109
  William, 78, 109
LAMAR
  Mirabeau B., 18
  President M. B., 134
LAMB
  Alexander, 85
LAMPKINS
  Pauline, 107
  William, 107
LAND
  Jackson D., 78
  John, 117
  Matilda, 117
  William E., 78
LANDERS
  Sarah, 99
LANDFORD
  Eleanor, 86
LANDRUM
  Willis, 106
  Willis H., 134
LANE
  David, 141
  James, 102
  Jane, 139
  John, 106
  John W., 141
  Martha Miles, 102
  William, 141
LANGFORD (LANKFORD)
  Mary, 107
LANGHAM
  Wily W., 116
LANI
  Alfred, 75
LANIER
  Benjamin, 75
LANKFORD
  Asa, 84, 160
  Benjamin, 86
  Ellenor, 118
  Garrett P., 140
  William, 120
LARGE
  Abraham, 109
  Crucilla, 109
  Deborah, 109
  Isaac, 109
  Jacob, 109
  Rebecca, 109
LARKIN
  Peter, 79
LARNODIER
  Maria Clemencia, 39
LATHAM
  Alca Large, 109
  James, 111
  Jeremiah, 107
  John, 43, 110,
    159
  John, Jr., 84
  King, 111
  King H., 110
  Latham, 84
  Lewis, 83, 105
  Marguerite
    Rosalie Simms
    (Rosey), 110
  Mary, 110, 111
  Maston (Mastin), 105
  Sarah, 105
  Sarah Ann, 111
LATIMER
  Albert Hamilton, 114, 125
  Elizabeth Richey, 114
  James L., 126
  Jane (Hamilton), 126
LATTEMER
  Elizabeth Gates, 118
  Henry Russell, 118
  James, 114
  Jane Hamilton, 114
LAURENCE
  Jos., 76
  P. T., 82
LAVANIE
  George, 104
  Sarah, 104
LAVIGNE
  Pierre, 43, 154
LAW
  John, 105
LAWHORN
  Elizabeth Rebecca
    Arnett, 113
  J. C., 66
  John (Juan)
    Creed, 113
  Nancy, 108
  Thomas, 108
LAWRENCE
  Joseph, 169
  Mary, 64
LAWS
  John, 105
LAWSON
  Josiah D., 86, 117
LAYTON
  Isabel, 56
LAZARIN
  Ensign Juan, 68
  Joseph, 68
  Juan Maria, 68
  Juana Maria
    (Rivas), 68
  Julio, 133
LAZARINE
  Joseph, 72
  Juan Maria, 72
  Juana Maria
    (Rivas), 72
LEACH
  Evand, 117
  Joseph, 117
LEAL
  Antonio, 43
LECLERC
  Marie Diana, 127
LECLERE
  Rosine, 96
LECONTE
  Maria, 38
LEE
  Abner, 119
  John, 106
  Thomas, 79
  William, 142, 159
  William L., 81
LEGG
  Seneca, 107
LEGRAND
  Edward Oswald, 125
  Edwin O., 113
  John, 125
  Margaret
    (Chambers), 125
  Martha McGehee, 125
LEIBA
  Isabel, 34
LEMMONS
  Samuel, 114
LENEAR
  Benjamin, 171
LENY
  Henry, 62, 157
LEONE
  Samuel, 35
LEPIN
  Jacques, 153
LEPINE
  James, 44
LEPLICHER
  John C., 99
LEROY
  William, 79
LESLEY
  James, 105
LETHEY
  Lewis, 102
  Polly Lowe, 102
LEVA
  Anastacia
    Mansola, 31
LEVAN
  Juan Babtista, 133
LEVENS
  John, 116
LEVINS
  James, 118
  James, Jr., 118
  Jas, Jr., 86
  Jas, Sr., 86
  John, 87, 119
  Joseph, 86, 116
  Mary, 49
  Nicholas, 86, 117
LEWIS, 19
  A. A., 77
  Barbara C., 162
  Charles, 114
  Elizabeth, 83, 160
  George W., 77
  Harman, 85
  Herman, 102
  Jacob, 106
  James, 85
  John T., 103
  Kendall, 142
  Lourany Taylor, 102
  Mariah Stark, 103
  Martha, 65
  Martha (Patsy), 106
  Martin B., 103
  Martin Bury, 72
  Nancy Moore, 103
  Samuel S., 72, 94, 103
  Sarah (LeMaster), 72
  Sarah (Sally)
    Lemasters, 103
  William, Jr., 85
  William, Sr., 85
LICK
  John, Sr., 87, 118
LIGHTENING BUG, 18
LIMBOY
  Richard, 108
LINDLEY
  Sam, 140
LINDSAY
  Benjamin, 109
  Eliza, 72
  Mary Amy, 109
LINDSEY
  Benjamin, 66, 69, 78
  Charles, 111
  Easter, 108
  Isaac, 43, 65, 108, 111
  Mariah, 109
  Micager
    (Micajah), 111
  Micajah, 155
  Nancy, 111
  Pennington, 111
  Polly, 111
  Sarah, 111
  Thomas, 109
LINN
  Isaac W., 77
LINNEY
  Henry, 108
  Lavica, 108
LINSE
  Jesusa, 56
  Manuel, 56
  Maria, 56
LINTOT
  Bernard, 41
  Frances, 41
LIONS
  James, 99
  Polly Miller, 100
LISONADE
  Manuel, 28
LISONDE
  Manuel, 152
LITTLE
  John, 81, 84, 100, 159, 160
  Mary (Polly), 104
  William Hiram, 104
LITTLE JACK, 19
LITTLE JIM, 19
LITTLE JOHN, 19
LITTLETON
  White, 78
LLOYD
  Elias, 56
  Maria, 56
  William, 69
LOBO
  Pedro, 35
LOCKE
  Richard H., 140

207

INDEX

LOCKRIDGE
  Henry H., 113
LOGAN
  Bennett T., 117
  Maria (Mary)
    Bell, 99
  William G., 99
LOMAX
  Maria, 73
LONG
  Dr. James, 42
LONGORDIA
  Francisco, 87
LONGORIA
  Juan, 133
  Phelipa, 33
LOOKAN
  John, 109
  Sarah, 109
LOOKING AT US, 19
LOONEY
  James, 90, 91
  Samuel, 69, 90, 91
  Sarah, 92
LOPES
  Jose Angel, 53
  Jose Luterio, 53
LOPEZ
  Gergie, 133
  Gregorio, 24
  Juan, 133
LOSOYA
  Francisco, 27, 152
  Maria, 57
  Sgt. Manuel
    Antonio, 24
LOUCOUVICHE
  Marie, 39
LOUIS, 18
  Frederick K., 75
LOURA
  Wash., 18
LOUT
  Alfred, 84
  Elizabeth, 107
  George, 157
  John A., 65
  Levisa
    (Anderson), 97
  Martin V., 77
  Pinckney, 107
LOVE
  David W., 82
  James Marshall, 113
  John G., 65, 76, 77
  John Gilbert, 113
  Rebecca Exam, 113
LOW
  Barry, 69
  Drusela Cook, 105
  Eli, 105
  Elizabeth
    Parsons, 105
  Isaac, 105
  Jesse, 105
LOWE
  Barney, 102
  Elizabeth, 82
  Elizabeth
    (Parsons), 158
  Isaac, 158
  Jesse, 158
  Joel, 158
  Margaret Carlock, 102
LOWERY
  Even, 160
LOYD
  Benage, 87, 118
  Doyal T., 142
  Hiram, 87, 118
  William, 66
  Wm. M., 77
LUCOBICHE
  Jose, 43, 153
LUMPKIN
  Richard C., 78
LUNA
  Antonio, 24
  Juan, 133
LYNCH
  Stephen, 61, 157
LYNDSY
  Benjamin, 61
  Isaack, 61
LYNDSY (LINDSEY)
  Benjamin, 156
  Isaac, 156
LYNN
  Benjamin F., 115
  Julietta F., 115
LYONS
  Daniel, 168

-M-

MABBIT
  L. H., 66
  William, 49
MACADAMS
  John D., 82
MCADAMS
  Elizabeth, 104
  James, 104
  John, 104
  Martha, 104
MCANICA
  Alexander, 115
MCANIER
  J. H., 139
MCANULTY
  Sarah Sparks, 100
MCBEE
  William, 119
MCBRIDE
  Edward, 79
MCCABE
  Matthew, 119
MCCELBY
  Hugh, 119
MCCELVEY
  Jesse, 83
  Mary, 112
  Susannah, 84
MCCELVY
  Ezekiel, 112
  Jesse, 160
  Sarah, 112
MCCELY
  Hugh, 87
MACCLANAHAN
  James, 47
MCCLELAN
  Allen, 115
  M. G., 115
MCCLENNON
  A., 139
MCCOLLISTER
  Rice, 113
MCCOMBS
  Robert, 107
MCCREARY
  Cyrena, 111
MCCRENERY
  Wilson, 117
MCCUNE
  James, 150
MCDANIEL
  Elijah, 119
  Eliza Ann, 107, 112
  James, 86, 116
  John, 107
  Robert C., 107, 112
MCDAVID
  Dortrick, 83
  John, 79
  Patrick, 107, 160
MCDONALD
  Andrew, 141
  Donald, 65, 70, 73, 77, 90, 106
  Elizabeth, 109
  John, 155
  Maria Louisa
    Maximillan, 106
  Thomas, 109
  William, 61, 156
MCDONOUGH
  William, 78
MCELROY
  William, 78
MCFADDEN
  Andrew, 111
  Clary, 112
  Elizabeth, 63
  Jane, 111
  William, 112
MCFADDIN
  Andrew, 84, 160
  Bailey, 84, 160
  Elizabeth, 172
  James, 169, 170, 172
  Jonathan, 160
  Margaret, 110
  Samuel, 83, 110, 160
  William, 170
MACFARLAND
  William, 119
MCFARLAND
  John, 44, 153
  Thomas S., 70
  Widow, 56
  William, 76, 77, 87, 90, 113
MCGAFFEY
  John, 172(2)
  Sarah, 172
MCGALLIN
  Elizabeth
    Strother, 102
  Thomas, 102
MCGEE
  Jesse, 104
  John, 101, 110
  Joseph, 85
  Malinda, 104
  Sally Winfree, 101
  Susan, 110
MCGEGOR
  John, 163
MCGHEE
  Hulda Ford, 101
  Joseph, 101
MCGINNES
  John, 77

MCGINNIN
  John, 66
MCGINNIS
  Anna, 108
  John, 108
MCGOWAN
  John, 106
  Mary Thompson
    Floyd, 106
  Rebecca, 119
MCGREW
  John, 84
MCHENRY
  Andrew, 78
MCINEAR
  John B., 115
MCKAY
  Charles, 81, 158
MCKEAN
  John, 81, 158
MCKENNY
  George Y., 115
  Nancy, 115
MACKEY
  Charles, 73
  Matilda F., 73
  Naoma, 105
  Naomi, 73
MCKIM
  Charles, 81
  James, 81, 158
  William, 81
MCKIMM
  Charles, 158
MCKINNEY
  Abraham, 59
  Anna G. Gibbs, 155, 156
  Blackly, 86, 114
  Collin, 115, 125, 138, 139
  Collin J., 138
  Daniel, 86, 114, 119, 127
  David, 138
  Dorothy, 114
  Eleanor
    (Prather), 59
  Elizabeth Ann, 114
  Elizabeth Lee
    Coleman, 115
  G. Y., 86
  H. C., 86
  Hiram C., 114
  Jas., 86
  Margaret (Peggy)
    Dooley, 155
  Margaret (Polly)
    Dooley, 117
  Massie
    (Blatchley), 127
  Melson Watts, 155, 156
  Mrs. Nancy
    Wilson, 155, 156
  Peggy McClure, 119
  Politico, 56
  Thomas, 155
  Thomas F., 56, 61, 156, 169
  Thomas Freeman, 59
  William, 86
  William Coleman, 117, 155
  Younger S., 115

INDEX

MCKINNY
  Ashly, 115
  James, 118
  Mary McKinney, 118
  Sally, 115
MCKINZIE
  Abner, 140
MCKINZY
  Abner H., 116
MCKIRBY
  George W., 115
MCLAIN
  James, 78
MCLAUGHLIN
  Archibald, 113
  Stephen, 113
MCLAURIN
  Elvira, 77
MCLEAN
  Daniel, 161
  Hannah, 162
  Lucinda, 161
MCMAHAN
  James B., 70, 73, 105
  Matilda, 105
  Pheoba R., 106
  Phoebe (Young), 73
  Samuel Doak, 73, 106
  Tabitha, 73
MCMAHON
  James, 119
  Samuel D., 66
MCMANUS
  William, 170
MCMILLAN
  Sarah, 128
MCMULLEN
  Charles, 79
  Horatio, 103
  Joseph, 79
MCMULLIN
  Elias, 113
MCNEAL
  Daniel, 85
  Neal, 66
MCNEEL
  Daniel, 155
  John, 155
  Pleasant, 155
  Sterling, 155
MCNULTY
  James, 43, 154
MCQUEEN
  David, 57
MCRE
  John, 78
MCWILLIAMS
  John, 62, 157
MADDIT
  T. (L?.) H., 113
MAGEE
  William, 42
  William Augustus, 41
MAGRUE
  John, 62, 157
MAHURIN
  Thomas, 119
MAJOR
  Vicente, 32
MAJORS
  J. P., 139
MALDONADO
  Jose Luis, 34

MALIGE
  Maria Josefa, 39
MALISSE (MALIGE)
  Maria Louise Angelica, 39
MALONE
  Eliza, 108
  John, 163
  Thomas, 66, 108
MALVIN
  Johnson, 78
  Richard, 78
MAN
  John, 160
MANCHACA
  Antonio, 69
  Ensign Antonio, 68
MANNA
  Robert, 78
MANNING
  Noel, 78
MANSELL
  Robert B., 140
MANSOLO
  Joaquin, 153
  Juaquin, 28
  Pedro, 27, 152
  Victor, 28, 153
MANSON
  Reubin, 82
MARCHANT
  Edward, 135
MARGATE
  Lucy, 160
MARGRAVE
  Lucy, 84
MARIANA, 35
MARINO
  Jose, 112
  Mary, 112
MARIOTINE
  Mary A. O., 150
MARLEY
  Louis, 47
MARO
  Maria S., 38
MARQUEZ
  Juan Joseph, 24
MARSHACK
  Tabashak K., 159
MARSHAK
  Tebosha, 81
MARSHALL
  Leonard, 156
MARSHEL
  Leonard, 61
MARTIN
  Daniel, 150, 164
  Elizabeth Brown, 100
  Gabriel, 86, 117
  Henry, 81, 104, 158, 161
  James, 169
  Josiah C., 169
  Mary, 104
  Mary Coffee, 99
  Mary Eleanor Ayers, 164
  Neil, 69
  Neil, Sr., 100
  Philip, 99
  William, 119
MARTINES
  Ceyetano, 133
  Delores, 55, 133
  Marcos, 27(5)

MARTINEZ
  Juan, 27, 152
  Juan Jose, 31
  Marcos, 152
MASK
  Jas. V., 79
MASON
  Elizabeth, 104, 158
  Fannie, 104
  James, 81, 104, 158
  John, 104
  John S., 78
  Judith R. (Judy), 104
  Judith Route Blackaby, 158
  William, 81, 104, 120, 158
MASSANET
  Father Damian, 2
MAST
  Jacob, 101
  Rebecca Robbins, 101
MASTERS
  Elizabeth Shaw, 161
  Jacob, Jr., 161
  Jacob, Sr., 161(2)
  Lawrence, 78
MATHIS
  Billy, 140
MATTHEWS
  Elbert, 118
  S. S., 77
MATTOX
  Wiley A., 141
MAXAMILIAN
  Claire, 106
  John, 106
MAXAMILLAN
  John, 81
MAXIMILLIAN
  Claire, 158
  John, 69, 158
  Maria Luisa, 73
MAXWELL
  Adeline Catherine, 127
  Catherine, 96
  Thomas, 113
MAYFIELD
  John E., 101
  Mary, 101
MAYHON
  Francis, 105
  Lettis, 106
MAYO
  Nancy, 160
MAYS
  Nancy, 84
  Squire, 86, 117, 138
MEANS
  Frances Amelia Blackburn, 106
  Hugh, 106
  Martha, 106
  William, 106
MEBANE
  J. H., 139
MECIA
  Carlotta, 46
MEDDLE
  Eliza, 110

  John, 110
MEDINA
  Bisenta, 33
  Juan Jose, 33
  Micaela, 33
MELTON
  Elizabeth, 81, 104, 158
  Levanna, 104
  W. K., 104
  William, 113
MENARD
  Hypolite, 96
  Marguerite (de Noyer), 127
  Michael, 127
  Michael Branamour, 125
MENCHACA
  Antonio, 72
MENCHACCA
  Pedro, 32
MENDEZ
  Manuel, 27, 152
MENDOSA
  Jose, 36
  Santiago, 36
MENNARD
  Pierre (Patrick) J., 95
MERCHANT
  E. A., 83
  Edward A., 111, 160
  Elizabeth, 111
  John D., 111
  Sarah Walker, 111
MEREDITH
  Daniel, 163
MERRILL
  Amos, 140
MEYA
  Dimas, 27, 152
MEZIERS
  Maria Delilah, 56, 59
MICHELI
  J. Vicente, 133
  Vicente, 165
MICHELLI
  Maria (Lengeven), 38
  Vicente, 37, 38, 101
MIDKIFF
  Candace, 149, 162
  Candice, 100
  Isaac J., 100
  Latha Jones, 100
MIER Y TERAN
  General Manuel, 4
MILAM
  Ben, 80, 138
MILES
  Mrs. Charles, 84
MILHOMME
  Francis, 99
MILLARD
  Henry, 95
  Josiah, 96
  Nancy, 96
MILLER
  Betsy Barnett, 102
  J., 111
  Jane, 111
  John, Sr., 102
  Leroy, 107, 109

INDEX

MILLER (continued)
  Matthew S., 107, 109
  Robert, 116
  Solomon, 66, 107, 109
MILSPAUGH
  William, 169
MINCHE (MINCHEY)
  David, 170
MINCHEY (MINCHEW)
  David, 169
MINTON
  Andrew G., 116
MIRES
  John, 103
MITCALF
  Thomas D., 115
MITCHELL
  Calpurnia Franklin, 100
  James, 106
  James B., 100
  Reuben, 86, 116
  Thomas, 161
MONROE
  John, 78
  Peter, 78
  William T., 78
MONTAGUE
  David, 140
MONTGOMERY
  William, 77
MOODY
  Isaac, 142, 143
MOONEY
  James, 77
MOORE
  Daniel T. D., 77
  David L., 78
  Jane, 85
  John, 105, 162
  Levi, 141
  Lewis W., 141
  Lucy, 105
  Mary A., 91
  Nancy, 72, 113
  Nathaniel, 155
  Nathaniel B., 78(2)
  S. D., 113
  Samuel F., 114
  Samuel T., 78
  Uriah, 163
  William, 75
MOORES
  Eli, 139
  Thomas, 139
MORA
  Antonio, 35
  Ensign Juan, 68
  Francisco, 53
  Gregorio, 34
  Jacinte, 30
  Jacinto, 28, 153
  James, 69
  Jose Maria, 73, 172
  Juan, 27, 73, 152
  Juan Maria, 70
  Manuel, 27, 152
  Maria Refugia, 35
  Nicholas, 28, 153
MORALES
  Crecencio (Cresences), 133
MORBAN
  Widow, 47

MORGAN
  Henry G., 103
  James, 91(2)
  Martha (Prudun), 91
MORILLO
  Augustin, 28, 153
  Francisco, 25
MORIN
  Barbara, 33
  Jose, 34, 133
  Maria, 33
  Maria de la Censousion, 34
  Melchor, 27, 34, 152
MORING
  Charles, 78
MORNEN
  Lavinia, 118
MORRIS
  Alfred W., 104
  Daniel, 114
  Elisha, 103
  Francisco Manuel, 133
  Granville, 119
  Harriet Alexander, 100
  Lee, 86, 114
  Mary, 105
  Robert, 86, 115
  Samuel, 80
  Sarah Ann Taylor, 104
  Shadrac, 105
  Silas, 100
  Susanna, 80
  Susannah Dunn, 103
  William F., 119
MORRISON
  Edmond, 101
  John C., 99
  Patsy Devore, 101
MORSE
  Willie, 78
MORTON
  Cynthia Wilson, 116
  James, 61, 156
  John, 116
  Peter, 79
  Susanna, 79
MORTON (MARTIN)
  James, 170
MORVAN
  Francois, 37, 39, 43
  Jose, 47
MORVANN
  Francis, 153
MORXIN
  Estevan, 34
MOSES, 18
MOSS
  James, 114
  John, 99
  Sampson, 118
  Samuel, 77
  Silas, 78
MOTT
  B. Franklin, 102
  Joseph, 103
  Morgan, 119
  Parthena, 103
  Zelpha Wiggins, 103

MOURHOUSE
  S., 82
MOWERY
  Malinda Giddens, 118
  Mathias, 118
MOZ
  Captain Frederick, 68
  Frederick, 70
MUDD
  B. H., 103
  Elizabeth Robuck, 103
MUNSON
  Elizabeth, 169, 170
  Henry W., 170
MURFREE
  Priscilla Dickson, 106
  Willis, 106
MURFY
  Isaac, 87, 118
MURPHY
  Edward, 40, 44, 48
  Frank, 61
  Joseph, 119
  Priscilla, 158
  Willis, 65, 81, 158
MURRY
  William, 118
MURVOIR
  Pierre, 83
MUSGROVE
  Jacob, 133
MUSQUIZ
  Lieutenant Miguel, 41
MUSSETT
  William S., 106
MYERS
  Henry, 163
  James R., 119

-N-

NAIL
  Abner, 111
  Andrew Jackson, 111
  Elizabeth, 84
  Martin G., 117
  William A., 111
NALL
  Barkley, 118
  Barley, 87
  John, 86
  John H., 118
  Martin G., 86
  Robert, 118
NAME
  Basilio, 154
NATIONS
  Joseph, 107
NAVARRO
  Jose, 36
  Lorenzo, 133
NEAL
  Margaret (Griffin), 96(2)
NECKLIS (NICHOLS)
  Henry, 105
  Nancy, 105
NEELEY
  Charity, 108

John M., 108
NEELY
  John M., 81
  Joseph, 107
NEIVES
  Maria, 32
NELS
  William, 99
NELSON
  Elizabeth, 105
  Samuel, 105
  Sarah, 105
  William, 57, 99
NEVILL (NEVIL/NEVILLE)
  Alexander, 142
NEWELL
  David, 79
  Samuel W., 82
NEWLIN
  Johnson, 105
NEWMAN
  Felix, 76
NEWTON
  Elizabeth, 71, 112
  Jacob, 78
  John, 78
NEYETTO
  Jose, 133
NICHOLAS
  Robert, 82
NICOLET
  Chief, 16
NIGHT KILLER, 19
NOBLE
  Dixon, 119
NOBLES
  E. M., 81
  John, 79
NOFSEN
  Miranda, 105
NOGGIN
  Lewis, 61
NOLAN
  Philip, 35, 41, 130
NOLIN
  John, 70
NORRIS
  Celeste Stockman, 101
  Edmund, 58(2), 59
  Jesusa, 56
  John, 56, 59, 101
  Jose Augustin, 56
  Juliana, 57
  Lieutenant Nathaniel, 68
  Maria Glorendia, 55
  Maria Juliana, 56
  Maria Priscilla, 56
  Maria Puarie, 101
  Nathaniel, 56, 58, 70, 133
  Raymond, 56
  Samuel, 52, 53, 84, 144, 145, 160
  Sarah, 58
  Sarah (Rogers), 59
  Sarah H., 160
  Susanna (Jesusa), 58
  Susannah, 128

210

INDEX

NORRIS (continued)
  Thomas, 56, 59, 101
  William, 56
NORTH
  Mary, 38
NORTHROP
  Orvil, 82
NOWLAND
  John, 103
  Milla Teal, 103
NUGENT
  John M., 117
  Quintas Cincinatus, 155
NUGERT
  John, 86
NUGGIN
  Lewis, 157
  Lewis, Sr., 157
NYRO
  James R., 87

-O-

OACHELLA, 19
OATES FAMILY, 162
OCHILTREE
  District Judge William B., 136
O'CONNOR
  John, 44, 45, 154
ODELL
  Benjamin, 106
  Sarah, 107, 109
ODOM
  Bretain, 106
  Kinchin, 163
  Margaret, 106
OGDEN
  Abraham, 87, 119
OLDHAM
  Benjamin, 141
OLIVER
  Anne, 70
OMENT
  Washington, 81
ONSTATT
  Elizabeth, 119
  John, 118
  Mary, 118
  William, 119
ORGAN
  William, 155
ORR
  George, 76, 168, 170(2)
ORSON
  Robert, 170
OSBORNE
  Bushrod W., 118
OSGOOD
  James, 87, 119, 138
OTTERLIFTER, 18
OTUSTUKE, 19
OVER THE BRANCHES, 19
OWEN
  Edward, 119

-P-

PACE
  Elizabeth, 105, 158
  Hardy, 102
  Isaac F., 158
  J. F., 82
  John, 81, 158
  Mahaly Isaacs, 102
  William, 81, 158
  William I., 105
PACHECO
  Juan Josef, 152
PACHERO
  Juan Josef, 27
PACKARD
  Emily, 71
PADILLA
  Antonio, 34
  Christoval, 27, 34
  Cristoval, 152
  Dona Maria, 30, 31
  Francisco, 33
  Gabriel, 28, 153
  Isabela, 34
  Juan Manuel, 152
  Magdalena, 32
  Maria Gertrudis, 30(2)
  Mariano, 27
  Miguel, 152
  Patricio, 28, 153
  Pedro, 35
  Xavier, 32
PAILLAR
  Joseph, 44
PAIN
  John, 105
  John C., 106
PAINE (PAYNE)
  Esther, 108
  Thomas, 108
PALACIO
  Juana, 35
PALLER
  Joseph, 154
PALVADOR
  Anastacia Tesie, 54
  Jose, 54
  Juan, 54
PALVADORE
  Joseph S., 83, 160
PAMPLIN
  Dorcus Coleman, 102
  William, 102
PANTALEON
  Agraye, 56
  Bernardo, 56
  Chrisanta, 56
  Ysur, 56
PANTALION
  Bernard, 59
  Bernardo (Bernard), 59
  Eusebio Ysur, 59
  Margueritte (Detchou), 59
  Marugeritte Grillet (Torin), 59
PANTELEON
  David, 56
  Moriel, 56
PANTHER
  Capt., 19
PARAKEET, 18
PAREZ
  Concession, 66

PARK
  George, 116
PARKER
  Ann, 113
  Argalus, 101
  Daniel, 97
  Elzira, 101
  Ira, 113
  Isaac, 99
  Jesse, 89
  John, 97
  Mary (Issacks), 158
  Mary Isaacs, 105
  Matthew, 81, 105, 158
  Peter, 48
  Rachel, 113
  Rebecca, 105
  Richard V., 79
  Sarah, 89
  Sarah (White), 97
  Thomas, 113
PARMER
  Colonel Martin, 16, 53
  Levinia Anderson, 113
  Malindy, 110
  Martin, 96, 113, 125
  Milly (Hardwick), 96
  William, 110
PARRON
  William E., 78
PARROT
  Latney, 48
  Lattney Anthony, 45
PASSING
  James, 78
PATILLO
  George A., 172
PATRICK
  George Moffit, 95
PATTERSON
  John, 107
  Lewis Y., 78
PATTISON
  James, 113
PATTON
  John McCoy, 113
  Robert, 139
PAULIN
  Juan, 25
PAURIE
  Maria, 56
PAXTON
  Hansford L., 116
  Jesse M., 116
  John, 116
  William J., 116
PAYNE
  John C., 83, 160
PEACE
  James, 119
PEAR
  John, 112
  Martha, 112
PEARCE
  Rufus, 78
PECK
  Ancil, 87
  Ancil C., 120
  Solomon Rice, 99
PEMBERTON
  John J., 103

PENA
  Beatrice, 32
  Matias, 35
PENDERGRASS
  Sarah, 86, 117
PENN
  Eli, 81, 159
PENNINGTON
  Sydney O., 125
PERALTA
  Rita, 34
PERDUE
  James, 79
PERES
  Francisco, 55
  Maria Sultana, 55
PEREZ
  Candelario, 133
  Francisco, 30, 31, 133
  Josefa, 35, 45
  Maria Concepcion, 38
  Pedro, 25
PERKINS
  James, 66
PETERS
  Etheldred, 116
  Margaret, 116
  Richard, 114
  Samuel, 115
  Stephen, 116
PETETAH, 19
PETIT
  John L., 47
PETTETT
  Kizeah, 111
  M., 111
PEW
  John, 116, 139
PEYTON
  Jon C., 155
PHARISH
  John, 101
  Oprey Smith, 101
  Samuel, 101
  Squire, 101
PHARRIS
  Daniel, 108
  Kiziah, 108
PHILLIPS
  Nathaniel, 82
PIERSON
  J. W. F., 138
  John Goodloe Warren, 155
PIFERMO
  Baptiste, 37
  Jean Ignacio, 43
  Jean Ignance, 153
  Juan Baptiste, 39
PLEASANT, 19
PLOWDEN
  Tamora Elizabeth, 73
PLUMMER
  Moses, 155
POCAWAH, 19
POISSON
  Atanacio, 153
POISSOT
  Marie, 47
  Marie Isabelle, 47
  Sousan, 47
  Thomas, 47
  William, 47
POLLARD

INDEX

POLLARD (continued)
  F. H., 103
  Nancy Parrish, 103
POLLONIO
  Jose, 133
POLLY
  Joseph W., 155
POLVEDORE
  John (Juan), 111
  Joseph, 111
  Juan Batiste, 111
  Louisa Tessier, 111
  Luiza, 111
  Susan de los Santos Coy, 111
PON
  Nicholas, 37
PON(T)
  Nicholas, 39
PONT
  Nicholas, 154
POOL
  Beverly, 163
  G., 81, 159
  Jonathan C., 155
POOR
  Elizabeth, 118
  Ira S., 117
POPE
  Cesar, 78
PORTER
  Alexander, 103
  James G., 81, 159
  John S., 117
  Mary, 110
  Mary Smith, 103
  Samuel, 110
  Steven, 82
POSSATATAH, 19
POSSUM, 19
POTTER
  Robert, 125
POWE
  A., 81, 159
POWELL
  Elizabeth, 104
  Isaac, 104
PRADO
  Jose Anselmo, 133
  Juan, 133
PRATHER
  Isaac, 169
  Mary (Phillips), 73
  Stephen, 61, 66, 70, 73, 155, 156
  Tamora Elizabeth Plowden, 155, 156
  Thomas, 73
PRATOR
  Thomas Freeman, 108
PRENTISS
  George W., 82
PRESE
  Jose Antonio, 82
PRESELA
  Maria del Pilar, 31
  Pedro, 31
PRESTON
  Elijah, 78
PREWITT
  Beasley, 169
  Jesse, 169

PRICE
  John, 118
  Mary, 118
PRIDGON
  Sophia Waller, 103
  William, 103
PRIETO
  Catarina, 34
PROCELLA
  Maria Theresa, 73
  Melchor, 32
PROCTOR
  Henry, 117
PROPHET
  John, 119
PRUDHOMME
  Baptiste, 46
  Catherine (Miller), 39
  Francis, 153
  Francisco, 37, 39
  Francois, 44, 46
  Jean Phillipe, 39
PRUETT
  Jacob, 162
  Jesse, 75
  Martin, 161
PRY
  Elizabeth Berry, 102
  Peter B., 85
  Peter P., 102
PUARIE (PORRIER)
  Baptiste, 57
PUERES [POIRIER]
  Maria, 59
PUERIE (POIRIER)
  Juana, 58
PURIO
  Juana, 56
PURIVAL
  Elisha, 141
PURNELL
  Charles S., 78
  William S., 78

-Q-

QUELLEN
  Charles, 119
QUINELTY
  James, 44, 101, 153, 156
  James (Santiago Conelte), 45
  Maria Manuela Fleet, 101
QUINILTY
  James, 133
  John, 133
QUINLETY
  James, 61
QUINNONES
  Manuel, 34
QUIRK
  Edmund, 43, 44, 45, 48, 113, 153
  Henry, 45, 57
  John, 45
  Jose Antonio, 57
  Martha Maria, 45
  Rebecca, 45
  William, 77
QUIROS
  Juana, 32

-R-

RABLO
  More, 133
RACHON
  Farrow, 118
RADDLE
  Archibald, 77
RAGSDALE
  Amanda M., 115
  Edward Baxter, 163
  John, 117
  Martin, 119
  Robert, 115
  Thomas, 115
  William, 117, 138
RAGUET
  Henry, 99
  Marcia Ann Towers, 99
RAINER
  Mary Horton, 114
  Samuel, 114
RAINES
  Emory, 66
  Joel D., 113
RAINS
  E., 83
  Emory, 109, 155, 160
  James, 81
  Mareener, 109
RALPH
  Samuel, 103
  Sophia W. P. Dean, 103
RAMBIN
  Louis, 39
  Maria Barbara, 39
  Marie Francoise Clairmont, 39
  Michel, 44, 153
  Mickle, 46
RAMERAS (RAMIREZ)
  Jinio (Ginio), 133
RAMEREZ
  Francisco, 152
RAMIRES
  Jose Guadalupe, 33
RAMIREZ
  Maria Lucia, 31
RAMON
  Jacinete, 32
RAMOS
  Juan Antonio, 24
  Miguel, 27, 152
RANDOLPH
  Elizabeth, 106
  John, 106
RANKIN
  Elizabeth Smith, 155
  Frederick Harrison, 155
  James M., 76
RARIDAN
  Thomas M., 159
RARIDEN
  Thomas M., 81
RATAN
  Larklin, 139
RATCLIFF
  Evelina (Eveline), 108
  William D., 108
RAY
  Allen S., 79

REAL
  Jonathon, 106
  Sarah, 106
RECHAR
  Maria Luisa, 55
REDMAN (REDMOND)
  Frances, 108
  Zachariah, 108
REED
  Cynthia Ann (Humphries), 13
  Elizabeth Harper, 164
  Isaac, 163
  Isaac H., 100
  John A., 115
  Joseph, 136, 138, 142
  Martin T., 78
  Miles, 116
  Pervilla Herrin, 100
  Reverend Isaac, 151, 164
  Sally, 138
  Sarah, 116
REESE
  Joseph, 44
  Joshua, 45
REEVE
  James R., 81
REEVE(S)
  James R., 159
REEVES
  Green, 108
  James, 139
  Sarah Jane Johnson, 108
REID
  Isaac, 118
  Joseph, 115
  Sally, 116
RELIQUET
  Louis, 44, 46
RENFRO
  David, 65, 76, 82
  Isaac, 65, 81
  Issac, 106
  Martha, 77
  Priscilla, 106
RENGLAN
  Robert, 154
REOLO
  Theresa, 31
REVIER
  William R., 117
REVO
  Antoner, 62
  Antonio, 157
RHODES
  Elizabeth, 108
  James, 118
  James, Jr., 87
  Richard, 87, 119
  Sarah, 118
RIAS
  Esparza, 35
RICE
  Claiborne, 78
  Clinton, 112
  Jane, 112
  Joseph, 112, 161(2)
  Lemuel, 112
  Levi M., 87, 115
  Mary, 112
  Willie Masters, 112

INDEX

RICHARDS
  Jacob, 82
  Maria S., 155
RICHARDSON
  Andrew, 85
  Benj., 85
  Benjamin, 103
  Lemuel, 82
  Lewis, 87
  Rebecca, 103
  Rupert N., 176, 177
  William, 85
RICHE
  Samuel, 114
RICHEE
  Samuel, 115
  William, 115
RICHEE (RICHEY)
  James, 116
  Sarah Ann Truit, 116
RICHEY
  Elizabeth, 126
  J. S., 81
  John M., 115
RICHMOND
  Francis, 108
  John R., 82
  Truman, 82
RICKEY
  J. S., 159
RIDDLE
  John, 107
  Mary Jane, 96, 127
RILEY
  Isaac, 141
  James, 158
RINCOS
  Pedro, 28, 153
RINEON
  Joaquina, 30(2)
RIO
  Maria Delores, 39
RIPLEY
  Ambrose, 142
RIVERA
  Juan, 31
ROARD
  William, 162
ROARK
  John, 99
  Margaret Reed, 100
  Nancy Chambliss, 99
  William, 100
ROBARDS
  Adam, 61
ROBARTS (ROBERTS)
  Abram, 156
  Elisha, 156
  Lucrecia Brown, 156
  Martha "Patsy" Gill, 156
ROBBINS
  John, 116
  Lucy, 97
  Nathaniel, 97, 139
  Rebecca, 97
ROBERTS
  Charles, 105
  Charles S., 161
  Elisha, 60, 61, 65, 73, 76, 77,
93, 155
  Ester Jane, 60, 73
  Harriet, 55
  Harriet F. Callier, 99
  Harriet Fenley, 155
  Isaac, 110
  John, 55, 57
  John F. (Callier), 58
  John S., 55, 57, 70, 80, 99, 125
  John S., Sr., 57
  Luke, 87, 119, 138
  Lycurgus, 58
  Major John S., 53
  Mark, 140
  Mrs. Noel G., 64
  Rhoda, 110
  Richard, 81, 159
  W. P., 139
  William, 65, 81, 93, 155, 158
ROBERTSON
  Edward, 110
  Elizabeth, 104
  James, 169
  Joel, 102
  S. J., 104
  Samuel, 104
ROBERTSON (NEGRO)
  Joshua N., 133
ROBINETT
  Calvin C., 103
  Mary Donoho, 103
ROBINSON, 19
  Helen, 55
  James, 55, 76, 169, 170
  James W., 97
  Joel, 85
  John B., 85
  Joseph, 55, 57
  Margaret (Newell), 97
  Moses, 55, 57
  Samuel, 97
  W. M., 133
ROBLEAU
  Helena, 38
  Pierre, 44, 153
ROCKWELL (ROCKWALL)
  Chester, 102
RODES
  James, 87
  Mastin, 159
RODRIGUES
  Juan Jose, 133
  Juana, 33
RODRIGUEZ
  Cristobal, 25
  Guillermo, 24
RODRIQUES
  Andres, 36
ROGERS
  Bethany, 107
  Elizabeth, 83, 160
  Elizabeth C. Sparks, 100
  James, 75, 79
  John, 18
  Ransom, 142
  Robert, 75
  Samuel, 100
ROGET
  Estevan, 37
ROLAN
  Vicente, 47, 48
ROLAND
  Christopher, 119
ROLAND (ROLLAND)
  John, 113
ROSALES
  Antonio, 32
  Gertrudis, 35
  Ignacia, 33
  Jean, 44, 153
  Joseph, 24
  Julian, 32
  Maria, 32
  Serafina, 36
ROSE
  Joannie, 154
  Moses, 155
ROSS
  John, 86
ROTH
  Jacob, 99
ROUBDAUX
  Nelson, 119
ROUBDOUX
  Nelson, 87
ROUBEAUX
  Pierre, 47
ROUSSEAU
  Francis, 87, 119
ROWE
  Joseph, 112
  Livinia Burditt, 112
ROWLAND
  John, 117, 139
  Sherrod, 115, 139
ROWLET
  Daniel, 140
ROWSON
  K., 81
RUDDIE
  George, 163
RUEG
  Henry, 99, 155
  Louis, 99
  Marie Louise Flores, 155
RUGG
  Sarah, 104
RUIS
  Andres, 36
  Maria Antonia, 33
  Paula, 34
RUIZ
  Gaspar, 35
  Gasper, 27, 152
RUNNELS
  Edmond S., 139
  Hardin R., 139
  Hiram, 139
  Howell W., 139
RUOFF
  Anna Maria, 74, 89
  Eva Catherine Rosine, 69, 99
RUSK
  General Thomas J., 18, 132, 134
  John, 98
  Mary (Sterritt), 98
  Mary F. Cleveland, 99
  Thomas J., 97,
99, 125
RUSSELL
  Dr. Samuel Price, 40
  Emily, 104
  Jane, 104
  Jesse, 104
  Jonathon, 104
  Margaret, 104
  Reddin, 139
  Reuben R., 161
RUSSET
  Francis, 154
RUSSLE
  John, 119
  Levi, 120
RUTHERFORD
  John A., 139
RYAN
  Mrs. Polly, 85

-S-

SADLER
  Felix G., 116
  Hiram, 116
  James C., 116
  James M., 116
ST. CLAIR
  Duncan, 169
ST. DENIS
  Louis, 171
  Maria Emmanuela Sanchez de Navarre, 171
SALVADOR
  Jean, 153
SAN GERMAIN
  James, 76
SAN MAGUEL
  Candide, 152
SAN MIGUEL
  Augustin, 33
  Candide, 28
SANCHES
  Bentura, 55
  Felicina de los Santos, 72
  Manuela, 54
  Maria Gregoria, 54
  Maria Josefa, 54
  Richardo, 55
SANCHEZ
  Antonio, 133
  Augustin, 27, 152
  Beatrice, 30(2)
  Joseph, 24
  Juan Jose, 27, 34, 152
  Louisa, 31
  Luis, 33
  Manuel, 34
  Maria, 32, 34, 36, 152
  Mariano, 34
  Matis, 27
  Pedro, 152
  Santa, 34
  Trinidad, 31
SANDERS
  Charity, 77, 108
  John, 62, 66, 119
  John, Sr., 157
  Julian, 44
  Rachel Willingham, 157
SANDOVAL

213

INDEX

SANDOVAL (continued)
  Policiano, 32
SANTA CRUZ
  Francisco, 30
  Jose Antonio, 30
  Juan Josef, 28, 153
  Juana, 36, 39
  Manuel, 32
  Marcos, 31
  Maria, 34
  Mariano, 33
SANTOS
  Bernino, 55
  Jose, 83
  Juan, 55
  Manuel, 55
  Maria Antonia, 55
  Maria Carmel, 55
  Ygnacia, 55
SARGENT
  Frederick, 82
  Ralph, 82
  Thomas, 82
SARNAC
  Jean, 44, 153, 154
  Maria Josefa, 56, 60
SATTERWHITE
  Thomas, 116
SAUL
  Drey Methreana Sutherland, 101
  James B., 81, 159
  Jno., 76
  John, 101
  John, Jr., 155
SAWL
  Rachel, 85
SCAIFE
  Martha, 96
SCARBERY
  Middleton, 116
SCARBROUGH
  Felix, 116
  Noel, 119
SCATES
  Elizabeth, 128
  Joseph, 128
  William Bennett, 125
SCHRIVERS
  John, 102
  Matilda Isaacs, 102
SCOTT
  George, 111
  Margaret, 113
  Rozelia, 75
  T. W., 81, 159
  W. L., 113
SCRITCHFIELD
  John, 61
SCRUTCHFIELD
  Fleming, 155
SCURLOCK
  William, 112
SEATS
  Precious, 119
SEATS (SEETS)
  Precous, 106
SEGUIN
  Juan, 51
SELF
  Jacob, 170
  Jacob E., 75, 169, 170

Taylor B., 75
SEPEDA
  Caystane, 30
SEPULBEDA
  (SEPULVEDA)
  Simona de, 26
SEPULVEDA
  Felice Segumendo, 54
  Jose Antonio, 53, 54
  Maria Antonia, 54
  Maria Rernave, 54
  Maria Torvina, 54
  Sequemundo, 133
SEQUEAH, 18
SERNAQUE, 31
SEWELL
  John C., 82
SEXTON
  Samuel, 66
SHACKLEFORD
  Joseph, 106, 109
SHANNON
  Jacob, 61, 155, 157
  John, 156
  Owen, 61, 157
SHARNAC
  Marfil (Margil), 133
SHAW
  Hugh B., 87(2), 118
  James, 75
  Susanna, 118
  William, Jr., 87, 118
  William, Sr., 118
SHEID
  Manston, 113
SHERIDAN
  Elizabeth, 45
  John, 161(2)
SHERIDAN (EDWARDS?)
  Charlotte, 95
SHERWOOD
  Wilkenson, 115
SHIPP
  Joseph, 109
  Manerva Williams, 109
  Sophia Thompson, 109
  William, 109
SHIT ASS, 19
SHITTING
  Samuel, 76
SHOCKEY
  Henry, 139
SHOCKLEY
  Henry, 118
  Rachel, 118
SHOEMAKER
  Evin (Evan), 111
  Matilda, 111
SHOTE
  James, 157
  Thomas, 61
SHY BUCK, 19
SIBLEY
  Dr. John, 48
  Mary (Pate), 59
SIERRA
  Jose Maria, 33
  Juna Maria, 35
  Maria Antonia, 31
  Philipe, 25

SIGLER
  Julia Ann, 94
  Julian, 106
  William N., 94, 106
SIMES
  Jesse, 62, 157
SIMMONS
  Clark, 118
  Elisha, 118
  Richard, 101
  Susan Guthrie, 101
SIMMS
  Candelaria, 56
  James, 77
  Josiah, 61
  Richard, 43, 153
SIMPSON
  Bartlett H., 111
  Gains, 78
  Holloway, 78
  Jane M. Brooks, 101
  John Jordan, 101
  John P., 140
  Mary, 111
SIMS
  Alfred, 100
  Anastacia, 66
  Ignacio, 133
  Jerusa Roble, 156
  John, 38
  Jose, 108
  Joseph, 61, 156
  Josiah, 157
  Marguerite (Chisley), 38
  Maria Candelaria, 59
  Richard, 37, 38, 66, 108
  Susan, 108
SINGLETON
  Ira, 82
SITZER
  Martin, 117
SKELTON
  Jane Alexander, 100
  John, 100
SKILLERN
  Isaac C., 107
  James A., 107
  Lucinda White, 107
  Nancy Alcorn, 107
SKINNER
  Jinny Webb, 100
  Thomas, 100
  William, 100
SLACK
  Daniel, 140
SLAUGHTER
  Elizabeth, 104
  Richard, 104
  Thomas, 61, 156
  William, 104
SLAYDON
  John, 85
SLEDGE
  Isom D., 113
SLINGLAND
  William, 86, 116
SMITH
  Abner, 155
  Abraham, 111
  Alexander, 119

Amos, 103
Archibald, 110
Charles, 140
David, 111
Edwin, 103
Eli N., 104
Elritta, 126
Ensign B., 119
Felix, 78
Frances Grigsby, 102
Frances Rutledge, 103
George W., 102, 119
Godfrey G., 141
Hugh, 119
James, 81, 113, 150
James N., 119
Jane, 111
John, 104, 159
John T., 115
Joseph, 104
Luther, 40, 100, 162
M. C., 106
Major, 81, 158
Malinda, 110
Manaen Turnbull, 110
Manen Turnbull, 155
Mary, 104, 119, 159
Matilda Haley, 110
Nancy, 104, 160
Philip, 81, 158
Rachel, 104
Rachel Roberts, 103
Reuben H., 78
Robert, 111
Robert W., 150
Sam W., 140
Sarah, 105
Sarah Ann, 111
Silas, 75
Sion, 105
Stephen, 75
Theodicia Clardy, 128
Thomas F., 140
Thomas S., 120
Tillman, 142
William, 75, 100, 133, 160
William D., 170
William M., 75
SMYTH
  Archibald, 84, 160
  Frances M. Grigsby, 127
  George W., 85, 173
  George Washington, 125
  Montair, 83
  Nancy, 84
SNAILUM
  Thomas C., 100
SNEED
  William, 70, 99
SNIDER
  Sarah, 97
SNODDY

INDEX

SNODDY (continued)
  William, 37
SNYDER
  John, 78
SOLGES, 19
SOLIS
  Clara, 36
SORELLE
  Parson Wiley J., 141
SOTA
  Gregorio, 28, 31
SOTO
  Barte, 28, 153
  Gregorio, 153
  Paula, 31
SOWELL
  Jno. T., 79
  M., 79
SPAIN
  W. R. D., 113
SPARKS
  Aaron, 78
  Elizabeth Cooper, 100
  James Hawkins, 100
  Massey C. Wadlington, 100
  Richard, 100
  William F., 100
SPEARS
  Andrew, 77, 108
  Mary, 108
SPENCER
  Elender, 119
  Margaret, 108
  Thomas, 65, 108
  Thomas W., 61, 156
SPINKS
  B. M., 76, 170(2)
SPROWL
  John, 66, 155, 157
SQUIRES
  Joseph, 108
  Sarah Carroll, 108
ST DENIS
  Louis Juchereau de, 79
STAGNER
  Henry, 103
  Sarah Pennington, 103
STALLINGS
  Jacob, 155
STANHAM
  William, 117
STARKS
  Moses, 78
STEADMAN
  Samuel, 70
STEARN
  John W., 82
STEARN FAMILY, 162
STEDHAM
  Samuel, 66
STEELE
  David, 108
STEPHEN
  Elias, 78
STEPHENS
  Carbet, 108
  Edward, 140
  John, 140
  John B., 142

STEPHENSON
  Elisha, 75
  Gilbert, 172
  James, 172
  John, 172
  William, 172
STERNE
  Adolphus, 70
  Emanuel, 69
  Ensign Adolphus, 68
  Helen, 69
  Nicholas Adolphus, 69, 92, 99
STERNES
  Nancy, 89
STEWARD
  J. W., 119
STEWART
  Jackson P., 82
  John, 141
STIBBENS
  Benjamin, 82
STIDDUM
  Samuel, 77
STILES
  John, 138
  Nancy, 138
STINSON
  John, 106
  Milla, 106
STIVERS
  Samuel, 66, 112
  Sarah, 112
STOCKMAN
  Anthony, 55
  C. C. F., 57, 163
  Catherine, 84, 160
  Catherine (des Bonnet), 57(2)
  Catherine des Bonnet, 163
  Celeste, 56, 59
  Dorcas Trebite, 163
  Epps G., 82
  Frederick, 57
  Harriet, 55
  Henry, 55, 57, 149, 150, 163
  Henry Samuel, 55
  Henry T., 84
  Joseph Anthony, 57
  Peter, 55, 57, 83, 160
  Tabitha, 55
STONE
  William J., 82
STONEHAM
  James, 117, 139
STORY
  Benjamin, 82
  Ephriam, 160
  Rachel, 83, 160
STOUT
  Henry, 87, 138
  James, 87
  Sealin, 141
  W. W., 142
  William, 139
STOVALL FAMILY, 162
STRANG
  Samuel, 75
STRICKLAN
  David, 83

STRICKLAND
  Amos, 83, 84
  Benjamin, 160
  David, 111, 119, 160
  David C., 87, 120
  Joseph, 119
  Mary, 83, 112
  Rachel, 111
  Samuel, 83, 84, 112, 160
STRICKLEN
  Joseph, 87
STRICKLIN
  David, 87
STRONG
  Samuel, 171
STROUT
  Henry, 118
  James, 118
STUBBLEFIELD
  Thomas, 75
STYLES
  John B., 116
  Sally, 116
SUBLETT
  Catherine, 56
  Philip, 56
  Philip A., 70, 76
  Phillip A., 60, 65, 73, 90, 93
SUDDETH
  Henry, 103
  Sally Golden, 103
SULLIVAN
  Richard F., 119
SUMMERS
  Henry, 81, 159
SUPULVADORE
  Juan, 46
SURDO, 165
SUTTON
  James, 78
  Philip, 78
SUTTONFIELD
  Laura, 140
  Sophia, 140
  William, 140
SWAGERTY
  Joseph, 119
SWAIL
  Amy, 75
  William, 171
SWAINSBURY
  John R., 85
SWETENBURG
  F., 113
SWIFT
  Mrs. Margaret, 85
SYTHE
  Francis, 77

-T-

TABLER
  Adam R., 117
TAHCHEE (DUTCH)
  Chief, 15
TALAMANTES
  Manuel, 36
TALBORN
  Thomas, 117
TALBOT
  Elijah W., 118
  Margaret, 118
  Wesly, 118
TANNER
  Charlotte

  Guthrie, 102
  Daniel, 81, 159
  Edward, 75
  James R., 76
  Thomas, 102
TARGENTER
  Burden, 75
TARRANT
  Edward H., 139
TAYLOR
  Anna Maria Ruoff, 99
  Ansen, 76
  Charity, 58
  Charles S., 70, 99
  Charles Stanfield, 74, 88, 125
  Dunston, 142
  Isaac, 87, 119
  Isabel A., 126
  Jane, 76, 169
  John, 82, 104
  John M., 61, 102, 156
  John W., 85
  Julian, 56
  Louisiana, 104
  Maria, 56
  Nancy Octavia, 70
  Owen, 102
  Pamela, 104
  Spicey McQueen, 102
  Spicy, 85
  Truman, 82
  William, 104, 155
TEAL
  Edward, 66, 114
  Fanny, 114
  George, 66, 70, 113
  Henry, 77
  Lucette, 71
  Porter, 107
  Rebecca Johnson, 113
TEAL (TEEL)
  Peter, 109
  Sarah Brooks, 109
TECIER
  Jose, 44, 153
TEKIANSTRA, 18
TENELOTE
  Juan, 36
TERRY
  Elizabeth, 108
  Jesse, 108
TESIE
  Leonora, 54
TEVIS
  George W., 169
  Nancy, 169, 172
  Noah, 169, 172
TEXADA
  Gertrudis, 54
THACKER
  Isaac, 66
THAYA
  Michel, 77
THEY HAVE SHOT THE DOG, 18
THOMAS
  Amos, 64
  Andy, 140
  Benjamin, 61, 65, 113, 156

215

INDEX

THOMAS (continued)
  Benjamin, Sr., 64, 155
  Elizabeth E., 113
  G. F., 61, 156
  Garry, 66
  Iradel D., 64
  Iradell, 66, 70
  Iredell D., 112
  Iredell Divisor, 107
  J. Francis, 82
  Jackson, 77
  James, 105, 108
  John, 66, 113
  Major Theophilus, 64
  Martha, 71
  Mary, 105, 107
  Mary Ann Dickinson, 155, 156
  Mary Brown, 156
  Mary Rogers, 64
  Mrs. Lucretia Brown, 156
  Nancy, 108
  Penelope, 64
  Penelope (Ashmore), 64
  Penelope (Penny), 107
  Penelope Edwards, 112
  Sarah, 64, 156
  Sarah Holman, 108
  Shadrac D., 77
  Shadrac(k) Dickson, 108(2)
  Shadrack, 65, 76
  Shadrack D., 156
  Shadrick D., 61, 64
  Susan Winn, 155
  Theophilus, 70, 77, 155
  Wiley, 65
  Wiley S., 61, 156
THOMASON
  Henrietta M., 56
THOMINSON
  Francis, 87
THOMPSON, 19
  Bartlett T., 107
  Burnell J., 155
  Burwell J., 66
  Charlton, 113
  Cynthia, 118
  Daniel, 78, 87, 119
  Dinsmore, 107
  Dr. Samuel, 74
  Ephriam, Sr., 102
  Hiram, 83
  Jack, 70
  John H., 74
  Jospeh E., 85
  Lewis, 110
  Molly, 110
  Nancy, 108
  Phenats, 106
  Precious (Wofford), 74
  Precous Wofford, 106
  Samuel, 106
  Susan Susannah Grigsby, 102
  William, 76
  William A., 106
  Wily, 118
THORN
  Frost, 52, 56, 58, 99
  John S., 99
  Susan Wroe Edwards, 99
THORNBERRY
  Alexander C., 112
  Elizabeth, 112
TIDWELL
  Erasmus, 119
TIER
  Polly, 76
TIJERINA
  Juana, 46
TILTON
  Charles, 76
TIMMONS
  Thomas, 163
TIMMS
  Amos, 61
TIMS
  Amos, 156
TINNIN
  Lawrence, 139
TINSLEY
  Nathaniel, 78
TIPPS
  Thomas, 77
TISDALE
  Ann, 116
  John, 116
TITTLE
  Elizabeth, 90, 93
  George, 93
  Mary (Cooper), 93
TITUS
  Andrew Jackson, 142
TIVIS
  Washington, 99
TOARVE
  Jose, 31
TOBAR
  Juan Francisco F., 133
TODD
  Martha, 110
  William, 110
TOMLINSON
  Thomas, 119
  Wm. S., 79
TONTIN
  Widow, 47
TORRES
  Andre, 55
  Carmel, 55
  Cleto, 55
  Feliciana, 45
  Jose Natavio, 55
  Maria Anna, 55
  Miguel, 133
TOTEN
  Maria Modesta, 53
TOVAR
  Juan Sanchez, 24
TRAMMEL, 149
TRAMMEL
  Robert, 115
TRAMMELL
  Philip, 119
TRAVIS
  Elizabeth, 50
TREBITE
  Dorcas, 55, 57

TREVINO
  Carmel, 55
TREW
  Damion, 81, 159
TREXE
  Manuel, 28, 152
TRUWORTHY
  T. T., 82
TUCKER
  James B., 111
TULLY
  Henry, 48
TURNER
  Edmond, 78
  John, 160
  Joseph W., 102
  Mary Jane Gilchrist, 102
TURNOVER, 18
TUTT
  Clement, 84, 112, 160
  Milla, 112
TWISTER, 19
TYLER
  Edward, 161
  Isaac, 119
TYRES
  James, 78

-U-

UCEBIO
  Narua Glee y Sur, 53
UCEBIO Y SUR, 53
URBIDE
  Maria Josefa, 42
  Marie, 42
UTALAH, 18
UXTALLE, 18

-V-

VALDEZ
  Francisco, 133
VALENTINE
  Andre, 44
  Andres, 46
  Andres (Andrew) Francois, 39
  Andrew, 37, 153
  Francois, 39
  Joseph, 84
  Maria Louis (Totin), 39
VAN
  Jane, 111
  Mason, 111
  Mason M., 83
  William, 84, 160
VAN SICKLE
  Maria Elena, 60
VANCEL
  Daniel M., 70
VANDINE (VANDYNE)
  John, 116
VANN
  Manson M., 160
VANPRADELLES
  A. G., 171
VANVIENTE
  Mickle, 46
VANWRINKLE
  Aaron, 119
VASCOCU
  Melani, 48
VASHERRY

  Nancy, 89
VASQUEZ
  Ambrosio, 28, 153
VAUGHN
  Theo, 77
VAUGHT
  John, 163
VEATCH
  Charlotte Sheridan Dean, 103
  John A., 103
  John Allen, 94
  Lucinda (Ramsey), 95
  Reverend Isaac, 95
VEHLEIN
  Joseph, 161
VERERO
  Ramos, 28, 153
VERNUELLA
  Andres, 133
VICKER(S)
  Harris, 104
VILLAFRANCA
  Gayitgano, 33
VILLANOVA
  Chisanto, 133
  Estevan, 133
VILLAPANDE
  Anna Maria, 32
VILLAPANDO
  Francisco, 35
VINCENT
  Henry, 87, 119
  Katherine, 128
VINNING
  Wade H., 115
VOLLENTINE
  Peter, 112
  Susan, 112

-W-

WADE
  Elizabeth, 111
WAGGONER
  David, 116
  Luther, 140
WAGLY
  Abraham, 118
  John, 117
  Joseph, 119(2)
  Martha, 119
  Martha Starks, 119
WALES
  James, 37
  Joseph, 37, 38, 153
WALKER
  Claborn, 111
  Elizabeth, 105
  Hiram P., 100
  Jacob, 81, 158
  James, 155
  John, 87, 110, 163
  Jonn, 118
  Joseph, 105
  Judah George, 100
  Leonard, 78
WALLACE
  James, 38
  Jesse, 120
  Joseph, 38
  Santiago (James),

216

INDEX

WALLACE (continued)
  47
  William, 169
WALLES
  William, 76
WALLET
  Jose, 44
WALLING
  Ann Chisum, 101
  John, 101
WALLIS
  E. H. R., 76
WALTER
  Hezekia, 119
WALTERS
  Lemuel, Sr., 102
  Sally Turner, 102
WALTHINGTON
  A., 82
WALTMAN
  David, 157
  Isabel Bebe, 158
WALTMANN
  David, 154
WARD
  James, 86, 115
  James J., Senr., 116
  James S., 169
  Jas. J., 86
  Jas. J., Sr., 87
  Jim, 137, 138
  Joseph J., 87, 116
  Morris, 119
  William B., 86, 115
  William C., 115
WARDEN
  Jesse, 107
WARE
  Ann, 115
  Hardy, 162
  John, 115
  Mary, 161
WARMSKY
  Jonathon, 105
WARREN
  David O., 76, 106, 109
  Davis, 78
  Eliza, 106
  Elizabeth, 81, 109
  Jesse, 82
  Lewis, 106
  Louis, 158
  Nehemiah, 82
WATCH, 19
WATKINS
  James, 110
  John, 119
  Joseph, 119
  Minerva, 110
  Rhoda Jackson, 128
WATSON
  Coleman, 114
  Evan, 119
  Evan, Jr., 119
  Harrison E., 66, 113
  Jason, 114
  Jesse, 119
  Lucy, 114
  Mary Cooper, 113
  Nancy, 110
  Rev. Benjamin, 141
  Wilis B., 110
  William, 107, 118
WATTS
  Hiram, 85
  John, 76, 102
  Mary Netherland, 102
  Melson, 56, 60
  Susan Hutchins, 102
  Thomas, 85
  Thomas, Sr., 102
  William, 115
  William H., 113
WEATHERSPOON
  Wily, 118
WEAVER
  John W., 115
WEBB
  William, 105
WEEKS
  Gracy Owens, 100
  Joseph, 100
WELCH
  C. P., 76
WEMBLE, 44
WEST
  Berry, 101
  Claiborne, 91, 95, 125, 172
  David, 115
  Elizabeth Jourdan, 101
  Gadi, 101
  Gardi, 85
  Jefferson, 102
  Nancy Sudduth, 102
  Polly Bivens, 101
  Richard, 102
  Sarah (Sally) Holden, 101
WETMORE
  Alex, 49
  George, 49
WHEAT
  Ester, 115
  Josiah, 115
  Martha Fletcher, 115
  Robert, 139
  Robert H., 116
  William, 115
WHET STONE, 19
WHETSTONE
  A., 83
  Edica, 107
  Peter, 83, 107
  Silas, 78
WHITAKER
  Benjamin F., 100
  Elizabeth Hammond, 100
  John, 98
  Martha Wilcoxson (Wilson), 98
  Peter, 168
  Saletha W. Easter, 100
  William, 97, 100, 155
WHITCHER
  N., 76
WHITE
  Benjamin, 81, 158
  Durant H., 118
  Elizabeth, 106, 158
  G. L., 81, 159
  James, 106
  James T., 76
  James Taylor, 168, 169
  Martha, 95
  Martin, 109
  Martin D., 81, 158
  Matthew G., 95, 171
  Matthew W., 169
  Nancy, 106
  Peter, 155
  Reuben, 169
  Sarah, 109
  William F., 81
  William H., 76
  William T., 159
WHITE MAN, 19
WHITING
  Samuel, 92
WHITLEY
  Elizabeth Little, 104
  Mills, 104
WHITLOCK
  Mary, 76
  Robert, 76
  William, 171
WHITMAN
  Mary, 60
WHITMORE
  Alex. O., 87
  Geo. W., 87
WHITTLEY
  Sarah Little, 105
  Sharp, 105
WICK
  Samuel, 113
WICKS
  John, 112
  Sarah, 112
WIDEMAN
  E., 139
  Edward, 117
  John, 117
WIGGINS
  Julian, 107
  L. H., 111
  Mary, 111
  Rodric(k), 107
WILBURN
  Matilda, 169
WILCOX
  Charles, 76
WILKASON
  David, 83
WILKENSON
  David, 112
  Malinda, 112
WILKINSON
  Amos, 160
  Anne (Herbert), 42
  Jane Herbert, 42
  William M., 42
WILLBURN
  Daniel, 100
  Elizabeth, 100
WILLET
  Andrew, 87, 118
WILLIAM, 18
WILLIAMS
  Alta Zera, 95
  Barbary Hooter, 103
  Brooks, 162, 164
  Cary W., 78
  Delila Palvador, 157
  Eliza, 105
  Eliza Emberson, 117
  Elizabeth, 109
  George, 141
  Henry, 109
  Hezekiah, 76
  James, 61, 155, 157
  John, 105, 107, 155
  John A., 61, 65, 155, 157, 169, 170, 171
  John D., 141(2)
  John H., 139
  Johnson, 81
  Leonard, 149, 150, 163
  Lucinda Isaacs, 103
  Maria, 109
  Mary (Polly), 103
  Moses, 119
  Mrs. Owen, 149, 163
  Penelope, 94
  Rebecca Wilson, 101
  Richard, 101
  Samuel, 70
  Selvester, 118
  Sittina Southern, 101
  Solomon, 155
  Standly, 119
  Stephen, 85, 101
  Stephen, Jr., 85
  Stephen, Sr., 103
  Sterling, 141
  Sylvester, 119
  T. J., 76
  Thomas, 85, 103, 149, 150, 163(2)
  Tilmon, 79
  W. W., 140
  Warren, 141
  William, 101, 103, 109, 150
  William M., 117, 119, 139
WILSON
  Catherine, 126
  Dr. S. P., 66
  George W., 161
  Isaac, 117
  James, 126
  James B., 85
  Jason, 138
  John, 138
  Mary, 107
  Mary Lee, 102
  Nancy, 60
  Rebecca, 126
  Robert H., 78
  Samuel, 115
  Stephen P., 107
  Thomas, 119
  William, 66, 85, 86, 116
  William, Sr., 102
WIMBY
  James, 87
WINDSOR

217

INDEX

WINDSOR (continued)
  Sarah, 70
WINFREE
  Isaac, 101
  Isabella Guthrie, 101
WINFREY
  A. E., 85
  Mrs. Sarah, 85
WINFRIE
  A. B. J., 76
WINN
  John H., 113
  Robert, 64
  Susan, 64
WISEMAN
  Baker, 169
  Robert, 61, 76, 156
WITHERSPOON
  Wiley, 139
WITMORE
  Alexander O., 119
  George C., 117
  Henrietta Wright, 117
WOOD
  Caleb, 139
  John S., 66
  Joseph, 87, 118
  Mrs. George, 149, 163
  Prissa, 81
  Reuben D., 66
WOODBURY
  Jesse, 92
WOODIFF
  John, 112
WOODRUFF
  Zachary, 79
WOODS
  Augusta, 96
  Caleb, 114
  James B., 95
  Joseph, 118
WOOTEN
  Margaret, 109
  Moses, 83, 156
  Moses (Moss), 109
WOOTON
  Moses, 61, 160
WORRELL
  William, 78
WORTHINGTON
  Mary (Polly)
    Barnes, 119
  Samuel, 119(2)
WREN
  Johnson, 140
WRIGHT
  Adam, 87, 119
  Alex. W., 87
  Alexander, 85, 103
  Anna Clark, 103
  Claiborne, 49, 137, 138
  Francis G., 87
  George, 138
  George W., 86, 115
  Hardin, 111
  Henietta, 50
  Henrietta, 50
  Henrietta (Claiborne), 50
  John, 85
  Mary, 109, 117, 119
  Mary Nail, 111
  McQuinney Howell, 141
  Moses D., 117
  Polly Winfree, 103
  Sarah Jane (Membrane), 115
  Sherod, Sr., 103
  Thomas, 109
  Thomas G., 117
  Travis, 50
  Travis G., 87, 119, 138
  William, 50, 138
  William F., 87
  William Fowler, 117
WRINKLE
  Charity Ann, 89
WYCHE
  Sarah, 108
WYRES
  Harriet, 114
  Robert, 114

-Y-

YALIS
  Caintha, 106
  Thomas, 106
YANCY
  Archibald, 107
YBANEZ
  Lazaro, 24
Y'BARBO
  Anastacio, 54, 133
Y'BARBO
  Antonio Gil, 26
Y'BARBO
  Antonio Gil, 27, 28, 29, 30, 36, 42, 52
  Benigno, 133
  Benino, 54
  Candelario, 133
  Damasio, 54
  Francisco, 54
  Gil Antonio, 151
  Jose, 54
  Jose Antonio, 54
  Jose Gregorio, 54
  Jose Ignacio, 54
  Jose Luciano, 53
  Jose Maria, 133
  Jose Remigio de Jesus, 53
  Juan, 133
  Juan Antonio, 54
  Juan Jose, 54
  Juan Pablo, 54
  Juana Bautista, 54
  Leonisio, 54
  Luciano, 133
  Manuel, 54
  Manuel de los Santos, 133
  Manuel Mariana, 133
  Manuel Monetre, 53
  Maria Cantu, 53
  Maria Carmel, 54, 73
  Maria Feliciana, 54
  Maria Josefa Lionicia, 53
  Maria Teresa, 54
  Martina, 53
YBARBO
  Mateo, 25
Y'BARBO
  Matheo Antonio, 26
  Maximilano, 54
  Norin, 54
  Pedro, 53
  Thomas, 28, 153
  Vicente, 54
YBARVO
  Tiburcia, 35
YELLOW JACKET, 19
YOCUM
  Jesse, 48
  John, 48
  Mathias (Mathew), 48
  Thomas D., 48
YORK
  John, 169
YOUNG
  Carolina, 104
  Dorothy "Dolly", 72
  Elijah, 118
  George S., 117
  Horatio, 81
  Phoebe, 73
  Pleasant, 104
  William C., 140
YOUNG BIRD, 19
YOUNG SHY BUCK, 19
YOUNGBLOOD
  Andrew J., 103

-Z-

ZANBERRY
  Cintha, 112
  Swanson, 111
ZEKIEL, 18
ZEPEDA
  Josef, 27, 152
ZIEGLER
  Edmund, 79
ZOTO
  Juan Ygnacio, 55
ZUBER
  Abram, 66

www.ingramcontent.com/pod-product-compliance
Lightning Source LLC
Chambersburg PA
CBHW051636230426
43669CB00013B/2324